* Reach millions of customers directly with your online store *
* Boost traffic, sales, and profits for your online business *
* Expand your brick-and-mortar store to the Web easily and effectively *

How to make
Money
Online
with
eBay, YAHOO!,
& GOOGLE

A STEP-BY-STEP GUIDE
to Using Three Online Services to Make One Successful Business

Peter Kent and **Jill K. Finlayson** Former eBay Senior Category Manager

How to Make Money Online with eBay, Yahoo!, and Google

A Step-by-Step Guide to Using Three Online Services to Make One Successful Business

This page intentionally left blank

How to Make Money Online with eBay, Yahoo!, and Google

A Step-by-Step Guide to Using Three Online Services to Make One Successful Business

Peter Kent
Jill K. Finlayson

McGraw-Hill

New York   Chicago   San Francisco   Lisbon
London   Madrid   Mexico City   Milan   New Delhi
San Juan   Seoul   Singapore   Sydney   Toronto

0-07-226444-6
The material in this eBook also appears in the print version of this title: 0-07-226261-3.

All trademarks are trademarks of their respective owners. Rather than put a trademark symbol after every occurrence of a trademarked name, we use names in an editorial fashion only, and to the benefit of the trademark owner, with no intention of infringement of the trademark. Where such designations appear in this book, they have been printed with initial caps.

McGraw-Hill eBooks are available at special quantity discounts to use as premiums and sales promotions, or for use in corporate training programs. For more information, please contact George Hoare, Special Sales, at george_hoare@mcgraw-hill.com or (212) 904-4069.

TERMS OF USE

DOI: 10.1036/0072262613

 **Professional**

Want to learn more?

We hope you enjoy this McGraw-Hill eBook! If you'd like more information about this book, its author, or related books and websites, please click here.

About the Authors

Peter Kent is the author of more books about the Internet than any other writer. His titles include *Search Engine Optimization for Dummies*, the bestselling *Complete Idiot's Guide to the Internet*, and the most widely reviewed and praised title in computer-book history, *Poor Richard's Web Site: Geek Free, Commonsense Advice on Building a Low-Cost Web Site*. In all, he is the author of around 50 books and hundreds of newspaper and magazine articles.

Kent has worked in e-commerce and online marketing for over a decade. He set up his first web-based store in 1997, and in 1999 he founded an e-Business Service Provider funded by one of the world's largest VC firms. Kent currently consults with businesses about their Internet marketing strategies, helping them to avoid the pitfalls and to leap the hurdles they'll encounter online. For more information, visit http://www.PeterKentConsulting.com/.

Jill K. Finlayson is one of the founders of M Networks, a media company that provides training seminars, books, and distance learning on online retailing, in addition to hosting the Small eBusiness World Conference and Expo designed for small business owners and entrepreneurs. Finlayson worked at eBay from 1998 to 2003 as Senior Category Manager in charge of the Toys, Dolls, Hobbies, and Crafts businesses, a segment that generates more than $1.5 billion in transactions annually. Finlayson is co-author of *Fundraising on eBay* (McGraw-Hill), and she writes much of the curriculum and training materials for eKnowledge Institute's Academy and Business School courses in eBay. Finlayson also worked for The Learning Company, an educational software company. She lives in Fremont, California, and is a graduate of the University of California at Berkeley.

This page intentionally left blank

For Nick and Chris

This page intentionally left blank

Contents at a Glance

Contents

This page intentionally left blank

Acknowledgments

I'd like to thank Roger Stewart for many amusing hours on the phone…and for giving me the opportunity to work on what turned out to be a very interesting project (in the Chinese sense). I'd also like to thank Agatha Kim, Acquisitions Coordinator, and Mark Karmendy, Project Editor, for going easy on me. And, of course, I'd like to thank the many publishing staff members who work in the background, anonymous yet essential to the whole process of getting a book off a computer and into the bookstores.

This page intentionally left blank

Introduction

Have you ever thought about setting up a business online? If not...where have you been for the last five or ten years? It's the new American dream, encompassing all the usual ideas of independence, freedom, and wealth. And sometimes, you know, Internet-based businesses really do bring all these things to their owners.

Not always, though, which is why you need this book. It's easy to stumble around on the Internet for months or years, and never quite get anywhere. What's the difference between those who stumble and those who leap into online success? Knowledge. You can't succeed unless you do the right things, and while some very successful online businesses have been built by people who serendipitously stumbled onto the right formula, why leave such an important factor to chance?

This book describes the basic principles, ideas, and tools that you'll need to succeed online. In addition, it lays out a roadmap; the book focuses on certain tools that many other successful businesses have employed:

- **eBay**   This, the world's most important online marketplace, has been used by tens of thousands of people to launch new careers and businesses.

- **Yahoo!**   You've heard of Yahoo!'s search system, of course, but did you know that tens of thousands of businesses use Yahoo!'s e-commerce tools to manage their online sales?

- **Google**   A business needs traffic, whether it's "foot traffic" to a brick-and-mortar store or web traffic to an e-commerce store. Google—and the other "Pay Per Click" advertising systems—can help you generate that traffic.

We've split this book into three main parts. In Part I, you'll learn how to begin working through eBay, selling your wares through auctions, Buy It Now sales, and the eBay store.

In Part II, you'll find out how to set up a Web store using Yahoo!'s low-cost Merchant Solutions software.

And in Part III, you'll find out how to generate traffic through Google's AdWords Pay Per Click system...as well as how to get traffic from Yahoo!'s Search Marketing Pay Per Click system through free search-engine traffic, from the price-comparison sites, and via a variety of other online marketing techniques.

So let's not waste time...your future beckons. Turn to Chapter 1 and find out how to get started.

This page intentionally left blank

Part I

Building an eBay Business

This page intentionally left blank

Chapter 1

How Your Business Fits Online

Launching a business online can be exciting and profitable. It's a great way to supplement an existing income stream or even to become one's sole occupation. Many individuals and small businesses have met with tremendous success, some making literally millions of dollars a year, even after starting at ground zero, with no knowledge of the Internet beyond the very basics, if that. There are no guarantees, but it can be done. It does require patience and a willingness to go through the steps to get it right, though. That's what we're going to teach you here.

Why Three Services?

In this book we explain how to use three different "channels" to build your business online:

- Selling products through eBay auctions
- Setting up an online store using Yahoo! Merchant Solutions
- Promoting your business through Google, other search engines, and various other online-marketing mechanisms.

Why three channels? There are a number of reasons:

- Few businesses are simple enough to survive with a single method for finding business. If you sell hot dogs to people who eat hot dogs, you may need only to place your hot-dog stand on a busy street. But if you sell hot dogs to businesses that sell hot dogs to people, you would use many different ways to reach those businesses.
- What works well for one business may not work so well for another. Using multiple channels to sell and to reach people increases the likelihood that you find the best one.

■ Multiple channels provide multiple opportunities. If you can find people to buy your products more than one way, why leave money on the table by only using one method?

■ You'll find some of the things we suggest in this book can be implemented very quickly, in some cases in just a few hours. Having a range of different options helps you get your toes wet and work your way in slowly. For instance, an already established business could begin selling online with eBay over a weekend, gradually build the online business, then investigate other sales channels later.

While it's true that some businesses have done very well by finding something simple that works and doing it over and over again for decades, most businesses are not so fortunate. Thanks to competitive pressures—other people want your customers too; remember—most businesses have to do many things in order to survive and thrive. What works today may not work tomorrow. Some method you try for finding more business may not work, or may not work well as something you haven't yet tried. Business is an evolutionary process, with the notion of natural selection replaced by the degree of initiative of the business owners and managers. A business gradually evolves as the people running the business try new things, discard things that don't work or that no longer work, and adopt techniques that show promise.

The three-channel method outlined in this book provides a great way to get started with an online business, showing you a number of essential techniques for surviving—and thriving—online.

In particular, companies succeeding online often use a number of strategies to do so. These are the sort of things you may one day find yourself doing:

■ Selling through **online auctions**

■ Selling through **discount channels**, such as Overstock.com

■ Selling through **merchant sites** such as Amazon.com

■ Selling through a **web store**

■ . . . or, in some cases, *several* **web stores**, for different audiences or perhaps different pricing strategies

■ Buying **Pay Per Click ads** to bring buyers from the search engines to your store

■ Using **Search Engine Optimization** to bring buyers from the search engines without paying a click fee

■ If you own an **offline business**, using various techniques to integrate online and offline operations, pushing business from the offline business to the online, and vice versa

■ Using an **affiliate program**, paying other web sites commissions for purchases made by buyers arriving at your store through affiliate sites

■ Publishing an e-mail newsletter to keep in touch with customers and promote your products to their friends

■ Marketing through PR campaigns targeting e-mail newsletter editors

■ Promoting your products through discussion groups

■ And many other things . . .

One thing you can say about doing business online is that however successful you become, there's always more to learn!

What Makes a Good Online Product?

Just about any product can be sold online. But let's be quite clear; some products sell much better than others. Let's think about some product characteristics that both help and hurt products when selling online:

- **Price:weight ratio**   The price:weight ratio needs to be high; that is the price, in comparison to the weight, needs to be high. Books have a very high price:weight ratio—a book might be worth, say, $30/lb. Sugar might be around 35 cents/lb. The price:weight ratio issue is why it's hard to sell sugar, cement, and charcoal online.

- **Availability**   Less available is good. Available everywhere is bad. That's why it's hard to sell candy bars online.

- **Information products**   Products that are essentially information sell well online. Books, reports, reference materials . . . even music is an information product, really. Why do they do well online? Because online technology provides a very efficient way to deliver information. It's fast and it's cheap. It's no wonder that books were the first major product category online and remain one of the primary categories.

- **Complicated products requiring research**   The Internet is the perfect research tool, of course. Products that require careful selection—products with many different features—often do well online.

- **Wide selection of specialty products**   An example is one of the earliest small-biz successes, HotHotHot.com, an online success for over a decade. Sure, you can find hot sauce in any grocery store. But can you find *Jamaican Hell Fire, Rigor Mortis Hot Sauce, 99%,* or *3:00 AM*? (The company provides 100 different brands.) Have you even heard of these? Another example is RedWagons.com. Certainly you can find two or three different Radio Flyer wagons in most toy stores, but where else can you find *every* Radio Flyer product made—steel wagons, plastic wagons, trikes, scooters, retro rockets, roadsters, and everything else?

- **Deals**   There's a class of goods that crosses all classes, and even covers products that you might think of as *Not Good Internet Products*. If you can sell a particular product at a very low price, you may have a good Internet product. Hey, if you can get the price of sugar down low enough, you might be able to sell that online.

- **"Cool" products that sell themselves through word of mouth**   There are some products that are just so cool, people tell their friends. One company that gets fantastic word of mouth is ThinkGeek.com, which sells tons of really cool stuff (Figure 1-1). Another example of a great word-of-mouth site is Despair.com. This company sells products that people put on their office walls and laugh about with their friends.

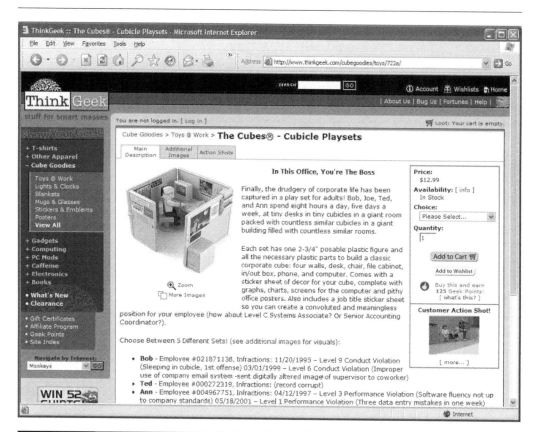

FIGURE 1-1 ThinkGeek.com is a classic word-of-mouth site—people love it and tell their friends.

■ **No need to touch, smell, or even see clearly.** Products that really require a close view generally don't sell well online. That's why it's hard to sell furniture online and difficult to sell unique works of art or perfume. And that's why well-known brands can sell online . . . because people know what they're getting. In other words, although it's hard to sell perfume that your potential buyers have never smelled, it's not hard to sell perfume from Christian Dior.

■ **High value products are good.** You may do better selling a $500 product than a $5 product. You'll have less competition—making it easier to compete using Pay Per Click (see Chapter 22) and in natural search—and will make much higher "margins" (gross profit). Low-price products can be very difficult to deal with online. Think very seriously before selling anything below, say, $50, unless you're pretty sure you can really pump out high volumes.

- **Junk is hard to sell.** This may sound obvious, but it's amazing how many merchants just post any kind of junk online and hope to make a business out of it. Mass produced statuettes of kittens from China, junk jewelry, handicrafts from the wilds of Wisconsin . . . *come on*, you can do better!

- **Products you understand and love.** These are easier to sell. If you have a passion for skydiving, there's a natural business for you selling skydiving products.

Having said all that, it's important to realize that every rule can be broken. Groceries *can* be sold online, for instance. Diamonds, products that most jewelers would say need to be looked at carefully before purchase, are selling very well online. And though Furniture.com crashed and the big grocery-store sites (PeaPod.com and WebVan.com) went down with it, some companies *are* selling furniture online and some companies *are* selling groceries online. (PeaPod, for instance, was bought up by a grocery chain.) So, you *can* break the rules. But you'd better have a good reason to believe that it will work.

The Perfect Online Product

Okay, so there's no such thing as perfect online product. But considering what *would* be perfect might spark ideas of what products are close to perfect. Here, then, is the perfect online product:

- **It's valuable, with high margins.** You're not making a dollar or two per sale; you're making dozens, perhaps hundreds of dollars.

- **It's in demand.** It's a product people want and are willing to pay for.

- **It's not widely available.** Buying online may be the only way to find the product, or the particular variety of the product.

- **It's a "research" product.** People are looking online for this product right now. (Most products are *not* research products. At this very moment, out of hundreds of millions of Internet users, probably only one or two are trying to find out how to buy sugar online.)

- **It's light and non-fragile, so it's cheap and easy to ship.**

- **There's little or no competition online.**

- **People love the product so much they're going to tell their friends about you.**

- **There's no smell or texture, or anything else that makes the product one that "just has to be seen."**

- **You are intimately connected to the product in some way.** The product is related to your hobby or passion.

- **Oh, and it's legal!** While a number of illegal substances match the perfect-product criteria, we're assuming the risk outweighs the benefits.

Understanding the Price Sensitivity of the Online Buyer

Online buyers are far more *price sensitive* than offline buyers. That is, the price of the product is much more important for the online buyer than for someone walking into an offline store. When someone buys a product and has to select a particular merchant, they are "sensitive" to various factors, such as these:

- The **price of the product** from that merchant
- The **convenience** of purchasing from the merchant
- The **confidence** they have in the merchant (whether the merchant "backs" the sale, for instance, if anything goes wrong)
- The **additional costs**, such as sales tax and delivery

Price is only one aspect in the decision to buy. But on the Internet, the weight given to price is much greater. This is a perfectly natural, and much predicted, state of affairs. Consider the buyer walking into a brick-and-mortar store who finds a product he's interested in:

- Many buyers don't care about pricing much at all. They are more interested in convenience, selection, location, and sales environment.
- Many buyers want the product now and don't care *too* much about price, as long as it's "in the ballpark." If the buyer finds the product, there's a good chance the sale is made.
- Even if buyers are shopping for price, there's a limit to how much driving around they're willing to do. Again, if the price is "in the ballpark," price may be trumped by convenience.
- Buyers don't think too much about how much confidence they have in the merchant; if the business can afford a storefront and take credit cards, they've already reached a certain level.

We know all this is true, because offline prices *are* often higher than online prices. And haven't we all been in stores and thought, "How do they sell at that ridiculous price?" The online sales environment is very different, though:

- **Buyers can jump from store to store *very* quickly.** It's very easy to find a low-priced product extremely quickly.
- **There are many sites that will even do the price comparison for you.** There are the shopping directories (see Chapter 25) and the merchant sites (Chapter 28), where buyers, more and more, are beginning their shopping.
- **Many buyers are used to, and now expect, a low price.** Price is a much more important factor for them than for most offline shoppers . . . they are much more *price sensitive*. In fact getting a low price is why many online buyers are willing to delay gratification (to wait for delivery).

■ **Many buyers now do a little research to settle on the exact product they want, then use a shopping-directory comparison tool to search for the product.** Then they'll ask for the system to show the products sorted lowest-price first and work their way through the merchants one by one. They often won't even go past the first few low-price merchants before buying.

Understanding these concepts naturally leads to a couple of conclusions:

■ **If you have a really good price, you're in a good competitive position.**

■ **If you don't have a good price, many of the marketing techniques won't be open to you;** you'll find it very difficult to sell through eBay, shopping directories, and merchant sites, for instance.

 tip   *eBay in particular is a very price-sensitive forum. Your products will be listed alongside other products, the same or similar, so buyers can quickly see the price at which products sell.*

Does this mean price is always important, that you can't sell a product unless you sell at a low price? No, not necessarily. It means you'll have trouble with sales channels that compare your product with others based on price, such as eBay, the shopping directories, and merchant sites. But it's possible to position your business—on your own web site—in ways that are not directly related to price. The lowest price does *not* always get the sale.

■ **The big merchants have a real brand advantage.** Many buyers buy everything at Amazon, under the (not unreasonable) assumption that it's a pretty good price, if not necessarily the best.

■ **Selection holds value.** Web sites that have a wide selection have an advantage; if people discover a hard-to-find product on your site, they may stop looking.

■ **Focus is important.** Sites that focus tightly on a particular type of product—and have a wide selection of a very small range of products—have an advantage, too, for the same reason. It makes the unfindable findable.

■ **A classy site trumps a trashy site.** Trashy sites make buyers feel uneasy. Classy-looking sites make them feel more comfortable. Even if your product, in your trashy-looking site, is listed in one of the shopping directories above a product from a really classy-looking site, it probably won't matter how cheaply you sell; the classy site is getting some (much?) of the business.

■ **Recommendations count for a lot.** If a buyer recommends your site to someone because they're so happy with buying from you, you'll get sales regardless of price.

■ **Simplicity is good.** Making it easy to buy helps turn visitors into buyers. AllAboardToys .com, for instance, sells products you could buy on Amazon.com if you wished, but they make it much easier.

■ **Brand differentiation matters.** Look for ways to make your business stand apart. ShaneCo.com, for instance, a national jewelry chain, doesn't compete on price directly; it competes on value and unique designs. They've positioned themselves as the price leader *for high-quality jewelry,* so they don't have to compete head to head.

To Ship or Not to Ship

Here's an interesting strategy, one that has worked well for many companies yet also represents some risk: Take orders, but don't ship.

No, we're not talking about scamming buyers; we're talking about acting as an order taker, not a shipper. This can, in some cases, make perfect sense. You operate the web site, the e-commerce store, the auctions, the shopping-directory listing, and so on. You carry out the marketing campaigns to bring in the sales, and you process the sales. But you *don't* ship the products; rather, you send the order to a manufacturer, wholesaler, distributor, or even retailer, who manages the shipment. (This is known as *drop shipping*; you take the order, your partner "drop ships" it.) This type of business has some huge advantages:

- **Lower initial investment**   You don't have to buy your initial inventory.
- **Less hassle**   Packing, shipping, and managing returns are nuisances you can do without.
- **Tighter focus**   You get to focus on Internet marketing and sales, not managing inventory, packing, shipping, and returns.

note   *Of course there are different ways to play this game. Another scenario is to put everything from sales transaction to shipping to customer service in the hands of the supplier. All you do is manage the store and the marketing and let the supplier do everything else, including running the transaction through their own credit-card merchant account, almost totally absolving you of all responsibility.*

Conversely, there are dangers and disadvantages:

- **If the supplier doesn't ship it, you get blamed!**
- **You get a lower cut of the sales price and profit.**
- **You have less control of the quality of the products shipped to your customers.**

warning   *Watch out for the scams! There are plenty of companies that will be happy to sign you up, to act for you as a drop shipper or wholesaler. Most of these are bad deals, selling junk. Be very careful and only get into business with reputable companies. In fact, you're probably not looking for a company that touts itself as a drop shipper. You're looking for a company that already ships products, that is willing to also ship for you.*

How would you find an arrangement like this? Keep your eyes open, research local companies, spend a lot of time looking in stores, reading mail-order catalogs, and so on. Then, when you think you've found a good opportunity, you'll have to make personal contact.

tip   *WorldWideBrands.com is a well-respected directory of drop-ship wholesalers. For $69.95 you'll get a lifetime membership to the directory, which contains information on thousands of actual wholesalers that have agreed to drop ship for small businesses.*

Drop shipping has got a bad name, but that doesn't mean there aren't good drop-shipping arrangements. This, in fact, is how online music sales got started. The first major success in online music sales was CDnow.com (type that into your browser and you'll arrive at Amazon .com, which bought them up a few years ago). CDnow found a wholesaler that was willing to ship small, individual orders, which the retailer already did anyway, when a music store called up and ordered one or two CDs.

This relationship provided CDnow with an enormous selection, almost all the music sold in North America, with minimal investment (at the time the company was being run by two 24-year-old brothers from their parents' basement). And the wholesaler also provided CDnow with a ready-made shipping department. All CDnow had to do was focus on taking the sales and transmitting the orders electronically to the wholesaler.

Another company that used this strategy very well is RedWagons.com (which started with a Yahoo! store and to this day still uses Yahoo! for its e-commerce needs). The company went into business selling Radio Flyer products; they convinced the company to ship for them, so RedWagons.com simply took the orders and forwarded them to Radio Flyer for fulfillment.

This page intentionally left blank

Chapter 2

Creating Your eBay Presence

The world's largest online market is eBay; the largest market of any kind, really. At any moment literally millions of items are on sale. Billions of dollars' worth of property are sold through eBay not merely every year, but every month.

eBay is an unusual e-commerce site because it doesn't actually sell anything; it simply provides a mechanism through which other people can sell online. It's allowed millions of people to sell online, and eBay claims that 400,000 of these people make a living by selling through eBay. Besides the relatively low-dollar individual sales of collectibles and "garage sale" items, many established merchants sell cars and real estate, computers and antiques, and electronics and jewelry. And not just in the United States, either. eBay operates around the world, in Western Europe and—through an investment, MercadoLibre.com—in Latin America, Hong Kong, Malaysia, Australia, and India. It's a vast, international marketplace, in which millions of individuals and merchants sell millions of products.

Why Sell Through eBay?

Why would you want to sell through eBay? For a number of reasons:

- **Hundreds of thousands of people** have made money through eBay, many of them enough to live on.

- **It's very easy to get started** selling through eBay. You can literally post your first product in a matter of minutes.

- **eBay provides a number of different ways to sell.** You can sell through an auction or fixed price, through the main listings, or in an eBay store.

- **eBay provides tools to increase the likelihood of safe transactions,** such as PayPal Buyer protection, eBay Standard Purchase Protection, and a feedback mechanism about buyers and sellers. You get paid, and the buyer can purchase with confidence.

- **eBay makes getting paid easy;** you can easily set up a PayPal account within minutes, allowing you to accept credit-card transactions for sales.
- **You have a vast audience.** Millions of people browse and purchase through eBay.

There's a reason that millions of people have sold through eBay: it's easy and it works. By the way, there *are* other auction sites. Both Yahoo! and Amazon have auction sites at the moment (auction.yahoo.com and auction.amazon.com), but these sites only have a fraction of the listings and transactions eBay does. In point of fact, there is *nothing* to match eBay.

 note   *In order to be an eBay merchant, you must be at least 18.*

Registering as an eBay Member

Let's look at how to register as an eBay member—whether buying or selling, the initial process is the same.

1. On the eBay home page, click the <u>Register</u> link near the top of the page.

 tip   *Visit the eBay Learning Center for audio tours and tutorials about selling through eBay. See http://pages.ebay.com/education/.*

2. The registration form appears. Enter all your information, and then click the Continue button at the bottom of the page.

3. The Choose ID & Password page is displayed.

 tip   *The User ID that eBay suggests is likely to be a combination of your name and a number. It won't be particularly memorable or distinctive, so we suggest you devise something better.*

4. eBay will offer a number of IDs from which you can choose, but we suggest you click the **Create your own ID** option button and type the user ID of your choice.

5. Type a **password**; make sure you use something you can remember (write it down somewhere safe, or use a password-protection program). Don't use anything obvious that someone can figure out.

6. Select something from the **secret question** drop-down list box. This will be a question that eBay's staff may ask in order to identify you.

7. Type the answer to the secret question in the **Secret answer** box.

8. Click the **Continue** button.

9. eBay now sends you an e-mail message to confirm the account; doing so ensures that the e-mail address you provided was valid and accessible by you. (If you entered a bad e-mail address, click the <u>Change your email</u> link to correct it.) You can check your e-mail within a few moments since the confirmation should arrive pretty quickly.

10. Click the **Complete eBay Registration** button in the e-mail message. (If the button doesn't work, as it may not in some e-mail programs, use the link and the confirmation code eBay provided below the button.)

11. You've created a basic account. You can now buy, but in order to sell you need to continue. Click the <u>Start selling</u> link.

What would you like to do next?
- <u>Start selling</u> - Create a seller's account to sell on eBay

 note *In this step, you're going to need your credit-card number and checking-account information (routing number and account number). eBay uses this information to confirm who you are and to charge seller's fees.*

12. On the page that next displays, click the **Create Seller's Account** button to see the Enter Credit or Debit Card page.

13. Enter your **credit-card information** into the page, and then click the **Continue** button. The Enter Checking Account screen appears.

14. Enter your **Bank name**, **Bank-routing number**, and **Checking-account number**. Be careful to enter the routing number and account number into the correct fields.

 tip *eBay saves money if you pay your fees from your bank account, so they encourage you to do so. Currently they will reduce your seller's fees by 1 percent for a couple of months if you agree to use your bank account.*

15. On the next page, you select which account you want to use in order to pay your **selling fees**, either the bank account or the credit-card checking account. Select the appropriate option button, and click the **Continue** button.

16. If you selected to pay from the bank account, you'll see a Direct Pay Authorization form, giving eBay permission to access your bank account. Click the **Authorize Checking Account** button once you've read the information.

That's it. You've created your account. You're now approved to sell on eBay. You can continue to set up an item for sale, if you wish, or build an eBay store, but there's no need to do so at this point. In fact, you'll probably want to set up a PayPal account, which is what we'll be covering in the next section.

Setting Up a PayPal Account

Somehow, you have to get paid. The best way for new merchants to collect money is through PayPal. PayPal, an Internet startup in 1998, created a simple payment system that allowed individuals to e-mail money to each other. Members could "load" their account with money, then tell PayPal to, say, "pay this e-mail address $10." PayPal would look up the e-mail address, and if it belonged to someone with an account, it would transfer the money to that account.

If the owner of the recipient e-mail address didn't have an account, PayPal would send an e-mail message saying, essentially, "Come to PayPal and set up an account, and we'll give you $10." The perfect "viral marketing" tool! Who, on being told by a friend or colleague that he'd be "PayPalling" money, and on receiving the notification message, *wouldn't* set up an account?

note   *There are fees associated with PayPal transactions, which vary from 30 cents plus 2.9 percent to 30 cents plus 1.9 percent, depending on your sales volume. PayPal has a much simpler fee structure than the credit-card merchant accounts (see Chapter 18), though the base rate is a little higher than for credit cards (if you do more than $3,000 in transactions a month, the rate is comparable or lower). Cross-border transactions are 1 percent more.*

Although money transfers were not part of the company's main business plan, PayPal found that people on eBay had discovered the system, and were recommending it to each other. It eventually became so popular that eBay actually bought PayPal. Today, PayPal has 65 million account holders in 45 countries around the world; one in three U.S. online buyers has a PayPal account, and 90 percent of eBay sellers accept PayPal. An even higher percentage of regular merchants use it. And, of course, it's easy to set up your own account.

1. Click the **My eBay** tab at the top of the page.

2. Click the <u>PayPal</u> link in the Related Links box at the bottom left of the page.

Related Links
PayPal
Buyer's Guide

tip   *Accepting PayPal means you can accept credit cards, too. If a buyer doesn't have a PayPal account, he can pay PayPal with a credit card, and the money is placed into your PayPal account.*

3. Click the **Sign Up for a PayPal Account** button.

4. Create an account **Password**—you must use at least eight characters—click the check box at the bottom of the page (acknowledging that you have read the Privacy Policy and User Agreement), and then click the **Register** link at the bottom of the page.

5. A page appears telling you that your account has been set up. You haven't finished yet, however. Check your e-mail for a confirmation message, and then click the activation link. A page opens in which you must enter your password to log in. When you do so, the Enter Security questions page opens.

6. Similar to setting up your eBay account, you also need to provide **Security Questions**. Choose the two questions from the drop-down list boxes, and then type the answers into the **Answer** boxes.

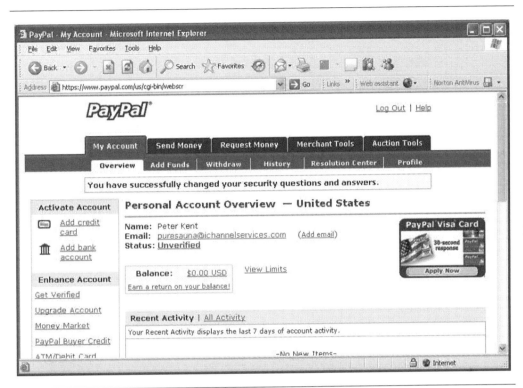

FIGURE 2-1   Your PayPal account page

7. When you click the **Submit** button, you'll be placed into your account page (see Figure 2-1).

 Being verified protects you against unauthorized withdrawals. You'll be considered more trustworthy by eBay buyers and sellers this way, and you'll be able to transfer money to and from your bank account.

8. Your account is currently unverified. You can verify the account by adding bank-account information; you may want to add credit-card information, too. You'll be able to transfer money between PayPal and your accounts.

9. Click the Add bank account link to see the page in Figure 2-2.

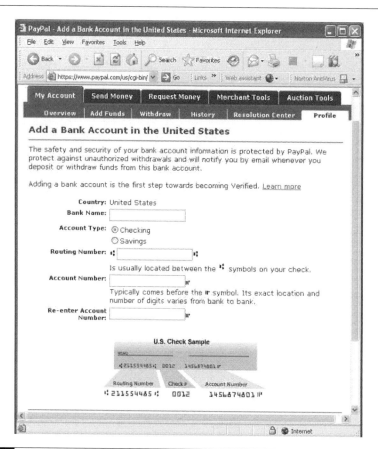

FIGURE 2-2   Enter your bank account information here.

10. Again, add your bank-account information: the **Bank Name, Account Type, Routing Number**, and **Account Number**. Then click the **Add Bank Account** button at the bottom of the page.

11. Though the process will seem complete, it actually isn't. It still has a few days to go since PayPal will place a couple of small deposits into your bank account—essentially only a few cents. When you see the deposits—in a statement, online, or through phone banking, perhaps—log back into your PayPal account and click the Confirm Bank Account link that appears, and then enter the amounts deposited (thus proving you have access to the account).

12. To link a credit card to your account, follow a similar procedure, beginning with clicking the Add credit card link. This process only takes a few moments with eBay contacting the credit-card network to verify the card.

PayPal provides a number of services to assist and protect eBay merchants, including the following:

- **Automatic PayPal logo insertion**   When you create an eBay listing (see Chapter 5) and select PayPal as a payment method, the logo appears automatically.

- **Offer PayPal Buyer Credit**   PayPal pays you, and the buyer pays PayPal over time.

- **Seller Protection Policy**   PayPal guarantees you won't be hit with a chargeback caused by fraudulent use of an account, as long as you follow certain steps (require a delivery signature for goods over $250, keep proof of delivery, and so on).

- **Invoicing**   You can send customers invoices, which are paid through PayPal.

- **Shipping Center**   Calculate costs, pay for shipping (UPS and the post office), and print packing slips.

- **ATM/Debit Card**   You can get a free debit card that allows you to take money out of your PayPal account at any ATM machine, or at any store that takes MasterCard. Plus, if you use PayPal Preferred in your eBay listings (see Chapter 5), you'll earn 1 percent back on your purchases.

There are other handy services, too. See the PayPal site for more information.

Using My eBay

The My eBay page (see Figure 2-3) is your home on eBay. You'll see the **My eBay** tab at the top of eBay wherever you go, so you can quickly return.

Buy	Sell	My eBay	Community	Help

From My eBay, you can get to wherever you need to go. For instance, you can

- View **reminders** about items you are buying and selling.

- View **messages** to you from the eBay staff and other eBay members.

- View items you are **watching**, are **bidding on**, have made **offers on**, that you **have won**, and items that you are **selling**, and **have sold**, and so on.

- **Manage your account**—change your **personal information** (including checking and credit-card account information), change your **address**, view and leave **feedback**, and so on.

My eBay is your personal eBay organizer, putting everything you need in one place.

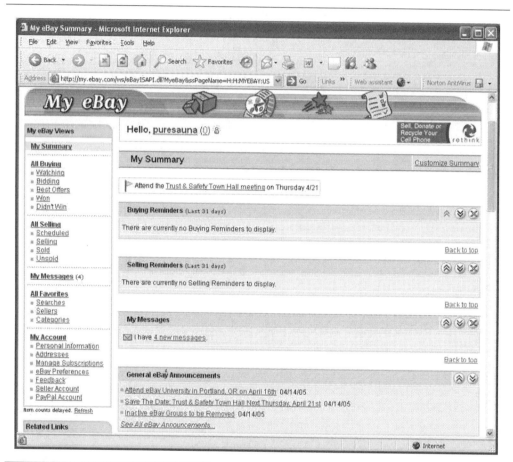

FIGURE 2-3 The My eBay page is your home page on eBay.

Creating an About Me Page

One of the challenges in an anonymous forum such as eBay is making it a little less anonymous. When someone sees a product they want to buy, particularly a new eBay user, it's natural for them to wonder, if they buy from you, will they ever see the product.

tip *To see some example About Me pages, go to http://hub.ebay.com/community, the eBay Community page. In the **Find a Member** box near the top, type an eBay member ID and click the **Find a Member** button. If you don't know a particular ID, type a word (toy, stamp, car, antique, and so on . . . there are millions of accounts so you're bound to find a match). When you search, you'll see a list. Some will have little **me** icons. Click those icons to see the About Me pages.*

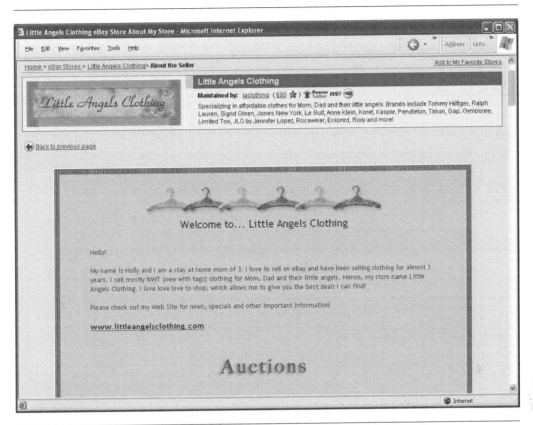

FIGURE 2-4   An example of an About Me page

The About Me page is one way to alleviate some concerns, and to make the transaction a little more personal (you can see an example in Figure 2-4). Buyers can see the page by clicking the little colored **me** icon in the Seller Information box on every product-listing page.

So, here's how to set up your **About Me** page.

1. On your **My eBay** page, click the Personal Information link in the left column under **My Account**.

2. On the page that appears, look for the **About Me page** line and click the Change link on the right.

About Me page: --   Change

3. On the page that appears, click the **Create Your Page** button.

note   *HTML is the basic web-page creation language. If you don't understand HTML, you can always have a web designer create a page for you. You can then customize the page this way more than with the step-by-step process, perhaps by adding extra images and links.*

4. You have a choice of creation methods. You can either use a simple **step-by-step process**, or you can, if you understand HTML, **enter your own HTML code** into an edit box. Select the method you want to choose, and click the **Continue** button.

Let's first look at the **step-by-step process**. Its opening page (shown in Figure 2-5) allows you to add a number of items to it:

- A page title
- Two text paragraphs
- A labeled picture
- A list of up to 100 buyer-feedback comments

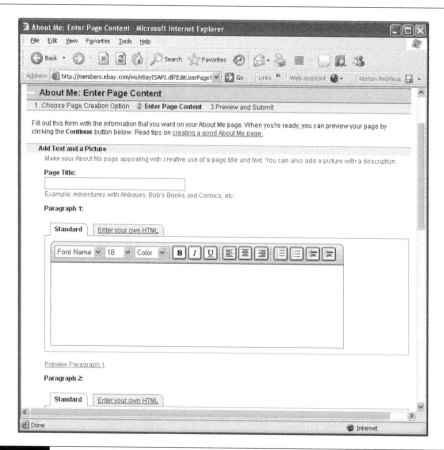

FIGURE 2-5   The step-by-step process is a simple way to create an About Me page.

■ A list of up to 200 of your product listings

■ Three links to other sites; if you have a web site, you can link to the site. (However, you may not link to a particular product page.)

5. Enter a **Page Title**.

6. Type your **Paragraph 1** text. You can use the editing tools to select a font typeface, size, and color, and format the text with bold, italics, or underline. The buttons also allow you to change paragraph settings, make the text left-justified, centered, or right-justified, create a numbered or bulleted list, and indent the text.

7. If you wish, can click the <u>Enter your own HTML</u> link to open a box into which you can input HTML.

8. When you've finished the text, click the <u>Preview Paragraph 1</u> link to see what the text will look like on your page; a window opens to display it.

9. Enter the text into **Paragraph 2**. When you're finished, scroll down and you'll see more controls (Figure 2-6).

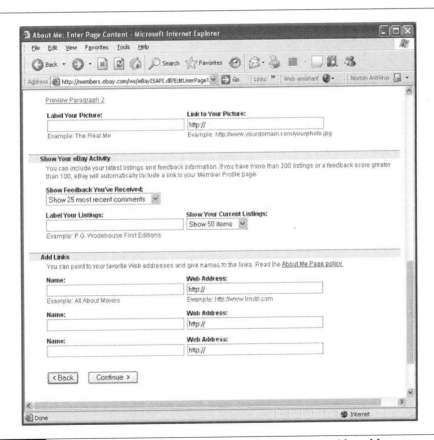

FIGURE 2-6   You can add feedback comments and listings to your About Me page.

10. If you wish, you can place a picture onto the page, as long as it's hosted somewhere else. That is, you have to enter a URL in the **Link to Your Picture** text box that points to the picture on another site. You can **Label Your Picture** if you wish.

11. You can also choose to include your feedback comments, using up to 100 of the most recent comments. Select from the **Show Feedback You've Received** drop-down list box.

12. If you plan to include your listings on the About Me page, enter a label in the **Label Your Listings** box and then select the number—up to 200—that you want to include from the **Show Your Current Listings** drop-down list box.

13. If you wish, you may add up to three links to your page. For each, provide a **Name** and the URL (**Web Address**) to point to. The **Name** is the actual link text that people can click. Remember, don't use these links to promote products for sale on other sites.

14. Click the **Continue** button and you'll see the next page (Figure 2-7).

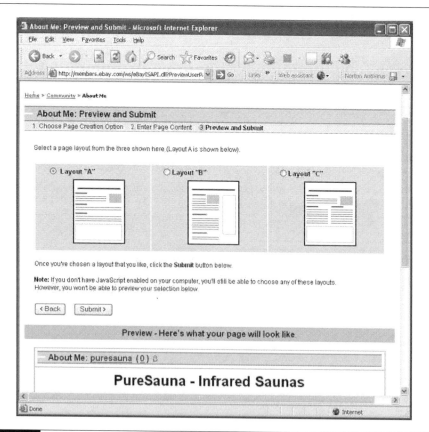

FIGURE 2-7   Pick the About Me layout you want to use.

Later, in Chapter 29, we'll discuss cross-channel marketing. If you have a web site, you cannot put information about your web site in your listing. You can, however, encourage people viewing your listings to go to your About Me page, and include a link from the About Me page to your site.

15. eBay provides three basic layouts for the page. When you select one, the **Preview** at the bottom of the page changes to show you the result.

16. You can use the **Back** button to go back and modify what you have entered, or click the **Submit** button to complete the process.

17. You can now view your page at http://members.ebay.com/aboutme/*your_eBay_ID*.

Using ID Verify

Another way to increase credibility is to use the ID Verify system. This system verifies, to some degree, that you are who you say you are, and gives buyers a little more assurance that the transaction will not be a problem. It costs $5 and is charged to your eBay account. ID Verify, a third-party firm, will check your personal information against certain public databases. Once verified, the ID Verify logo appears in your Member Profile information and is visible to buyers.

ID Verify is also required if you want to bid on auctions over $15,000 or access eBay's Mature Audiences category. Note also that once you have been verified, you cannot change your contact information for 30 days. After that you will lose your verification status if you do so, forcing you to re-verify.

There are other advantages to verification, too. If you want to sell using the Buy It Now feature, for instance, you generally need to be ID Verified.

1. Click the Services link at the top of any eBay page.

2. On the Services page, click the ID Verify link, near the top left.

3. Click the Sign Up Now link.

4. Click the **I Agree** button on the following page.

5. A **Choose a digital certificate** dialog box *may* appear. If so, simply click the **Cancel** button.

6. You'll see the Verify Account Information page. Enter your information. You'll provide your address and phone numbers, date of birth, Social Security number, and driver's license state and number. Click **Continue**.

Other verification systems, such as SquareTrade (www.squaretrade.com), are also available. SquareTrade costs $25/month, and provides a logo that is placed in your listings. This links to a page about the detailed verification, which includes a letter that is exchanged and a utility bill that must be submitted.

7. On the next page, confirm your information, and click **Continue** again. At this stage, ID Verify actually looks up your credit information.

8. On the following page, ID Verify asks questions based on information it found in your credit record. For instance, it may come back with a partial credit-card number and ask you to add the next two digits, as well as enter the card's credit limit. You may also have to provide an earlier street address. Enter the answers and click **Continue**.

That's it. You're now verified and the logo has been automatically added to your Member Profile.

Getting Help

eBay is a huge, complex system, with many different services and options. It's easy to get lost. Unfortunately, there's no way to call eBay for help. In order to reduce customer-service costs, eBay provides all its assistance online. There are, however, a number of other ways to get help.

For instance, you can click the **Help** button in the bar at the top of almost every eBay page to enter the main help area.

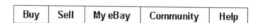

Once in the help area, you can **type a phrase and search for help** on that subject. You can also click links **to popular questions and major subject** areas.

Using the links in **the eBay Help box and Related Links box** in the Help area, you can find different types of assistance such as a list of topics, an index, a list of acronyms and a glossary, links to the Learning Center and eBay University, and so on.

You can also use the Site map and Services links at the top of most pages to find information on many subjects. In addition to this, in many areas of eBay, **little information boxes** are available that will link you to information about the process you're involved in.

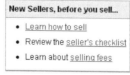

Perhaps one of the best things you can do, though, if all this fails, is to use the **Live Help** system. On many pages, you'll see a little <u>Live help</u> link. A lot of these tend to appear on pages where eBay knows people get stuck. These will open little chat windows that put you in touch with a real person.

You can also e-mail customer support, if needed. In the Help area, simply click the <u>Contact Us</u> link (inside the **eBay Help** box). You'll have to select a category of question and then two subcategories, and on the page that next appears you'll be given an <u>Email</u> link.

You're now ready to sell on eBay. But before listing that starting item, there are a few things you should learn first about selling formats, fees, and strategies, which are the subjects covered in the next chapter.

This page intentionally left blank

Chapter 3

Preparing to Sell

You've set up your account with eBay, but you're still not quite ready to buy. You need to be more familiar with the system, for a start; if you don't understand how to buy on eBay, it will be hard to sell, so we recommend you start buying right away (in fact, whatever you buy, see if you can buy it through eBay). As you'll learn, there's an added advantage: you'll boost your feedback rating.

You also need to understand the different ways you can sell through eBay, primarily Auctions, Fixed Price Listings, and a hybrid "Auction with Buy It Now." Each has its advantages and disadvantages, of course. This chapter also explains the fees you'll have to pay eBay, both when you list and when you sell your items. You'll learn about different selling and timing strategies, too, and before we move on to actually listing an item for sale, we'll discuss setting a few preferences.

Learning How to Buy on eBay

We recommend that you learn to buy on eBay. Each time you need to purchase something— a toner cartridge or a book, pens and paper, a CD—begin your online search at eBay, and buy from an eBay merchant. There are three important reasons to do this:

- ▪ You'll find great deals on eBay.
- ▪ You'll learn to understand the system from the buyer's perspective, and in general get more comfortable working with eBay.
- ▪ You'll boost your feedback rating.

In Chapter 2, we discussed using the About Me page and ID Verify to boost your credibility. Another important way to do so is to have a high feedback rating. You'll learn more about feedback in Chapter 7, but essentially the system is one in which buyers and sellers rate each other. You can get good feedback, and you can get bad feedback. People feel more comfortable buying from someone with a lot of good feedback, of course, and lots of bad feedback will eventually kill your chance of doing business through eBay (see Figure 3-1).

As a new merchant, you're at a real disadvantage—with no feedback, you're an unknown entity. But you can get feedback by making purchases through eBay, and then asking for

Member Profile: msrs_online (667 ☆) 🏆 Power Seller me			

Feedback Score:	667	Recent Ratings:			
Positive Feedback:	99.9%		Past Month	Past 6 Months	Past 12 Months
Members who left a positive:	669	⊕ positive	72	326	493
Members who left a negative:	1	◎ neutral	0	1	1
All positive feedback received:	697	⊖ negative	0	1	1
Learn about what these numbers mean.		Bid Retractions (Past 6 months): 2			

FIGURE 3-1   This merchant has great feedback. With 669 positive remarks and one negative, the negative score disappears in most people's minds.

feedback. Thus, you should get into the habit of making all your online purchases through eBay—you may even save money, and you'll build a better reputation as a *seller*.

Understanding the Selling Formats

You can sell through eBay using several different formats, as shown in the following list:

Auction	The most common form of eBay transaction
	Has the potential to get a high price
	Preferred by many eBay buyers
	Has low listing fees
	Seller can set a reserve price (for an additional fee)
Fixed Price	Involves no bidding—either someone buys or they don't
	Often leads to quicker sales
	Convenient for customers who want to buy quickly and move on
	Good for listing multiple items
Combination—Auction and Buy It Now	An auction that can be cut short if someone meets a fixed price (We'll discuss this a bit later.)
Real Estate Advertising	Not a sales tool so much as a lead generator (We won't be covering this form of selling.)

tip *Though we'll be talking here about eBay listings, you can also sell through an eBay store. We'll look at this subject in Chapter 9.*

note *A reserve price is the minimum at which you are willing to sell. If the bidding on an item doesn't reach its reserve price, the auction is cancelled.*

How do you decide which format—auction or fixed price—you should use?

Consider using an auction when . . .

- You don't know for sure what price the product can be sold for. In this instance, an Auction uses the market to set the price.

- The product is likely to have a high price if exposed to enough people. This is particularly true if the item's a hard-to-find or especially valuable product.

- It's likely that buyers will be excited to see the listing.

- You have only one copy of the item to sell.

- You can afford to wait for the sale.

Consider using a fixed price when . . .

- The item is a "commodity" item, where nobody cares to bid on it.

- It's a low-cost item.

- You have multiples of the same item.

Using Buy It Now—BIN

You can also combine a Buy It Now function with an auction, creating a sort of auction/fixed-price hybrid. BIN listings have a little **Buy It Now** icon next to them and a **Buy It Now** button on the product page. If someone clicks the Buy It Now button, the auction's over and the item is sold for the specified Buy It Now price. On the other hand, if nobody clicks it before bidding begins—or, if you have a reserve price, before the bidding passes the reserve price—then the Buy It Now option is removed.

Buy It Now price: **US $309.99**

Buy It Now >

(immediate payment required)

 tip   *You can use Listing Tools software (see Chapter 8) to automatically re-list a product as soon as it's been purchased, allowing you to keep a product posted at all times and thus maximize sales.*

BIN can be useful . . .

- For commodity items that many people want to buy without having to bid for them.

- For items that have a pretty predictable price, meaning there's no need for an auction to set the price.

- For items that people may want quickly. This way they can buy them now rather than having to wait for the auction to end.

- For speeding up product turnover. Products are often sold much more quickly in this manner, allowing you to push through a greater number of products.

Buy It Now is often used for commodity items, where pricing is fully understood. You know what the price is likely to be if sold at auction, and you know a reasonable starting price. You set the BIN somewhere around the maximum—a little below perhaps or a little above—which lets many people simply click the button rather than being made to wait.

Different Quantity Options

You can list an item, sell just one of the item, or sell multiple products simultaneously. The following list outlines the different ways to sell multiple items:

- **In an auction**   Bidders specify how much they're willing to pay, and how many of the item they want. A bid must have a higher *Total Bid Value* than the prior bid—that is, the number of items multiplied by the price must be greater than the previous bid. (This often doesn't come into play since people often bid on one item.) Buyers don't necessarily pay the bid price, though; everyone pays the lowest successful bid price.

- **Fixed price**   You can provide a fixed price for multiple items. Buyers can buy the number they want, at the price you fixed, and the listing doesn't end until they're all gone. (Particular criteria exist for this type of listing—you must be ID Verified, for instance.)

- **Lot sale**   You want to sell multiple items to a single buyer as a "lot," rather than one by one to different buyers.

 Selling multiple items through an auction is typically known as a Dutch Auction.

eBay Fees

eBay is not a charity, of course; it's going to charge you to list and sell your products. Essentially, two main fees must be paid: an **Insertion Fee**, charged when you list your item, and a **Final Value Fee**, charged when you sell the item.

 You can find a listing of all the fees at the following web address: http://pages.ebay .com/help/sell/fees.html.

You pay the Insertion Fee whether or not you sell the item. Plus, you pay a fee for *each* category into which you place the product. An example of this type of pricing is shown in the following listing:

Starting or Reserve Price	Insertion Fee
$0.01–$0.99	$0.25
$1.00–$9.99	$0.35
$10.00–$24.99	$0.60
$25.00–$49.99	$1.20
$50.00–$199.99	$2.40
$200.00–$499.99	$3.60
$500.00 or more	$4.80

What if you're listing multiple items? (You'll see how to do that later, in Chapter 5.) You simply multiply the price by the number of items. Even then, you never pay more than $4.80 for one listing.

The Final Value Fee is charged when you sell the item. If you don't sell, you don't pay the fee, of course. The Final Value Fee is based on the actual price you sold the item for; this doesn't include any shipping charges. Some examples of Final Value Fees are shown in the following listing:

Selling Price	Final Value Fee
$0.01–$25.00	5.25%
$25.01–$1,000.00	5.25% of the initial $25.00 ($1.31), plus 2.75% of the rest
Over $1,000.00	$28.12 plus 1.50% of the price above $1,000.00

These fees are for most products, but some items have a different fee schedule. For instance, the following list shows the current fees for vehicles:

Category	Insertion Fee	Transaction Service Fee
Passenger Vehicles	$40.00	$40.00
Motorcycles	$30.00	$30.00
Powersports	$30.00	$30.00
Pocket Bikes	$3.00	$3.00
Other Vehicles	$40.00	$40.00

 tip *Remember, other fees are involved in completing a transaction. If you're using PayPal, for instance, you'll probably be paying 2.9% of the transaction price, plus 30 cents.*

In the case of vehicles, eBay charges a Transaction Service Fee, payable, whether or not the item is actually sold, when the first bid is placed, or, if using a reserve price, when the reserve is met.

Another special category is that of Business & Industrial products, such as farm machinery and manufacturing equipment, which have $20 insertion fees and a 1-percent Final Value Fee with a $250 maximum.

Other fees to keep in mind are those for ancillary services and for using specific categories on eBay. The following shows a more comprehensive list.

Reserve Fees	$1 for items up to $49.99, $2 for items up to $199.99, and 1% of the reserve price above that (to a maximum of $100). But note that if you sell the item, these fees are refunded.
Buy It Now Fees	From 5 cents to 25 cents depending on the Buy It Now price.
Picture Services Fees	When you list an item, you can include one picture free. You can add more, though, for 15 cents each, "supersize" a picture (75 cents), create an animated picture show (25 cents), or purchase a special Picture Pack that allows you more images than these other image services for $1 or $2.
Listing Upgrade Fees	You can "tart up" your listing by including a photo in the search results (Gallery), adding bold to your listing text, putting your item in the Featured Items section of a category (Featured Plus!), adding the item to a special placement program that may see it placed onto the home page, and so on. These fees vary from 10 cents to $80.

Selling Strategies

As you've seen, there are different ways to sell through eBay and different strategies you can use. Now we'll discuss a few concepts and things to know.

 tip *When you list an item on eBay, you are committing to sell it under the conditions you set. If you set a $10,000 product with no reserve, and someone bids $1, you're obliged to sell! Of course, eBay won't send thugs around to your house to beat you up if you refuse, but you could find yourself getting kicked off eBay if you don't honor your commitments.*

Traditional Auction, No Reserve, Low Opening Bid	No-reserve auctions get a lot of bidding; reserves often put people off, because they feel that there's little chance of getting the product at a price they want to pay.
	Paradoxically, because these types of listings get bidding rolling quickly, they often end up with a high sales price.
	There's a danger, however: you may end up selling the product very cheaply.

 note *Studies carried out by eBay have shown that low starting prices combined with no reserve generally pay off for merchants that sell a lot of products. For instance, merchants selling diamonds starting at $1 with no reserve generate a lot of bidding excitement, which carries the price up. These merchants may lose on some transactions, but in the end make more money than if they had listed with a reserve price.*

Auctions with a Reserve	You can set a reserve price, letting you limit your liability.
	Often used on expensive items.
	If bids don't reach the reserve price, the item isn't sold.
	Reserves tend to discourage bidding.
Auction, No Reserve, Higher Opening Bid	These help limit your potential losses.
	Merchants often set prices from 20–40% below market.
	Because there's no reserve, you're still likely to get good bidding.
Auction with Buy It Now (BIN)	Decreases sales time.
	In some cases, it may decrease sales price.
	Merchants sometimes post a high BIN price to make buyers think the item is more valuable. However, this can backfire and lead to low bidding and a lower sales price.
	Merchants often use an average selling price as the start price and then a BIN price that's a few dollars above.
	Don't place the BIN price too low because the BIN acts as a cap; nobody's going to bid higher than the BIN.
Fixed Price	You'll never see the highest prices generated by enthusiastic bidding.
	Involves no liability and has a totally predictable selling price.

Timing Strategies

The timing of an auction is also important. When you list an item, you define when the auction starts and how long it will last. The following are a few ideas:

- More people browse and search through eBay during evenings and weekends. Thus, letting an auction extend over a weekend is often a good thing.

- The longer something is on sale, the more people will see it. However . . .

- If an item is very popular, with heavy bidding, you need less time.

 tip   *Once you're selling a lot of products, you should consider the effect of timing on your workload! You don't want to have all your auctions end at the same time and be unable to process them quickly.*

Setting Your Preferences

Before you're ready to sell, you should at least check your preferences. Go to your **My eBay** page, and click the **eBay Preferences** link (in the **My Account** links, on the left). The **eBay Preferences** page is shown in Figure 3-2.

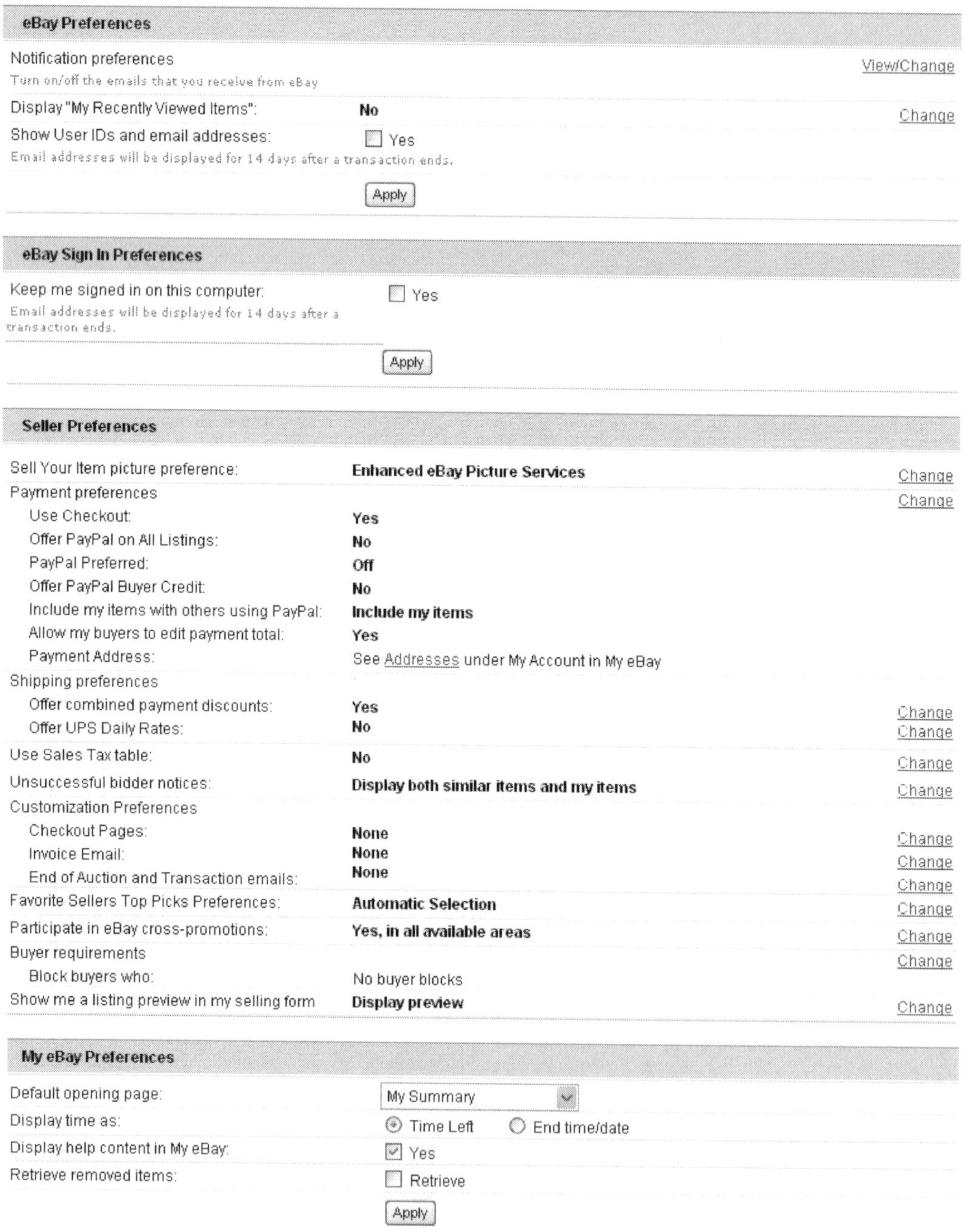

eBay Preferences

Notification preferences   View/Change
Turn on/off the emails that you receive from eBay

Display "My Recently Viewed Items":   **No**   Change

Show User IDs and email addresses: ☐ Yes
Email addresses will be displayed for 14 days after a transaction ends.

[Apply]

eBay Sign In Preferences

Keep me signed in on this computer: ☐ Yes
Email addresses will be displayed for 14 days after a
transaction ends.

[Apply]

Seller Preferences

Sell Your Item picture preference:	**Enhanced eBay Picture Services**	Change
Payment preferences		Change
Use Checkout:	**Yes**	
Offer PayPal on All Listings:	**No**	
PayPal Preferred:	**Off**	
Offer PayPal Buyer Credit:	**No**	
Include my items with others using PayPal:	**Include my items**	
Allow my buyers to edit payment total:	**Yes**	
Payment Address:	See Addresses under My Account in My eBay	
Shipping preferences		
Offer combined payment discounts:	**Yes**	Change
Offer UPS Daily Rates:	**No**	Change
Use Sales Tax table:	**No**	Change
Unsuccessful bidder notices:	**Display both similar items and my items**	Change
Customization Preferences		
Checkout Pages:	**None**	Change
Invoice Email:	**None**	Change
End of Auction and Transaction emails:	**None**	Change
Favorite Sellers Top Picks Preferences:	**Automatic Selection**	Change
Participate in eBay cross-promotions:	**Yes, in all available areas**	Change
Buyer requirements		Change
Block buyers who:	No buyer blocks	
Show me a listing preview in my selling form	**Display preview**	Change

My eBay Preferences

Default opening page: [My Summary   ▾]

Display time as: ⦿ Time Left   ○ End time/date

Display help content in My eBay: ☑ Yes

Retrieve removed items: ☐ Retrieve

[Apply]

FIGURE 3-2   Check your preferences here before you get started.

You don't need to worry about everything here—when you have a spare moment, click a few Change links and read through the descriptions. But there are a few things you should adjust.

- **Add PayPal.** If you've set up a PayPal account, click the Change link next to Payment Preferences, and select the **Offer PayPal as a payment method in all my listings** check box to automatically place the PayPal logo in your pages. You may also mark the **Tell Buyers that I prefer PayPal payments** check box if you wish (doing so gets you a rebate on your PayPal debit card; see Chapter 2).

- If you're going to accept **mailed checks**, enter a **Payment Address** on the same page.

- If you have a **UPS Daily Pickup Account**, see the UPS options at the bottom of this page, too.

- Specify how much you plan to charge for sales tax, in what states, and whether you have to apply sales tax to shipping fees. Click the Change link on the **Use Sales Tax table** line. For a more detailed discussion of sales tax, see Chapter 19.

- You can **customize** your checkout pages, invoice e-mails, and end-of-auction and transaction e-mails if you wish, adding logos and personalizing the messages. Use the Change links under **Customization Preferences**.

You're almost there . . . almost ready to sell. But there's one last important thing you must do: decide how to ship your products. It's a good idea to know how you'll ship something *before* you sell it! So that's just what we'll look at in the next chapter.

This page intentionally left blank

Chapter 4

Planning Your Shipping

You must think about shipping *before* you start selling, for a couple of reasons. You have to know what it's going to cost to ship; you don't want to guess at this, and then discover that shipping the item is eating up the profit of the sale you've just made. And in order to know how much it costs to ship, you have to know *how* you're going to ship. Also, you don't want to make a sale and then think, "Now, how am I going to get this book/computer/llama to the buyer?" In fact, if you don't figure all this out first, you probably won't get the sale anyway. Who buys without having a reasonable estimate of the final cost?

In this chapter, we'll examine these issues, from packing carefully to shipping affordably. The good news is that all this is *much* easier than it was way back in the 20th Century. Shipping services are competing heavily, and the free market seems to be doing its job—all the major shipping services have introduced online tools to let you pack, label, and ship, without ever leaving the comfort of your cave.

 tip   *eBay and PayPal, combined, make shipping via UPS and the post office very easy. For this reason, many merchants, perhaps most, use these methods. However, you should still consider other services. You may find, in some circumstances, that you can ship a particular type of product more cheaply using another service.*

The Internet Shipping Revolution

If you haven't looked closely at shipping services in the last few years, you may have missed what's going on. The Internet has revolutionized the shipping industry, due to a few of the following reasons:

- **Businesses and shipping services can now connect directly,** providing a way for these services to market to businesses and for businesses to make their shipping operations more efficient.

- **There are more small merchants now than five years ago.** Services such as eBay, Yahoo! Merchant Services, Amazon Marketplace, and thousands of others, have created a new merchant class: small online businesses, shipping products to their customers.

Here's a list of the more obvious online services available to small businesses:

■ **Print stamps online.** The post office lets you buy stamps online and print them on your laser printer.

Here's the quickest way to track a package (if you haven't been given a direct link to a tracking page in an e-mail or web page). Don't go to the shipping service web site. Rather, begin by installing the Google toolbar; you can download it from toolbar.google.com. Now, whenever someone gives you a tracking number, enter it into Google toolbar and press ENTER. Google checks all numbers used in searches to see if they match various different formats. If Google thinks the number is a UPS, FedEx, or USPS tracking number, it links directly to the tracking page.

■ **Print labels online.** All the major shipping services let you print shipping labels online.

Getting a tracking number into the hands of your customers will reduce your customer-service costs. Most buyers will use the tracking number, rather than contacting you when they're impatient and the package hasn't arrived yet!

■ **Track packages.** You can track packages online at all the major services.

■ **Combine everything.** As you'll see in Chapter 7, eBay, PayPal, the post office, and UPS have teamed up to create the following process:

1. On eBay, select **Print Shipping Label**; you're then taken to PayPal.

2. Once at the PayPal site, select the shipping service, UPS or USPS.

3. Provide the address information.

4. Provide the package weight and size, pick a shipping method, and calculate the cost.

5. Print the shipping label.

6. Automatically send the recipient a notification e-mail, with a tracking link.

7. Order a package pickup.

8. Pay for the shipping.

Consider that this process can be accomplished in literally minutes, and does not require you to step away from your desk, let alone drive to a shipping center or post office miles away. The shipping world has truly undergone a revolution. Standing in line for stamps is just *so* 20th Century!

Picking Packing Materials

The first thing to consider is how you will pack the product. Until you know that, you don't really know the cost, because you won't know the size and weight. You have several conflicting goals here. You want to:

■ **Ensure the product is well protected.** Handling products that are damaged in shipping is time-consuming and expensive.

■ **Package in a way that looks professional.** If your packaging appears shoddy, it may be the last sale you ever make to that buyer.

- **Pay as little as possible for packing materials.** Packing materials can be a significant cost, which eat into your profits or may increase your sales price too much.

- **Pay as little as possible for shipping.** The same goes for shipping—the lower the cost, the better.

Clearly, these goals conflict with each other. You can cut the cost of packing dramatically, but doing so may increase your damaged-goods rate, and may reflect poorly on you. Or you can package the product in a large box with a huge amount of padding, thus greatly increasing your shipping costs.

tip *Don't overpack! The package may look fine when it leaves your business, but after it's traveled a couple of thousand miles, it can get beaten around a bit. For instance, if you pack books too tightly into a padded envelope, they may, after rubbing against other packages for a few days, start to tear at the tight points. Dealing with bad packaging often costs more than expensive quality packaging, so do the job right.*

You should experiment with packaging before you get started by doing the following:

- **Visit an office-supply store.** To see what sort of packaging is available, stop by one of your local office suppliers.

- **Talk with a shipping center.** The best way to find out how a shipping office typically packages items is to contact them directly. Since they do this all day every day, they know what they're talking about.

- **Check the pricing of packaging online.** You can check packaging pricing through eBay or by using the various search engines available.

- **Visit eBay's Packing & Shipping page.** You can find loads of information about how to package well and affordably at the following address: http://pages.ebay.com/sellercentral/shipping.html. You'll also find links to packing-supply vendors.

- **Look at how other companies package the same sort of products.** Large, well-established companies learned long ago how to pack their products to minimize breakage and claims. So even if their packing materials seem excessive, there may be a good reason for it.

- **Ask a shipping company.** Visit a shipping service—the post office, or a UPS or FedEx office, for instance—and ask how to ship an item, what the best methods are for shipping, and the regulations related to the different types of shipping. For instance, officially Media Mail packages cannot include advertising (though probably a huge proportion of Media Mail packages contain advertising inserts).

- **Visit the shipping companies' web sites.** At shipping company web sites you can find rates, regulations, and advice.

You should actually pack an item yourself first—it's surprising what you can forget if you don't actually do it. You might even go so far as to ship the product—perhaps to a friend across the country and back—and see how it fares.

We can't suggest how you should package your products; every product is different, but a little investigation and a few questions posed to the right people should lead you to the right answer. Either way, you need to completely prepare your shipping department beforehand. The following is a reminder list of the sort of materials you might need:

- Padded envelopes
- Bubble wrap rolls
- Shipping scales
- "Peanut" packing material

tip *Ideally, you'll be printing shipping labels directly from the service you work with, rather than filling them out by hand; all the major services let you enter shipping information, print the label, and pay at the same time. You might consider buying self-adhesive labels for your printer, and then printing the shipping label directly onto these; it'll save you having to tape the label to the box, and will reduce the chance of the label being torn off.*

- Shipping boxes (remember to allow for multiple-item orders; one size is rarely enough)
- Packing tape
- Box cutters (to cut boxes, tape, bubble wrap rolls, and so on)
- Self-adhesive address labels
- Stretch film
- Inflatable packaging (plastic air bags, as Amazon currently uses)
- Styrofoam packing sheets
- Plastic bags
- Shrink-wrap
- Wooden crates for particularly heavy items

tip *The major shipping companies all offer some free shipping materials. For instance, FedEx, UPS, and the post office all provide envelopes and boxes. You may need to provide the packing material inside, but why pay for the outside if you can get it for free? Of course, the free packing material is generally for premium services, not the lowest-cost methods. The post office even provides "co-branded" boxes—boxes with the eBay logo on them—for free. You can order them online and they'll deliver them to your door (see http://ebaysupplies.usps.com/).*

Once you learn the packing business, you'll never look back. There are all sorts of weird and wonderful products; whatever you're shipping, from leather to llamas, someone, somewhere, has created a packing material for it.

Remember that you will package products differently according to the shipping method. For instance, if you're shipping books via "Media Mail"—the cheapest way—you'll have to provide your own packaging. If you're shipping via Express Mail or Priority Mail, you can let the post office provide some of the packaging for you.

Packaging "Best Practices"

Whatever you're shipping, you have to pack carefully, but some items are more challenging than others—for instance:

- Fragile items
- Valuable items
- Large items
- Heavy items
- Posters/flat items

tip *Visit the eBay Shipping Tips page at http://pages.ebay.com/help/sell/shipping.html for some sage advice.*

tip *Packing materials can be expensive, so it's tempting to skimp. Don't give into the temptation! Do it right, and you'll save money in the long run.*

The following are a few tips to help you pack properly:

- **Use *clean* packing material.** Packing materials should preferably be new (or at least appear new).

- **Don't use newspapers.** See the first tip! Newspaper is *not* clean.

- **Use a sturdy container.** The heavier the item, the sturdier it needs to be.

note *While some shipping services provide free insurance up to a certain value, the insurance is dependent on the item being packed correctly. If there's damage, the company may choose to inspect the shipment and deny your insurance claim if it was badly packed.*

- **Use the correct size.** In most cases, use a container that includes a little extra room for the object. Squeezing into a tight package can lead to damage en route.

- **Double-box fragile items.** Think about how computer companies ship computers— they place the computer into a box, then they place that box into a much larger box, suspended in some kind of packing material. And be realistic—the outside box needs to be more than ¼" larger than the inside.

- **Make sure padding material totally suspends the item.** The item, or interior box, should not touch the shipping container on any side.

- **Send posters in tubes.** You should buy very sturdy tubes for posters; some merchants believe the free tubes provided by the postal service aren't sturdy enough.

- **Make sure your staff follows the rules.** If you employee someone to do your packing and shipping, make sure they do it right, every time.

- **Include paperwork.** Remember to include clear documentation within the package—an invoice, for instance, providing contact information (your phone number and e-mail address), your eBay ID, returns information, a packing list, and so on.

Who Will You Ship With?

The United States is dominated by three major shipping services: USPS (United States Postal Service), UPS (United Parcel Service), and FedEx. The vast majority of all shipments go through these organizations. However, there are others vying for your attention, which may be worth checking with, such as:

- **DHL/Airborne Express**   Similar to FedEx, these companies recently merged.
- **TSI**   TSI focuses on items that are too big or heavy for most "parcel" services, but too light or small for a moving company.
- **DAS**   DAS stands for Dependable Auto Shippers, which is eBay's vehicle shipper of choice. Check them out at www.dasautoshippers.com.

Specialty shippers are also available, and can ship just about everything. Need to send that llama to Norway? Contact AnimalTransportation.com.

Estimating Shipping Costs

Once you've figured out how you're going to ship the product, you can estimate shipping costs. Once again, however, you'll face contradictory goals. The ideal shipping service is one that is

- **Fast**   You want to get the product into your buyer's hands as soon as possible.
- **Reliable**   Problems cost you time and money.
- **Cheap**   Cheap, as always, is good. The cheaper you can get the product into their hands, the better for both of you.

Before you start comparing prices, you'll need the following information:

- The packed-item weight
- The package dimensions
- The value of the contents (for calculating insurance)
- The origin ZIP code and the delivery ZIP code or country

With this information, you can now compare rates. You may want to create a simple little table with, say, five or six shipment types compared against three or four services, like that shown next:

	USPS	FedEx	UPS	DHL
One item, standard shipping				
One item, three-day				
One item, overnight				
Two items, standard				
Two items, three-day				
Two items, overnight				

Why two columns for each package? You'll want to see the effect of different ZIP codes. Try one in your state for instance, and one from the other side of the country. By the way, don't worry; this won't take long. Once you've determined all the criteria you plan to use for each shipment—size, weight, value, ZIPs—you can actually fill in this form very quickly.

note   *You may end up using two or three different services, depending on what you're trying to do. For instance, you might use the USPS for your cheapest shipments and FedEx for your fast shipments.*

Now, it's time to compare rates. Here are a few good places to do that:

■ **iShip.com**   This service provides a quick way to compare rates for the USPS, UPS, and DHL/Airborne Express (see Figure 4-1). It will show you different days and delivery times and the costs for various services from each company.

■ **The U.S. Post Office web site** (www.USPS.com)   We're happy that they finally hired a decent web-design firm and now have a very easy-to-use and useful web site that's comparable to the major commercial shipping services.

■ **FedEx**   www.Fedex.com

■ **UPS**   www.UPS.com

■ **DHL/Airborne Express**   www.DHL.com

tip   *Don't forget discounts! Some shipping services will provide you with a discount off the regular rate table if you set up an account (which you'll probably want to do anyway if you're shipping a lot). Some professional and trade associations also have discount agreements with large shippers.*

When you have all the numbers, go through them and consider various issues:

■ Remember that some services provide **free shipping containers**. Factor these reduced packing costs into the equation. Thus, you may find that shipping quickly is often slightly less expensive than it at first appears, thanks to the free boxes.

■ **Can you work with the service online?** You should be able to print shipping labels, pay, and order pickups online.

■ **Look for shipping methods that are comparable.** For instance, First Class Mail is generally much cheaper than Priority or Express, but it is still reasonably fast.

■ **Will the shipper pick up the packages from your location?** Is there a minimum pick-up quantity or other requirements, and is there a charge?

■ **Consider insurance.** Some services include a level of free insurance; others don't. How much will additional insurance cost, and can you buy it online?

■ **Investigate tracking services.** All the major services now provide tracking services, but some are better than others. (There's a long time-delay on tracking USPS orders, for instance.) Consider how you will deliver tracking numbers to the buyer; shipping through the eBay/PayPal system automates this, sending a tracking e-mail to the buyer when you print the label.

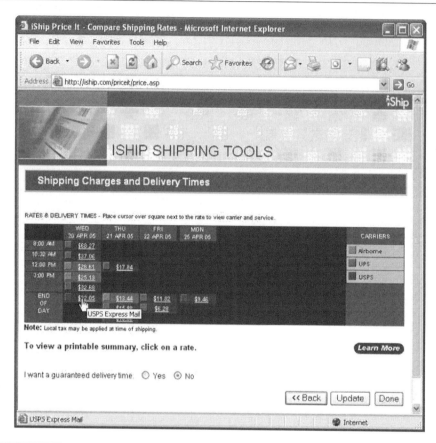

FIGURE 4-1 The iShip Shipping Calculator compares several shipping methods.

 tip *Even services, such as first-class mail and Media Mail, that don't normally have tracking, often have delivery confirmation available. In fact, if you create your USPS shipping labels online, delivery confirmation is free. (With full-tracking services, of course, delivery confirmation is included.)*

Calculating a Packaging and Handling Fee

Once you know how much each service costs, you should create a schedule of fees for different services. Depending on your products, you'll probably want to offer several shipping methods (not necessarily using these terms, of course):

- **Cheap and slow**   For buyers who want the lowest price, and don't care too much when it arrives. If selling books, for instance, this could be Media Mail.

- **Overnight**   For customers who simply have to have it immediately.

- **3-day**   For customers who can't decide! They really, really want it, but they don't want to pay the huge overnight fees.

 tip   *It's a good idea to let customers know just how slow the "cheap and slow" method actually is. Media Mail, for instance, can take up to nine days. Don't assume buyers will realize this, or you may spend time dealing with upset customers.*

Now you need to calculate your final shipping charges. Note that there are basically three ways to do this when working through eBay:

- **Method 1: Calculate shipping fees after the sale.** When sending an invoice to a buyer, you can figure out what it will cost to send the item to the buyer's location, and then add it. *This is a bad way to ship the product!* Worse, you'll reduce the number of bids on your item. If someone else is selling the same product, and they clearly state their shipping fees, they'll get the sale!

- **Method 2: Provide a flat fee for the product.** Everyone, wherever they are, pays the same for a particular shipping method. This is better than Method 1, but still isn't great in some cases. It may work well for small items—for instance, it costs the same to ship a Media Mail package anywhere in the country—but it's a problem with shipping methods that vary according to the distance shipped. Either you'll charge some people more than necessary in order to make sure you don't lose money, or you'll lose money on some shipments.

- **Method 3: Provide a base fee, and then let eBay calculate postage.** This is the best method. You'll charge as little as necessary and no more—you won't lose money, and buyers will pay the minimum.

You'll find out how to calculate shipping fees in Chapter 5, but for now the following shows the basic process:

1. For each shipping method, calculate how much it will cost you to package the product. Remember, some methods come with free packing materials.

2. Figure out how much time and effort it takes to pack the item, or how much you have to pay someone to do it for you. (Remember, using your own children is cheap, and they rarely complain to the Department of Labor.) Come up with a handling fee.

3. Add these two numbers together to calculate your base fee. This will be your *Packaging and Handling fee.*

4. You'll provide this fee to eBay as the base fee when listing a product (see Figure 4-2).

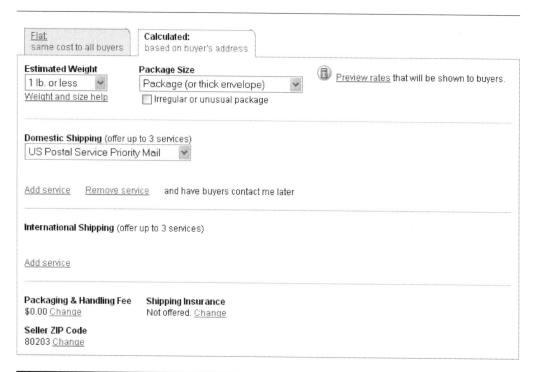

FIGURE 4-2 When setting up shipping calculations, you can enter your Packaging and Handling fee near the bottom of the page.

 Buyers don't see these two fees; they just see a single shipping charge. In many cases, merchants actually make a little money on the shipping and handling. But remember, you're often competing with merchants who sometimes cut or eliminate their shipping fees in order to get the sale.

5. When eBay calculates the buyer's shipping charge, it looks at the origin and delivery ZIP codes and calculates the actual USPS or UPS shipping fee. It then *adds* your Packaging and Handling fee to calculate the total shipping charge.

Considering "Shipping Strategies"

Shipping is not just a necessity and a nuisance; it can also be considered a competitive differentiator and a marketing tool. Many companies use shipping in various ways to grab the attention of prospects, and to turn first-time customers into repeat buyers. Here are a few ideas:

■ **Offer "free" shipping.** This is hard to do with auctions, of course, but easier with fixed-price listings.

■ **Offer free shipping as an incentive.** This can be set up as buy two items and get free shipping, get free shipping on automatic reorders, receive free shipping on orders over $50, and so on.

The following are a few more useful shipping resources on eBay: the USPS Shipping Zone (pages.ebay.com/usps/), the UPS Shipping Zone (pages.ebay.com/ups/), and the eBay Shipping Center (www.ebay.com/shippingcenter).

■ **Offer fixed-price shipping.** Offer a single price for shipping, regardless of how much the customer buys. Whether one or a thousand products, the shipping rate is still $5.95, for example.

■ **Explain packing in your listing description.** With hundreds of thousands of people selling online at any time, eBay has its fair share of bozos who will throw the product into any old box and pad it with newspaper, old plastic bags, or junk-food wrapping. Some merchants believe that explaining that you only use new, clean packing material helps persuade buyers that you're professional.

■ **Make shipping costs simple for your customers.** As you'll see in Chapter 5, you can have eBay calculate shipping costs for the customer. eBay claims that doing this increases the likelihood of a sale because buyers are more comfortable bidding when they know exactly what it will cost to ship.

■ **Pack to impress.** Some merchants actually use their packing and shipping as a differentiator. They pack extremely well, and they let potential customers know this in their listing and in their About Me pages; some merchants even claim to get a lot of good feedback mentioning their packaging.

■ **Sell again with your packaging.** Both the inside and outside represent opportunities to promote your business. Include flyers, a request for the buyer to leave feedback, as well as catalogs, samples, and bonuses.

Amazon used to advertise on TV. Not any more. They decided that offering free shipping to customers was more valuable than getting their name on TV, so they took the TV-ad budget and poured it into their free-shipping offers.

Some shipping strategies may be easier to use for some merchants than others. If you're selling books or gold coins, for instance, free shipping is certainly a possibility. If you're selling slabs of granite and marble, it's more of a problem.

Shipping Overseas

Shipping overseas is definitely more of a problem, but many businesses ship a considerable amount of their products outside the United States. So, unless it's simply impractical—for instance, you're shipping guns, or those marble and granite slabs we mentioned earlier—you should probably consider it. A few things to watch for include the following:

- This probably won't be a surprise, but it's **more expensive to ship outside the country**. It's still viable for high-value goods, but not so much for low-cost goods.

- It can take **a long time to ship to the other side of the world**. To get a general idea just how long, take a look at the post office's International Priority Mail and International Express Mail services, which provide fairly quick shipping times at a reasonable cost.

- Don't forget **customs declaration forms**. This is one more step needed before you can ship overseas. And also be aware that some countries want to charge a custom's duty on items. Buyers must be aware that they are responsible for these fees; there's no practical way for you to deal with them.

- Some third-world countries, such as Canada, have a tendency to **stop everything crossing their borders** and try to extract a fee.

- **Consider fraud.** Though not a shipping issue, fraud is still an important concern. Western Europe has very low fraud rates, but some countries (we might mention eastern Europe) have very high rates. This is something we talk about in more detail in Chapter 18.

tip   *The major shipping services provide customs forms online. For instance, to find the U.S. Postal Service custom forms, visit http://webapps.usps.com/customsforms/. You can even fill in the form online and print out the completed document.*

Finally, we're done! We're now ready to sell through eBay. In the next chapter, we'll look at exactly how to go about listing your products on the site.

Chapter 5

Listing Your Items Effectively

In this chapter you're going to learn how to submit an item for sale in eBay. There's a lot to cover. We're going to discuss how to create your photographs, the different ways in which you can list items, how much eBay charges, how to enter information and pictures for your listing, specifying payment and shipping, and so on.

This chapter is not intended as a quick step-through process. We're going to show you the process step-by-step, but we'll be stopping and explaining various concepts and issues in detail as we go. So, we advise you read through this once before you begin listing your first item, otherwise eBay may timeout and make you start again.

Creating Your Photographs

You're going to need photos of the products you're selling; you can *try* to sell without pictures, but you'll regret it—in general they're unlikely to sell well.

In many cases you can get product photographs from a supplier; in many other cases, you'll have to get the photos yourself. That's not necessarily difficult.

You *don't* need the very best digital camera for your pictures. Digital photography has advanced tremendously over the last few years, which means the top-end equipment is amazing . . . but it also means that good equipment, good enough for taking pictures to post on a web page, is cheap.

The basic requirements are pretty simple:

■ **2.0 megapixels**   Get a camera that produces images with 2 megapixels or more.

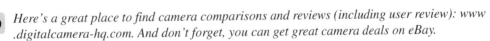 *Here's a great place to find camera comparisons and reviews (including user review): www .digitalcamera-hq.com. And don't forget, you can get great camera deals on eBay.*

■ **Optical zoom**   Optical zoom is more important than digital zoom.

■ **Macro mode**   Macro, or close-up, mode, lets you take photographs very close to the object, allowing you to get fine details.

- **Optical viewfinder**   You need a camera with an optical viewfinder (a glass viewer you look through, like on a film camera).
- **Manual flash**   You should be able to control the flash, so *you* determine when the flash is used and when it isn't.

A camera tripod can be very useful, too! They're pretty cheap and will help you steady the camera while you take photographs, ensuring the sharpest photo possible.

- **Well-known brand**   Picking a brand that is well known and has a good reputation ensures you'll get something decent.

Taking Great Photographs

Here are a few tips for taking great photos:

- **Lighting**   Poorly lit products are going to look bad. Just hitting the item with a flash usually isn't good enough, as it often creates reflections, high spots, and dark spots. You might try outside light. Bright but cloudy days are often good, because the light is more diffuse; you don't want heavy shadows.

Getting lighting just right is very tricky for the amateur photographer. There's a great little tool that might help, though. Take a look at the Cloud Dome and Cloud Cube (www .CloudDome.com). You place the object into the dome or tent, shine lights on the outside, and snap the picture through a porthole. You'll get diffuse, even light.

- **Focus**   Make sure your pictures are in focus. Use a tripod to keep your camera still while you snap.
- **Background**   Remove the clutter! Before you snap, look at the object and the background. Cluttered backgrounds are both distracting and look amateurish.
- **Plenty of shots**   The great thing about digital "film" is that it's cheap. Take plenty of pictures: you want to make sure you get some good ones, and you want to provide several pictures to your potential buyers.

The Selling Process

Once you've sold a few times, it will become natural. But there are actually a number of steps in the entire process you need to understand. When you want to list an item in eBay, you're going to have to do the following:

1. Choose a **selling format**.
2. Select a **listing category**.

3. Create a **title and description**.

4. Enter **pricing information**.

5. Specify **when the item will sell**.

6. Specify **item quantity and location**.

7. Add one or more **photographs**.

8. Selecting the **listing layout and options**.

9. Provide **payment, shipping, and returns details**.

10. **Review and submit** the listing.

We'll look at these one by one.

tip   *There's a way to test the process that we recommend you use. When you list an item, place it into a Test category, so you can view it and experiment with it. You must label the item as a test in both the Title and Description fields. Do not test by putting an item into a live category; when you do so you are committing to deliver the item, and if you don't do so you could be penalized. Also, do not use a live account to leave or receive feedback; you must use a test account to do this.*

Choosing a Selling Format

In order to bring some semblance of order to the hundreds of millions of items sold through eBay every year, eBay built a categorization system. You can easily see this by going to the eBay home page and clicking on a product category—say, *Dolls & Bears*. In the page that appears (Figure 5-1), you'll find subcategories of different kinds. In some cases there's yet a third, fourth, or fifth level of categorization, too.

The first step in listing a product is selecting a category, or perhaps two, in which you want to list the products. Here's how:

1. Click the **Sell** button on the button bar at the top of the eBay screen.

Buy	Sell	My eBay	Community	Help

2. In the following page, click the **Sell Your Item** button. You'll be taken to a page with your Selling Format options (Figure 5-2).

3. You have up to four options here (if you have an eBay store, the **Sell your items in your own eBay Store** option button will be present; see Chapter 9). We're going to assume that you are selecting either **Sell item at online Auction** (you'll be able to select Buy It Now later) or **Sell at a Fixed Price**, then click the **Continue** button to see the Select Category page.

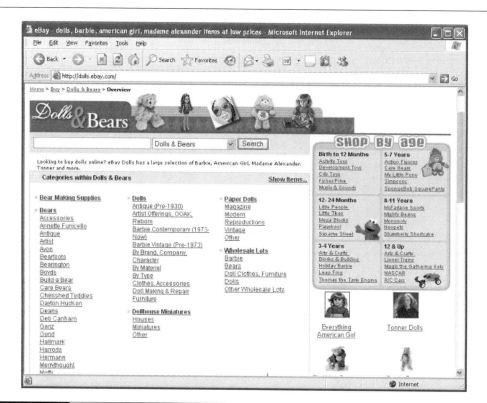

FIGURE 5-1   The Dolls & Bears page

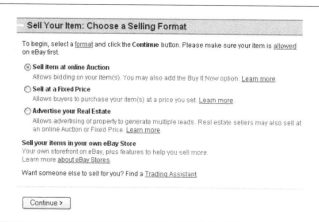

FIGURE 5-2   Selecting your Selling Format options

Selecting a Listing Category

The next step is to select the category into which you want to place your item (in the page in Figure 5-3).

tip *Listing in two categories ensures that the product is more likely to sell, but in many cases it probably isn't worthwhile unless the category is a major one for your product type. Experiment to see if this works for you.*

1. The first thing you may want to do is search using your product name; enter it into the text box in the top right and click the **Search** button. eBay searches for matching products, then opens another window and shows you where these items have been listed (see Figure 5-4). If you find two really strong categories, as in the screen shown, you may decide to list the item in both; otherwise, in most cases, you'll just want to list it in one.

note *Listing in two categories increases your fees. You'll pay two insertion fees, and some of the optional fees are doubled, too—most upgrade fees will be doubled, such as the fee for bolding text. Click the fee varies link to see details.*

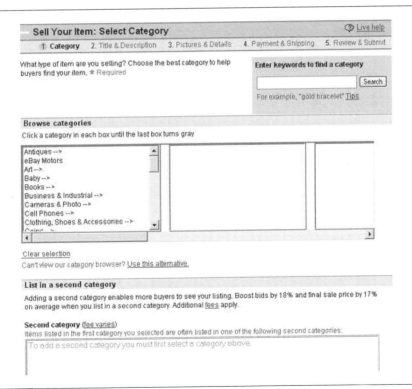

FIGURE 5-3   Begin selecting your category here.

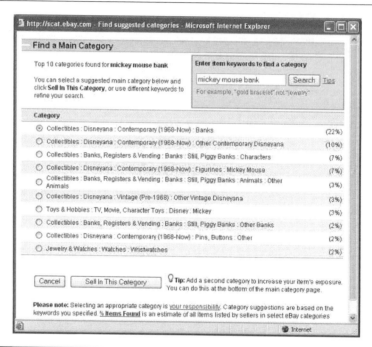

eBay can help you select an appropriate category, and show you when a single product is strong in more than one category.

2. Select a category into which you want to place the item, and click **Sell In This Category** button. The other way to select a category is to click in the first list box in the main window, which then displays subcategories in the box to the right, from which you can select.

tip   *To list the item in a test category, click on the **Everything Else** category in the first list box, then in the next text box select **Test Auctions**. In the third box select, for example, **General**.*

3. If you decide to place the item in a second category, click the Select from all categories . . . link under the **Second category** box. When you've finished, click the **Continue** button to move on to the Describe Your Item page.

Creating a Title and Description

The next step is to enter your title and description (in the page in Figure 5-5).

1. Enter an **Item title**, up to 55 characters.

2. Enter a **Subtitle** if you wish, though you'll pay an extra 50 cents ($1 if you are using two categories).

tip *You can also include pictures in your description and not pay a picture fee. See "Adding Photographs," later in this chapter.*

3. Enter your **Item description**, using the built-in editor if you wish, or the HTML box.

4. Notice the **Inserts** drop-down list box. This allows you to create blocks of text that you'll use again. Select **Create an Insert . . .** and another little window opens. Enter a title and the block of text, and click the **Save** button. You can now select the insert from the Inserts drop-down list box, in this (and later) listings.

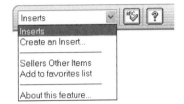

5. Check what your listing looks like so far; click the Preview description link under the description box.

6. Click the **Continue** button to move to the next screen.

tip *Remember to spell check; if someone is searching for a digital camera, they won't find your digtal camera. And avoid terms that are likely to be misunderstood.*

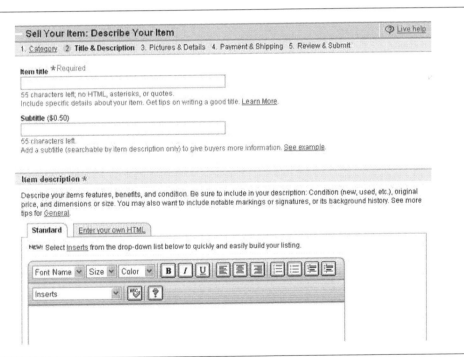

FIGURE 5-5   Describe the item you are selling in this page.

tip *eBay does not allow you to use a different product's name in the title. For instance, you can't name a product as being* like *another product, as it's misleading. You can't say, for instance,* Digital Camera, Similar to the Nikon PowerShot SD110.

Let's consider a few ways to make your listing sell. First, consider these issues when creating a **Title**.

- You've got **55 characters** to work with; use as many as you can.

- Get as **many keywords into your title as you can**, to help people find your products and to "sell"—you need to think about what terms people are likely to use when searching.

- Get **specific product characteristics and brand names** into your title. Don't just say *Canon Digital Camera,* say *Canon PowerShot SD110 3MP Digital Elph w/ 2xOpticalZoom.*

- Include **the generic term,** too. Some people will search for the *Canon PowerShot,* others will search for *Digital Camera.*

- Put **strong words in the title**, and leave the more expansive details for the description.

- Avoid **descriptive terms** that people aren't searching for—*Great condition, cool, fantastic deal,* and so on.

- Remember, **the title will appear on listing pages**, not just your product page; you must have enough information in the title to draw people into the listing page.

If you wish, you can add a subtitle, a second line that appears in the listing and in the listing page and at the top of your product page. Many merchants who sell expensive equipment do this—it's only another 50 cents—but it may not make much difference for lower-cost products or for products with little competition.

Acuson 128 XP/10 - ART - Color Flow Ultrasound System
"New Skin", Cardiac, Vascular W/2 Probes

How about the product description?

- **The more detail the better.** Make it easy for someone to make a decision.

- **Add the descriptive text here that you didn't have space for in the title.** Now's the time to talk about what a great condition the product is in, how well it's been looked after, the warranty, and so on.

- **Discuss shipping and payment information.**

- **Don't make the customer wonder.** Provide answers to their questions before they have to ask.

You can type directly into the box and use the basic formatting tools. More advanced merchants often use the HTML box; they create their description in an HTML program, then paste it into the box. This allows them more flexibility over the description. Using HTML you could, for instance, create a feature table.

Entering Pricing Information

When you move to the next page, eBay tries to load a little image-upload program; although we'll be looking at pricing information first, then timing, the page also includes a photograph-upload area.

Allow eBay to load this. If you're using Internet Explorer, it may initially block the download; you'll see a yellow bar at the top of the page. Click on the bar and then select **Install ActiveX** to continue, then click the **Run** button in the dialog box that opens. Once the program has installed, you'll see a page with the **Pricing** information shown in Figure 5-6 (if you selected an auction) or Figure 5-7 (if you are listing a fixed price item).

Here's how to set **Auction Pricing** (Figure 5-6).

1. Enter a **Starting price**. You *must* have this number. Remember that the lower the price, the more bidding you're likely to get.

2. If you wish, enter a **Reserve price**, the minimum price at which the product must sell for. If the bidding doesn't reach this high, the product is not sold. Remember, you'll be charged a fee for a reserve price, although it will be refunded if the item sells.

 note *Not all merchants can use the Buy It Now process; you must either have a feedback score of 10 or use a PayPal account and have a score of 5. You must also have verified your ID with ID Verify (see Chapter 2).*

3. You may also enter a **Buy It Now price**. As soon as someone buys it at the Buy It Now price, the auction ends, *unless* bidding begins and, if applicable, passes the reserve price, at which point the Buy It Now option is removed.

Pricing and duration

Price your item competitively to increase your chance of a successful sale.

NEW! Get ideas about pricing by searching completed items...

Starting price *Required

$ [   ]

A lower starting price can encourage more bids.

Reserve price (fee varies)

$ [   ] Remove

The lowest price at which you're willing to sell your item is the reserve price.

Buy It Now price (Fee Varies)

$ [   ]

Sell to the first buyer who meets your Buy It Now price.

FIGURE 5-6   This is what you see for an auction format.

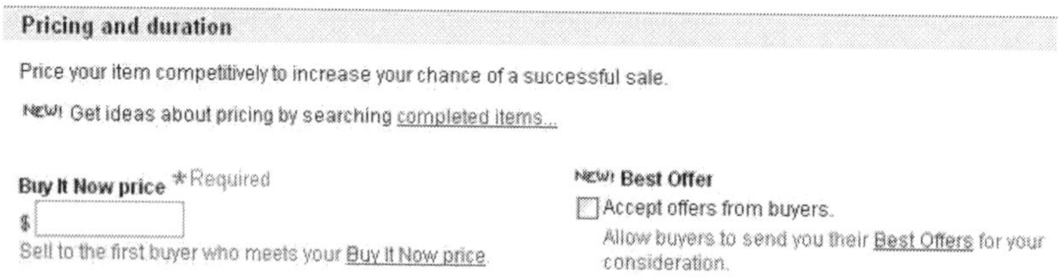

Pricing and duration

Price your item competitively to increase your chance of a successful sale.

NEW! Get ideas about pricing by searching completed items...

Buy It Now price *Required   NEW! **Best Offer**

$ [   ]   ☐ Accept offers from buyers.

Sell to the first buyer who meets your Buy It Now price   Allow buyers to send you their Best Offers for your consideration.

FIGURE 5-7   If your item is fixed price, you'll see this.

note   *Not every merchant can use fixed pricing; you must have a feedback score of 10 or more or be ID Verified to sell a single item this way. If you want to sell multiple items, you'll need a score of 30 or more, and either be ID Verified or have been a registered merchant for at least 30 days.*

Here's how to set **fixed pricing** (Figure 5-7):

1. Enter a **Buy It Now** price. This is the fixed price you are asking.

2. If you wish, select the **Best Offer** check box. This allows buyers to send you an offer, which you may accept or decline. There's no cost for this feature.

Specifying When the Item Will Sell

Next, you'll specify when the listing will begin (Figure 5-8), lower down on the same page. There are two ways to do this:

- Begin immediately, and specify a duration.

- Specify a start date, time, and duration (there's a 10-cent fee for this).

Either way, listings can last 1, 3, 5, 7, or 10 days; if you want a 10-day auction, you'll have to pay a 40-cent fee.

Duration *   **Private listing**
[7 days   ▼]   No private listing. Change

Start time
◉ Start listing when submitted

○ Schedule start time ($0.10) [Select a date... ▼] [Select a time... ▼] PDT
   Learn more about scheduled listings.

FIGURE 5-8   Enter the sale timing information.

Note that you can also create a **Private listing** in this area. This term's a little ambiguous; it actually means that a bidder's ID is not listed, so observers cannot see who is bidding on the item. PayPal discourages its use, recommending it for specific sales such as pharmaceuticals and very valuable items. If you want to use it, click the <u>Change</u> link.

Specifying Item Quantity and Location

Next, you'll specify how many items you are selling and, perhaps, where they are, lower down on the same page (see Figure 5-9; we discussed different quantities in Chapter 3).

- If you have **multiple items that you are willing to sell separately** to different people, enter the number into the **Quantity** box.

- If you have **multiple items that you want to sell to a single person, as a "Lot,"** leave 1 in **Quantity** box, click the <u>Lots</u> link, and enter the number of items into the **Number of items per lot** box that appears. (If you have a box with 20 books in it, enter 20.)

- If you have **multiple lots**—such as five boxes of books, with 20 books in each box— enter the number of lots into the **Quantity** box and the number of books in each box into the **Number of items per lot**.

Finally, enter **Item location** information. Click the <u>Change</u> link and you can enter a ZIP code; also choose whether to let eBay enter the city and state into your product page for you, based on the ZIP, or whether you want to enter a location yourself.

Item location

ZIP Code: Not specified
Location display: , United States
<u>Change</u>

The address information is particularly important for items that are very large or unwieldy— the sort of item people are probably only going to want to buy locally—because this allows people in your area to find the product listing.

Quantity * ⊠ Minimize

| **Individual Items** | NEW! <u>Lots</u> |

Quantity *
1
Learn more about <u>multiple item</u> listings.

Selling similar or identical items together in a "lot"?
Help buyers find your listing - just enter the number of items you have in the <u>Lots tab</u> above.

Item location

ZIP Code: Not specified
Location display: , United States
<u>Change</u>

Tip: Adding a ZIP Code makes it easier for buyers to find your item when they search by distance.

FIGURE 5-9 Enter the quantity and, optionally, the location.

Adding Photographs

On the same page, lower down, you'll find controls for uploading photographs (see Figure 5-10). There are two ways to place images into your listings:

■ Let eBay host the pictures for you.

■ Host your pictures on another web site.

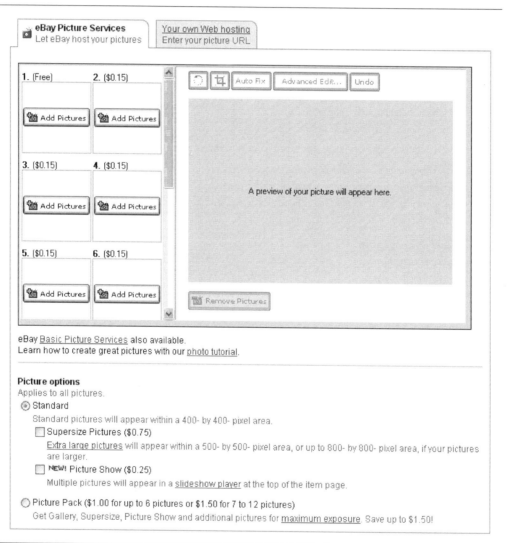

FIGURE 5-10   Specify your pictures here.

To host pictures with eBay:

1. Click the **Add Pictures** buttons to upload pictures from your hard drive. Remember, each one after the first costs 15 cents.

 tip   *If these image-upload controls don't work, click the <u>Basic Picture Services</u> link to use more basic controls.*

2. Once uploaded, you'll see a **Preview**, and can modify the image using the editing tools.

3. You can enlarge the pictures if you wish by clicking the **Supersize Pictures** check box (there's a 75-cent fee).

4. If you want to use the **Picture Show** feature (it costs 25 cents), click the check box; all your images will be placed into an animated picture display at the top of your product page.

5. Select **Picture Pack** and you'll get the Supersize, Picture Show, and Gallery features (otherwise, you add the Gallery a little later), and get either six images ($1) or 12 images ($1.50).

Hosting Your Own Pictures

If you have hosted pictures elsewhere, you can point to one of them to be used in your listing. Where do you place these images? On your web site, or perhaps in a personal hosting area provided by your ISP. There are also image-hosting services, such as Pongo.com, Twaze.com, and PixHost.com. You can specify a single image on this page, which will be used as your primary picture—the picture that will appear at the top of your product page, and in your listing in a category or search-results page if you choose the Gallery feature later.

 tip   *You may want to test the URL first; copy and paste it into the Address bar in your browser and press ENTER. If the image doesn't appear, there's something wrong with the URL.*

1. Click the <u>Your own Web hosting</u> link and you'll see the information in Figure 5-11.

2. Enter the URL to the picture into the **Picture Web address (Free)** text box.

3. If you entered a URL into your description, you can click the **The description already includes a picture URL for my item** check box, and eBay will use that URL; there's no need to enter anything into the **Picture Web address (Free)** text box.

 tip   *There's another way to add hosted pictures to your listing—by entering the URL into the description in the earlier step.*

4. If you want to the **Picture Show** feature (it costs 25 cents), click the check box and several more text boxes appear, into which you can enter URLs. The Picture Show feature puts an animated picture display at the top of your product page.

FIGURE 5-11   Enter your picture URL here.

Specifying the Listing Layout and Options

Next, you can specify your listing layout and options. Scroll down the page a little further (see Figure 5-12).

These are the options you'll find in this area:

Listing designer	For ten cents you can select a theme—colors and border styles—and a layout, which defines where the pictures sit in relation to the text. Use the Preview listing link to see what it will look like.
Increase your item's visibility	In this area you can select a variety of options related to how and what will be displayed.
Remember my selections	Check this, and eBay will save your selections for subsequent listings.
Preview your listing in search results	This area shows you what buyers will see in the search results or when they are browsing categories. As you make selections below, this area changes to show you the effect.
Gallery	Select this and your picture will appear next to your product title in the search results.
Subtitle	Here's another chance to enter a subtitle to appear under your title.
Bold	Add bold text to the item title.
Border	Place a frame around your listing.
Highlight	Put a colored background behind your information in the search results.
Show as a gift	Puts a little gift-box icon in your listing. Plus, information about gift wrapping, express shipping, and shipping to the gift recipient will be added to the product description.
Gallery Featured	Adds the standard Gallery feature, *and* the listing will sometimes appear above the main listings, in the Featured area.

Featured Plus	This adds your listing to the Featured area, though without a picture.
Home Page Featured	Select this and your product *may* appear on the eBay home page.
Page Counter	Click the <u>Change</u> link to see page-counter options. A page counter shows how many people have viewed your page. Probably not a great idea, as it may sometimes indicate to someone that few people are viewing your pages and lead people to hold off bidding until later. You can, however, add a hidden counter; you can see the results, buyers can't.

Click the **Continue** button to save your settings.

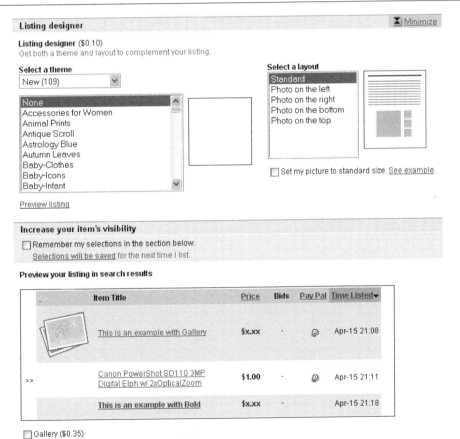

FIGURE 5-12 Now you get to specify your listing layout.

Providing Payment, Shipping, and Returns Details

Finally, time to enter payment and shipping details (see Figure 5-13).

1. If you set up a PayPal account and changed your preferences earlier (Chapter 2) you'll see PayPal included. You can click the <u>Add other payment methods</u> link to choose Money Order/Cashiers Checks, Personal Checks, and, if you have a merchant account, Credit Cards.

2. By default, **Will ship to the United States** is selected; click the check boxes for other areas if you want to ship to them.

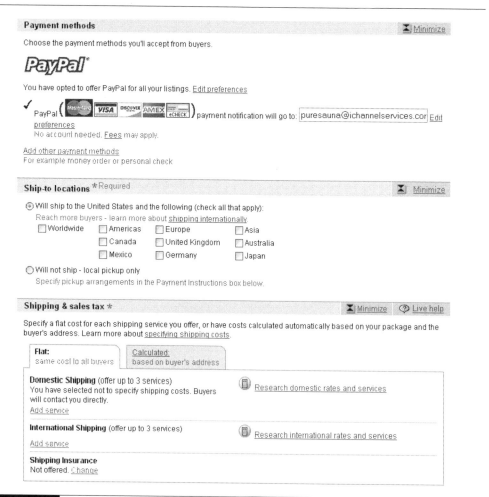

FIGURE 5-13   Enter payment and shipping details here.

3. If you don't ship your products—but expect people to pick up locally—click the **Will not ship—local pickup only** option button.

4. There are two ways to specify shipping costs, **Flat** shipping rates and **Calculated** shipping rates. We're going to look at this issue in a moment.

5. We looked at **Sales Tax** in Chapter 3, so your tax rates are probably already set.

6. Specify your **Return policy** (see Figure 5-14). If you're willing to accept returned items, click the **Returns Accepted** check box; you can then select the return period and how money will be refunded, and enter Return Policy Details text.

7. Enter **Payment instructions**. The clearer you can be, the better. Don't make people guess at how you want them to pay you.

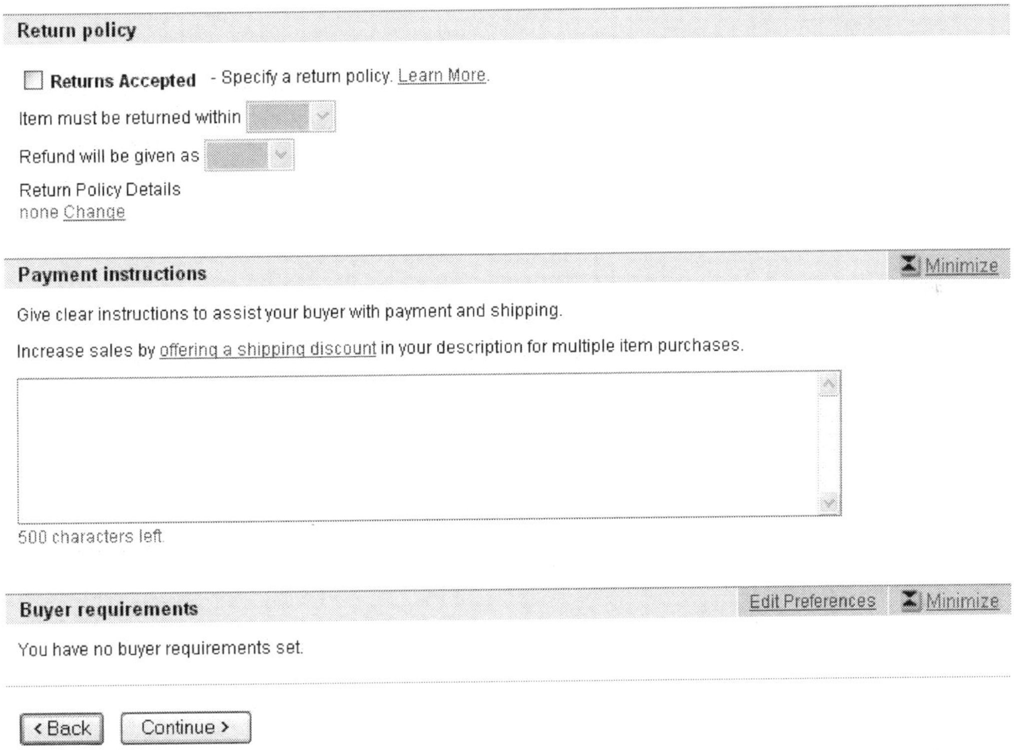

Return policy

☐ **Returns Accepted** - Specify a return policy. Learn More.

Item must be returned within [   ]

Refund will be given as [   ]

Return Policy Details
none Change

Payment instructions   ☒ Minimize

Give clear instructions to assist your buyer with payment and shipping.

Increase sales by offering a shipping discount in your description for multiple item purchases.

[   ]

500 characters left

Buyer requirements   Edit Preferences   ☒ Minimize

You have no buyer requirements set.

[< Back]   [Continue >]

FIGURE 5-14   Finally, enter the return policy, payment instructions, and buyer requirements.

tip *If you are creating a test listing and want to bid on it, you must, according to eBay's policies, create a* buyer requirements exemption list, *which you can do on the Buyer's Requirements page. This defines which accounts may bid on your product. Click the buyer requirements exemption list link, then, on the next page, click the Add an item to my Pre-approved Bidder/ Buyer List link. Create a test account that will be used to bid, then place it into this pre-approved list of accounts that may bid.*

8. It's worth blocking some buyers. On the **Buyer requirements** line, click the Edit Preferences link. You can block buyers based on these criteria.

- **Buyers in countries to which I don't ship.**

- **Buyers with a negative feedback score;** either this is a new buyer with some bad beginner's luck, or this guy has real problems.

- **Buyers with unpaid item strikes.**

- **Buyers who may bid on several of my items and not pay for them;** be careful with this one; there may be a good reason why people would be bidding on a lot of your items.

- **Buyers without a PayPal account.**

Entering Your Shipping Information

Let's look at how you can specify shipping fees. First, we'll look at **Flat shipping fees**. Click the Add service link in Figure 5-13, and you'll see a new drop-down list box (Figure 5-15). You can add up to three services like this for each of domestic and international shipping.

note *See Chapter 4 for a discussion of shipping issues.*

Simply select the service from the **Domestic Shipping** drop-down and the price for that method. Then click Add service if you want to add another method.

Flat: same cost to all buyers	Calculated: based on buyer's address

Domestic Shipping (offer up to 3 services)

US Postal Service Parcel Post ▾ $ [   ]   🖩 Research domestic rates and services

Add service   Remove service   and have buyers contact me later

FIGURE 5-15 You can add up to three different domestic shipping services and three international.

Entering **Calculated shipping costs** is a little more complicated. eBay can calculate costs based on the location of the buyer and the information you provide. It can calculate for a variety of **UPS** and **US Postal Service** shipping methods; the buyer selects the method and eBay calculates the costs. Click the <u>Calculated</u> link to see the area shown in Figure 5-16.

Here's how to use this area:

1. From the **Estimated Weight** drop-down list box, select the shipping weight of the product and shipping materials combined.

2. From the **Package Size** drop-down, select the package type or size. For information on specifications—for instance, what is a *Large Package*—click the <u>Weight and size help</u> link.

3. If the product doesn't match any of these options, click the **Irregular or unusual package** check box.

4. Click the <u>Add service</u> link to see the **Domestic Shipping** drop-down list box, and select a shipping method.

5. Use the <u>Add service</u> link to add up to three domestic shipping methods and three international shipping methods.

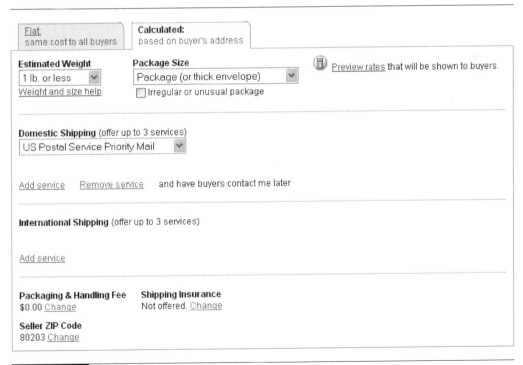

FIGURE 5-16   Setting up calculated shipping costs

6. Under **Packaging & Handling Fee**, click the <u>Change</u> link and add how much you want to *add* to the calculated costs to pay for your packaging and the time it takes to handle the shipping.

7. Under **Shipping Insurance**, click <u>Change</u> if you want to allow or require buyers to purchase shipping insurance; this will be calculated automatically, according to the UPS and USPS rates.

8. The **Seller ZIP Code** should already be correct, based on the ZIP code you entered on the previous page. If not, click the <u>Change</u> link.

Reviewing and Submitting Your Listing

This is the final step; on the next page you can review your submission. We suggest you look through this carefully; it shows exactly what will be in the listing and under what conditions it will be run. You can edit anything from this page if you find a mistake.

Look carefully at the fees to make sure you know what you're being charged for the insertion, then click **Submit Listing** and you've finished.

Now you can sit back and wait. Don't expect to see people bidding right away; in fact, many people hold off bidding until the last moment. So don't be discouraged if you don't see any action until the last day. In the meantime, read on to learn how to monitor, modify, and manage your listings.

Chapter 6

Monitoring, Modifying, and Managing Sales

You've listed your items . . . the game is on. Now it's a matter of waiting to see what happens and reacting when it does. Of course, what you're hoping is that you get the price you asked for, and quickly, or that your product is bid up way above what it's reasonably worth. Someone wins, you take your money, and you ship the product.

Actually running an auction is a little more complicated than that. How do you keep an eye on the auction? What if you feel you need to modify your listing? How about ending the auction early or handling bids from members you don't feel particularly comfortable with? There are many possibilities, so this chapter explains how to monitor, modify, and manage your auctions.

Checking on Your Listings

You'll find information about your listings in your My eBay page, as in Figure 6-1. You can quickly scan down this page and see the **Quick Stat** summary of what's going on in your page. This area is broken down into several areas:

- **Scheduled Listings**   Listings that have not yet gone live
- **Active Listings**   Those that are currently live
- **Ended Listings**   Listings that ended, whether sold or unsold
- **Sold Items**   Items that have been sold but not yet processed
- **Sold Items: Past Due**   Items that have been sold but that have not been paid for within the allotted time

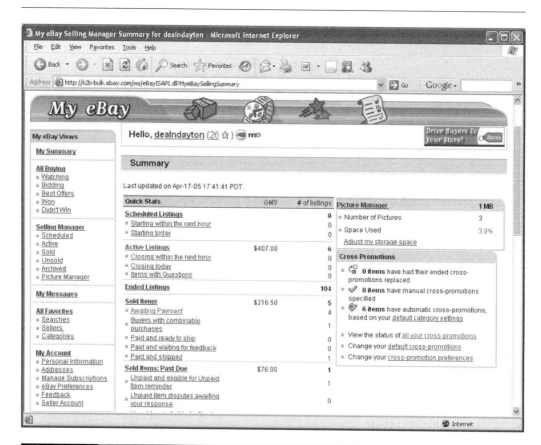

FIGURE 6-1   Monitor your sales in the My eBay page.

Click on any of these links to see the actual listings and orders (we'll be looking at how to process orders in Chapter 7).

Changing a Listing

You can modify your listing even after you've submitted it, but there are some rules about what can be changed when. You can't change the selling format at any point once listed, but you can do the following:

	Any change you wish	Add to description (not modify or remove info)	Place in second category	Add optional selling features
12+ hours before closing, no bids	✓	✓	✓	✓
12+ hours before closing, bids received	✗	✓	✓	✓
Less than 12 hours before closing, no bids	✗	✓	✓	✓
Less than 12 hours before closing, bids received	✗	✗	✗	✓

Here's how to make changes to your listing:

1. Open your **My eBay** page.

2. Click the <u>Active</u> link in the **My eBay Views** to see all the items currently selling.

3. Find the item you want to modify and click the little down-arrow button at the end of the listing line (Figure 6-2).

4. Click <u>Revise</u> if you want to make multiple changes or to change the description, or click <u>Add To Description</u> if a bid has been received or it's less than 12 hours before closing—you'll be able to add to the description but not modify what's already there. Select <u>Edit Promotions</u> to modify the cross-promotions set up with this product.

Canceling and Rescheduling Listings

If you have scheduled a listing but it has not yet started, you can cancel or reschedule it at any point up until it begins; click the <u>Scheduled</u> link in the **Selling Manager** area of the navbar on the left side of the My eBay page. But what if it's already begun running? It is possible to cancel a listing even after it's begun, under some conditions.

 tip *There's one reason that is not all right to cancel the sale: you cannot cancel a sale simply because the bids are not high enough. You need to either use a reserve price or establish a reasonable minimum bid, but once you place a listing you have committed to sell. If you cancel an item for this reason (in particular, if you do it repeatedly), you may be penalized.*

eBay understands that sometimes there are good reasons to cancel a sale, such as these:

- The item is no longer available for sale.

- There was an error in the starting price or reserve amount.

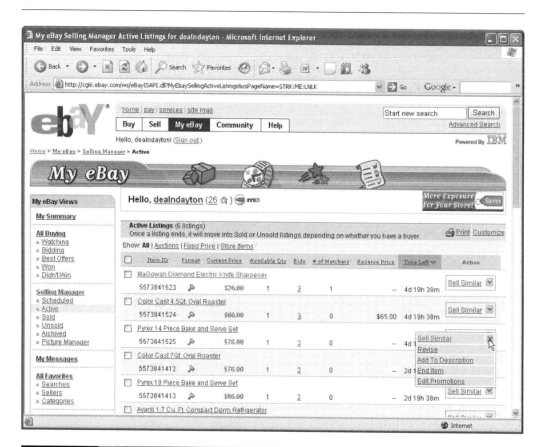

You can modify a listing here.

■ There was an error in the listing.

■ The item was lost or broken.

■ You discovered that the item is a fake or non-functioning.

■ Sickness or family emergency stops you from shipping.

In order to close an item, find the item you want to modify and click the little down-arrow button at the end of the listing line (Figure 6-2); click the <u>End Item</u> link.

tip *You can also choose to end an auction and sell to the highest bidder so far.*

If there are no bids, the listing is simply removed. If bids have been received, the listing remains but with a notification message explaining what happened.

Reviewing the Auction Status

You can watch the auction in progress, of course, and see how bidding on your listing is going. Here's how:

1. Click the Active link in the **My eBay Views** to see all the items currently selling.

2. Find the item you want to review and click on the number of bids in the Bids column (see Figure 6-3).

3. The Bid History page appears; see Figure 6-4. This page shows you who has bid, and how much.

4. Click on a bidder's name to see their profile (Figure 6-5).

note *You want to be sure that the bidder is going to follow through—that he will pay and isn't out to scam you in some way. Of course, the more expensive the product, the more of a concern this is.*

5. You can review bidders in various ways:

■ Look at the **Bid Retractions**; does this bidder have a habit of bidding and then reneging on the bid?

■ Look at the **Feedback Score**; are there many negative ratings? If necessary, scroll down and see the feedback comments. Is there a trend? A common theme?

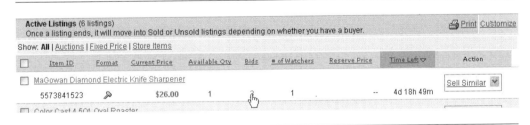

FIGURE 6-3   Finding the bid history; click the number of bids.

Bid History   Item number: 5573841523

Email to a friend | **Watch this item** in My eBay

Item title: MaGowan Diamond Electric Knife Sharpener

Time left: 4 days, 18 hours 44 minutes 21 seconds

Only actual bids (not automatic bids generated up to a bidder's maximum) are shown. Automatic bids may be placed days or hours before a listing ends. Learn more about bidding.

User ID	Bid Amount	Date of bid
sumakimi (2)	US $26.00	Apr-15-05 13:59:44 PDT
tshipman44 (2)	US $25.00	Apr-15-05 13:56:15 PDT
sumakimi (2)	US $14.00	Apr-15-05 13:59:36 PDT

See how to cancel bids if you need to.

FIGURE 6-4   The Bid History page

■ Look at **Member Since**; has the bidder been a member very long? You may also see a **New Member** (a member who joined within 30 days) or **Changed ID** icon.

■ Click the ID History link; has this person been working on eBay under different IDs?

tip   *Just because someone has some bad reviews doesn't mean you shouldn't sell. If someone has five bad reviews out of five thousand, it doesn't mean much. If someone has five bad reviews out of six, there's a problem!*

6. If you want to follow up with a bidder, click the **Contact Member** button. You'll be able to send an e-mail through eBay to the bidder. If you wish, you can request a phone number or e-mail address so you can communicate directly.

FIGURE 6-5   The Member Profile page for one of the bidders

*You can also tell eBay to show you the e-mail addresses of people who bid on your listings. Click the <u>eBay Preferences</u> link on the left side of the My eBay page. Check the **Show User IDs and email addresses** check box and click the **Apply** button.*

Canceling a Member's Bid

If you decide that you really have to cancel a bid because you simply don't trust the bidder, or perhaps you cannot make contact with the bidder, or maybe even the bidder has asked you if you would cancel his bid, here's how to do it:

1. Copy or note the **Item ID**—the ID of the listing.

2. Open the **Bid History** page and note the **User ID** of the person making the bid you want to cancel.

It's possible for a buyer to retract a bid, but that doesn't look good on the Member Profile. So some buyers will ask the seller to cancel the bid instead.

3. Click the <u>cancel bids</u> link.

Sometimes eBay cancels accounts if the members have been up to no good in some way. You may get a message saying a bid has been removed due to administrative cancellation.

4. In the **Cancel Bids** page, click the <u>cancel bids</u> link.

5. In the following page, enter the **Item Number** (the Item ID), the **User ID**, and a **Reason for cancellation** (a message up to 80 characters).

6. Click the **Cancel Bid** button.

Blocking Bidders

You can also block members from bidding on your items. You can do this to carry out private auctions, for instance, or perhaps to block a member whom you've dealt with in the past and want nothing to do with any more!

Near the bottom of the My eBay page, you'll find a <u>Block or pre-approve certain bidders</u> link. Click this to find the Buyer/Bidder Management page (Figure 6-6).

Much of what we've covered in this chapter won't be necessary most of the time. Hopefully, all you need to do is check on your listings now and then, and then manage the sale when it closes . . . which we'll cover in the following chapter.

Click here to stop a member from bidding on any of your listings

Click here to create a list of members who may bid on a particular item

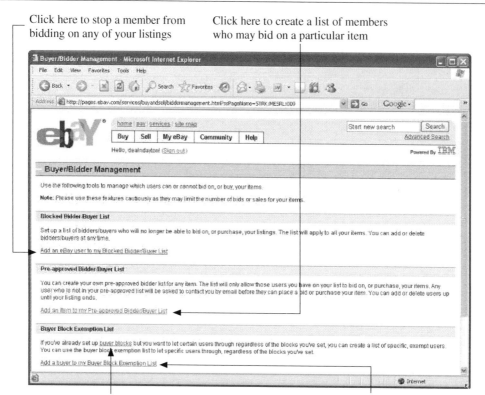

Click here to block classes of buyers from all your listings—buyers from certain countries, with particular feedback scores, with unpaid items, who have bid on several of your items at the same time, or those without a PayPal account

Click here to exempt particular members from the blocked classes

FIGURE 6-6   The Buyer/Bidder Management page.

Chapter 7

Payment, Shipping, and Feedback

When your auction ends, you'll have plenty to do. Luckily, eBay provides lots of handy tools to automate the entire process, from immediately after the listing has ended to once you've shipped the product. And if you're taking payments through eBay, you've even got a fantastic, automated tool for printing shipping labels and paying for shipping, in seconds.

In this chapter you're going to learn what to do once someone's bought the product you've just sold; how to send an invoice asking for payment, what to do when the payment arrives, how to ship the product, and how to leave feedback for the buyer. We'll also cover that critical subject, what to do when someone doesn't pay!

Viewing Your Sales

To find your closed sales, open your **My eBay** page and click the <u>Sold Items</u> link in the **Quick Stats** area. You'll see a list of buyers (Figure 7-1).

Notice the icons at the top of some columns; here's what they indicate:

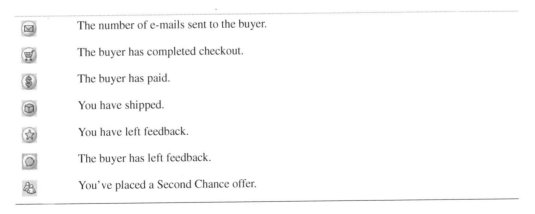

✉	The number of e-mails sent to the buyer.
🛒	The buyer has completed checkout.
$	The buyer has paid.
📦	You have shipped.
☆	You have left feedback.
◎	The buyer has left feedback.
🏷	You've placed a Second Chance offer.

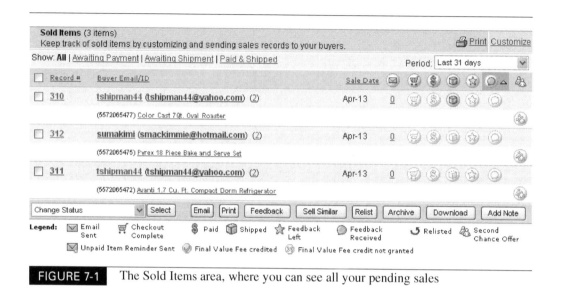

FIGURE 7-1   The Sold Items area, where you can see all your pending sales

Completing a Sale

Here's the process used to complete the sale:

1. Calculate the final charge and ask for payment.
2. Wait for payment.
3. Ship the product.
4. Provide feedback to the buyer, and ask for feedback from him.

We'll look at this process step-by-step.

Calculating the Final Charge and Asking for Payment

You may recall that there are two ways for the buyer to learn the final payment:

■ The buyer sees the final payment when the sale is complete because shipping charges are added automatically. The buyer receives an e-mail, with a **Pay Now** button.

■ You have to tell the buyer what the charge will be because you add charges *after* the sale.

In the first case, the buyer may well pay before you even review the auction. But in the second case—if the buyer hasn't yet paid—you should send an invoice. Here's how:

1. In the **My eBay** page, click the <u>My Summary</u> link at the top of the navbar; you'll see the My Summary page (see Figure 7-2).

2. On the **I am awaiting payment for *x* items** line, click the <u>*x* items</u> link. You'll see the Items I've Sold table (Figure 7-3).

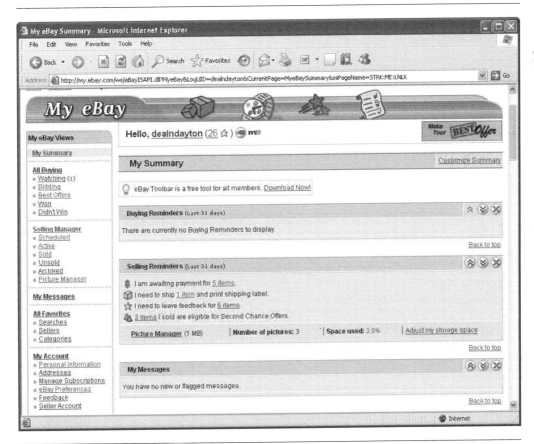

FIGURE 7-2   The My Summary page

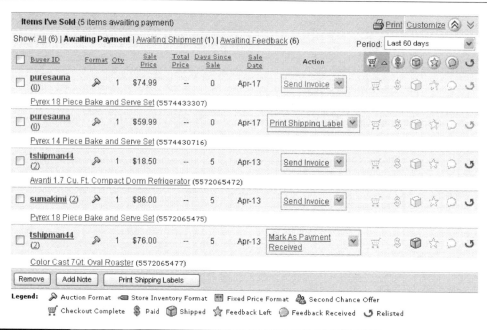

FIGURE 7-3   The Items I've Sold table

3. Find the item you want to work on and click the Send Invoice link under the **Action** column. You'll see the invoice page (see Figure 7-4). If the buyer has purchased more than one item from you, you'll see a slightly different page—the Combine Purchases page. It's almost exactly the same, except each of the items is shown on a separate line.

You can see the form displayed if the buyer has multiple purchases in Figure 7-5. You can modify the shipping fees accordingly in this form.

4. If you were presenting the buyer with shipping options, then the buyer will have already made a choice. Otherwise, you can enter a shipping fee, and of course the buyer will be notified of this fee when receiving the invoice.

5. Click the calculator icon to open the **Shipping Calculator** (which we discussed in Chapter 4).

6. Adjust the **Shipping insurance** as required.

7. If you have to charge **Sales tax**, select the state and enter a percentage; also, if the state requires that **Tax applies to the subtotal + shipping and handling**, select that check box.

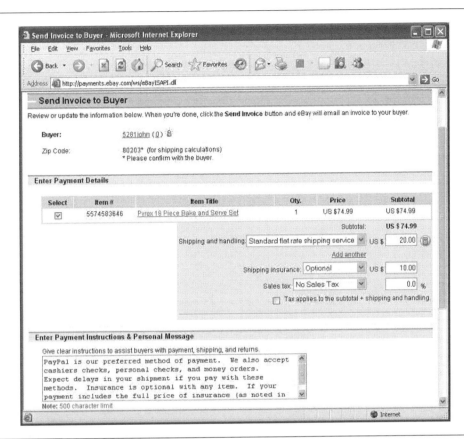

FIGURE 7-4   The Send Invoice to Buyer page

 tip   *You should provide a customized message. You want to make working with you as easy and as clear as possible. Create a simple set of instructions to make the process of paying you idiot-proof. While the old adage, "if you make something idiot-proof they'll just make better idiots," may be true, a personal e-mail from you outlining exactly what to do can go a long way to making the process go quickly and smoothly.*

8. Scroll down and you'll see the **Payment Instructions and Personal Message box**; this contains either a generic message provided by eBay, or the message you customized in the eBay Preferences area of My eBay (see Chapter 3).

9. By default, the **Copy me on this invoice** check box is selected, and you should probably leave it selected (at least when you first start selling).

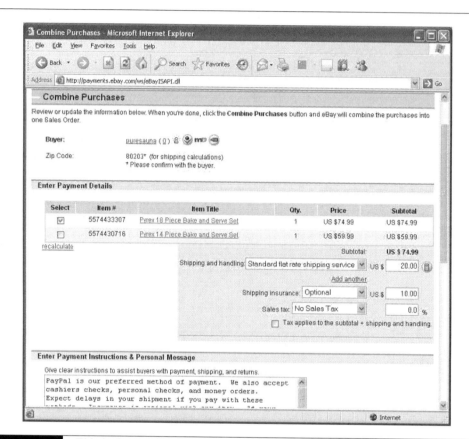

FIGURE 7-5   This is the way the form appears if the buyer has multiple purchases.

Receiving Payment

Next, of course, you'll wait for payment. When payment is received, you may have to mark the order as paid. If paid through PayPal, that's done automatically, but if you are, for example, processing credit-card orders through your brick-and-mortar's credit-card merchant account, you'll have to mark it as paid manually. Here's a quick way to do that:

1. In the **My eBay** page, click the My Summary link at the top of the navbar; you'll see the My Summary page (see Figure 7-2.).

2. On the **I am awaiting payment for x items** line, click the *x items* link. You'll see the Items I've Sold table (Figure 7-6).

	Items I've Sold (6 items awaiting payment)								Print Customize

Show: <u>All</u> (6) | **Awaiting Payment** | <u>Awaiting Shipment</u> | <u>Awaiting Feedback</u> (6)   Period: Last 60 days

	Buyer ID	Format	Qty	Sale Price	Total Price	Days Since Sale	Sale Date	Action	
☐	<u>5281john</u> (0)	🔨	1	$74.99	--	0	Apr-18	Print Shipping Label ✕	🛒 $ 📦 ☆ 💬 ↺
	<u>Pyrex 18 Piece Bake and Serve Set</u> (5574583646)							Mark As Payment Received ⤵	
☐	<u>puresauna</u> (0)	🔨	1	$74.99	--	0	Apr-17	Mark As Shipped Leave Feedback	🛒 $ 📦 ☆ 💬 ↺
	<u>Pyrex 18 Piece Bake and Serve Set</u> (5574433307)							View Payment Details	

FIGURE 7-6   Click Mark As Payment Received to indicate that the buyer has paid.

3. Find the buyer you want to mark as having paid, and click the down arrow in the drop-down list box under the **Action** column heading.

4. Click the <u>Mark As Payment Received</u> link.

Shipping the Product and Sending a Notification

Once you've received payment, you need to ship the product (we discussed shipping in detail in Chapter 4). Shipping promptly is not only a nice thing to do, it's required by eBay, PayPal, and the credit-card companies if the buyer paid with that method. (Even if you received a payment via PayPal, the buyer may have paid with a card.)

 note   *Why not just take the payment and ship, and forget about changing status? Because hopefully you'll be doing so much business that you need to keep all this straight. Changing status allows you to view products sorted by their status; for instance, you can click the <u>Awaiting Payment</u>, <u>Awaiting Shipment</u>, and <u>Awaiting Feedback</u> links at the top of the Items I've Sold table to see just orders with those statuses. Plus, of course, your Final Value Fees are assessed when the item is sold; if it isn't paid for, you have to report it as such (as we'll discuss a little later in this chapter). These statuses are a critical part of a sophisticated process designed to make managing your business simple.*

Here's how to print a shipping label and mark the item as shipped:

1. In the **My eBay** page, click the <u>My Summary</u> link at the top of the navbar; you'll see the My Summary page.

2. On the **I need to ship x items** line, click the <u>x items</u> link. You'll see the Items I've Sold table; find the buyer for whom you want to print a shipping label and click the <u>Print Shipping Label</u> link under the **Action** column heading.

3. If you have a PayPal account, you'll see a login page. Log into your account.

4. Choose which shipping method you want to use, U.S. Postal Service or UPS, and click the **Continue** button.

5. In the Print Your Label page (Figure 7-7), enter the shipping information, then click **Continue**.

When you create shipping labels like this, your buyer will get a confirmation e-mail, including a tracking number.

6. In the information page that appears, click the **Continue** button.

7. In the following page, confirm all the details; this page also shows you the charge.

If your browser has a pop-up blocker working, the label window won't open! Set your browser to always allow pop-ups from eBay.

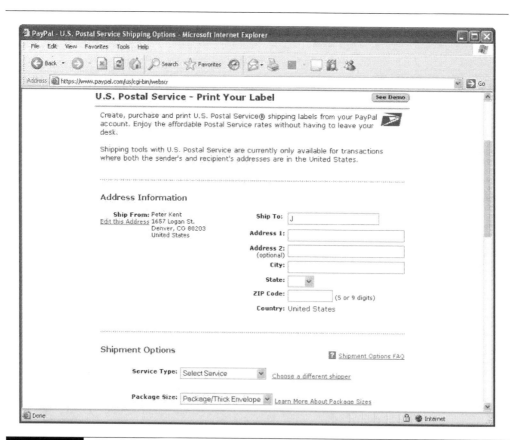

FIGURE 7-7   The Print Your Label page, for shipping via the post office

8. Click the **Pay and Continue** button. A secondary window pops up, containing your label.

9. If you wish to test your printer setup, click the **Print Sample Label** button. Otherwise, click the **Print Label** button.

note *You can void a shipping label and get a refund within 48 hours of printing the label. Find the transaction in your PayPal Recent Activity list, click on the* Details *link, and click the* Void Payment *link at the bottom of the page. You can also reprint the label from this page.*

10. In the main browser window you have a number of options:

   ■ Print the label again.

   ■ Create more labels for a multiple-box shipment.

   ■ Request a pickup.

   ■ Create a packing slip for the shipment.

Leaving Feedback

Feedback is critical to the entire eBay business model. It's a way to prove you're reliable, and also a way to weed out the unreliable or dishonest members. You need as much good feedback as you can get, which is why you should reciprocate—provide feedback to your buyers, and encourage them to do the same for you. Additionally, you should also provide *bad* feedback when warranted, to let other eBay buyers know that this buyer did something wrong.

tip *For a detailed discussion of feedback and how feedback scores are calculated, see http://pages.ebay.com/help/feedback/.*

Here's how to leave feedback:

1. In the **My eBay** page, click the My Summary link at the top of the navbar; you'll see the My Summary page (see Figure 7-2).

note *Feedback is hugely important to the entire eBay concept, and members recognize this. By early 2005, eBay buyers and sellers had left each other 3 billion feedback messages.*

2. On the **I need to leave feedback for *x* items** line, click the *x* items link. You'll see the Items I've Sold table.

3. Find the buyer for whom you want to leave feedback and click the Leave Feedback link under the **Action** column heading. You'll see the Leave Feedback form (Figure 7-8).

4. Simply select a **Rating**, type a **Comment**, and click the **Leave Feedback** button.

Feedback Forum: Leave Feedback   help

Rating other members by leaving feedback is a very important part of transactions on eBay.

Please note:
- Once left, you cannot edit or retract feedback; you are solely responsible for the content.
- It's always best to keep your feedback factual; avoid making personal remarks.
- Feedback can be left for at least 90 days following a transaction.
- If you have a dispute, contact your trading partner to try and resolve the dispute before leaving feedback.

| User ID: | 5281john | Show all transactions |
| Item Number: | 5574583646 | |

Rating: ○ Positive   ○ Neutral   ○ Negative   ● I will leave feedback later

Comment:
80 characters left.

[Leave Feedback]   Cancel

FIGURE 7-8   The Leave Feedback form

tip   *You can carry out all these feedback functions through the Feedback Forum. In My eBay, click on the __Feedback__ link (under the My Account area of the navbar), then click the __Go to Feedback Forum__ link. Click the __Feedback disputes__ link in the forum page.*

Things sometimes go wrong, but eBay has thought of everything. What if you get into an argument with a buyer, things get heated, you both leave bad feedback for each other . . . and then, after a few days, you both calm down? Was the fight worth the bad feedback? What if you both decide you'd rather remove the impact of the bad feedback?

It's possible to do a **mutual feedback withdrawal**. You and the buyer will have to first agree to this through e-mail and phone calls, perhaps, then both of you must go to the Mutual Feedback form and withdraw your feedback. Once *both* have done so, the feedback points are removed, although the feedback still appears in the Member Profiles. There's a time limit to these withdrawals; you've got until 30 days after the feedback was left or 90 days after the transaction, whichever is the longer.

There's another way to withdraw feedback, through **Square Trade's dispute resolution program**. This company claims to have managed over a million disputes, involving nondelivery of goods or services, misrepresentation, improper selling practices, unhonored guarantees or warranties, unsatisfactory services, credit and billing problems, unfulfilled contracts, and so on.

It doesn't cost anything to file a case with them. Once you do that, they contact the seller, and if the seller agrees to mediation, they'll charge you a $20 fee. The mediation is undertaken through a web-based chat tool, and the end result may be mutually-withdrawn feedback, one party withdrawing feedback, or neither party withdrawing; and unlike the eBay mutual-withdrawal tool, there's no time limit on this type of withdrawal.

How about if you get **retaliatory negative feedback**? That is, if you provide negative feedback for good reason and the seller gives you negative feedback in revenge? It's not easy to deal with this. eBay will rarely remove feedback comments. In order to avoid acting as an "editor" and thus becoming liable for every slander posted on their site, eBay has to take a hands-off position and only remove feedback in a few cases:

- **A court order** finds the feedback to be slanderous, libelous, defamatory, or otherwise illegal.
- The feedback comment contains **profane, vulgar, obscene, or racist language, or adult material**.
- The feedback comment contains **personal identifying information** about another member.
- The feedback makes reference to an **eBay, PayPal, or law-enforcement organization investigation**.
- The feedback comment **contains links or scripts**.
- A member accidentally leaves negative feedback for the **wrong member**.
- The feedback was left by someone **ineligible to participate in eBay transactions**.
- Feedback was left by a member with **false contact information**.
- Feedback was left by a member who bid with no intention of completing the transaction, **for the purpose of leaving bad feedback**.

As you can see, in most cases, eBay won't get involved but will point you toward the mutual-withdrawal process or mediation.

Handling Nonpaying Bidders

Now and then, someone won't pay. You'll send e-mails, call perhaps, and still they won't pay. They may even tell you they're going to pay . . . and still they don't pay. How do you handle this? There are several ways to deal with the unsold product:

- **Use the Unpaid Item process.** eBay has a process intended to resolve unpaid items.
- **Relist the item.** eBay will let you do this for free any time within 90 days.
- **Do a Second Chance sale.** Offer the item for sale to the next-highest bidder.

Using the Unpaid Item Process

Under the eBay agreement, buyers commit to paying for the product they agreed to buy. If they don't pay, that's a strike against their record that will appear in the Member Profile.

 note *There are a lot of rules related to the Unpaid Item Process; read them carefully before you report the first case. Click the* Unpaid Item Policy *link on the Report an Unpaid Item Dispute form.*

You generally cannot file an Unpaid Item dispute for at least seven days after the close of the sale, but you do have up to 45 days. (You can claim earlier if the buyer is no longer an eBay member or if the buyer is in a country you clearly stated, in the payment details area, that you would not ship to.)

To report an unpaid item, view the Items I've Sold table and click the little down arrow in the drop-down list box under the **Action** column heading. Then click the Report an Unpaid Item link. You can use this process to report an unpaid item—in which eBay investigates and encourages the buyer to pay—and to request an insertion-fee refund.

Relisting the Item

If your buyer doesn't pay, or even if the product simply didn't sell, you can relist it at any time within 90 days. If the item sells the second time, eBay will refund the insertion fees (so you end up paying the insertion fees just once). You'll only pay any additional costs—if you add features, for instance.

Before you relist an item, consider why it didn't sell. If you list it again and it still doesn't sell, you lose two insertion fees. Can you improve the listing title? Add more to the description? Lower the reserve price?

Here are a few more rules for relisting the item:

- You can only relist the same item for free once.
- The original item, and the relisting, must be in **auction of fixed-price format**; the policy doesn't cover store inventory or real-estate advertising.
- The original listing and relisting must be single quantity.
- The relisting starting price can't be more than the original listing.
- You can't increase the reserve price or add a reserve price if the original listing didn't have one.
- If the item doesn't sell on the relisting, eBay will not refund the insertion fees.

Doing a Second Chance Sale

Another way to deal with an unpaid item is to do a Second Chance sale to offer it to the other bidders. Once you've written off the first buyer, you can approach the second bidder—and third, and fourth, and however many more you want—and ask if they'd like to purchase.

Here are some guidelines:

- You should only use the Second Chance method after **attempting to resolve the unpaid-item problem** first.
- The price asked will be set to **the bidder's highest bid**.
- Don't send **more offers than items you have** to sell.
- There's **no charge for a Second Chance offer**; eBay wants you to sell so they can earn their Final Value Fee.

Here's how this process works:

1. In the **My eBay** page, click the <u>My Summary</u> link at the top of the navbar; you'll see the My Summary page.

2. On the *x* **items I sold are eligible for Second Chance Offers** line, click the <u>*x* items</u> link. You'll see the Items I've Sold (*x* items eligible for Second Chance Offer) table (see Figure 7-9).

3. You'll see both the name of the buyer and the item title. Click on the <u>Second Chance Offer</u> link under the **Action** column.

4. On the page that appears, click the **Continue** button. You'll see the Second Chance Offer page.

5. You're about to offer the item to other bidders (you'll see a list). Select a **Duration** for the offer, up to seven days. If the bidder doesn't respond in that time, the offer is retracted.

6. Click the check box for each bidder to whom you want to extend this offer.

7. If you want to see a copy of the e-mail, click the check box next to your e-mail address.

8. Click the **Continue** button.

Now, let's see what happens when you take what you learned in this chapter and repeat it over and over, dozens, hundreds, of times. As your business grows, you'll need to learn about tools eBay provides to help you. Read on to find out how to scale your business.

FIGURE 7-9   You can see the Second Chance Offers here.

This page intentionally left blank

Chapter 8

Automating and Scaling

If you've read the earlier chapters about eBay, you may be wondering, "This is great for listing an item or two, but what if I have hundreds?" With many millions of products being sold every year through eBay, there has to be a better way . . . and there is. eBay provides a number of tools to help you automate as your online business grows.

These tools manage not only listing items, but, if you use the right tool, virtually everything. You can manage your inventory, list schedules, track sales and post-sales management, and check reporting. Whatever needs to be done online, you can bet there's a tool for the process, whether provided by eBay or another company.

The Different eBay Tools

As your business grows, you'll find that managing data can become a big headache. Certainly there are plenty of other headaches—shipping, finding inventory, cash flow, and so on—but just managing the data can become a huge job. That's why eBay provides a number of products, shown in the following table, that you can use to automate sales.

Turbo Lister	Uploads listings in bulk. The program runs on your Windows PC. **eBay Pitch:** *List Multiple Items.*	Free to all members
Selling Manager	Manages the sales and post-sales process. Runs online. **eBay Pitch:** *Online sales-management tool that makes keeping track of your sales simple.*	$4.99/month
Selling Manager Pro	Includes the features of both Turbo Lister and Selling Manager, plus inventory-management features, automatic feedback placement, and so on. Runs online. **eBay Pitch:** *Do It All! A powerful way for high-volume sellers to list, manage sales, and make more informed business decisions.*	Free to Seller's Assistant Pro subscribers and members with Featured and Anchor eBay Stores (see Chapter 9). $15.99/month for others

Seller's Assistant Basic	Has Turbo Lister features, plus a minimal number of tracking and e-mail management features. The program runs on your Windows PC. **eBay Pitch:** *For the medium seller who wants to save time.*	$9.99/month
Seller's Assistant Pro	Offers complete sales management, bulk listing, and post-sales assistance. The program runs on your Windows PC. **eBay Pitch:** *For high-volume and business sellers.*	$24.99/month

The following table shows how eBay characterizes these tools:

Tool	Type of Seller	Features
Turbo Lister	For any merchant who wants to make listing multiple items faster and easier	Lists more in less time Quickly manages and organizes your listings Uploads multiple items in bulk
Selling Manager	Optimal for medium- to high-volume sellers	Tracks and manages your sales after they have been listed Can easily be paired with any listing tool
Selling Manager Pro	Optimal for high-volume and business sellers	A complete sales management tool that includes all the features of Selling Manager plus bulk listing, inventory management, reporting, and automated features
Seller's Assistant Basic	For the medium seller who wants to save time	Offers professional listings, tracking, and e-mail management
Seller's Assistant Pro	For high-volume and business sellers	Offers complete sales management, bulk listing, and post-sales assistance

 tip *Visit the Seller Tools page at http://pages.ebay.com/sell/tools.html for all the details and to subscribe.*

 tip *Yes, there's a lot of overlap among these tools. To compare them all, feature by feature, see the comparison table at http://pages.ebay.com/selling_manager/comparison.html.*

The single most important feature you need is the ability to "bulk list," that is, to upload dozens, even hundreds, of items at once. But there are plenty of other features. The following table provides a quick glance at a few, and shows which products have the feature:

	Turbo Lister	Selling Manager	Selling Manager Pro	Seller's Assistant Basic	Seller's Assistant Pro
Creates fixed-price listings for an eBay Store	✓	✓	✓	✓	✓
Warns when running out of stock	✗	✗	✓	✗	✓
Offers store sales and customer information	✗	✓	✓	✓	✓
Leaves feedback in bulk	✗	✓	✓	✗	✓
Automatically leaves feedback when buyer pays	✗	✗	✓	✗	✗
Shows monthly Profit and Loss reports	✗	✗	✓	✗	✓
Creates reusable feedback messages	✗	✓	✓	✗	✓

eBay provides a special utility to help you pick which tool to use. Visit http://pages.ebay.com/sell/toolrecommendations.html and follow the steps. eBay will suggest a tool for you to use.

Using Turbo Lister

A good way to get started is by using Turbo Lister. It's free, and deals with one of the most troublesome issues, listing many products at once.

 tip *Go directly to Turbo Lister at the following address: http://pages.ebay.com/turbo_lister/.*

Here's what you can do with this system:

- Format your description text using a "What You See Is What You Get" design tool
- Select predesigned templates for your listings
- Preview your listings before you post them
- Save listing information to reuse as a template—create it once, use it thousands of times
- Edit in bulk—select many items and change all the selling formats at the same time
- Save items in an inventory database, and then use the data over and over again
- Search your listings, both current and past, to find a particular item
- Duplicate and copy listings

- Upload many individual listings at one time
- Create a backup of your item database
- Keep records of what was listed and when

tip   *Even if you're not working with dozens or hundreds of listings at a time, you may still want to use Turbo Lister, as it makes the process so simple.*

You'll need a Windows PC to use Turbo Lister. Download the program and install it. It's really worth the effort and is very easy to work with. The following steps outline how to use the program.

1. When you first use the program, run the wizard. Along the way, you'll enter your eBay account ID and password, and Turbo Lister will go online to grab your information.

2. You can then import your current listings from the store, if you wish. You can even import listings that have ended as well. The Turbo Lister window will open (see Figure 8-1).

3. You can now create a single new item (select File | New | Item). But let's look at how to create a template, which can then be used to create items time and again. Select File | New | Template to see the Create New Template Wizard (Figure 8-2).

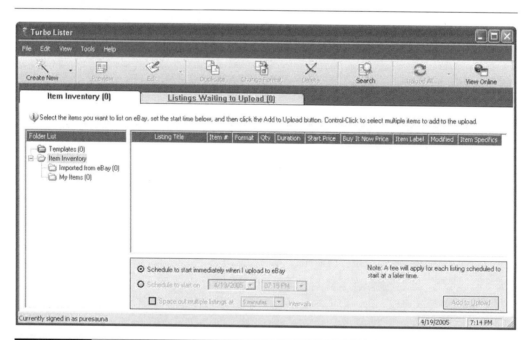

FIGURE 8-1   The Turbo Lister window

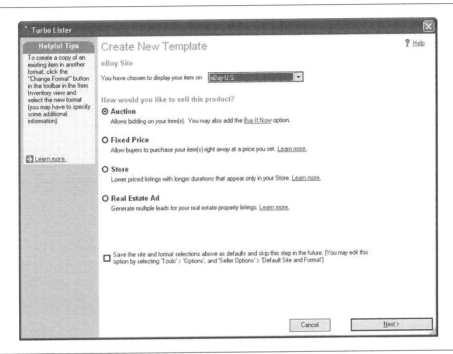

FIGURE 8-2   Start by creating a template for your products.

4. If you want to display the items managed by this template in eBay sites outside the U.S., open the **You have chosen to display your item on** drop-down list box, and select **Add site . . .**

5. Select one of the listing formats: **Auction**, **Fixed Price**, **Store**, or **Real Estate Ad**.

6. If you wish, click the **Save the site and format selections** check box. All your subsequent listings will use these criteria until you change the Seller Options in Turbo Lister's Options dialog box. Click the **Next** button and you'll see the **Create a New Item** box (Figure 8-3).

7. This is similar to entering a listing in the manner you learned in Chapter 5. You'll provide an **Item Title**, and maybe a **Subtitle** (but remember, there's a fee for subtitles).

8. Click the **Find Category** button to open the box in which you can select a category. It's the same concept as in Chapter 5, but with a different tool. See Figure 8-4.

9. Select a **2nd Category**, if you wish. Remember, there's an additional fee. If you have a store, you can select the **Store Category**.

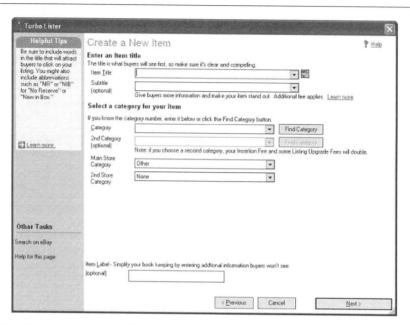

FIGURE 8-3   Enter your item information here.

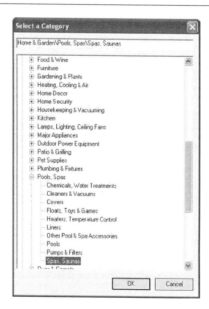

FIGURE 8-4   Selecting a category

10. There's also space for an **Item Label**. This is not part of your listing; it's simply a reference you can use to track listings. Click the **Next** button, and you'll see the Enter Your Description page (Figure 8-5).

11. Again, you've seen this before in Chapter 5. You'll enter the description and pictures, and select various special listing features. When you've finished here, click **Next** to see the final data-entry page (Figure 8-6).

12. It's on this page where you enter the pricing, duration, and all the other details we looked at in Chapter 5. When you've set all these items, click the **Save** button. You've now created a template. Continue with the remaining steps to find out how to use it to create many listings at one time.

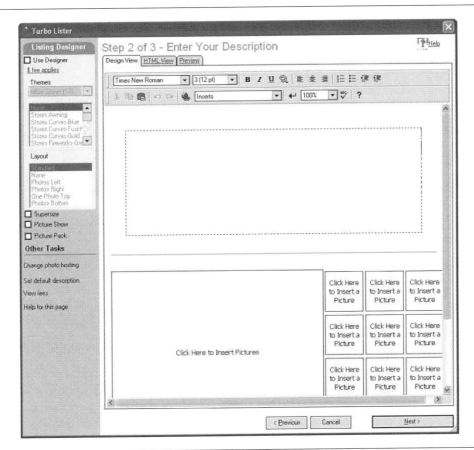

FIGURE 8-5   Here's where you enter your product description.

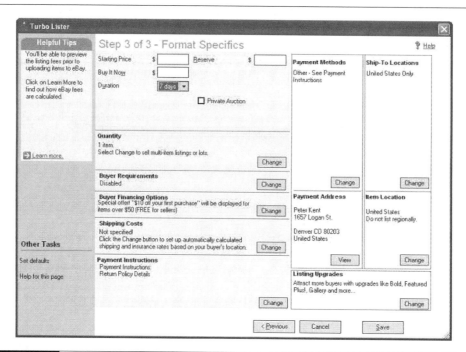

FIGURE 8-6   Enter pricing, duration, shipping details, payment instructions, and so on.

13. Select **File | New | Item(s) From Template**, and then select the name of the template you created.

14. In the box that appears, select the folder into which you want to enter the listings you are creating.

15. When you click the **Save** button, the Edit Item window is displayed (Figure 8-7).

16. You can now make whatever changes you want to the listing you're about to add—change the description or title, for instance, modify the listing features, or whatever you want to do.

17. Click the **Save** button, and the item is placed into the folder you created.

18. Right-click the folder, and select **Duplicate Item(s)**; the Duplicate Item box appears.

19. Type the number of items. If, for instance, you want to list 30 items and auction them individually, type **30** and click **OK**. Turbo Lister places all the items onto your list.

20. When you're ready to upload your items, select the listings you want to upload and click the **Add to Upload** button. These are the placed onto the **Listings Waiting to Upload** tab. In the confirmation box, click the **Go Upload Listings** button, and the Listings Waiting to Upload tab is opened (Figure 8-8).

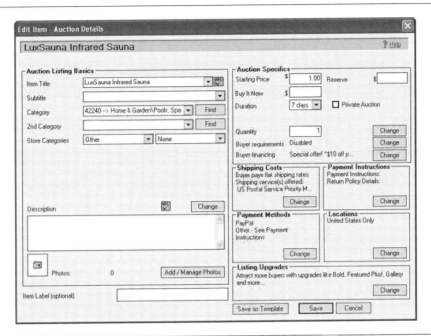

FIGURE 8-7   The Edit Item window

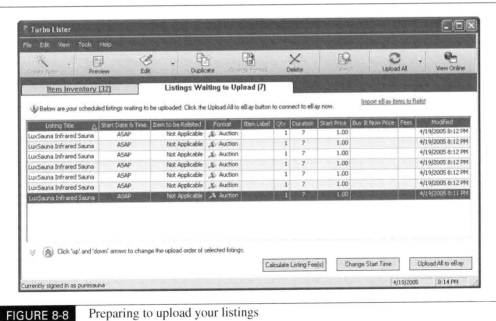

FIGURE 8-8   Preparing to upload your listings

21. Click the **Calculate Listing Fee(s)** button. Turbo Lister goes online, and checks to see how much your listings are going to cost you. The fees for each listing are entered into the **Fees** column.

22. Click the **Upload All to eBay** button to upload the listings.

There's more to Turbo Lister, of course. In particular, these other features may be of use to you:

■ **Import from a spreadsheet.** You can create listings in a spreadsheet or database program, export the data from that program, and select **File | Import Items | From CSV** to import the listings.

■ **Preview listings.** Choose the listing, and then click the **Preview** button.

■ **Create pre-filled items.** You can create listings for some classes of products—books, cell phones, DVDs, music CDs, and so on—and Turbo Lister will fill in some information for you. For instance, provide a book's ISBN, and Turbo Lister grabs the book title. Turbo Lister can insert basic facts—titles, movie descriptions, film credits, and so on—and even grab images in some cases. Select **File | New | Multiple Items**.

Using Selling Manager

Selling manager has two versions. The basic version is, according to eBay, intended for medium-to high-volume sellers, while the Pro version is for high-volume and business sellers. The basic system—which runs online, through a series of web forms—"tracks and manages your sales after they have been listed," and can "easily be paired with any listing tool," states eBay (see Figure 8-9). If you're using the basic version, you'll probably want to use Turbo Lister, too.

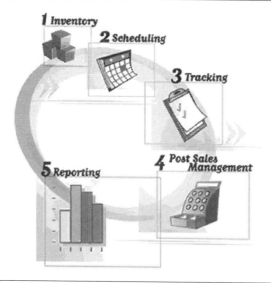

FIGURE 8-9   Selling Manager manages inventory, scheduling, tracking, post sales, and reporting.

The Pro version, though, has a bulk-listing tool included. It also has inventory management, reporting, and a couple of interesting automation tools, that none of the other tools has:

■ You can create **automatic payment-received e-mails and item-shipped notification e-mails**.

■ You can **automatically add feedback** for buyers when the buyer pays.

In addition, it has two reporting tools only otherwise available in Seller's Assistant Pro: a monthly Profit and Loss report, and the ability to export to Excel.

Using Seller's Assistant

Seller's Assistant is an offline tool (it runs on a Windows PC) that's described as a product "for the medium seller who wants to save time." Seller's Assistant Pro is eBay's top-of-the-line product and is intended for high-volume and business sellers. The Professional version contains just about everything the other tools have, and more. It can

■ Create listings and upload them, en masse

■ Manage your inventory

■ Track your sales information

■ Manage post-sales operations

■ Do reporting

Seller's Assistant Basic and Pro are eBay's all-in-one, desktop listing- and sales-management tools designed to save time. Seller's Assistant tools help medium- to high-volume sellers like you sell on eBay without the need for a constant Internet connection, and can be customized to how you do business.

Using Third-party Tools

Many other tools are available, provided by companies other than eBay, and are designed to help you manage your eBay business in many different ways. We recently found *85* different tools. Some tools attempt to do everything, while others specialize in a certain area, such as inventory management. Some integrate with QuickBooks, while some are adapted for Great Plains or Microsoft Office.

 tip *To find the Complete Selling Solutions list, go to solutions.ebay.com, and click the Complete Selling Solutions link near the top of the page.*

There's also another good reason to use these tools. As your business grows, you may find that you outgrow eBay. After all, eBay may be a huge market, but it's not everything. You may want to run your own web store, feed data to shopping directories such as Yahoo! Shopping and Froogle (see Chapter 25), sell through merchant sites such as Amazon.com and Overstock.com (see Chapter 28), and so on. Some of the third-party tools help you do just that.

The following products are some of the better-known eBay management tools:

- **Andale** (www.Andale.com)   This company has good research tools, too.
- **Marketworks** (www.Marketworks.com)   One percent of all eBay transactions are managed by this system. It doesn't just manage eBay sales, but other channels as well.
- **Channel Advisor** (www.ChannelAdvisor.com)   Also manages other channels.
- **Vendio** (www.vendio.com)   This product is used by 100,000 eBay users.
- **HammerTap Manager** (www.HammerTap.com)   This product also includes auction-research tools.

Notice that some of these tools are much more than eBay management tools. Perhaps the best known service provider is Marketworks (formerly Auctionworks). Their products manage 1 percent of all eBay transactions, for around 4,000 eBay merchants; that may not sound like a lot, but it comes in at around $340M worth of transactions every year. The Marketworks system (see Figure 8-10) combines the following functions:

- An online store
- An inventory management system
- Product-data entry
- Single-point order and customer management for all the sales channels
- Automated data feeds
- Reporting tools
- For more sophisticated companies, a way to tie in the Marketworks tools with the customer's existing systems

FIGURE 8-10   How Marketworks views their role in online marketing: they want to help data flow between different channels

What does all this mean? Well, it allows a business to enter and manage all their data in one place. That data is then fed to their web store, to eBay and Overstock, to the Google and Yahoo! PPC systems (this component is coming soon), to shopping directories such as Yahoo! Shopping, Shopping.com, Froogle, and Kelkoo (and they may have already added NexTag and Shopzilla by the time you read this), and even to private merchant sites (Marketworks has a tool allowing site owners to create their own Amazon-like merchant sites). They're also currently in the process of adding an interface to Amazon Marketplace, and can even feed data to Yahoo! Auctions (though that auction site is definitely a backwater in the auction world).

When sales are made, the flow of data is, in effect, reversed. Now transaction data comes from the channels—from eBay, from the web store, from Amazon Marketplace, from Overstock, and so on—back to the Marketworks tools, where all sales, from all channels, can be processed in the same way. Without a system like this, your clerical staff will be opening up the different order-management systems, and processing orders in different ways depending on the channel from which they come. Marketworks also has advanced inventory-management tools, allowing you to, if you wish, keep track of which systems inventory has been committed to and lock that so inventory cannot be listed on other sites.

This system is very much targeted at small and medium businesses. The startup costs vary from "$0 to $6,000," based on what you want. Do everything yourself and there's no fee; have Marketworks set up and design the store and you'll pay for their services. Marketworks charges a 2-percent fee on each transaction, with a $29.95/month minimum, so operational costs are reasonable, too. Marketworks claims its merchants quickly benefit from increased efficiencies—one seller, they say, boosted sales from $30,000/month to $150,000/month after using Marketworks.

If you shop around for a service, check each one carefully. In particular, find out the size of the company. Some companies comprise just a handful of people, meaning they may be stretched to the limit supporting their clients (and may not be around next year).

More Resources

For more information, visit the following pages:

- **Seller Central page**   http://pages.ebay.com/sellercentral/
- **Advanced Selling and Seller's Tools**   http://pages.ebay.com/sellercentral/techniques .html

Turbo Lister is a very easy tool to work with—you *must* check it out. And in the following chapter, we'll tell you about another very useful system provided by eBay, the eBay store.

This page intentionally left blank

Chapter 9

Opening an eBay Store

After selling through the auction listings for a while, many eBay merchants take the next step: setting up an eBay store. In many respects, it's a natural next step. You wet your feet with auction listings, discover your products are selling, start making money, and now want more. So you bring in more products and more inventory, and set up an eBay store. But are you sure it's the right step? What are the advantages and disadvantages? How will you get people into your store? These are the issues we'll cover in this chapter.

Why Set Up an eBay Store?

Should you set up an eBay store? Maybe. Let's consider some of the reasons merchants do just that.

■ **They want a web site.** Many merchants begin by selling through the auction listings, doing well, and then expanding. Selling online is more than just selling in auctions: they want to create a web site that they can direct buyers to, a site that can be promoted in many ways (see Chapters 22 to 29).

■ **It's fast and cheap.** Merchants can set up a web site through eBay very quickly and affordably.

■ **Merchants want to sell accessories.** A merchant may sell digital cameras through the auctions, then direct people toward their store where they can sell them accessories such as batteries, memory cards, camera cases, and so on.

■ **They want to sell many fixed-price items.** A merchant who sells mostly fixed-price items may find it easier to do so through a store.

■ **Merchants can sell multiples.** More like a regular store; merchants attempt to sell as many of each product as they can. Thus, they're not just selling "one off" products.

■ **Insertion fees are very low.** A merchant could list a thousand products for a month for just $20.

- **Final Value Fees are much lower.** As long as the buyer comes directly to a merchant's store and not through eBay, Final Value Fees are considerably lower.

- **Merchants end up selling to repeat customers.** Why should a merchant pay high Insertion Fees and Final Value Fees if they've done a good job of bringing customers back to their site?

- **eBay Stores is turning into a destination.** More people now know about eBay Stores, and eBay is doing more to educate people about it. So having a store provides another way to reach people.

- **eBay pays 25 percent of a merchant's advertising.** If a merchant owns a store, eBay will pay up to 25 percent of the cost of placing ads in newspapers and magazines.

Of course, there are always disadvantages to any choice in this world. Take, for example, the following:

- **Final Value Fees are higher.** If the buyer gets to a merchant's site after arriving at either the main eBay or eBay Stores site, the Final Value Fees are higher.

- **Store listings are not found in the main eBay site as easily.** Searches through eBay.com mostly find listings in the auctions. eBay Stores listings are only included if there aren't enough matches.

Pushing People to Your Store

If you set up an eBay store, how are you going to get people to visit it? There are two ways people can arrive at your store: through eBay's efforts, and through your own.

> **tip** *If you wish, you can create a domain name and point it to your eBay store—for example, instead of typing http://stores.ebay.com/really-cool-toys, your clients would only have to type really-cool-toys.com. To learn more, click the Register your domain name link in the Manage Your Store area of your My eBay page.*

In the early days, eBay Stores was a little-used backwater. These days it's much better known, and eBay is doing more to let people know it exists and push people toward it. eBay will direct people to your site in the following ways:

- By including a little **eBay Stores link in the Specialty Sites** box at the top of the eBay Home page.

- By including **various eBay Stores links in the Other Ways to Browse** box at the bottom of the main Buy page.

- By including the **Visit this seller's eBay Store!** link in the Seller Information box at the top of the items listed in auctions by eBay store owners.

Visit this seller's eBay Store!
stores **Buy Essex**

- eBay store items **are included in search results** when eBay can't find enough auction listings that match.
- Products are included in the **More on eBay** box in auction search results (see Figure 9-1).

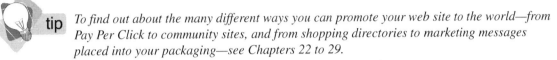

tip   *To find out about the many different ways you can promote your web site to the world—from Pay Per Click to community sites, and from shopping directories to marketing messages placed into your packaging—see Chapters 22 to 29.*

Of course, since this is your store you'll have your own URL—http://stores.ebay.com/ *storename*—so you can guide people directly to your store. This way, you can market directly to people, and cross-promote from your eBay listings. For instance, you can

- Promote your store in **all your auction listings**, prominently and multiple times.
- Promote your store in your **eBay auctions About Me page**.
- Use various **eBay marketing tools** (see Chapter 10).
- Market directly to existing customers **through postcards and e-mails**.
- Use **Pay Per Click systems** (see Chapter 22).
- Include **your store's URL** in ads.
- Promote your store to customers **with in-packaging flyers**.

Remember, this is your web site. You can promote it in any manner you see fit.

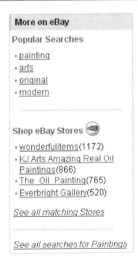

FIGURE 9-1   The More on eBay box appears on search-results pages.

Selecting a Store Type

eBay has three different store types—Basic, Featured, and Anchor—which range in price from $15.95 to $499.95 a month. The following table summarizes the differences between these stores.

Feature	Basic	Featured	Anchor
Price	$15.95	$49.95	$449.95
Fast template-based store production	✓	✓	✓
Merchandising and cross-promotion tools	✓	✓	✓
Sales reports	✓	✓	✓
Advanced sales reports (including eBay marketplace data to "benchmark" your store)	✗	✓	✓
Traffic reports, including search keywords	✓	✓	✓
Advanced traffic reports (w/visitor path analysis and bid and Buy It Now tracking)	✗	✓	✓
Fully customizable pages in your store	5	10	15
24-hour phone customer support	✗	✗	✓
eBay Selling Manager Pro included (see Chapter 8)	✗	✓	✓
Free eBay keywords (see Chapter 10)		$30/mo.	$90/mo.
E-mail marketing—e-mails/mo.	100	1,000	4,000
Place your logo at the top of the eBay Stores Home page and your category page (*Check Out These Stores*)	✗	✗	✓
Place your listing half-way down the eBay Stores Home page and your category page (*Featured Stores*)	✗	✓	✗

One of the most valuable features is probably the promotional placements.

■ **Anchor** stores appear in the Check Out These Stores area of the eBay Stores Home page and their category pages (their logos are displayed).

■ **Featured** stores appear in the Featured area of the eBay Stores Home page and their category pages (the store titles are displayed).

■ **Anchor and Feature stores** are more likely to appear in the various eBay promotional placements.

eBay Store Fees

The fees charged for the eBay store are a little more complicated than the regular fees we looked at in Chapter 3. Listing fees are actually much lower, and there are two levels of Final Value Fees: the fees you are charged for sales originating within eBay itself, and fees for sales originating from your own online promotional efforts (that is, sales to people who arrive directly at your store rather than through eBay). Let's look at all the fees.

Monthly Fees

As you've already learned, you're charged a monthly fee for the store:

Basic	$15.95
Featured	$49.95
Anchor	$499.95
Insertion Fees	

A listing can include multiple items, so you pay a single fee for the listing regardless of whether you are selling one item or one thousand. You simply pay a listing fee that depends on how long you keep the item listed.

30 days	2 cents
60 days	4 cents
90 days	6 cents
120 days	8 cents
Good 'til cancelled	2 cents every 30 days

For instance, let's say you have 100 different products listed at all times. You'll pay just $2 a month.

Listing Upgrade Fees

The fees charged for listing upgrades are often lower, too, and even when they are comparable to the eBay auction upgrade fees, they're still lower when you consider that the fees are charged for 30 days, not the few days that an auction lasts. For instance, to use the Gallery feature (which bundles several images into an animated slideshow-type picture) it costs just 1 cent every 30 days. To add bold text to the listing description is $1 for 30 days, as opposed to $1 for up to 10 days in the auctions.

Final Value Fees—Sales Originating Through eBay

The fee you pay eBay for the actual sale is higher than for auctions if the sale originates through eBay—that is, if someone comes to eBay and then follows a link to your store.

Sales Price	Fee
Up to $25	8%
Up to $1,000	$2 plus 5% of the amount over $25
Over $1,000	$50.75 plus 3% of the amount over $1,000

note *How does eBay know if a sale originates with eBay, or you drive people directly to the site? As soon as a buyer arrives at your site or at eBay, eBay sets a "cookie" on their computer (a small text file used for tracking). eBay can then track their travels through the eBay system. Whenever a sale is made at an eBay store, eBay checks to see how the buyer first arrived at the eBay system during that browser session.*

Final Value Fees—Sales Originating Through Your Own Efforts

If someone arrives directly at your store and buys from you, your Final Value Fees are considerably less, because you'll receive a 75-percent Store Referral Credit. The following table shows the effective rate, after you subtract the credit.

Sales Price	Fee
Up to $25	2%
Up to $1,000	50 cents plus 1.25% of the amount over $25
Over $1,000	$12.69 plus 0.75% of the amount over $1,000

Setting Up Your Store

Before you can set up an eBay store, you must have a seller's account, and either be ID Verified (see Chapter 2) or have a feedback score of 20 or above. Here's how to create a store:

1. Go to eBay Stores (http://stores.ebay.com/). There's an <u>eBay Stores</u> link on the home page (top left).

2. Click the **Open a Store** button.

3. You may be asked to log into your seller account. On the next page, click the **Open Your eBay Store** button.

tip *You can customize your store later. An easy option in this regard is to select one of the <u>Easily Customizable</u> themes.*

4. Select a theme—the layout and color scheme (see Figure 9-2). Note that some themes have **Color scheme** drop-down list boxes below them, allowing you to select different colors. You can click the links at the top left to select different groups of styles. Click the **Continue** button when you've selected one.

tip *Read the rules about store names (click <u>naming your Store</u>). The URL of the store will be based on the name you provide, so you may want to include a few keywords for the search engines to read. You can base it on your company name, but adding keywords may help.*

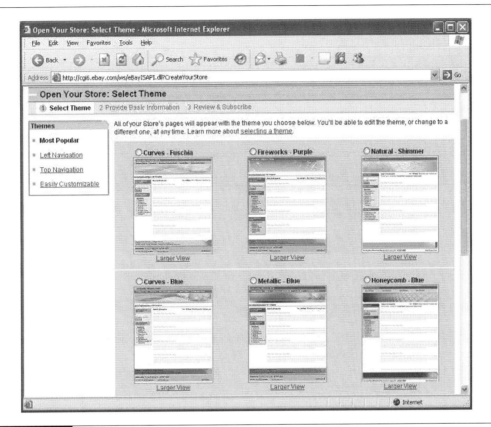

FIGURE 9-2   Select an eBay store theme.

5. On the following page, enter a **Store name** and **Store description**.

6. You should also provide a logo. eBay lets you use a generic or **Predefined** logo, but you shouldn't use this more than temporarily when you set up the store. Your logo is too important—it appears at the top of every page in most layouts, and in the Check Out These Stores area at the top of your category if you choose to buy that position (see Figure 9-3). So, have a designer create an image that is 310-pixels wide and 90-pixels high, and then upload it to your store. You want your logo to be a sales piece, because if you buy a placement in the Check Out These Stores area, the logo will be displayed there.

FIGURE 9-3   Store logos, shown in the Check Out These Stores area at the top of the Antiques category

7. Click the **Continue** button to see the **Review & Subscribe** page (Figure 9-4).

8. Select the subscription level for the store (click the <u>benefits of each subscription level</u> link to learn more).

■ **Basic store** $19.95/month, the cheapest store; you may want to select this to begin.

■ **Featured store** $49.95/month

■ **Anchor store** $499.95/month

9. Click the **Start My Subscription Now** button and your store will be built.

10. You can now customize your store. Click the **Customize Your Store** button or go to My eBay to see the new options that have been added.

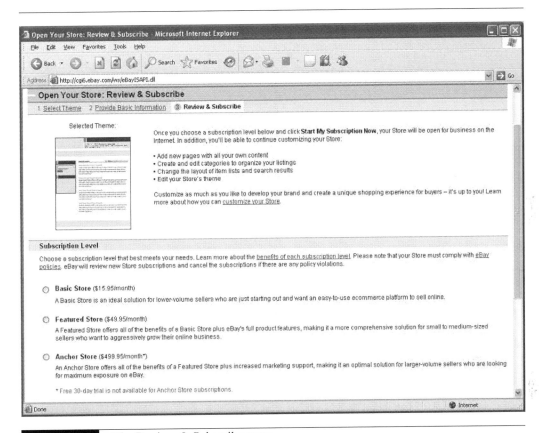

FIGURE 9-4   The Review & Subscribe page

Customizing Your Store

You've only half-finished your store. You now need to finish the customization. Enter the My eBay page and look for the **My Subscriptions** box on the left side. Click the <u>Manage Your Store</u> link and the Manage Your Store box appears (Figure 9-5).

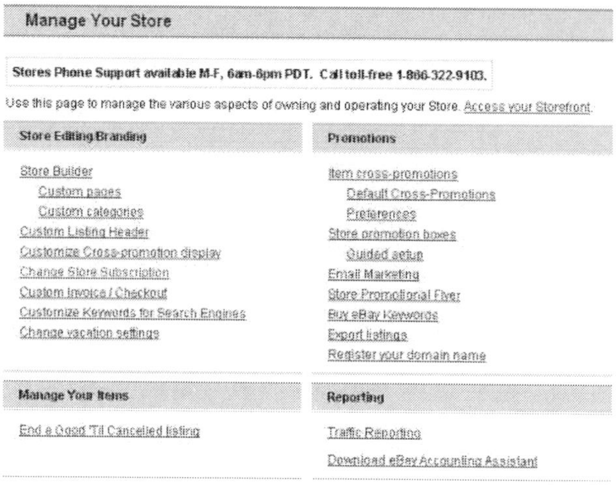

FIGURE 9-5   The Manage Your Store box

From here, you can customize your store by completing various tasks shown in the following table:

Option	Description
Store Builder	Edit the basic information you entered when you created the store.
	Change your listing layout.
	Change the header style; if you have a Featured or Anchor store, you can make the eBay header at the top of your store smaller.
	Add custom pages, and change the navigation.
	Organize listings into custom categories.
	Add product-promotion boxes to the store.
Custom Listing Header	Create a custom header for your listing pages—add a logo, include links from the header to particular categories, and incorporate a store-search box.
Customize Cross-promotion display	Set up your cross-promotions box, which appears on the product pages (see Figure 9-6).
Change Store Subscription	Switch from one store type to another (Basic, Featured, Anchor).
Custom Invoice/Checkout	Add a logo and custom message to your checkout pages and invoice e-mail.
Customize Keywords for Search Engines	Edit your category pages' TITLE tags and DESCRIPTION and KEYWORDS metatags to help your ranking in the search engines. See Chapter 26 for more information.
Change vacation settings	If you're running a one-person operation and going on vacation, you can turn off your store.

FIGURE 9-6 The cross-promotions box. This appears on product pages in both your eBay store and auction listings.

Listing Your Items for Sale

We explain in Chapter 5 how to list items for sale in the auctions. Listing items in your store is very similar.

1. Click the **Sell** button on the button bar at the top of the eBay screen.

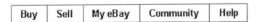

2. On the following page, click the **Sell Your Item** button. You'll be taken to a page with your Selling Format options (Figure 9-7).

3. Select the **Sell in Store Inventory** option button, and then click the **Continue** button to see the Select Category page.

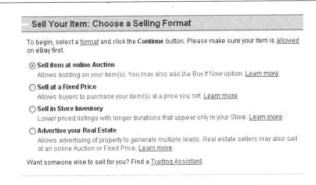

FIGURE 9-7 Select your selling format.

tip *eBay provides a tool that can push items from your store to auction listings. See http://pages .ebay.com/help/specialtysites/sending-store-inventory.html.*

From here on, the process is much the same as listing for auctions (see Chapter 5 for more information). However, if you've set up a store, there's a good chance you have more than a handful of products. You'll want to use the Turbo Lister to load your products. We'll cover that in Chapter 10.

Chapter 10

Marketing, Keywords, and Promotions

At its most basic, the eBay system is simply a matter of listing an item and then waiting for someone to come and buy it from you. But there's more you can do to generate interest and sales. For instance, you can promote your listings a number of ways in order to catch the attention of buyers and bring them to you. Once you have their attention, you can encourage them to buy from you.

In this chapter, we'll look at a variety of techniques to market and promote your business. Some of them cost money and should be used carefully—eBay's new Pay Per Click *eBay Keywords* program, for instance. Other things have no direct cost, however. In fact, one of them may even earn you additional income: if you promote eBay's *service plan* to buyers of electronics and jewelry, you'll actually earn a cut of the sale *and* encourage potential buyers to purchase from you.

Using eBay Keywords

The online advertising world is going PPC—Pay Per Click. Billions of dollars are spent on PPC ads every year, primarily through Google and Yahoo!. eBay now offers PPC ads through their *eBay Keywords* program, and tens of thousands of eBay merchants already use it. You can find details about PPC advertising in Chapters 22 through 24, but for now here's what you must understand. When a buyer enters a search term, if your ad matches the keywords entered, it will appear on the search results page. This doesn't cost you a thing; however, if the buyer clicks on the ad . . . *then* you pay.

> **tip** *For details about the eBay Keywords program, see https://ebay.admarketplace.net/.*

So, how much do you pay? Well, that depends. The *minimum* you'll pay is 10 cents, but ad pricing is set through bidding. You can set the maximum bid—your bid defines the frequency with which your ad appears. Thus, people who bid more will have their ads displayed more often when the specified keywords are entered into a search box. As a result, they'll pay more when someone clicks their ad.

eBay currently provides three ad types:

- A 120 × 60 pixel text box. Two are placed at the top of the search results, to the right of the large image banner.

- A larger text box is displayed to the left of the search results.

- A 468 × 60 pixel image banner is shown at the top left of the search results.

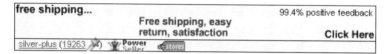

Experiment with eBay's Pay Per Click system carefully. It may not work well for low-cost goods, unless you do a really good job of getting people to look through your store once you've grabbed their attention. If you're listing just two or three $20 books, for instance, it's very unlikely you'll find eBay Keywords worthwhile. If you have a store selling hundreds of digital cameras and accessories, and work hard to turn visitors and buyers into long-term customers, it may be good for you.

Using Store Promotion Boxes

You can create product-promotion boxes that can be placed into your store to do different things, such as:

- Promote particular products

- Announce special offers

- Provide links to particular areas of your store

 note   *Click the <u>Store promotion boxes</u> link in the Manage Your Store area of My eBay to create promotion boxes.*

These boxes can be placed near the top of your store pages (you can place two boxes here, or combine them into one large one; see Figure 10-1). You can also place promotional boxes below the navigation bar on the left. Again, two can be placed below the navbar and they'll appear on every page with a navbar.

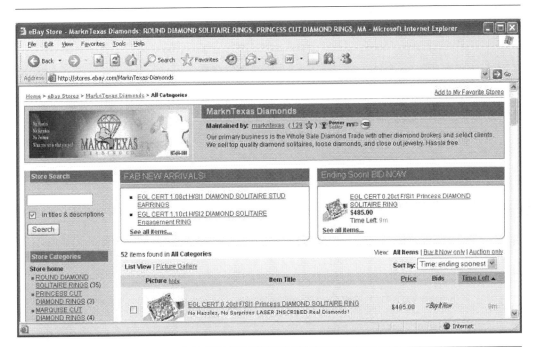

FIGURE 10-1   A couple of promotion boxes displayed above the product listings in this eBay store

Setting Up Cross Promotions

eBay automatically cross-promotes your products. That is, when someone looks at one of your products, eBay displays other items you're carrying, displaying them in a **See More Great Items From This Seller** box (see Figure 10-2). You may, if you wish, specify *how* items are cross-promoted by employing the following criteria:

■ **Specify *where* the ads appear.** You can choose whether ads will appear in the checkout or elsewhere (such as the product place).

■ **Determine which types of products are cross-promoted.** These items can be from the Store inventory, can be Buy It Now items, or any type.

■ **Determine how the items should be sorted.** You can sort items by when their listing ends, their price, and so on.

■ **Determine how many items should be shown.** You can determine how many items are shown (up to 12).

FIGURE 10-2   The cross-promotion box. This appears on product pages in both your eBay Store and your auction listings.

The cross-promotion box is a very useful tool, and there aren't many good reasons for *not* displaying it . . . though you can turn it off if you wish.

Using eBay's E-mail Marketing Tools

eBay provides a useful little tool that allows you to send attractive e-mails to your customers. eBay Stores can send a certain number of e-mails for free each month:

- **Basic Store**   400 e-mails/month
- **Featured Store**   1,000 e-mails/month
- **Anchor Store**   4,000 e-mails/month

If you go over your limit, you'll pay 1 cent per e-mail—so a Basic Store that sends 10,000 e-mails a month would pay $96.

Creating an e-mail is quite straightforward since eBay provides a tool that automates the process. More of the problem derives from getting the various e-mail addresses to send to in the first place.

The big question is then: Who do you send e-mails to? eBay does provide tools to create and manage various mailing lists. In fact, you can create up to five different groups—perhaps one for a *Monthly Newsletter*, one for *New Products*, one for people who have subscribed to your *Special Offer Bulletin*, and so on. But how do you get e-mails into this list?

There's an e-mail list subscription tool built into the Favorites page. Visitors to your store can subscribe to one or more of your lists at the same time they set you as a Favorite store, or they can sign up *without* adding you to their Favorites just by clearing the **Add to my Favorite**

Sellers Top Picks check box. Of course you have to let people know this, because it isn't widely known. So here's how to use this feature.

1. In your **My eBay** page, click the <u>Manage Your Store</u> link in the **My Subscriptions** box.

2. In the Manage Your Store page, click the <u>Email Marketing</u> link in the **Promotions** column.

3. Click the Mailing Lists link, and create up to five different lists.

4. Go to the page where you want to tell people about your mailing lists—for instance, you'll probably want to put it into your About Me page. (In the My eBay page, click the <u>Personal Information</u> link, and then on the About Me line, click the <u>Change</u> link.)

5. Enter some text promoting your newsletters, and include a link to the Favorites page. You have to add this link as HTML. The preceding URL would appear something like this:

```
<a href="
http://my.ebay.com/ws/eBayISAPI.dll?AcceptSavedSeller&amp;sellerid=
YOURSELLERIDHERE&amp;sspageName=DB:FavList">Click here to sign up
for our newsletters!</a>
```

 How do you find the URL of your Favorites page? Log into your account, and then open one of your pages that contains the <u>Add to Favorite Sellers</u> link—for instance, a store page or an auction-listing page. Click the link to go to the Favorites page, and then copy the URL you see in the browser's address page. It should look something like this (your merchant ID should replace YOURSELLERIDHERE, of course):

```
http://my.ebay.com/ws/eBayISAPI.dll?AcceptSavedSeller&amp;sellerid=
YOURSELLERIDHERE&amp;sspageName=DB:FavList
```

If you're planning to use e-mail marketing, then promote the e-mail lists wherever you can—on your store page, your About Me page, in all of your product listings, and so on. The clearer the list and the more often you promote it, the more subscribers you'll get.

You can also sell product warranties to customers. This will make customers feel better about buying from you, and make you a little extra money at the same time! See http://pages .ebay.com/help/warranty/seller_overview.html for more information.

Looking for Ways to Differentiate Your Listings

You're competing against thousands of other merchants selling products similar to yours, right? So, how do you get the sale? There are a numbers of ways you can encourage people to buy from you: have a lower price, have a high Feedback score, use ID Verify, have a very professional About Me page, and so on.

But there are many other ways to go about this, too. For instance, successful merchants keep their eyes on their competitors, and then look for ways to *differentiate* their products from their competitors' in some manner, or make their listings stand out more when compared to others. If you know what you're up against, you'll have a better feeling for what you need to do to differentiate yourself, and can then employ some of the following techniques:

- **Use product bundling.** A merchant selling scrapbooks might put together particular packs that include a scrapbook plus various other useful products. Someone selling cameras might bundle a camera with film, batteries, and a case. Merchants selling video games could bundle three or four games together, and so on.

- **Offer free shipping.** Some merchants provide free shipping and include that information in the listing title. Sometimes eBay runs *Free Shipping* promotions, and links to free-shipping listings. Also, some buyers search using the term *free shipping* along with the product they're looking for. We recently found over 42,000 product listings with this term.

- **Use holiday tie-ins in your descriptions.** People often search for specific, calendar-related gifts. For instance, if you sell stuffed animals during Christmas and Valentine's Day, you might use those terms in the listing: *Stuffed Teddy Bear . . . Great Valentine's Day Gift!* Also consider Easter, Mother's Day, Father's Day, Hanukkah, and so on. Think about terms such as *Easter basket* and *stocking stuffer*.

- **Include "bonuses".** The bonuses concept is similar to bundling, but this time you "throw in" an extra product, some relatively low-cost item that you tell the buyer he'll get for free—perhaps a free memory card with a high-priced digital camera, free poker chips with a poker table, a free variety pack of paper with a laser toner cartridge, and so on. In some cases, the freebie can actually be used as a sample to bring people back to your store.

- **Combine shipping.** Clearly state that you'll combine shipping if the buyer purchases more items. In the case of light but valuable items, you might offer to waive shipping if the buyer purchases two or more, or charge a single shipping fee for as many items as the buyer wants to purchase. In other cases—that are more appropriate for heavier and lower-cost items—you might lower the shipping cost on multiple purchases.

Using Your Store to Build Relationships

An eBay store can be used as a tool to build long-term relationships. For instance, let's say you sell office supplies. Someone comes to eBay, searches the auctions, and buys printer ink from you. You can use your product-listing page to encourage people to visit your store, and also attempt to get them to sign up for your special-offer's bulletin. Ultimately, you want the customer to *come back* the next time they want ink, so you might also put a fridge magnet in the shipment.

 tip *eBay can be a little confusing to buyers. Many people think of each listing as being independent, and sometimes may not realize that you actually have a store (essentially a permanent location) that they can return to. The next time they want the same sort of product you sell, they may come back to eBay and search again. You don't want them to do that. You want them to return directly to your store. If they search again, you've probably lost them, and even if they do find you, your Final Value Fees will be much higher than if they'd come directly to your site. We recommend you register a domain name (see the Register your domain name link on the Manage Your Store page), point it to your store, and heavily promote that domain to all your customers.*

Do everything you can to bring people back to the store, to stop them from searching eBay again when they need products you carry. This idea now brings us to the issue of fees. If you direct someone to your store to buy additional items, you'll pay higher Final Value Fees on the store items than you would if they had been bought at auction; the base fee is 8% for store sales as opposed to 5.25% for auction sales. So why not just list all your items in the auctions, and *not* push people to the store? Well, for the following reasons:

- Many accessory items don't sell so well at auction. They're better off being sold from the store, and may fetch a higher price there anyway.

- If you're carrying many different items that don't always sell well in auctions, it would be expensive to list them permanently in the auctions. By contrast, listing them in the store is very cheap.

- The ultimate goal for many merchants is to encourage repeat sales through your store, and if you can get people to come directly to the store you'll pay very low Final Value Fees—a base of just 2 percent compared with 5.25 percent through the auctions.

We recommend that you promote your store heavily in your auction listings. Many merchants list their major items for sale in the auction, and link back to the store for the smaller accessory items, of which they stock many and that probably won't sell well at auction.

tip *Keep an eye on the eBay Merchandising Calendar (which you can find at http://pages .ebay.com/sellercentral/calendar.html). It lets you know what eBay has planned during the year, and which special promotions will appear on the eBay Home page.*

Selling Wholesale Lots

eBay has a special area for wholesale products: the Wholesale Lots portal. You can reach this area using the Wholesale link on the eBay Home page (near the bottom of the left-side navbar).

This area provides another way to sell your products. For instance, instead of selling directly to individuals one sale at a time, you might experiment with selling larger lots of products at a wholesale price. Getting listed in this area is simple: you use the same process as you do when listing in any other category (see Chapter 5). In the first step, when you pick a category, choose the general product category—Coins, Sporting Goods, Toys & Hobbies, whatever—and then when eBay shows you the list of subcategories, select the **Wholesale Lots** category. (Note, though, that not all primary categories have a Wholesale Lots subcategory.) You'll then find a list of subcategories within the Wholesale Lots category.

Chapter 11

Power Selling, Consignment Selling, and Analyzing Your Business

We hope your business grows. We hope it grows so much, in fact, that you can join the honored fraternity of PowerSellers. It only takes $1,000 a month to reach the point at which you can be considered for this program—although eBay has several levels of PowerSeller, with some merchants selling tens or hundreds of thousands of dollars' worth of product a month. As your business grows, you'll need to keep an eye on your statistics, too; if you don't know what's going on with your sales, you don't know how to manage and grow your business. We'll take a quick look at the reports available to you. Finally, we'll also discuss another interesting way to grow your business. by acting as a *trading assistant* and selling other people's products through eBay.

Becoming a PowerSeller

A *PowerSeller* is a merchant that consistently sells a lot of product through eBay and maintains a good feedback rating. There are various benefits, from being able to use the PowerSeller logo—a real credibility builder—to health benefits for you and your employees. (If you're a PowerSeller, there's a good chance you're employing someone to help you.)

 tip *To find all the PowerSeller details and sign up, go here: http://pages.ebay.com/services/ buyandsell/welcome.html.*

To qualify to be a PowerSeller, you must meet certain criteria, both specific and general:

- You must average **at least $1,000 in sales each month**, for three consecutive months.
- You have a **feedback rating of at least 100**.
- You have at least a **98-percent positive feedback**.
- You have been an **active member for at least 90 days**.

- You have your account in **good financial standing**.
- You maintain an average of **at least four listings** for the past three months.
- You must also "Uphold **the eBay community values**, including honesty, timeliness, and mutual respect."

 note *PowerSeller feedback ratings are actually calculated differently from normal feedback ratings. The standard calculation only includes a single rating from each person. If a buyer gives you five good ratings, for instance, only one counts in the feedback calculation. The PowerSeller calculation, however, would include all five good feedbacks.*

Once you're in, you don't necessarily stay. Eligibility is reviewed every month. You must maintain your account in good standing, maintain your 98-percent positive feedback, and maintain the average monthly sales amount of at least $1,000.

The Five PowerSeller Levels and Their Benefits

There are five different PowerSeller levels, and each comes with different benefits. The levels are based on the monthly sales of each:

Bronze	$1,000/mo.
Silver	$3,000/mo.
Gold	$10,000/mo.
Platinum	$25,000/mo.
Titanium	$150,000/mo.

There's no charge for the PowerSeller program, but there are real benefits:

- **Priority eSupport** provided to all PowerSeller levels.
- **Toll-free phone support** for all levels above Bronze.
- An **assigned account manager** for all levels above Silver.
- **The PowerSeller logo**; place it everywhere you can, in all listings, the About Me page, and so on. It will appear in your Member Profile automatically.
- **Personalized sales and Feedback** information.
- Use of the **PowerSeller icon** next to your User ID on your About Me page.
- Use of the **PowerSeller logo** in your item listings and on your About Me pages.
- **PowerSeller logo letterhead and business card** templates.
- PowerSeller-only **discussion board**, where you can discuss sales strategies with other merchants who really know what they're doing.

■ **Monthly PowerUp! e-mail newsletter** and a **Quarterly-printed PowerUp!** newsletter.

■ **eBay Co-op advertising dollars**; eBay will pay 25 percent of your print advertising, up to $32,000 at the Titanium level.

■ eBay **keyword banner ads** up to $200/quarter.

■ **Health insurance** for PowerSellers and employees.

■ Special **eBay events**.

Reviewing Your Sales Reports

You should sign up for your free sales reports and consider subscribing to the more advanced, paid reports. (These are free if you have a store, but they cost $4.99 for other merchants; the first month is free, though, so you could try the reports for three months for just ten dollars.) These reports provide a lot of useful information that can help you plan your marketing strategies:

■ Sales

■ Ended listings

■ Successful listings percent

■ Average sale price

■ eBay and PayPal fees paid

■ Metrics by category

■ Metrics by format (fixed price, auction, store)

■ Metrics by category and format

■ Metrics by ending day or time for all formats

■ Buyer counts

■ Detailed eBay fees

■ Unpaid item credits requested

 note *Find more information about sales reports at http://pages.ebay.com/salesreports/ welcome.html.*

Knowing exactly what's going on with your sales is incredibly important; for instance, you can quickly see which types of sales are more profitable for you, which categories are doing best, and even which listing ending times work best.

There are also companies that provide more extensive data, not only about your business—they can analyze your sales data—but about eBay commerce in general. These services can tell you what's hot on eBay, and how to price, promote, and even source your products. Two of the better known are HammerTap (www.HammerTap.com) and Andale (www.andale.com).

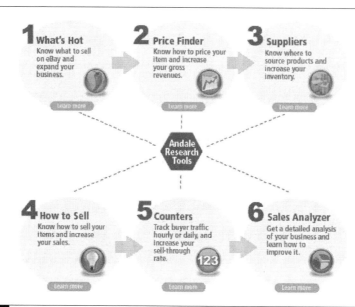

FIGURE 11-1 The Andale Market Research Pack's six services

The Andale Market Research Pack (Figure 11-1), for example, is just $9.95 a month, and provides these tools:

- **What's Hot** Reports on the best-selling products in every category (see Figure 11-2)
- **Price Finder** Helps you figure out what a product is worth on eBay before you sell it
- **Suppliers** Helps you find suppliers of the products you are selling on eBay
- **How to Sell** Tells you which categories you should list in, and which listing features to use, to get the best price
- **Counters** Detailed traffic statistics showing how many people view your listings
- **Sales Analyzer** Detailed sales statistics—number of items listed and sold, percent sold, your best-performing items, recommendations to improve your selling price and number of sales, and so on

tip *HammerTap has some other interesting services: BayCheck Pro (find detailed statistics about any eBay merchant), BayMail Pro (e-mail management for mailing to eBay members), Fee Finder (a fee-analysis tool).*

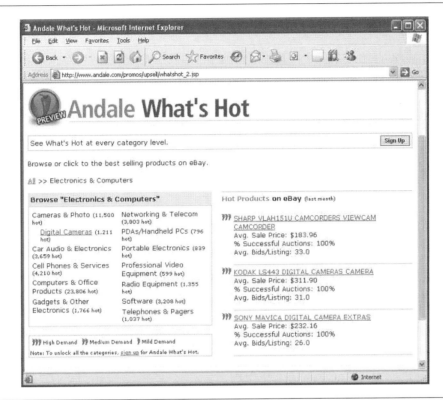

FIGURE 11-2 A small part of the Andale What's Hot report

HammerTap has a Windows-based tool called DeepAnalysis (see Figure 11-3) that focuses on eBay data rather than your sales data, and can provide a wide range of detailed statistics:

- See what competing merchants are doing: total sales, sell-through rates, average sales price, etc.

- Get information about particular auctions, showing starting prices, total sales, number of bids, etc.

- Find out success rates for different sales strategies—Buy It Now, Reserve prices, Dutch Auctions, etc.

If your business is growing and you're serious about growing even more, you really should spend some time understanding the statistics available to you. They are very affordable—Andale is $9.95/mo., HammerTap is $180 for the software and the first year of service.

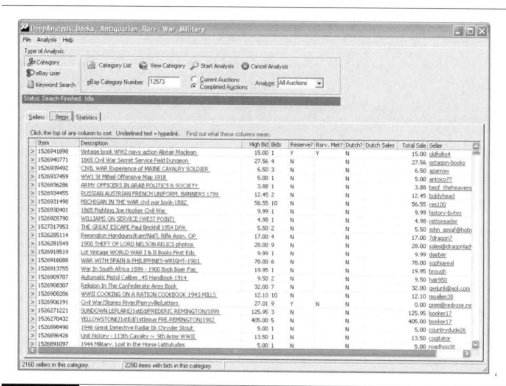

FIGURE 11-3   HammerTap's DeepAnalysis

Consignment Selling and Becoming a Trading Assistant

Consignment selling is the process of listing other people's products for them and paying them when the product finally sells. eBay has formalized this process with their *Trading Assistant* program. This program has various benefits, but of course there's nothing to stop you being a consignment seller even if you don't join the program.

tip   *Being a trading assistant may be illegal in some states, unless you are a registered auctioneer! eBay is currently fighting a number of absurd regulations in a few states. See ebay.com/sellercentral/governmentrelations/auction-regulation.html for more information.*

note   *To find the Trading Assistant program, click the services link at the top of any eBay page, then click the Trading Assistants link under **Listing Solutions**.*

eBay provides a directory of trading assistants; sellers can enter a ZIP code and, if they wish, select a product category—many trading assistants specialize in particular product types. They can also choose to view only trading assistants who have drop-off locations. (See Figure 11-4.)

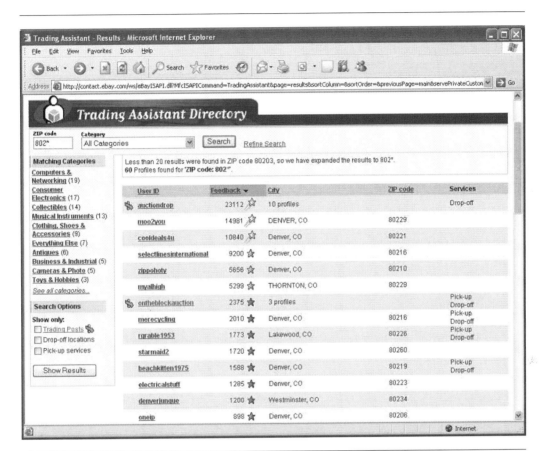

FIGURE 11-4   Sellers can quickly find an assistant to help them sell the item.

In order to make selling on consignment work, of course, you have to be selective. Trading assistants generally have certain criteria that the product must meet:

- **Many only sell in particular categories.** Their experience in those categories helps them estimate pricing and salability.

- **They have a minimum value.** Trading assistants generally won't accept products that they feel won't sell for more than, say, $75.

- **They have a maximum weight.** Most trading assistants try to avoid very heavy items—over, say, 25 lbs.—because of the shipping problems. Some may take larger items if they feel they can sell them locally, with the buyer picking up.

- **The item must be sellable!** The product has to be in a condition that will allow it to be sold.

How much can you make if you sell other people's products? Typically trading assistants deduct a sales commission and the insertion and final-value fees from the sale price; the item's owner gets the rest. For instance, here are a few fee schedules, from major eBay trading assistants:

QuickDrop	38 percent of the first $200, 30 percent of the next $300, 20 percent of the rest.
AuctionDrop	38 percent of the first $200, 30 percent of the next $300, 20 percent of the rest, plus a payment-processing fee of 2.9 percent of the total transaction value (sale price, shipping, handling, and sales tax). A minimum $19.99 commission.
iSOLD It	30 percent of the first $500, 20 percent of the rest, plus a payment-processing fee of 30 cents plus 2.9 percent. A $5 minimum commission.

In addition to these fees, the trading assistants deduct the eBay insertion fees, the final-value fees, the payment-processing fees (typically 2.9 percent of the total transaction value—sale price, shipping, handling, and sales tax—plus 30 cents), and the shipping and insurance fees. They may even charge the item owner for packaging.

Acting as a trading assistant is very attractive to some eBay merchants. If they are selling, packing, and shipping already, adding more products isn't hard. The process is already in place, and you get to keep a sizeable chunk of the sales price. Your responsibilities are these:

- ■ Taking product photographs
- ■ Listing the item
- ■ Paying the original insertion fees (You'll get these back when the buyer pays.)
- ■ Paying the final-value fee (You'll get this back when the buyer pays.)
- ■ Processing the order and payment
- ■ Packing and shipping the product
- ■ Sending the owner a check for what's left over

What you *don't* have to do is pay for the original item in the first place, providing, in effect, free inventory in exchange for a smaller cut of the pie. When you consider, however, the cost of the inventory if you were buying products to sell, your final cut is still quite substantial. Of course eBay won't let just anyone join. If you want to become a trading assistant, you need to meet these criteria:

- ■ Sell four or more items in the last 30 days.
- ■ Have a feedback score of at least 50.
- ■ Have at least 97-percent positive feedback.
- ■ Have an eBay account in good standing.

 tip   *Remember, you can sell on consignment without every joining the Trading Assistant program. However, as the criteria to join are pretty easy to meet, you should join as soon as you can.*

To stay in the program, you'll have to sell at least one item every 30 days, retain your 50-or-higher 97-percent feedback score, and keep your eBay account in good standing. If you meet the initial requirements, it's very easy to join.

Becoming a Trading Post

There's another category of trading assistant, the *Trading Post*. eBay requires that these companies have drop-off locations or stores with regular business hours. Some of these have hundreds, even thousands, of drop-off locations around the country. For instance:

- **AuctionDrop (www.AuctionDrop.com)** This 75-person company has been given $17M in funding by several Venture Capital companies, and uses UPS stores as drop-off locations . . . 3,800 locations around the country.

- **QuikDrop (www.QuikDrop.com)** This company has about 50 drop-off locations around the U.S., as well as one each in Canada, Australia, and China.

- **Instant Auctions (www.InstantAuctions.net)** This company uses an UPS, FedEx, USPS, or DHL drop-off point; the item is shipped to their headquarters. Note that they are also setting up local stores.

- **zTradingPost (www.zTradingPost.com)** They have around 120 drop-off locations around the country.

- **iSOLD It (www.i-soldit.com)** There are over 400 locations either already open or opening soon. They claim to be eBay's #1 seller.

There are also many smaller trading posts—one-location outfits or organizations—such as On-the-Block Auction (www.ontheblockauction.com/), which set up arrangements with local packing and shipping stores to let people drop off items around the region. If you find your trading assistant business doing well and already have a retail location, you might decide to become a trading post; it's not much more effort and may increase your chance of getting the business. Some people who are using the Trading Assistant Directory choose to search just for trading posts, so you'll be more likely to be found; in addition, your directory listing will show the little trading-post icon.

Building Your Trading Assistant Business

You might consider becoming a franchise location of one of the major trading-assistant companies; several have franchise stores. The big drawback, of course, is the hefty fee to get started; you'll need $50,000 to get started with QuikDrop. The advantages are marketing, ready-made management systems, and so on. But right now there's no dominant brand in this area, so you don't know for sure what you're buying into—McDonalds or Joe's Burger Shack? If you do buy in, make sure the backup you get from the company is worth what it's going to cost you.

How can you get into this business? Here are a few ideas to get you started:

■ **Make sure you're ready!** Don't start until you have an operation that works smoothly and can easily add additional listings.

■ **Join the Trading Assistant program.** You'll get a listing in the directory.

■ **Use the Trading Assistant logo.** Place it in your About Me page, throughout your eBay store if you have one, and in all your product listings.

■ **Advertise.** eBay recommends using small-city newspapers, school and church newsletters, and bulletin boards.

■ **Use the eBay Co-op Ad program.** eBay will pay up to 25 percent of your print advertising budget under this program. (You must be a PowerSeller.)

■ **Use signs.** Get a sign for your car, for instance, saying something like, "We'll sell for you on eBay. Call 800-555-1234." Make up T-shirts with the same message; if you have a brick-and-mortar store, put prominent signs inside and out.

■ **Approach businesses.** Keep your eyes open for local businesses that might want to partner with you, with you becoming their online channel.

■ **Promote through schools, churches, and charities.** The non-profits can solicit donations; you sell them and the non-profit gets the fee.

■ **Get a story about your business in the local paper.** This may be hard to do in big cities but probably quite easy in small towns. Call the editor!

And that, as they say, is that. You've learned how to list and sell products on eBay. But that's not the only way to sell online, of course. In the next section of the book you'll begin to learn how to sell online through a Yahoo! Merchant Solutions store.

Part II

Building Your Yahoo! Store

This page intentionally left blank

Chapter 12

Getting Started with Yahoo! Merchant Solutions

So you're selling on eBay. Is that enough? Maybe. But many businesses selling online use multiple channels, which really is what this book is all about. If you're only selling through eBay you may be leaving money on the table. Using multiple sales channels can both increase revenues—that is, grow your business larger, faster—and make your business more stable. Fluctuations in one channel are easier to handle when you have several channels bringing you business. So, in the second part of the book, we're going to look at how to set up an online store . . . using Yahoo! Merchant Solutions.

Yahoo! Merchant Solutions provides a quick and easy way to start selling online through your own store. You can present your products to the public, take orders using credit cards, view sales statistics, and do everything else required when building a successful online business. You can see an example of a store created using Merchant Solutions in Figure 12-1.

You have plenty of choices when picking an e-commerce system . . . so why use Yahoo! Merchant Solutions? Yahoo! Merchant Solutions has many advantages and is a good choice for many small merchants:

- **It's Yahoo!.** You've got a big brand behind you, which means . . .

  - **Stability**   They'll still be around next year, and the year after that, while plenty of e-commerce service providers have gone out of business!

  - **Great support**   Toll-free, 24 hours a day, seven days a week, there's always someone you can talk to, and in most cases, they'll answer quickly. They also provide a dedicated "consultant" you can talk to for the first 30 days—you'll get a real person's name and direct phone number.

  - **Solid infrastructure**   Yahoo!'s web servers are fast and stable. Interruptions in service are likely to be rare and brief. And Yahoo.com is the world's most popular web site, so the company knows how to handle huge amounts of web traffic and enormous traffic surges (so you know your site won't go down at Christmas!).

FIGURE 12-1 A Merchant Solutions store

- **It's proven.** Some people who started small e-commerce stores with Yahoo! are now doing millions of dollars' worth of business each year . . . and are still with Yahoo!.

- **You're in good company.** Merchant Solutions is probably the most popular e-commerce system on the Web; more merchants use this software than any other product.

- **It can handle volume.** Merchant Solutions can handle catalogs of up to 50,000 products, as well as rapid transaction frequencies. Some companies sell millions of dollars' worth of their products through this system each year, and have been doing so for five years or more.

- **You're on a development path.** You can start with the basic Store Editor creation tool now (as explained in Chapter 14), and shift to more advanced HTML-development tools later, as the business grows.

■ **You're with a consulting community.** Yahoo! has been selling an e-commerce system for a number of years now (in fact, the system they use has probably been on the market for around ten years). There's a large community of Yahoo! Merchant Solutions developers, so it's easy to hire someone to help with your store.

■ **It's affordable.** You can begin selling online for as little as $40 a month with a $50 setup fee.

■ **It's flexible.** In this book, we'll be looking at the basic page-creation tool, Store Editor. However, Merchant Solutions allows you to create web pages with *any* HTML tool, and to use Perl and PHP scripts and MySQL databases.

■ **It's simple.** Actually, Yahoo!'s most basic page-creation tool can be difficult to learn if you have to do so on your own. You don't. This book leads you through the Yahoo! Merchant Solutions setup, making it into an easy-to-use system.

■ **It offers a simple credit-card processing setup.** Some systems make setting up credit-card transactions complicated. Merchant Solutions makes it easy.

■ **Web hosting is included.** When you sign up for a Merchant Solutions account, you get a full-featured web-hosting account, too.

■ **You get Yahoo! Shopping integration.** Yahoo! makes it very easy to submit products to Yahoo! Shopping; in fact, Yahoo! Shopping will check your product information up to four times a day to ensure it has the most recent data (see Chapter 21).

■ **There are lots of discounts.** Yahoo! Merchant Solutions members get special discounts on various services. For instance, you'll save 20 percent on click fees through Yahoo! Shopping (see Chapter 21), You'll also get a three-month free trial on an e-mail marketing tool, as well as a 33-percent discount on a "keyword analysis" tool.

So let's get moving right away and begin building your Yahoo! Merchant Solutions store.

Choosing a Merchant Solutions Package

Yahoo! has three different packages available: Starter, Standard, and Professional. All three packages allow you to take credit-card orders, provide you with an equal number of e-mail accounts, provide automated UPS-shipping processing, come with 24-hour, toll-free support and 30 days "consulting" assistance, and so on. You can find details about these features online (http://smallbusiness.yahoo.com/merchant), but the following list provides a quick summary of the sort of features you'll find in *all three* packages:

■ Free domain name with your store

■ Free support by 24/7 phone line and e-mail

■ Web-hosting space where you can store image files and create web pages, along with 10GB of disk space to store your files and 200GB of data transfer per month

■ One hundred e-mail accounts, with 2GB storage space per account

■ A shopping-cart system that allows buyers to purchase products using credit cards

- An order-management system in which you can process orders
- A way to receive orders by fax and e-mail
- Integration with UPS's shipping system for price calculations, shipment tracking, and label printing
- Statistics related to traffic in your store and sales made

note   *Make sure you look at Yahoo!'s policies (http://store.yahoo.com/vw/guide.html). Yahoo! won't let just anyone use one of their Merchant Solutions stores. Some products are banned from the Yahoo! system.*

All packages have these features . . . so what are the differences? There are only a few ways in which they vary, which makes it relatively easy to choose among the packages. Table 12-1 summarizes the differences among the three packages.

With the Starter package, you won't be able to export orders to the UPS WorldShip service (useful if you ship a lot of packages through UPS, not so important when first starting out). You also won't be able to automatically export transaction data to other software programs. You won't be able to accept orders faxed to you. The statistics provided to you won't be as good; you won't be able to see the *click trails*—the path taken by visitors through your site—and won't be able to see search terms people used to find your site or to search within your site. You also won't be able to use gift certificates, the *cross-sell* feature (which allows you to suggest related items when someone selects a product), or coupons, and you won't be able to create *trackable links*—a tool that helps you build simple "affiliate relationships" through which you can pay other web sites a commission for sending buyers to your store. There's another important difference, too. When you sell a product, Yahoo! takes a transaction fee: sell a $100 product and Yahoo! will take $1.50 if you have the Starter, $1.00 for the Standard, and just 75 cents if you have the Professional package.

	Starter	Standard	Professional
Export to UPS WorldShip	No	No	Yes
Transaction-Data Export	No	Yes	Yes
Accept Fax Orders	No	Yes	Yes
Click-Trails Statistics	No	Yes	Yes
Search Statistics	No	Yes	Yes
Gift Certificates, Cross-Sell, Coupons, Trackable Links	No	Yes	Yes
Transaction Fee	1.5%	1%	0.75%
Monthly Fee	$39.95 + one-time, $50 setup fee	$99.95 + one-time, $50 setup fee	$299.95 + one-time, $50 setup fee

TABLE 12-1   Yahoo!'s Merchant Solutions Packages

So which do you choose? You *only* need the Professional package if you do a *lot* of shipments through UPS, or if the savings in the transaction fees outweigh the additional monthly fee. So, most people just starting out can forget this option. The Standard package has useful features—fax orders, better statistics, gift certificates, coupons, cross-sell, and trackable links— all of which are missing in the Starter. But for many, a good choice is the Starter because you'll pay *much* less while you build the store and learn how to use it. When you're ready, you can contact Yahoo! and upgrade to the Standard package, and once you do a lot of business, you can upgrade to the Professional package with no additional setup fee. (In this book we're going to be using the Standard package.)

If you'd like to see a chart listing all the features and comparing the three packages, click one of the **Features** buttons you'll see when you first enter the Merchant Solutions home page (http://smallbusiness.yahoo.com/merchant/), then click the **Compare** button on the page that appears.

tip *If you run into problems during the sign-up, call and chat with Yahoo! at 1-866-781-9246. Also, note that Yahoo! will provide 30 days free consulting with any of the packages; you can ask them to look at your site and suggest improvements.*

Do You Need a Web Site, Too?

Merchant Solutions, in essence, provides two things:

- A "store" account, in which you can create your web store
- A web-hosting account, in which you can create a web site using a variety of different tools

The "store" account contains the following items:

- A store catalog
- A shopping-cart system
- All the mechanisms needed to handle sales tax, shipping rates, transaction payments, and so on
- The ability to create additional pages, which can contain contact information, a privacy policy, and so on

The Merchant Solutions store account creates a special form of e-commerce web site; it provides a very fast way to build a store web site. However, it doesn't provide as much flexibility as other methods for building web sites, so some business owners combine the two. They still need Merchant Solutions to provide the shopping cart and other tools for processing sales, but they also create a separate web site and combine the two pieces. They use a web-design tool to create a web site and the store's catalog pages, but use Merchant Solutions to manage transactions—to set up sales-tax rates, shipping rates and methods, and payment methods. Because Merchant Solutions includes a full-featured web-hosting account, you can create virtually any kind of web site in association with your store. You can use a plain old text editor to create your HTML pages if you understand how to do that, then upload them to your hosting account. To create pages, you could use Microsoft FrontPage or Dreamweaver, or any of hundreds of other web-creation tools.

Deciding How to Build Your Store Pages

There are four ways to build your store's catalog pages—the pages that actually display your products:

- Use the Store Editor provided by Merchant Solutions.
- Use Yahoo!'s SiteBuilder tool to build pages, then upload them to your web-hosting account.
- Use Macromedia Dreamweaver, combined with the Yahoo! Merchant Solutions Extension, then upload pages to the hosting account. The Extension automates some catalog functions.
- Use some other kind of HTML tool, such as Microsoft FrontPage, along with Merchant Solution "store tags" to define products, then upload pages to the hosting account. (Connecting to the Merchant Solutions product catalog is a bit more work than using the Dreamweaver Extension.)

The following table summarizes the pros and cons of using the various methods:

	Store Editor	SiteBuilder	Dreamweaver	Another HTML Tool
Expense	The cheapest method because you can create a store very quickly, if you don't mind sacrificing design uniqueness	SiteBuilder software is free and can be used to create pages relatively quickly, too.	Depends; you may have to pay for software. Dreamweaver and FrontPage are commercial products, although there are other HTML tools available free.	
Speed	The fastest method	Fairly quick	Slower	*Much* slower
Flexibility	Not very flexible	More flexible, but still limited to a great degree	Total flexibility; build whatever you want.	
Knowledge	Quick to learn. No HTML knowledge required (although it's helpful, allowing you to create more attractive pages)	Another tool to learn, although relatively simple	Learning these tools can take a considerable investment in time and cause brain damage.	
Size of Catalog	Any number of products	Fewer than 100 products	Any number of products	

note   *We've said that you can learn to use the Merchant Solutions Store Editor quickly, and you can . . . with this book. Store Editor, for a variety of reasons, is actually quite complicated in many ways, but this book steps you through the process of setting up a store, explaining how to work with the system much more clearly than the existing Yahoo! documentation.*

One issue needs a little explanation. We've mentioned that Store Editor is both a quick and simple way to create pages, and is a system that provides little flexibility. This isn't entirely true, but *in effect* it's true! Strictly speaking, Store Editor provides tremendous flexibility, allowing you to create pages that look exactly the way you want them. However, in order to do this you need to learn RTML, a special coding language that the original software designers created for this purpose. Creating pages using RTML is not quick and simple; it can be very complicated. In practice, few people learn RTML these days because if you want total control over your Merchant Solutions pages, it makes more sense to use Dreamweaver or another HTML tool, *not* RTML. The great majority of RTML users—and there really aren't many—are people who learned to use it when it was the only way to create customized pages for what was then Yahoo! Store (the early version of Merchant Solutions).

We don't discuss RTML and the advanced Store Editor customization of pages in this book. If you need total control, you should use one of the web-hosting options.

Making Your Decision

How do you decide which method to use? You should simply use the Merchant Solutions Store Editor and forget about working with an HTML tool if . . .

- ▨ Your overriding concern is getting your store online quickly and cheaply, or

- ▨ You know nothing about HTML or any kind of web-design tool, don't have the time to learn, and don't have the money to pay someone else to do the work, or

- ▨ You want to get up and running quickly, and are willing to worry about unique site design later.

note   *SiteBuilder provides a much easier way to create your store's pages than Store Editor. However, the 100-product limit is a real problem. Even though you may have a small number of products now, if your store is successful, you will probably expand the number of products over that 100 limit at some point . . . and you'll have to throw away the store and build it again using another method.*

Consider one of the other options if . . .

- ▨ A unique site design is your overriding concern, or

- ▨ You want to build a web site with a great many web pages in addition to the store, or

- ▨ Money's no object, or

- ▨ You're in no hurry; you just want a perfect site, or

- ▨ You're an HTML guru and enjoy messing around with this stuff.

Poor Man's Site Integration

There is another way to integrate a Merchant Solutions store into a web site. Treat the two as separate entities, and simply link from your web site to your store using an ordinary HTML link.

Let's say you already have a web site and now need a store. There's no need to throw away your site and rebuild in Merchant Solutions. And there's no need to learn complicated tools to integrate your catalog into the existing site. Rather, quickly set up the store using Merchant Solutions Store Editor, then simply link from your site into the store when needed. You might even register a domain name that is similar to your original name. For instance, let's say you own the RodentRacing.com domain name. Register RodentRacingStore.com for the Merchant Solutions account, and on your original site, link to RodentRacingStore.com when you direct people to your online catalog.

And the Choice Is . . .

In this book we're going to focus on the first method, building your store entirely within Merchant Solutions. If you want to use SiteBuilder, Dreamweaver, or some other HTML tool, refer to Yahoo!'s online documentation for the details.

Remember, though, whichever of the four methods you use, you will still be doing a lot of work within Merchant Solutions. You'll be entering product data into the product database—Catalog Manager. You'll be setting up shipping methods and rates, sales-tax rates, and payment methods. You'll use Merchant Solutions to process orders, view statistics, set up coupons and discounts, and so on. In fact, one great strategy for many businesses is to focus on Merchant Solutions and Store Editor for now . . . and worry about using more advanced catalog-building tools later when you're comfortable with the basics.

Picking a Domain Name

You'll need a domain name for your store. A domain name is the "*something*.com" piece of a web address (or .org, .biz, *.whatever*). For instance, in the URL www.yahoo.com/index.html, the domain name is the yahoo.com piece. If you've already registered a domain name with a service, that's fine; you'll be able to point it to your Yahoo! store later. Or you can register a domain name during the sign-up process, and Yahoo! will throw it in at no extra charge. But how do you pick a name? Spend a little time thinking about this. It's not easy picking a domain name because most good ones have already been taken! Here are a few things to consider:

- Pick a name that is easy to understand. If you read the domain name on the radio, would listeners be able to understand (and spell!) it?

- If you already have a business name, you really need a domain name that matches (which isn't always possible, of course).

- If at all possible, pick a .com domain, not a .org, .biz, or *.anything else*. The world thinks .com, and if you select a different one many people may not notice and might end up at the wrong site.

You may want to spend a little time thinking about your domain name before signing up. Go to domains.yahoo.com to get to Yahoo!'s domain-registration service. There are also many services online that help you select a name; www.nameboy.com is a good one to try. Whether you register with Yahoo! before setting up your Merchant Solutions account or register with any other service, you'll still be able to use it with Yahoo! when you're ready. However, if you register the domain at the same time you set up your Merchant Solutions account, you'll pay no registration fee, and Yahoo! will pay the renewal fee each year as long as you still have a Merchant Solutions account.

■ If all the domains you want have already been purchased, try combining words. Try mixing your primary word with a color or location name (city, state, etc.), a store-type word (store, depot, warehouse, shop, etc.), or something else. Sometimes the only way to get a domain that works for you is by building a combination.

Before you register your Merchant Solutions account, check to see if the domain name you want is available. You can search at http://smallbusiness.yahoo.com/domains/.

■ If your domain name can be confused with any other name—in particular plurals, singulars, and common spelling mistakes—you need to register *both* terms. You need the one you want *and* the "confused" term. Registering *cooldoll.com*? Then you also need *cooldolls.com*. Getting *jobadvisory.com*? You also need *jobadvisery.com, jobsadvisory .com*, and *jobsadvisery.com*.

■ Yahoo! provides a pretty good "brainstorming" tool; you tell it what domain you want, and it suggests alternatives. Spend a little time to make sure you get a good domain name.

Avoid "domain confusion." Don't register a domain name that is likely to be confused with another. Don't register royalsaunas.com *if someone else owns* royalsauna.com, *or* bluesauna.org *if someone else has* bluesauna.com. *If you market heavily using the domain name, some of the traffic will go to the other domain, possibly a competitor!*

Registering for a Yahoo! Merchant Solutions Account

To register for an account, navigate to http://smallbusiness.yahoo.com/merchant, click the <u>Merchant Solutions</u> link, and follow the instructions. The forms will lead you through the process of picking a domain name and will try to "upsell" you on a more expensive Merchant Solutions account. Remember that all packages come with 24-hour, toll-free support, 30 days of consulting, and the ability to be upgraded later (with no setup cost).

After you have registered your account, you should receive several e-mails from Yahoo! Read these carefully—and save them—as they include important information.

tip   *If you can't find your way back to your Manage My Services area, go to the Small Business Home (http://smallbusiness.yahoo.com/), then click the **Manage My Services** button in the top right.*

The Manage My Services page, shown in Figure 12-2, is the central "control panel" for all your Yahoo! services. The list that follows shows what you can do from this page.

■ You'll see a <u>Store Manager</u> link; this is where you'll work with your Merchant Solutions e-commerce system.

■ There's a <u>Web Hosting Control Panel</u> link. This takes you to where you'll manage your web-hosting account.

■ The <u>Domain Control Panel</u> link takes you to an area where you manage your domain name, if you registered it through Yahoo!.

■ Every Merchant Solutions account comes with 100 e-mail accounts; the <u>Email Control Panel</u> link takes you to where you can manage these.

■ Use the <u>Check Email</u> link to read e-mail messages using the Yahoo! Small Business Email system.

■ Click <u>Compose Email</u> to create an e-mail message.

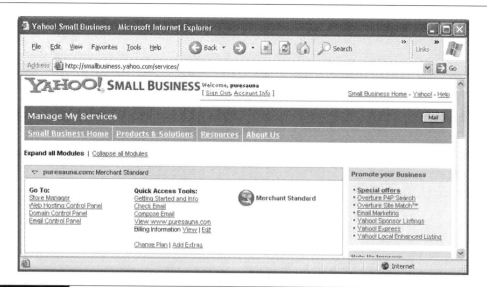

FIGURE 12-2   The Manage My Services page, from where you can administer all your Yahoo! services.

- Click <u>View www.*domain*.com</u> to open a browser window containing your store. (Remember, when you first set up the account, you'll see an *Under Construction* message.)

- Use the Billing Information links to view or modify the information used to pay for your Merchant Solutions account each month.

- Click the <u>Change Plan</u> link if you want to upgrade to the next Merchant Solutions package.

- Click <u>Add Extras</u> to add e-mail accounts or disk space.

When you first view the Manage My Services page, you'll find that the Status is set to *pending*. You can begin working on your account, but it takes a little while for the domain name to point to the store. In other words, if you open a browser, type the domain name into the browser (store.puresauna.com, for instance), and press ENTER, the browser will *not* load a web page from your store; you may see an error page or a Yahoo! Under Construction page. It will take a few hours, perhaps a day or so, before the domain name points to the site.

Pointing Your Domain to Your Store

If you already own a domain name—and therefore did not register one for the store during your Merchant Solutions account setup—you need to *point* the domain to the store. In other words, you have to change the domain's settings so that when someone types the domain into a browser, the main page from your store will be loaded.

In order to point a domain to a web site, you have to change the DNS settings for the domain. *DNS* means *Domain Name System*; it's the system used by the Internet to specify where a web site can be found. When you change DNS settings, you are telling the Internet which web server has your site so that a browser knows where to go to find it. In order to point your domain to your Merchant Solutions store, you have to change the nameserver information associated with your domain to use the Yahoo! nameserver information.

This sounds a little complicated, but don't worry too much about the technical aspects. Yahoo! should send you an e-mail providing the nameserver information if you told Yahoo! that you intended to use an existing domain. (If you can't find this information, call and talk to their customer support people.)

Provide this information to whoever manages your domain name. If that's you, go to the registrar's web site and look for a page where you'll see "Set Nameservers" or something similar, and follow instructions there.

note   *You can only point a single domain to a Yahoo! Merchant Solutions store. However, you can forward as many domains to the store as you wish. With forwarding, you don't change nameserver information; you simply tell the registrar to forward browsers to another domain name.*

Pointing www to the Store

By default, Yahoo! sets up your domain so that it points in two different "directions":

- Type **www.*yourdomain*.com** into a browser, and the browser goes to your web-hosting account at Yahoo!.

- Type **store.*yourdomain*.com** into a browser, and the browser goes to your store pages.

What if you're not planning to use the web-hosting account? If you have decided to use Merchant Solutions alone and want to point www.*yourdomain*.com to the store itself, you can change this setting:

1. In Store Manager, click the <u>Domain</u> link (near the top-right corner) to open the Domain Control Panel.

2. Click the <u>Manage Domain & Subdomains</u> link.

3. You'll see the domain listed in a table; click the <u>Edit</u> link.

4. In the following page, select the **Change the destination to my Store Editor home page** option button.

5. Click the **Submit** button at the bottom of the page.

The change won't be immediate; the switchover may take a few minutes or could take eight hours or more to complete. Eventually, however, when anyone types www.*yourdomain*.com into a browser, they'll end up at your store's home page.

Finding Your Way Around the Store Manager

The Store Manager is where you build and manage your Yahoo! Merchant Solutions store. You can get there by opening the Manage My Services page and then clicking the <u>Store Manager</u> link, but we recommend that you bookmark the page so you can go directly there. (In Internet Explorer, select Favorites | Add to Favorites.)

You can see the different areas of the Store Manager page in Figure 12-3.

Creating a Store Security Key

When you created your Merchant Solutions account, you had to either provide information about an existing Yahoo! account or create a new account. The Yahoo! account has an ID (to identify you), and a password (to ensure that only you can access the account). There's one more form of account protection that you're going to need, a *security key*. The security key is required for access to many, although not all, areas of your Merchant Solutions account. This allows you to set up a store account that can be used by, for example, a web designer, but that will give you sole access to important areas.

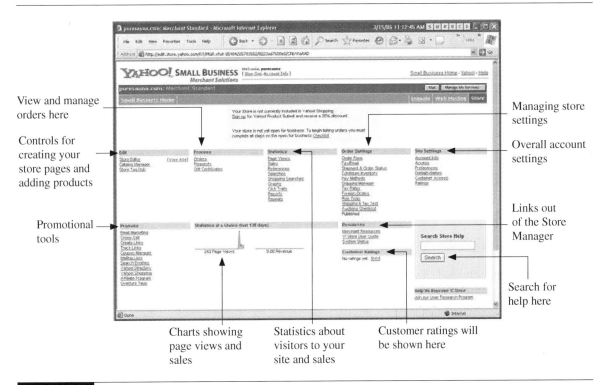

View and manage orders here

Controls for creating your store pages and adding products

Promotional tools

Managing store settings

Overall account settings

Links out of the Store Manager

Search for help here

Charts showing page views and sales

Statistics about visitors to your site and sales

Customer ratings will be shown here

FIGURE 12-3 The Store Manager

 tip *Do you have several people who are going to be working on your store? Maybe a couple of web designers, someone who updates your product list, a staff member responsible for inventory, and so on? You can create different accounts for each person, providing different permissions to each. Each staff member must set up a Yahoo! account and check the **Add this profile to the Yahoo! Member Directory** box in their Edit Public Profile page. You can then set up an account in the store using the* Access *link in the Site Settings column.*

The security key is required to view orders—for instance, to set up payment methods or to change basic account information. It is *not* required for access to the Store Editor—where you can create store pages—or to some other less sensitive areas.

It's a good idea to set up your security key right away, before you allow other people access to the Store Manager.

1. Click the Pay Methods link in the Store Manager.

2. Yahoo! will ask you for your account password, to verify that you have the right to create a security key. Type the password and click **Continue**.

3. Provide a security key, another password. It must contain at least six characters and cannot match or contain your Yahoo! ID or password, nor include your first or last name.

4. Provide all the other information requested. Yahoo! asks you to confirm some basic information, including the credit card used to set up the account.

5. Click **Submit This Form**.

Spend much time online at all, and you'll end up with a whole lot of account IDs and passwords. Ideally, these should not be easy to figure out and should vary, so eventually you have a problem—how do you remember them all? Write them down, and the paper may be found; don't write them down, and you'll eventually forget some of them. A more effective way to store them is to use a password-management program. One great program is Password Depot (http://www.password-depot.com/). You can find others at any good download site, such as WUGNET.com and Tucows.com.

Setting Up a Credit Card Merchant Account

In order to sell, you need a way to take money. While there are a number of different ways to take payments—we'll discuss your options in Chapter 18—in order to have a functional Merchant Solutions store, you *must* set up the store to accept credit-card payments. (Yahoo! won't allow you to open until you do so.) As this may take a few days to sort out, it would be nice if you could start the process right away.

One thing you may need to prepare—you'll need a land-line phone number. If you, like so many people these days, only have a cell number, you'll have to set up a land line before you can apply for a merchant account if you want to use Paymentech, Yahoo!'s recommended merchant-account provider (it's one of Paymentech's policies that you must have a land line). On the other hand, the second recommended company, 1st American Card Service, does not require this.

Unfortunately, you cannot complete the merchant account setup until some key items are present—your store must be "ready for business with clear product and pricing information available for viewing" so that the company issuing the merchant account can review it. Even if you don't have everything complete when you apply, you must at least have a site that looks complete—one or more products, a contact page, privacy page, and so on. So go ahead and build your store, and when you're ready, refer to the information in Chapter 18. Or perhaps get the paperwork in now, but be aware that the process will grind to a halt fairly quickly.

You are backing up data, aren't you? You need to protect your business information. What if you lost all your product-catalog data, or lost the program that stores all your passwords or all your accounting information? Would it hurt? Would it take much time to recover? If you're serious about doing business online, you need to find some way to back up data. And that means off-site! One good strategy is to buy two external USB hard drives and do a full backup onto both. Store one in your office and back up every day, and store the other somewhere else, such as a safe-deposit box. Switch them every week or two.

In the following chapters, we'll see how to enter your products into the store catalog.

Chapter 13

Adding and Importing Products

You've set up your account and done a few preliminary bits and pieces. Now let's get started by adding products to your store. Why add products before you create pages? Because Merchant Solutions will create pages for you automatically—both section (category) and product pages—based on the products that you create and import. Once the pages have been created, you'll see how to modify them in subsequent chapters.

There are actually two ways to get products into Merchant Solutions—you can type them by hand, or you can import them from a database or spreadsheet file. In this chapter you'll learn both methods. If you are setting up a very small store with just a handful of products, entering them by hand is probably fine. If you have a larger store, with hundreds, or even thousands of products, you should almost certainly be using the second method, storing product data offline, and importing the data into Merchant Solutions.

Understanding the Product Database

All the information about your product has to be stored somewhere so that Merchant Solutions knows what you are selling, how much to charge for it, and, in some cases, additional information such as how much it weighs (so it can figure out how much to charge when shipping it). It needs to show your products to potential customers—that is, create catalog pages containing product information—and it needs to use the product information when checking out a purchase.

This information is stored in a product database, hidden away on Yahoo!'s servers. A *database* is a computer file that is specially designed to store information in a manner that allows the information to be pulled out as needed. Imagine a printed document with a table— each product is stored on one line of the table, and each piece of information about a product is stored in one of the table cells; price in one cell, description in another, weight in yet another, and so on:

Each cell is a *field*

id	code	taxable	ship-weight	label	price	sale-price	headline	name
lx-201	LX-201	Yes	32	The LX-201 2-Person Sauna	3495	2796	The Brand New LX-201	The LX-201 2-Person Sauna
lx-202	LX-202	Yes	32	The LX-202 2-Person Sauna	3495	2796	The Brand New LX-202	The LX-202 2-Person Sauna
lx-204	LX-204	Yes	32	The LX-204 4-Person Sauna	4495	3495	The Brand New LX-204	The LX-204 4-Person Sauna

Each product
line is a *record*

- For each product, the database contains a *record*, the equivalent of a line in the table.

- Each piece of information within a record is stored in a database *field*, the equivalent of a cell in the table.

Don't worry too much about the database. You'll never see it and don't even know where it actually is—it's on one of Yahoo!'s computers somewhere. All you need to know is that Merchant Solutions stores your product data and can retrieve it whenever and however it needs to.

There are three ways to put products into this database:

- Type the product into Store Editor.

- Type the product into Catalog Manager.

- Import a file containing product information into Catalog Manager.

Whatever method you use for entering product information, the data is saved in the same product database. Enter it through Store Editor and you'll see the same data in Catalog Manager, and vice versa . . . it's all stored in the same place.

note *Yahoo!'s tech-support staff have been trained to tell you* not *to use Catalog Manager if you are creating your pages with Store Editor. However, the Yahoo! documentation department clearly recommends that you* do *use Catalog Manager. Furthermore, the tech-support people have a poor understanding of Catalog Manager and what you can and can't do with it, and frequently provide misinformation—information that is demonstrably wrong—about working in Catalog Manager. We've chosen to go with the documentation department and what we've observed, and recommend Catalog Manager!*

However, while you *can* enter products through Store Editor, we recommend that you don't. Rather, work primarily with Catalog Manager. It makes working with your products much easier.

Adding an Item to the Product Database

Here's how to add your first product to the database.

1. In Store Manager, click the <u>Catalog Manager</u> link.

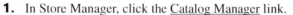**note** *Don't worry about tables right now. Tables provide a way to help you group or categorize products, an advanced subject that we won't be covering here.*

2. Click the <u>Manage Your Items</u> link. You'll see the Items page, showing the content of the default-table (right now, nothing).

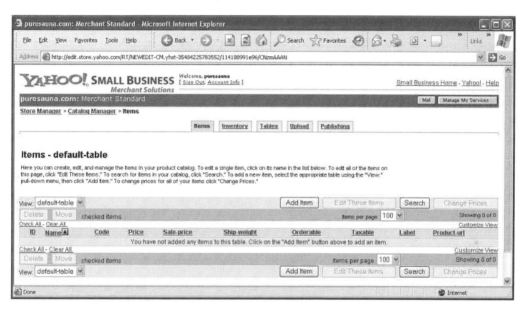

3. Click the **Add Item** button to open the Add Item page. This page contains fields into which you will enter information about the product. Type the information into each field, or use the appropriate control, as explained in Table 13-1.

note *When you are in the Add Item page, you are adding a* database record. *Each piece of information entered goes into a particular database* field.

4. When you've finished entering all the product information, click the **Save** button at the top or bottom of the page.

5. You'll be taken back to the Items page. Click the **Add Item** button to begin adding the next item.

tip *Even if you don't have product data ready yet, go ahead and put some fake data in, so you can see how the system works.*

Field	Description
ID	This field is a unique identification code for the product. It's also used to create the product-page filename. For instance, if the ID is 27166-00-00, the page URL becomes http://store.*yourdomain*.com/27166-00-00.html. Use only letters, numbers, and dashes. You may want to use the same information as the Code field. On the other hand, it's a good idea to use a product name, with each word separated by a dash (but don't use more than, say, three or four words). As you'll learn in Chapter 26, it may help a little in the search engines to have a page named after the product.
Name	This is a required field that can include letters, symbols, numbers, and spaces. The product Name appears on the product page above the product Caption (if no Headline field is present), or above the Price (if a Headline *is* present). It also appears in a section/category page (clicking on the name takes the shopper to the product page). The Name also appears in your page's <TITLE> tags (something you'll learn about in Chapter 26), which means when someone loads the page into a browser, the Name text appears in the browser's title bar.
Code	Code is also unique, but this time it will be shown to customers. It's generally some kind of SKU or other product code. If you are selling books, it might be the ISBN number; if selling some other sort of product, it might be the UPC code, or perhaps some kind of internal company product code. The product Code appears on product pages before the price.
Price	This is the product's list price. Type only numbers and a decimal place—no commas or dollar signs. This is the price the product sells for *unless* you also enter something in the Sale-price field, as described next. You can add *incremental pricing* if you wish. Simply enter prices like this, where the first number is the base price, the second is a quantity, the third a price, the fourth a quantity, and so on: 12.00 2 11.00 5 10.25 You'll end up with a price line on the product page that looks like this: **$12.00, 2/$11.00, 5/$10.25**
Sale-price	If you enter a value here, the Price value is overridden—this is the price at which the product is sold. Also, if you enter a Sale-price, the Price will be displayed on a web page as the *Regular price*, in combination with the *Sale-price*. You can use incremental pricing in this field, too, as you can with the Price field. **tip** *If you plan to use export product data to Yahoo! Shopping, do not use the Sale-price field! See Chapter 21 for the reason why.*
Orderable	By default, this is set to Yes, but you can change it to No if the product is out of stock. The Order button will be removed from the product page.
Ship-weight	You only need to fill this field if shipping weight is in some way relevant; if the buyer needs to know it or if it affects your shipping calculations (which we'll discuss in Chapter 19). If you plan to use the UPS Online Tools, which calculate shipping charges for you, weights *must* be entered here and must be in pounds.
Taxable	Select Yes if the product is eligible for sales tax. (We discuss sales-tax issues in Chapter 19.)

TABLE 13-1   The Product Fields

Field	Description
Image	This is the full-size picture of your product. A reduced version will appear on your product page, and when the buyer clicks the image the full-size image appears. Clicking on the image loads a larger version of the same image; the shopper clicks the browser's Back button to return to the product page. Use the **Upload** button to upload the file into the store.
Options	You can create one or more drop-down list boxes that customers can use to select product options, such as colors and size. You can also use this to create monogram and inscription boxes, as well as set incremental pricing. To create a simple option drop-down list box, enter the option label, followed by the options, like this: **Color Red Green Blue**
	For more complicated settings, see "Working with Options—Monograms, Inscriptions, Incremental Pricing, and More," later in this chapter.

 tip   The Variables page contains all sorts of interesting settings that have a variety of effects, throughout your store. For more information, see Chapter 17.

Headline	The Headline is an optional title line that appears above the product description in the product page, replacing the product Name. However, if you *don't* use the Headline— in which case the Name appears above the Caption—the Name will *not* appear above the price. From a search-engine perspective, getting as many keywords into a page is a good idea (see Chapter 26), so you may want to place the text you use in Name in the Headline text too, so that it appears twice. Headline color is controlled by Display-color-text in the Variables page.

 tip   Provide as much information for your products as possible. The more words the better. As you'll learn in Chapter 26, search engines index words in pages; the more good words you can provide—words likely to be searched by people looking for products such as yours—the better. The more words, the more likely your pages are to be found in the search engines.

Caption	This is the product description, displayed in the product page. You can enter as much text as you wish and use HTML tags to format it; see Chapter 14 for more information.

warning   *Several of these items are converted to graphic images before being placed onto the page; the Name (when displayed above the Caption if no Headline is present), the Headline, and the Label are all converted to an image file with a single line of text. Although there's plenty of space in these text boxes, in particular the Headline and Label boxes, don't use it all! If you type too much text it will simply run off-page, past the right edge of the browser window. In the case of the Label, if you put a great deal of text it won't display at all; rather, a colored square will display in its place. How much is too much? It depends on the font size; experiment to see what fits.*

TABLE 13-1   The Product Fields (*cont.*)

Field	Description
Abstract	Abstract is a product description that is used on the store's home page if you set the product as a "special." (See Chapter 15 for information on specials.) It can also be used on your site's section pages to briefly describe an item, but it doesn't appear on the product page itself.
Icon	The Icon image is a small image that appears next to the product Name in a section (category) page. It will also appear on the home page if you set the product as a "special." Clicking on the icon takes the shopper to the product page. This could be a smaller version of the Image file. Use the **Upload** button to upload the file into the store.
Inset	The Inset image is a small, thumbnail-sized image that appears on your product page, alongside the larger picture (the Image). Clicking on the image loads a larger version of the same image. Use the **Upload** button to upload the file into the store.
Label	The Label text is used only on the home page when the product has been set as a "special." A graphic image is created from the text and placed onto the page, above the product price (*if* the home page's Edit page has Specials-format set to As-Thumbnails).
Download	If you are selling a downloadable product—a computer file such as a PDF e-book, an MP3 music file, or a software program, use the **Upload** button to upload the file into the store.
Gift-certificate	You can sell gift certificates by creating a gift-certificate "product." See Chapter 21 for more information about this.
Product-url	This is the address of the page where the product will sit in your store. It's required if you are submitting products to the Yahoo! Product Submit marketing program (see Chapter 21).

TABLE 13-1   The Product Fields (*cont.*)

You can see how these things lay out on the product page:

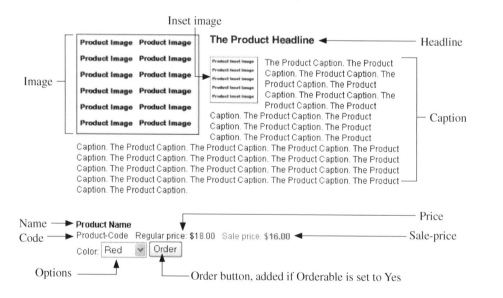

If you only have a handful of products, you'll probably want to enter them into Catalog Manager one by one, by hand. If you have more—dozens, perhaps hundreds—then you should probably *import* them into Catalog Manager. You'll learn about that later in this chapter, beginning with "Exporting Product Data."

Working with Options—Monograms, Inscriptions, Incremental Pricing, and More

As you saw earlier, you can create drop-down list boxes using the Option text box while entering product data. However, this text box actually allows you to do several things:

- Create a simple drop-down text box, with one-word options in the box (*Red*).

- Create a drop-down with multi-word options in the box (*Bright Red*).

- Create multiple drop-down list boxes.

- Create a Monogram box in which a buyer can enter three initials (for a product that will be personalized with a monogram).

- Create an Inscription text box into which the buyer can enter text to be inscribed onto the product.

- Set up Incremental Pricing options, which will allow buyers to select a particular option—color, product material, and so on—and different prices are applied.

- Specify codes for option combinations.

Simple Drop-down Text Boxes

To create a simple drop-down list box, type the name of the list, followed by the options within the list, all separated by spaces. If, for instance, you want a drop-down list box with the label *Size*, and the options *Small, Medium,* and *Large,* enter this:

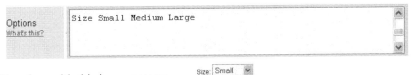

You'll end up with this in your store:

Multi-word Options

If an option uses multiple words, place the words in quotation marks, like this:

Multiple Drop-down List Boxes

If you need multiple drop-down boxes, separate each entry with a blank line, like this:

Monogram Boxes

If you offer the service of monogramming products, you can create a special option box that looks like the one shown here.

 note *Where does the price (in this case $10) come from? Don't enter this into the Options box. It comes from the Personalization-charge field in the Variables page. You'll learn about this later, in Chapter 17.*

The buyer can type three initials into these three text boxes; the initials will appear on your order forms so that you can engrave or print the monogram onto the product. Creating the Monogram line is easy; simply type the word **Monogram** on a line by itself in the Options text box.

Inscription Text Boxes

You can also allow buyers to provide an inscription to be engraved or printed on a product. In this case, you must enter the label (in quotation marks), the word **Inscription**, and the number of characters allowed, like this:

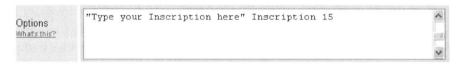

 note *Again, the inscription price (in this case $10) comes from the Personalization-charge field in the Variables page.*

The number at the end of the line defines both how long the text box will appear and how many characters the buyer will be able to type into it. You'll end up with this:

Type your Inscription here ($10.00): _____

Incremental Pricing

You can also associate a price with an option. For instance, enter this text:

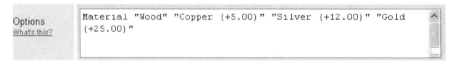

You'll end up with this:

When the buyer selects an option, the sum you've defined will automatically be added to the purchase price.

Assigning Codes to Option Combinations

There is an additional setting for your option drop-down list boxes if you want to use it. You can assign item codes to option combinations. Let's say your widget comes in red, green, and blue, and in three sizes, small, medium, and large. You can assign a code to Red/Small, Red/Medium, Red/Large, Green/Small, and so on. It's not necessary, but if this helps you manage your product inventory, then it can be done. Click the Enter Individual Item Codes link to see the Options Codes screen. Enter the code you want to use in the first column, then select the option combinations you want using the subsequent columns; when you've finished, click **Save and Continue**.

What if you have some combinations, but not others? You have Red/Small widgets but not Red/Large, you have Green/Large but not Blue/Large, and so on? How do you handle this situation? Rather than creating two option drop-downs, one for color and one for size, you'll have to create a single drop-down, showing all the different combinations.

Modifying Items

There are several ways to work with products once they are stored in Catalog Manager:

- **Change a single product's information.** Click on the Product ID in the ID column.

- **Change several products at once.** Click the **Edit These Items** button to see a table showing the products with editable fields. You can change multiple fields, in multiple products, and then click **Save**.

- **Search for particular products.** Click the **Search** button. You'll be able to search for a keyword in a particular field and see a table showing only products that match the search criteria.

- **Delete products.** Click the check box next to the product you want to remove from the product database, and click **Delete**.

- **Change all prices.** You can modify all the products' prices at once. Click **Change Prices**. In the Change Prices page, you can choose **Clear Sales Prices** (the sales price will be removed from all products) or **Apply Discount**—enter a discount rate (10%, 15%, or whatever), and Merchant Solutions will reset all the sales prices to the price minus this discount.

- **Change the columns shown in the table.** You can add fields to and remove them from the table; click the Customize View link on the right side of the table.

Publishing Your Product Data

If you've entered all your products or just entered a single product and now want to see it in the store, you must "publish" your data. Changes and additions made to the product database *do not* appear live in your web store until you published them. Here's how:

1. In the Catalog Manager home page, click the <u>Publish Your Changes</u> link (or click the Publishing tab elsewhere in Catalog Manager).

2. Click the **Publish Catalog** button. At this point, despite the note on the Publishing page, your data has *not* been added to your site. The data will appear in your Store Editor but not in your live store. You still have a few more steps to push the products onto the live store.

3. Exit Catalog Manager and return to Store Manager; click the <u>Store Manager</u> link in the top left of the page.

4. Click the <u>Store Editor</u> link in the Edit column.

5. In the Store Editor screen, click the **Publish** button on the right side of the command bar.

6. In the Publish Status window, you'll see a little status box; wait until all the lines are preceded by check marks, indicating the step has been completed.

7. Click the <u>Go to Manager</u> link to return to Store Manager.

Your changes and additions to the product database have now been published to your store.

Viewing the Data in Your Store

By now you should have at least one product in your product database, so let's see what it looks like in the store. Remember, we haven't customized the store yet. What you're going to see is rather crude . . . but it's a start. We're going to look at your product in a web browser, in your "live" store. Here's how:

1. Look at the bottom of the Order Settings column in Store Manager.

2. If the last entry is <u>Publish Order Settings*</u>, click this link to ensure that recent changes made to various Store Manager settings are uploaded.

3. When the page reloads (the entry now is <u>Published</u>), right-click on the [<u>View Site</u>] link in the Edit column on the left side of the page.

4. When the pop-up menu appears, select the Open in New Window option. A new browser window opens, showing your browser's home page—there won't be much on the page, but don't worry about that for now.

5. Click the **Index** button.

6. Click on a product link that appears in the Index page. The product page opens.

note   *Remember the publishing sequence. When you make changes to the store, you have to "publish" your changes before they will appear on the web site. Here's the sequence of "publish" commands you use in order to see all changes:*

*1. Catalog Manager: click <u>Publish Your Changes</u>, then click **Publish Catalog**.*

*2. Store Editor: click the **Publish** button.*

3. Store Manager: click <u>Publish Order Settings</u> (Order Settings column).

4. Click [<u>View Site</u>] (Edit column) to view the site.

Exporting Product Data

If you have a lot of products, you won't want to enter them all by hand. Rather, import them into the system en masse. It's much quicker to enter data into a spreadsheet or database program and import the information than it is to enter it into Catalog Manager one by one. (If you want to do this later, skip this section, continue building your store, and return here later.)

In order to import data to your database, you will use the Upload area of Catalog Manager. Note that this area allows you to both upload (import) data and to download (export) data. The best way to get started, in fact, is to create one product by hand (see "Adding an Item to the Product Database," earlier in this chapter), then export the information so that you now have a "template" to work with.

1. In the Catalog Manager home page, click the <u>Upload Items</u> link (or click the Upload tab elsewhere in Catalog Manager).

2. Click the **Download** button.

3. If you created multiple tables (which we're not covering in this book), select the table containing the data you want to export; otherwise, just ignore this setting.

4. Click the **Download** button.

5. A File Download dialog box opens. Click the **Save** button and save the data.csv file on your hard disk.

note   *Some text editors (such as Windows Notepad) won't open the file very well because of a problem with the line breaks; all lines are strung together in one long line. More advanced text editors and word processors can open it properly.*

6. When the file has been saved, click the **Open** button to open it in an appropriate program, such as Microsoft Excel, or even in a text editor. In Windows, by default a .csv file will open in Microsoft Excel if you have that program installed.

Open the file in a text editor and you'll see that the file is what is known as a *comma-separated variable* file. Every field in a record is separated from another by a comma. The first line in the file contains the column headers, showing what each field in the file is—the ID, the label, and so on.

Open the file in a spreadsheet program and you can see it a little more clearly. You can see that the first row contains headings and the second row contains product data.

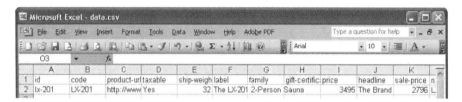

 note *If you export from Catalog Manager after you've already created sections (categories) in your store, Catalog Manager includes a line for each section in the export file; you might want to delete these, as they include no useful information.*

Importing Product Data

Once you've exported a product file, you have a template you can work with. If you can create a file in the same format as the export file, you can import the data into the store. Note these issues:

■ The export (download) file contains a *family* column. You can ignore this . . . your import file does *not* require this column of information. This is left over from an earlier version of Yahoo!'s small-business e-commerce product, Yahoo! Store, and isn't used with the more recent Merchant Solutions.

■ You do not enter any image information into this data file; for information on importing images, see "Importing Images," later in this chapter.

■ Some fields are required; others can be omitted from the import file. You *must* have these fields: Name, Sale-price, and Ship-weight. The Name field must contain something; the other two can be empty if you wish, but they must be included.

■ Fields don't have to be in the same order in your .csv file, but they must use exactly the same column titles in the first line so that Catalog Manager can recognize the fields.

 tip *We recommend that you use a spreadsheet or database program to create your import file. It's easy to make mistakes when working in a text editor. Many people have a copy of Microsoft Excel available, which is a good spreadsheet program for the task.*

Dealing with Options

You saw how to add options to a product in the earlier "Working with Options" section. You also saw how it's possible to create monograms, inscriptions, incremental pricing, and even codes for individual options and option combinations. How do you handle all this when importing data?

Let's put aside for the moment the situation in which you provide codes for option combinations. In general, you simply enter the text that would normally be entered into the Options text box in Catalog Manager, into the options field in your spreadsheet or database. Place line breaks between them, just as you would when typing into Catalog Manager.

Managing option-combination codes is a little different. In this case, you're going to enter all the code information into the Code field of your product database. Let's say the code for the product is 73086-15-00 and you're going to add a number after the code for each option combination (73086-15-00-01, 73086-15-00-02, and so on). First, place the base code into the field, followed by a semicolon:

```
73086-15-00;
```

Next, enter the first option combination:

```
Color:Red#Size:Small=73086-15-00-1
```

The above means, "if the color is red and the size is small, the code is "73086-15-00-1". Note that each combination is entered with the option name (Color), a colon, then the option choice (Red), like this: Color:Red. Different options are separated with a # symbol (Color: Red#Size:Small) and end with an = sign immediately before the code.

Each of the option combinations are separated with an & sign, like this:

```
Color:Red#Size:Small=73086-15-00-1&Color:Yellow#Size:Small=73086-15-00-2
```

Here's an example of the text you would enter into the Code field for two option choices (four colors and three sizes):

```
73086-15-00;Color:Red#Size:Small=73086-15-00-1&Color:Yellow#Size:
Small=73086-15-00-2&Color:Blue#Size:Small=73086-15-00-3&Color:Bright
Chrome#Size:Small=73086-15-00-4&Color:Red#Size:Medium=73086-15-00-
5&Color:Yellow#Size:Medium=73086-15-00-6&Color:Blue#Size:Medium=73086-
15-00-7&Color:Bright Chrome#Size:Medium=73086-15-00-8&Color:Red#Size:
Very Large=73086-15-00-9&Color:Yellow#Size:Very Large=73086-15-00-
10&Color:Blue#Size:Very Large=73086-15-00-11&Color:Bright Chrome#Size:
Very Large=73086-15-00-12
```

Creating Section Pages

When you import product data into Merchant Solutions, a page for every product is created. Of course, there has to be a link from somewhere to a product page, right? So where does the link to the page appear?

There are two places that your products can be linked from:

- From the home page
- From a section (category) page

Let's say your store sells cookbooks, and you want to categorize the books. Imagine you want this structure of sections and subsections (categories and subcategories) for your store:

- Specials
- Baking
  - General
  - Bread
  - Cakes
- Cooking by Ingredient
  - Cheese and Dairy
  - Fruits
  - Meat
  - Pasta

Each category of books would have its own section page; within the section page would be links to a variety of books, and to the subcategories' section pages, too. *Meals* is a category; its section page is linked to from the home page. *Breakfast* is a subcategory of the *Meals* category; its section page is linked to from the *Meals* section page. Here's an example of a section page; the top buttons in the navbar lead to other section pages:

This is from a real store, A2BScooters.com, and it shows the Electric Scooters page, a section page with a list of products; buyers can click on a product link to go to that product page.

There are two ways to create these section pages:

■ Manually, in Store Editor (as you'll see in Chapter 15).

■ Automatically, when you import products.

The simplest way to create a store structure is to import all your products in one go, and then specify which categories they are placed into (which section pages link to the products). Merchant Solutions will automatically create the necessary section pages for you. Now, that doesn't mean you've finished creating your section pages; you may also need to add information such as a section header and section introductory text, as you'll see in Chapter 15. But the pages are created automatically during the import, and so most of the store structure is there, waiting for you to drop data into it.

Here's how to specify into which section a product is placed:

1. Create a new column in your spreadsheet and name it Path.

2. Enter the category (section) name for each product into the Path field. For a book that you wish to place into the Baking category, you would type **Baking** into the Path field. If you want to place a book into the Bread category—a subcategory of Baking—you would type **Baking:Bread** into the Path field.

	A	
1	path	
2	Baking	
3	Baking	
4	Baking	
5	Baking	
6	Baking:Bread	
7	Baking:Bread	
8	Baking:Bread	
9	Baking:Cakes	
10	Baking:Cakes	
11	Baking:Cakes	
12	Deserts	
13	Deserts	

warning *Don't create too many top-level sections. For each top-level section, Merchant Solutions will create a button on the button bar, up to a limit of 14; if you have more than that, the extra sections won't get a button. Also, use short names for your sections or you'll end up with huge buttons extending to the right, shrinking your content area.*

That's all there is to it. Now, when you import your data file, Catalog Manager sees the path information and creates matching section pages—a Baking page, with a link to the Bread page.

So now you're thinking, "that's great, but how do I put a single product into multiple categories?" That is, how do you have a product page linked to from multiple section and subsection pages? For instance, you might want a particular book to be in your New Books category, your Baking category, and your Cooking by Ingredient category. Unfortunately, there's no simple way to do this. You cannot assign, in the import file, a product to multiple categories.

There are two ways to get around this problem. You can duplicate the product in your import file; the product will appear three times if you want the product in three categories. The problem with this method is that you must have unique product codes for each one. Or, you can manually create links from a section page to a particular product (explained in Chapter 16).

What if you don't provide a path? The product is imported into the database but is not assigned to a section page in your web site. Rather, it's assigned to the home page. For every product, up to 26 products, you'll find a button on the navbar that takes you to the product page. If you have more than 26 products, the additional products don't get a button and must be linked in some other way. Basically, importing more than a handful of products without a path is not a good idea.

Entering Inventory Quantities

In Chapter 19 you will learn how to manage inventory—how Merchant Solutions tracks inventory and even warns you, by e-mail, if stock levels drop too low. If you choose to use Database Inventory, the simplest method, you can upload inventory information into the system, as explained in Chapter 19. The database or spreadsheet used for that purpose is a very simple one, with just two fields: Code and Quantity.

While you are creating the product-import file, you might want to include the Quantity field—it's a good idea to manage all your product data in one place. You'll be able to import the file into the product database—it will ignore the Quantity field. When you are ready to import the inventory information, you can export the data with just the Code and Quantity fields (if working with a database program), or save the file (if using a spreadsheet) with all fields deleted but the Code and Quantity fields.

Creating and Importing the Data File

How, then, do you create an import file? Virtually all spreadsheet and database programs have a way to export to the .csv format. You could, in theory, create the file in a text editor, but you probably shouldn't; it's easy to make mistakes. The easiest program to use is a spreadsheet program, such as Microsoft Excel, but merchants with large product catalogs may already have their products in a database. If you exported a .csv file from Catalog Manager and have Excel installed on your system, you'll probably find the file automatically opens in that program.

Understanding how to use a spreadsheet and a word processor's search-and-replace function can make your data manipulation easy. For instance, let's say you want to use the same information in the Name field and in the ID field so your .html pages have words from the product name in the filename—Merchant Solutions uses the ID as the product page's filename. First, sort your data in the spreadsheet alphabetically by the Name column, then copy the Name column and paste it into a word processor. (You may be able to do the following search-and-replace functions in your spreadsheet, but generally the word processor's tools are better.) Use the search-and-replace function to remove commas, apostrophes, quotation marks, periods, & symbols, slashes (/), and non-important words such as articles and prepositions (the, with, by, on, in, for, and so on). Replace all spaces and slashes with a dash. Then replace any multiple dashes you may have with a single dash, and remove preceding and trailing dashes. Make sure you don't have any duplicates in the list, and then paste the column into your spreadsheet as a new ID column.

Here's how to get your product data into Merchant Solutions:

1. Create a spreadsheet or database file using all the field names from the file you downloaded from Catalog Manager (with the exception of the Family field, which you can ignore).

2. If you want to assign products to categories, use the Path field, too.

Remember that Merchant Solutions' IDs can contain only letters, numbers, and dashes. If the IDs in your data file contain other characters, those characters will be replaced with dashes.

3. Enter all your product data into the file.

4. Save the file as a .csv file.

5. In the Catalog Manager home page, click the Upload Items link (or click the Upload tab elsewhere in Catalog Manager).

6. Click the **Upload** button.

Upload

Click "Upload" to upload a spreadsheet containing revisions to your items. Once you have uploaded your spreadsheet and addressed any critical errors, click "Commit" to apply your changes to the database. (When the "Revert" button is active, you may revert to the last saved version of your catalog.) Click "Download" to download a spreadsheet containing your existing item information.

7. Select the table where you want the data to be imported (ignore this if you have not set up multiple tables).

Be careful with the Rebuild option; it throws away the existing data and replaces it with the data from the new file. In addition, any page formatting you've done in your product and section pages is lost; for instance, if you link from a product to another product (see Chapter 16), or if you create a product accessory (see Chapter 14), that information is lost. Also, if the data file you are importing doesn't include a product that is already in the store database, that product will be removed from the database. It's always safer to use the Add option—products can be changed, products can be added, but no products will be removed. The Rebuild option is an extreme measure that should only be used if you want to totally start over with your product database and store structure.

8. Click the **Add** button if you are adding new data to the product database or modifying existing products; click **Rebuild** if you want to completely remove all products in the store database and replace them with the new data.

9. Click the **Browse** button and find the file you want to import.

10. Click the **Upload** button.

When using the Add import, if you have a blank data field, the corresponding field in the database will be emptied. However, if you do not include a particular data column, the corresponding data in the database will be untouched. For example, if your spreadsheet doesn't include a Sale-price column and the existing data in the database does *include Sale-price data, the Sale-price data will be retained. If you want to clear the fields you must include the Sale-price column in the spreadsheet and make sure the fields in the column are empty.*

11. A table appears showing what you are importing and any error messages if the system found problems with your data file. In the example in Figure 13-1, the system has found a column of data that it doesn't recognize. It will still import the data but will ignore the unknown fields. If everything looks okay, click the **Commit** button.

12. In the confirmation page that appears, click the **Add** or **Rebuild** button.

13. Click the Items tab at the top of the page. Review your product data to ensure everything looks okay. If everything's fine, you're finished.

14. If you see problems, return to the Upload page. The previous Upload table is still present.

15. Click the **Revert** button to remove database changes and return to the previous product database.

16. In the confirmation page, click the **Revert** button.

Publishing Your Import Data

Once you've imported your data—assuming you *haven't* clicked the **Revert** button—you need to "publish" it in order for it to appear in Store Editor. Click the Publishing link on the tab at the top right of the page, then click the **Publish Catalog** button. When you return to Store Editor, you will find your data. Remember, though, that in order to see the products in the live store, you must publish from within Store Editor, too, using the **Publish** button on the Editor toolbar.

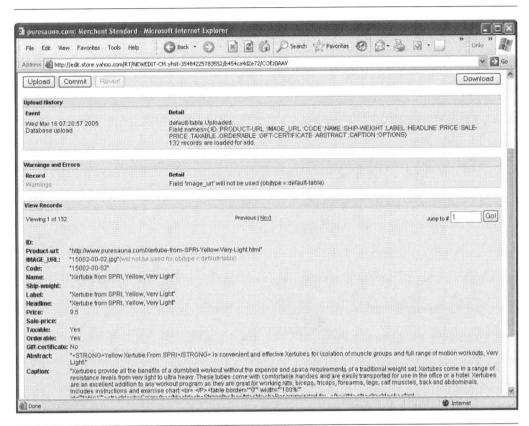

FIGURE 13-1   The Upload table shows you the data that will be uploaded and reports any problems.

Importing Images

When you import a data file, you can't import images, of course—it's just a text file. You can still associate a single image with each product, though. Use .gif or .jpg images. Although the Merchant Solutions documentation suggests you can work with a variety of other formats, it doesn't mean that web browsers can display them! Use .gif and .jpg, and you can be sure they will work in all image-enabled web browsers.

tip   *Once you have uploaded images to the system, you can import (using Add or Rebuild) your product files at will, and your images will remain. However, if you delete an entry in Catalog Manager, the associated image will be deleted, too. That means if you do a Rebuild import, you'll lose your images because the Rebuild function deletes products and then imports.*

Here's how to import your images:

1. For every product for which you need an image, create an image file named after the product's ID. For instance, if the product is a book, you may have used the ISBN number as the product's ID, 0764567586, for instance. If you have a .jpg image for the book, then the image file should be named 0764567586.jpg.

While you can only import one image file for every product, there is a way to display more images for a product. See Chapter 15 for how.

2. Compress all the images into a ZIP file. In Windows XP you can simply select all the images in Windows Explorer, right-click on the selected files, and choose the **Send To | Compressed (zipped) folder** option. (This actually creates a ZIP file, although Windows Explorer treats it as if it were a folder.)

Limit the ZIP file to under 14MB. If the file is larger than this, break it down into separate files.

3. In Store Manager, click the Store Editor link. You'll learn more about Store Editor later; for now, don't worry about what everything is that you can see, just follow the instructions carefully!

4. Click the little red triangle on the right side of the Editor toolbar.

5. A second row of buttons opens; click the **Controls** button.

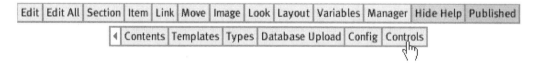

6. Scroll down the page that appears, to the **Multiple Image Upload** line. Click the Multiple Image Upload link.

7. Click the **Browse** button and find the ZIP file.

8. Click the **Send** button to upload the file. The upload may take a while, but eventually you'll be returned to the Controls page.

9. Click the **Update** button at the top of the page to return to the main Store Editor pages. Your images are now imported and should display in the product pages.

So, you've got your products into the catalog. The next step is to edit the store's design, which we'll begin to learn about in the next chapter.

Chapter 14

Working in Store Editor

As discussed in Chapter 13, you'll be using Store Editor to create your store's pages. In this chapter, you're going to come face-to-face with this tool, and you'll learn how to find your way around. Store Editor can be a trifle confusing to new users, so it's worth spending a little while getting used to how it functions.

You might think of Store Editor as a set of tools laid on top of your store's pages. While you work in Store Editor, you'll see your store more or less how it will appear when it's "live," except that a special toolbar—the Editor toolbar—is placed on the content area of the page, at the top or bottom (you get to choose . . . the top is generally the best place for it). You'll learn how to move around from page to page, how to use the Editor toolbar, and how to work with the various tools available to you. We'll also discuss an important choice—whether or not to use HTML in your pages.

Moving Around in Store Editor

You're about to begin using Store Editor to learn how to create pages, so let's take a quick look to see how it works. (You'll want to spend a little while getting a feel for this tool; make sure you read this material carefully, as Store Editor can be very confusing if you don't have someone to guide you!) Click the Store Editor link in Store Manager to open Store Editor, as shown in Figure 14-1.

Store Editor is designed to look like your final store pages. The same colors, same navigation buttons, the product information you add, and so on, will all appear inside Store Editor. The big difference is the presence of the Editor toolbar and the Help box, which summarizes the purpose of the currently displayed buttons in the Editor toolbar.

Here's how all this works . . . follow these steps to get a feel for what's going on:

1. When you first enter Store Editor, you see the Home page.

note
The term home page *means, these days, a site's* main page—*the page that appears when someone first arrives at your site using the domain name and no page reference. You might think of this as your site's* front *page. (Originally, in the first days of the Web,* home page *meant the page your browser opened every time you started the program.)*

The store's navigation buttons (*navbar*)

Your store name (stored in the Title field of the Variables page)

The content area

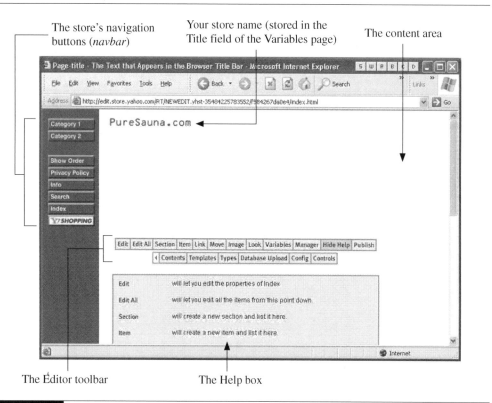

The Editor toolbar

The Help box

Store Editor, showing a store Home page

2. The Editor toolbar's buttons control what is done to this page. The **Edit** button edits the contents of the page; the **Section** button creates a new section (product category), linked to from the Home page; the **Item** button creates a new product page; and so on.

How do you know where you are at any point? Sometimes it's a little confusing, especially if you haven't yet entered much information yet. If there's no Home button in the navbar, you are on the Home page. If there is a Home button, you are on some other page, of course. Look in the browser's address bar, and you'll see a long string—something like http://edit.store.yahoo.com/RT/NEWEDIT.yhst-35484225783552/0973ce6cd3dc/—followed by a filename. This filename sometimes indicates the page name: privacypolicy.html means you are viewing the Privacy Policy page, exercise-equipment.html means you are in the Exercise Equipment category, 28631.html means you are in the product page belonging to the product with an ID of 28631, and so on. Oh, and don't confuse index.html (the Home page) with ind.html (the Index page).

3. Now, all this can get a little confusing—it's easy to lose track of where you are. For instance, follow this procedure:

Action	Location
In Store Manager, click the <u>Store Editor</u> link.	The first page you see is the Home page.
Click the **Edit** button, make changes, click the **Update** button.	You're still on the Home page.
Click the **Section** button, add information about the new section, click **Update**.	You are now viewing the new section page.
Click the **Section** button, add information about the new section, click **Update**.	You are now viewing the second new section page, a subsection page of the first section.
Click the **Up** button.	You are viewing the first section page.
Click the **Home** button.	You are viewing the Home page.

4. If you've entered products, you can get to them quickly by clicking the **Index** button on the navbar, then clicking a link to the product.

5. If you've created sections, you can get to them by clicking one of the buttons near the top of the navbar.

6. If you're not in the Home page, you can always return by clicking the **Home** button in the navbar.

It's important to remember these few points:

▪ In order to edit a page, you have to navigate to that page, then click the **Edit** button on the Editor toolbar.

tip *You may find the Editor toolbar easier to use if it's at the top of the page rather than the bottom, especially once you've entered products and information into your pages. Click the little red triangle to open the second row, then click the **Config** button, change **Edit-button-position** to **Top**, and click the **Update** button.*

▪ If you are in the Home page or a section/product category page, and you click the **Section** or **Item** button in the Editor toolbar, you'll be able to create a new section (product category) or item (product) that will be linked to the current section. When you do this, you'll end up in the new section or product page; click **Up** in the Editor toolbar to return to the previous section page.

▪ To return to Store Manager at any time, click the **Home** button to return to the Home page, then click the **Manager** button on the Editor toolbar.

To summarize, here are the different ways to move around your site while working in Store Editor:

- **Click on a navbar button.**

- **Click on a link.** You'll see both text links and image links in your pages; click on these to move to a page.

- **Use the Index button.** Click the **Index** button on the navbar, then click the name of the page you want to move to.

- **Use the Contents button.** Open the secondary bar of the Editor toolbar by clicking the red triangle, then click the **Contents** button. Find the page you want and click on the name or ID link.

- **Click Up.** Click **Up** on the Editor toolbar to go up one level.

- **Click Home.** Click the **Home** navbar button to return to the Home page.

Understanding Your Store Structure

In order to use Store Editor, you need to understand that a web site is built almost like a pyramid. Imagine the home page is at the top of the pyramid, with pages below it; below those pages are more pages, and below those pages could be more pages.

If you have been working with computers for some time, you probably understand the concept of a *directory tree*. On your computer, you have a disk drive, drive C:, let's say. In that drive you can create *directories*, perhaps more commonly known as *folders* these days. Inside those folders you can place document files, or more folders—*subfolders*. Inside the subfolders you can place more document files, and more subfolders.

Well, your store is similar. At the "top" is a Home page, the store's "front" page. That page can link directly to section (product category) pages and to item (product) pages. The sections that are linked from the Home page can also contain sections (this time, in effect, subsections) and more product pages. You can see this illustrated in Figure 14-2.

This description is what may be thought of as the core structure. However, you can also create links between pages that are not part of this "top-down" structure, as you can see in Figure 14-3.

There are various types of pages:

- **Home page**   The site's "front" or "main" page (commonly known as the Home page), has the filename *index.html*. There is, of course, only one Home page.

- **Section/Category page**   Merchant Solutions uses the term *section page* to refer to a "category" page in which a category of products can be grouped. A small amount of information for each product is shown for each product, with a link to the particular product page.

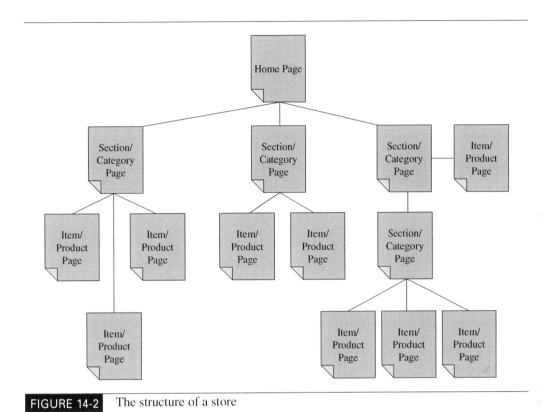

FIGURE 14-2   The structure of a store

■ **Item/Product page**   Item or product pages display information about a particular product.

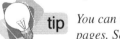

tip   You can create more pages to store any kind of information you want by creating new section pages. See Chapter 17.

■ **Ancillary pages**   Your store is already set up with several ancillary pages, pages that do not contain product-catalog information but that are related to your store nonetheless: the Show Order page (which displays information about a buyer's order), the Privacy Policy page, the Info page (which contains background information about your store), the Search page, and the Index page (which contains a link to every section and product page in your store).

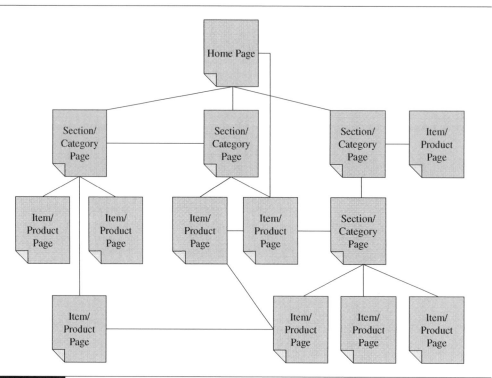

FIGURE 14-3   Links can also be built between pages in any direction.

Using the Contents Page

The Contents page provides a great way to both see your store structure and navigate around within it; it lets you go directly to a particular page. The Contents page shows all the pages—section pages, product pages, and ancillary pages—in your site. Pages are listed by the ID, so if you decided to make the ID match your product name (as suggested in Chapter 13), then the Contents page may look something like Figure 14-4. Obviously, the Contents page is easier to use if the IDs are clearly recognizable text, rather than just a jumble of numbers.

 note   *Yahoo! uses the terms* parent *and* child *to refer to pages. If a section page links to a product page, then the section is the* parent *and the product page is the* child. *If a section links to another section, the subsection is a* child *of the first—parent—section.*

 note   *The Contents page is displayed only in Store Editor, not in your live store.*

To get to the Contents page, open the second line of Editor Toolbar buttons by clicking the little red triangle on the right end of the first line, then click the **Contents** button.

The Home page; click on **index** to
return to the Home page in Store Editor

Click this button to return
to the page you came from

A section/category page

A product page with a
link to another product

A product page linked
from another product

A product page

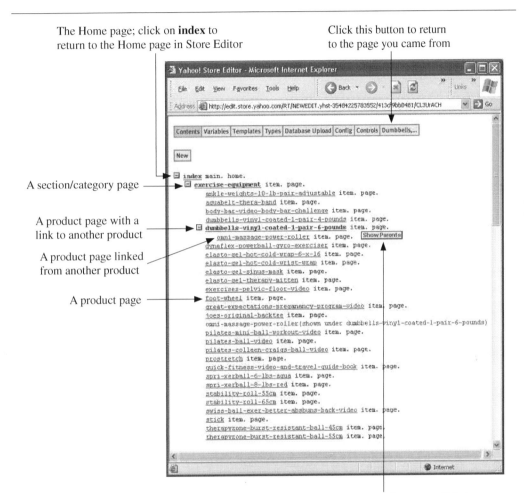

If the product is linked to from another page, click the
Show Parents button to see a list of the pages linking here

FIGURE 14-4   The Contents page, a good way to navigate around your store

Learning the Edit Toolbar Buttons

The Edit toolbar buttons carry out a variety of actions, depending on where you are at any point.
In fact, you'll see different buttons in different places as you build your site. When you first enter
Store Editor, you're in the Home page and you'll see this Editor toolbar:

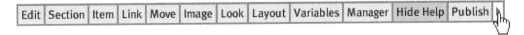

Click the little red triangle to open the second (Advanced) bar:

| Edit | Edit All | Section | Item | Link | Move | Image | Look | Layout | Variables | Manager | Hide Help | Publish |

◀ | Contents | Templates | Types | Database Upload | Config | Controls |

 tip   *Leave the Advanced toolbar turned on at all times! If you ever notice that the second bar is not present, click that little red triangle. If you* don't *leave it turned on, some fields will be missing in the Edit pages. Better still, make sure it's turned on by default. Click the* **Controls** *button on the Advanced bar, select* **Advanced** *in the* **Default Editor Mode** *drop-down, and click* **Update***.*

 tip   *You can move these buttons to the top of the page, if you wish, which is useful if your pages contain a lot of content. Click the* **Config** *button, change* **Edit-button-position** *to Top, and then click* **Update***.*

The buttons displayed on the bar vary, depending on where you see the bar: in the Home page, in a section page or product page, or in an ancillary page. Table 14-1 describes the buttons.

Button	Home	Section/ Category	Product/ Item	Ancillary	Purpose
Up	✗	✓	✓	✗	Displays the *parent* page, the one immediately "above" the current page.
Edit	✓	✓	✓	✓ (not Index)	Lets you edit the contents of the currently displayed page; when you first enter Store Editor, of course, that's the Home page.
Accessory	✗	✗	✓	✗	Creates a new product but without creating a product page. The Accessory information sits on the same page as the current product.
Edit All	✓	✓	✗	✗	Lets you quickly adjust basic information for all your products "below" the current page (all products if on the Home page, all products within a category if in a section/category page). We recommend that you use Category Manager rather than this tool, unless you have a small number of products.
Section	✓	✓	✗	✗	Creates a new section page and a link to it from the current page.

TABLE 14-1   The Store Editor's Edit Toolbar Buttons

Button	Home	Section/ Category	Product/ Item	Ancillary	Purpose
Item	✓	✓	✗	✗	Creates a new product and links to it from the current page.
Link	✓	✓	✓	✗	Creates a link to a web page, inside the site or elsewhere. In the Home page, the link is placed on the navbar, as a button; on section and product pages, it's placed within the page contents.
Move	✓	✓	✗	✗	On the Home page, it lets you move one of the buttons in the navbar to a different position in the navbar. In a section page, it lets you move an item on the page to another location. This is a little "sticky" sometimes, but there are other ways to move components on a page. (See Chapter 16.)
Image	✓	✓	✓	✓ (only Info page)	Places an image onto the page.
Special/ Not Special	✗	✓	✓	✗	Puts a link in the content area of the Home page to the current section, in effect making whatever is in this area a current "special." Clicking Not Special removes the product from the Home page.
Unexile	✗	✓	✓	✗	You'll only see this if you have used the Cut or Copy buttons. Clicking **Unexile** cancels the cut or copy operation, removing the page from the clipboard.
Cut	✗	✓	✓	✗	Removes the selected item from the current page, saving it for placement elsewhere in the store.
Copy	✗	✓	✓	✗	Copies the current page, saving the copy for placement elsewhere in the store.
Delete	✗	✓	✓	✗	Deletes the current page.
Look	✓	✓	✓	✓	Opens the Look button bar, allowing you to select a site template.
Layout	✓	✓	✗	✗	Lets you modify the layout of the content in the page.

TABLE 14-1   The Store Editor's Edit Toolbar Buttons (*cont.*)

Button	Home	Section/ Category	Product/ Item	Ancillary	Purpose
Variables	✓	✓	✓	✓	Lets you modify the store's design settings, such as colors and background images.
Manager	✓	✗	✗	✗	Returns you to the Store Manager page.
Hide Help/ Help	✓	✓	✓	✓	Removes/returns the Help box.
Publish/ Published	✓	✗	✗	✗	Publishes your pages to your live store (if the button is gray and says *Published*, the button is inactive as all changes have been published).
Red Arrow ▶	✓	✓	✓	✓	Click this to open the second row of Edit buttons.
Red Arrow ◀	✓	✓	✓	✓	Click this to close the second row of Edit buttons.
Contents	✓	✓	✓	✓	Displays the store's Table of Contents page, which lists all the store's pages and shows how they are related.
Templates/ Types	✓	✓	✓	✓	The Templates and Types pages allow you to create completely new page designs. We do not cover this subject as it's really a relic from an earlier version; if you need more design control, you probably should be working with SiteBuilder, Dreamweaver, or some other kind of HTML tool.
Database Upload	✓	✓	✓	✓	An old tool for uploading data into your store—it dates back to earlier versions of Yahoo!'s e-commerce products. Ignore this and use Catalog Manager for uploads.
Config	✓	✓	✓	✓	Use this to modify how Store Editor looks and works.
Controls	✓	✓	✓	✓	Set Store Editor properties such as mode and editor entry page, and access features such as search, multiple image upload, and edit multiple items.

TABLE 14-1   The Store Editor's Edit Toolbar Buttons (*cont.*)

Planning Your Strategy—to HTML or Not to HTML?

As you're about to learn, Merchant Solutions provides a lot of different component choices on each of four different types of pages. There are actually *five* types of pages, although you cannot modify one type:

- **The Home page**   Your site's "front door."

- **Section/category pages**   These pages are used to group products into different categories. If you have very few products, you don't have to use section pages.

- **Product pages**   Pages containing information about individual products. (It's also possible not to use product pages, but instead to put product information onto your section pages and allow buyers to order from there, as you'll learn in Chapter 16.)

- **Ancillary pages**   The Info and Privacy Policy pages.

- **Non-editable pages**   A number of pages, such as the Catalog Request page and the Help page are provided by Merchant Solutions "as is," with no editing available.

Each page has two basic areas; the navbar and the "content" area, as shown in Figure 14-5. On each of the first four types of pages, you can choose to include or omit various components in your content area. For instance, on the Home page you can choose to include these items (don't worry too much about where the Variables and Edit pages are for the moment; you'll learn this later):

- Text from the Address field, in the Variables page

- A list of links pointing to all the products in your store

- The text from the Final-text field in the Variables page

- The image uploaded through the Image field of the Home page's Edit page

- The text from the Intro-text field on the Home page's Edit page

- The text in the Message field of the Home page's Edit page

- The store's name, from the Title field in the Variables page

- A search box

- An area in which product "specials" will be placed

For instance, here's how you would get the Intro-text field into your Home page:

1. Enter the text into the Intro-text field of the Home page's Edit page.

2. Make sure Intro-text is one of the items selected in the Page-elements list in the Edit page.

At this point, you have a couple of choices. You see, Merchant Solutions was originally designed for use by people who know nothing about HTML, the Web's basic page-description markup language. If you know nothing about HTML, you can simply enter text into the appropriate fields and use various tools (which you'll be learning about soon) to position the fields on the page.

This is the navbar or buttons area   This is the content area

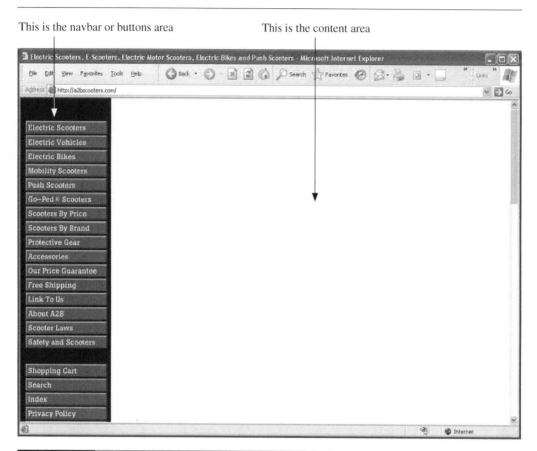

FIGURE 14-5   A page's navbar and content areas

However, you have very limited formatting options when you do this. For this reason, many people who create stores with Merchant Solutions use a slightly different method. They omit many of the page elements they can use and place HTML directly into one of the fields. For instance, in the case of the Home page, a store developer might completely ignore these elements:

- Text from the Address field, in the Variables page
- A list of links pointing to all the products in your store
- The text from the Final-text field in the Variables page
- The image uploaded through the Image field of the Home page's Edit page

■ The text from the Intro-text field on the Home page's Edit page

■ The store's name, from the Title field in the Variables page

Instead, the developer could use the following fields:

■ The text in the Message field of the Home page's Edit page; the developer would place HTML into this area, allowing him totally flexibility in the layout of the main area of the page.

■ A search box; this might be placed above or below the main text.

■ An area in which product "specials" will be placed. This could also be placed below the main Message, with a heading placed at the bottom of the message.

Here's an example. In Figure 14-6, you can see a real, live store, in which the developer has followed this process. All the text and images you can see in the content area were created as HTML and pasted into the Message text box in the Home page's Edit page.

FIGURE 14-6   The developer of this site has entered HTML into the Message field.

How do we know this? For various reasons:

- There are too many images on this page for Merchant Solutions to handle directly; the designer must have entered HTML in order to place all these pictures.

- The layout is too complicated; text wrapped around the image of the woman, with another large image on the right side, would be too complicated for Merchant Solutions to handle directly.

- The text formatting; some words have been bolded, italicized, and underlined, which Merchant Solutions couldn't do.

As we scroll down this page, we see more, as in Figure 14-7.

It looks like the HTML entered into the Home page's Message box probably ends at FEATURED SCOOTERS & BIKES. After that, the designer may have used Merchant Solutions' "Specials" feature to drop these product info blurbs and links onto the page. So the designer has used a combination of Merchant Solutions elements and HTML.

Now, Figure 14-8 shows what the page might look like if the designer *didn't* use HTML.

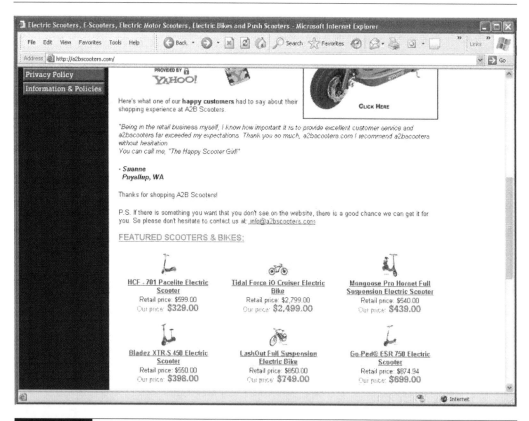

FIGURE 14-7   The designer has placed "specials" below.

FIGURE 14-8   What A2BScooters.com store might look like *without* HTML formatting

What a huge difference! The designer would still be able to drop the top image onto the page, but would lose the ability to format most of the page—the font formatting, the additional images, the "column" layout, and so on.

So here's the choice: you can use Merchant Solutions to set up a store without any HTML knowledge, but it's going to look a little bland. By working with HTML, though, you can spruce it up dramatically.

In this book, we're not going to be teaching HTML; that's a big subject on its own. But you should know that entering HTML into some of the large text fields in the Edit pages can make a big difference. It's worth learning how to use a simple HTML tool, or perhaps paying a student or young web geek a few bucks to format a few of your pages for you.

This page intentionally left blank

Chapter 15

Creating the Home and Section Pages

Time to get down to work. Now that you understand how to get around in Store Editor and use the Editor toolbar, you can get started setting up the Home page and section pages. The Home page is your store's "front" page; the section pages are product category pages. You'll learn in "Creating and Editing Section Pages" later in this chapter, how to create pages for various other purposes by creating section pages.

You're going to learn how to use HTML in message fields, a very important technique that, as you saw in the previous chapter, can make your store stand out. You'll also learn how to add, remove, and move components on the Home page, how to create a product "special" on the Home page, how to place products onto a section page, and how to move products between sections. By the time you finish this chapter, you should have a good feel for how to create pages within Store Editor; in the following chapters, you'll learn much more about how to define what sort of information is placed onto them and what the pages actually look like—the page design.

Setting Up the Home Page

Let's begin working in Store Editor by setting up the Home page. When you first open Store Editor, you'll be in the Home page; if you've moved around, you can get back there by clicking the Home button on the navbar. Then click the **Edit** button on the Editor toolbar. The page you can see in Figure 15-1 opens.

> tip *Look in your browser's Address or URL bar; do you see /index.html at the end? If so, you're definitely in the Home page. If not—if you see a scramble of letters, such as CMIqwAAC— you could still be on the Home page; in some circumstances Merchant Solutions doesn't show the index.html filename. Is there a Home button at the top of the navbar? If not, you're in the Home page.*

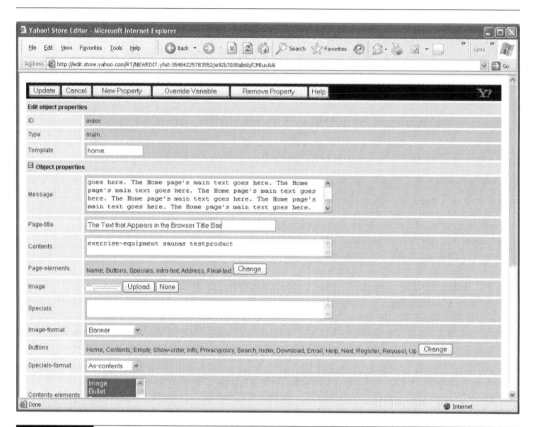

FIGURE 15-1 A typical Store Editor Edit page

 warning *The "Help" text under fields in the Edit pages is usually ambiguous and sometimes plain wrong! Stick with the field descriptions in this book.*

This is a typical Edit page. You'll see a lot of these while working in Store Editor. Wherever you're modifying a page, you'll see something similar to this; fields will vary, but essentially the pages all use the same sort of layout. Table 15-1 explains what the fields are when working in the Home page.

You can see the effect of most of the settings in this Edit page in Figure 15-2.

 **tip** *Remember, the Variables page is used to control settings throughout the store and is explained in Chapter 17.*

Field	Description
ID	Every page, as you saw with products earlier, has a unique ID. In this case Merchant Solutions has provided the ID.
Type/ Template	The Types and Templates pages are advanced features that allow you to create completely new page designs. We do not cover this subject as it's really a "relic" from an earlier version; if you need more design control you probably should be working with SiteBuilder, Dreamweaver, or some other kind of HTML tool.
Message	This is the main block of text that appears on the Home page. You can place HTML in here. See the "Using HTML in the Message and Other Text Fields" section for more information.
Page-title	This is the text that appears in the browser's Title bar when the page is displayed. (If you know HTML, you may know that this is the <TITLE></TITLE> text.) To help the search engines index your site, make sure you use good keywords here, rather than just your company name. See Chapter 26 for more information.
Contents	The list of sections (categories) and products that will be included on the navbar; each item has its own button. Some of these entries are put there automatically; when you click the **Section** or **Item** button on the Editor toolbar, for instance, you create a section or product page. The system puts a button onto the navbar for you (and thus places the appropriate section or product name in the Contents text box).
Page-elements	This setting controls which page elements will be displayed on the Home page and where each element will sit. The elements include items such as the Message and Image that you define in this Edit page, along with other items, such as a search box and an address block, which are created elsewhere. See Chapter 17 for information on how to use this tool.
Image	You can upload an image onto the Home page if you wish; click the **Upload** button.
Specials	A *special* is a section or product that you want to feature on the Home page. Simply type the ID of the section or product into this box, and information about that section or product will be placed onto the page. See "Making a Product or Section a 'Special'" later in this chapter for more information.
Image-format	This controls the format of the picture that you upload on the Image line. **Left** reduces the image in size and places it to the left of the text, wrapping the text around it to the right; select **Banner** and the image is shown above the text, larger, but constrained to the width of the text below it; select **Unconstrained** and the image is shown full size above the text.
Buttons	This line is where you define which buttons will be shown in the navbar on the Home page. We'll cover this later in a discussion about different ways to modify the navbar throughout the site; see Chapter 17.
Specials-format	If you enter *specials* in the Specials box, Specials-format defines how they will be displayed.
Contents-elements	This field defines what information is pulled in from a product or section that you have entered into the Contents box. In other words, when information about a product or section is displayed on the Home page, this is where that information comes from. See Chapter 17 for more information.

TABLE 15-1   The Fields Available While Working in the Home Page

Field	Description
Contents-format	The manner in which the product or section information is formatted; see Chapter 17.
Columns	The number of columns of information shown on the page.
Intro-text	Another block of text you can place onto the Home page; by default it's not used, but you can add it using the Page-elements control. You can also use HTML in this box. (See the "Using HTML in the Message and Other Text Fields" section that follows.)

TABLE 15-1 The Fields Available While Working in the Home Page (*cont.*)

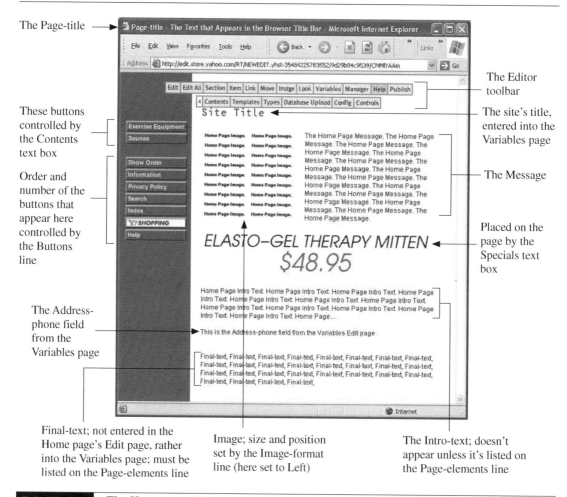

FIGURE 15-2 The Home page elements

Using HTML in the Message and Other Text Fields

You can place HTML text into a variety of fields in the Store Editor's Edit pages. In the Home page's Edit page, you can place HTML into the Message and Intro-text fields. This is very important because it allows you to do many things. You're not limited to having just plain old text on your pages; you can do anything that can be done with HTML.

note   *HTML means* HyperText Markup Language, *and it's the coding used to create web pages. In your browser, select View | View Source, and you'll see the code used to build the current web page. You can use it to modify the text in your store pages. For instance, enclosing text with <b> and </b> makes it bold. If you know HTML you can use it to format text, create tables, insert images, and more, in the Caption and Abstract fields.*

Using HTML, you could do the following:

- Drop an image into the page by pulling it from another web site. For instance, the following tag drops a picture into the page by pulling it from another web site or from a special directory you create in your store, in this case from images.*yourdomain*.com/littlepicture.jpg:

```
<img src="http://images.yourdomain.com/littlepicture. jpg">
```

(We'll explain this in more detail under "Working with Images and HTML" later in this chapter.)

note   *When you press* ENTER *after typing text into a text box that allows HTML, Merchant Solutions automatically enters a <br> tag, the line-break tag.*

- You can format text in many ways: bold, italic, underlines, different colors, different fonts, different sizes, and so on.
- You can format paragraphs anyway you wish: left, right, justified, and so on.
- You can create tables.
- You can insert Flash animation files.
- You can create bulleted or numbered lists.

tip   *Many store owners choose not to use most of the fields in the Home page. Instead, the only thing they place into the content area of the page is the Message, in which they put HTML, laying out the page exactly the way they want. To find out how to remove elements using the Page-elements line, see Chapter 17.*

Anything you can do with HTML, you can place into your text boxes and, therefore, display on your pages (see Figure 15-3).

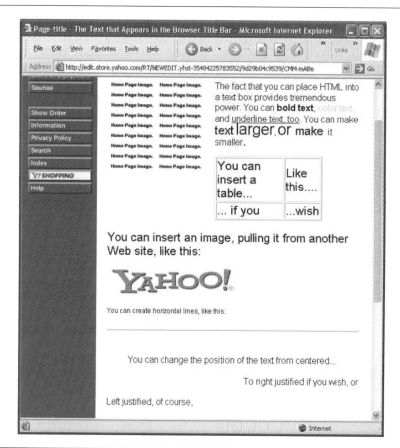

FIGURE 15-3   Placing HTML in text boxes allows you to format the content of your pages.

 tip   *How about products? If you import your products, how do you handle HTML fields? Just drop the HTML straight into the appropriate fields in your database or spreadsheet. When creating product data files, you can use HTML in the Caption and Abstract fields.*

This can't be stressed enough; the ability to use HTML in the text fields provides tremendous design power, allowing you to dramatically change the look of your site. You can create your blocks of HTML in an HTML editor, then copy and paste them into Merchant Solutions.

Moving and Removing Elements on the Home Page

The content area of the Home page has a variety of *elements* or components that you can choose to position or omit from the page—the Contents and Intro-text fields from the Edit page, the Final-text field from the Variables page, the store's Name field from the Variables page, and so on. These are modified—added to the page, removed from the page, or shuffled around on the page—by clicking the **Edit** button in the Editor toolbar, and then clicking the **Change** button on the Page-elements line.

note   *Unfortunately, sometimes these elements "stick." You add an element or move one, and nothing seems to change when you return to Store Editor. If you're absolutely sure that you did what you are supposed to do and the desired action was not carried out, try reloading the web page. Failing that, try exiting Store Editor (click **Manager** on the Editor toolbar on the Home page), then log out and log back in.*

   Table 15-2 shows the elements available to you, and Figure 15-4 displays the table in Store Editor.

Making a Product or Section a "Special"

A *special* is a product or section that is displayed on the Home page—it's "specially featured" on your site's front page. Creating a special is simple. Navigate to the product page and click the **Special** button on the Editor toolbar. Store Editor jumps you to the Home page and shows you how the special will appear.

tip   *To remove a special, navigate to the product or section page and then click the **Not Special** button on the Editor toolbar.*

Element	Purpose
Address	The text from the Address field in the Variables page (see Chapter 17).
Buttons	Defines where the navigation buttons sit on the page, but this setting probably only has an effect if you have created a horizontal navbar (by selecting Top-buttons in the Page-format drop-down list box in the Variables page)—some witnesses claim it sometimes works even with the vertical navbar! Generally speaking the setting is ignored because when you first open Store Editor it has a left-side navbar. We recommend that you leave this element listed in the table and use the Buttons line in the Edit page to control the buttons.
Contents	A list of links pointing to all the products in your store.
Final-text	The text from the Final-text field in the Variables page.
Image	The image uploaded through the Image field of the Home page's Edit page.
Intro-text	The text from the Intro-text field on the Home page's Edit page.
Message	The text from the Message field of the Home page's Edit page.
Name	The store's name, from the Title field in the Variables page, or the Name-image, also defined in the Variables page.
Search	Places a search box onto the page, which visitors can use to search your site.
Specials	Defines where product "specials" will be placed. You will learn about setting a product as a "special" next.

TABLE 15-2   The Elements Available in the Content Area of the Home Page

Edit List Position (page-elements)

Element	Position
Address	1
Buttons	2
Contents	3
Final-text	4
Image	5
Intro-text	6
Message	7
Name	8
Search	9
Specials	10

[Update]   [Cancel]

FIGURE 15-4   The Page-elements table

tip   *There's another way to enter a special. Go to the Home page and click the **Edit** button on the Editor toolbar. Then type the ID of the product or section you want to feature as a special into the Specials text box, and click **Update**.*

There are a number of settings that affect specials:

- **Label-color, Label-font, and Label-font-size**   Click **Variables** on the Editor toolbar to find these settings. They modify the color, the typeface, and the font size of the Label text. The Label text (a product field) is only used if the Home page's Edit page has the **Specials-format** drop-down set to **As-thumbnails**.

- **Specials-format**   Navigate to the Home page, then click the Editor toolbar's **Edit** button to find this setting. You can select **As-contents** (the special is laid out on the page according to the Contents-elements, Contents-format, and Columns settings in the Home page's Edit page), or **As-thumbnails** (the product's icon image, label, and price are shown).

note   *Sometimes specials may be shown as a little block, probably a blank red square. This is probably because you have too much text in the product's Label field (set in the product's Edit page or in the product import file). Keep the Label field short.*

Creating and Editing Section Pages

You now have at least one product in the product database, perhaps many more. It's now time to create your store pages. We'll begin by editing an existing section page or creating a new section page.

 note *What is a section? Merchant Solutions uses the term* section *but it might help to think of a section as a* category. *A section (category) page contains links to product pages. For instance, a section page in a cookbook store might be* Baking; *on this page shoppers will see links to books about baking; clicking one of these links takes a shopper to a product page.*

As you learned earlier, you can create your section pages when you import your product data, and in many cases—if you have more than just a few products—this is the best thing to do. Assign each product to a section (a category), then when you import the data file and "publish" your data, Merchant Solutions automatically creates a page for each section you built. You can then go into Store Editor and modify the section pages that were automatically created when you imported your products.

1. In Store Manager, click the <u>Store Editor</u> link. You'll be viewing the store's Home page.

2. Look on the left side of the page; you'll see a number of buttons—you should see one button for each section that was created. Click one of the section buttons that you created to load that section, and click the **Edit** button on the Editor toolbar. Or, to create a new section, click the **Section** button while on the Home page.

3. Enter or modify the information in each field, as described in Table 15-3.

Field	Description
Name	The section name. If the section is a first-level section—if it's added to the Home page—then this Name also appears on a button on the navigation bar. (These are known as the *Contents* buttons; see Chapter 17.) If a subsection of another section page, the name appears on the parent section page. The name is also displayed at the top of the section page, unless you've added a Headline (see below). The Name should be kept fairly short.
Image	You can place an image at the top of the page, if you wish. Click the **Upload** button to select it. This image size is controlled by the Item-height and Item-width settings in the Variables page.
Headline	The heading appears at the top of the section page if no name has been added. As with the name, it should be kept relatively short.
Caption	This is the full section description; it appears near the top of the page, under the name or headline. You can make this as long as you want, and you may include HTML tags to modify the text.

TABLE 15-3   The Fields Available When Creating a New Section Page

Field	Description
Contents	This box lists the contents of the section page—it can contain product IDs and section names (if you have placed subsections into this section). If you imported products from a data file and used the *path* field, the Contents box contains a list of the products that have been assigned to this section, each separated by a space. You can change product and section positions on the page by moving them around in the Contents list. See Chapters 16 and 17 for information on managing page contents.
Abstract	The Abstract text is used in place of Caption text on pages other than the section page, so typically it's a shorter block of text (although actually you can enter as much as you wish). For instance, if you set the section as a *special*, the Abstract text is used on the Home page (*if* Specials-format, on the Home page's Edit page, is set to As-content, *and* Abstract is selected in the Home page's Contents-elements list). You can also format Abstract text using HTML tags.
Icon	This image is used on pages other than the section page. For instance, if you set the section as a *special* (see "Making a Product or Section a 'Special'" earlier in this chapter), the icon will appear on the Home page, or if this is a subsection of another—parent—section, the icon will appear on the parent-section page.

In addition, if this is a first-level section—one below the Home page and not a subsection of another section—and if you set **Button-style** to **Icon** in the Variables page, the Icon image will be used as a navbar button. The Icon image size is controlled by the Thumb-width and Thumb-height settings in the Variables page. |
Inset	This image appears as a smaller image, next to the main Image, on the section page. This image size is controlled by the Inset-width and Inset-height settings in the Variables page.
Label	The Label text does not appear on the section page itself. Rather, it is used on the Home page when the section has been set as a "special", and on parent section pages if the section is a subsection. Furthermore, in the case of a special, the Label text is only used if the Specials-format setting is set to **As-thumbnails** on the Home page's Edit page. This text should be kept short, as it is displayed in the form of a one-line image.
Leaf	You can ignore this for now. It's an advanced feature that defines which settings apply to the page. See Chapter 16 for more information.
Product-url	This is the address of the page on which the product will sit in your store. It's required if you are submitting products to the Yahoo! Product Submit marketing program (see Chapter 21).

TABLE 15-3   The Fields Available When Creating a New Section Page (*cont.*)

Are some of the fields in the table missing from the page you're viewing? You probably have the Advanced toolbar turned off. Leave the Edit page and open the Advanced toolbar by clicking the little red triangle. Make sure the Advanced toolbar is always on: click the **Controls** *button on the Advanced bar, select* **Advanced** *in the* **Default Editor Mode** *drop-down, and click* **Update**.

note *You'll learn about the Variables page in Chapters 16 and 17.*

You can see how these various elements are laid out on a page in Figure 15-5.

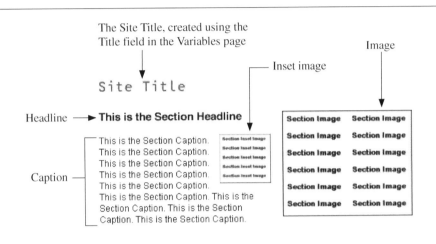

FIGURE 15-5   An example section layout

note *The manner in which items are laid out on the page can be modified. See Chapters 16 and 17.*

Working with Images and HTML

Merchant Solutions provides fairly limited help with images. If you enter a product by hand, you can provide three images—but you have only limited control over where they appear, anyway. Two of them, the Image and Inset images, will appear on the product page. If you import your products, you only get to define a single image (the Image field), by importing the images separately (see Chapter 13).

However, there's another way to drop product images into your product pages, and you can include as many as you want. You can create a special directory in your account to store images, and pull the images into your pages. Here's how you do it, assuming you understand basic HTML:

1. In Site Manager, click the **Manage My Services** button at the top right of the page.

2. In the Manage My Services page, click **Web Hosting Control Panel**.

3. In the Web Hosting Control Panel page (Figure 15-6), click the Create & Update link on a tab near the top.

4. Scroll down and click the File Manager link to open File Manager.

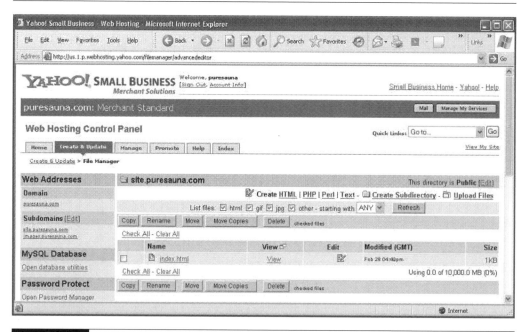

FIGURE 15-6 You can create a new folder using File Manager.

5. Click the <u>Create Subdirectory</u> link near the top.

6. Type **images** into the text box and click **Create Subdirectory**.

7. The File Manager page appears again; click the new **images** link.

tip   *If you know how to use an FTP (File Transfer Protocol) program and have a large number of files that you want to upload, you'll probably want to use that. To find the FTP settings you need, click the <u>Create & Update</u> link on a tab near the top of the Web Hosting Control Panel, then scroll down the page to find the **FTP Account Info** line.*

8. In the page that appears, click the <u>Upload Files</u> link (top right) to open the Easy Upload page. Use this page to upload the image files you want to work with into the images directory you have just created.

You have now loaded the files you want to refer to into your hosting account. The next step is to point a subdomain—such as images.*yourdomain*.com—to the new images directory.

note   *With these instructions you're going to create a subdomain to point to your images directory because we're assuming that you pointed your main domain—yourdomain.com— and the www. domain (www.yourdomain.com) to your store. Your store is actually placed in a different web server location (you won't see the store when you view the contents of your hosting account). You learned how to point these domains to your store in Chapter 12.*

1. Click the **Manage My Services** button at the top of the page to return to the Manage My Services page.

2. Click the <u>Domain Control Panel</u> link.

3. Click the <u>Manage Domain & Subdomains</u> link.

4. Click the **Add Subdomain** button.

5. Type **images** into the text box and then select **images** from the drop-down list box.

6. Click the **Submit** button.

That's it; you've uploaded images into a directory in your hosting area from which you can now pull images into your site. In order to refer to an image you would enter a URL like this:

`images.`*`yourdomain`*`.com/`*`imagename`*

For instance, let's say you have an image called bigpicture.jpg and your domain name is PureSauna.com. You would use this <img> tag to pull an image into your store:

`<img src="http://images.puresauna.com/bigpicture.jpg">`

You can test to see if everything's set up properly by typing the URL (http://images .puresauna.com/bigpicture.jpg) into the address bar in your browser and press ENTER. The image should load into the browser.

Once you have uploaded the images, here's how to actually use them in your HTML:

1. Create your HTML in an HTML-editing tool such as Dreamweaver or Microsoft Frontpage.

2. Where you want to insert an image, use an <img> tag, like this:

   `<img src="http://images.`*`yourdomain`*`.com/`*`imagename`*`.jpg">`

3. Enter this HTML into the product's Caption field. (You can also enter HTML into the Caption field in your spreadsheet and database, and import the product; see Chapter 13.)

 As with the Home page, you can create all your section-page content using HTML in the Caption field.

4. Publish your product data as normal; when you open the product page in your browser, you should see the images created by the HTML that you placed into the Caption field.

Placing Other Products on a Section Page

We're going to look at how to place a product in a section page, which is useful in two circumstances: if you are not importing a data file through Category Manager, or if you *are* importing a data file but want a product to appear in two or more section/category pages.

As you saw before, you can define which category (section) a product is placed into when you import data (see Chapter 13). But what if you want the product to appear in multiple categories? There are two things you can do.

 If you duplicate a product in your data file, you might add some little code to the duplicates. Let's say you are selling a book with the ISBN number of 0-764-56758-6 and using this number in both the ID and Code fields. The first duplicate might be D1-0-764-56758-6, the second D2-0-764-56758-6, and so on.

Place the product into your database once for each category where you want the product to appear. If you want the product to appear in three categories, make sure you have three entries for the product in the database, with a different *path* for each, of course. The problem with this method is that you'll have to use different ID and Code fields because these are unique fields;

Catalog Manager simply won't allow you to import a data file with duplicated ID or Code fields. Still, this method may be the most efficient if you want to place many products into multiple sections.

You can manually place a product into a section page. The product only appears once in the database, but a little instruction in the section page tells Merchant Solutions to place the product into that section.

Here's how to manually place an existing product into a section/category page.

1. In Store Editor, navigate to the section page into which you want to place the product.

2. Click the **Edit** button on the Editor toolbar.

3. Scroll down to the Contents field.

 tip   *Don't remember the code of the product you want to associate? Click **Contents** on the Edit toolbar and copy the product code from the list, or refer to your original import spreadsheet or database.*

4. Type the product ID into the field, in the position in which you want it to appear.

Contents What's this?	5300 5334 7125 6001 6003 6011 6013 26600 28630 28631 29004 29009 29012 29015 29018 40048 40050 40051 40052 66010 66102 66801 66804 66805 saunas-new-saunas

5. Click the **Update** button at the top or bottom of the page.

Here's another way to do the same thing, using Copy and Paste:

1. Navigate to the page containing the product you want to associate with the section.

2. Click the **Copy** button on the Editor toolbar. You'll see the Clipboard bar under the Editor toolbar.

tip   *You can navigate to multiple pages, clicking Copy on each one to "collect" them in the Clipboard bar.*

CLIPBOARD (CLICK TO INSERT):   Aquabelt by Thera-Band

3. Navigate to the section page into which you want to place the product.

tip   *If you copy an item to the Clipboard accidentally, how do you remove it? Click it to place it onto a section page, then go into that page's Edit page and remove the product from the Contents text box.*

4. Click the link in the Clipboard bar. Merchant Solutions automatically inserts the copied product into the current page. (It has entered the code for the product into the current product's Edit page Contents field.)

Moving Products Between Sections

You can also shift products around in your store, from page to page, using the Clipboard bar that you've just seen. This time, instead of clicking the **Copy** button, click the **Cut** button. Then, when you move to another page and click the link in the Clipboard, the product is actually moved to the new page.

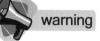 **warning**   *We recommend that you* don't *use this method for moving or copying products into sections* unless *your store only has a handful of products. In general, you should import products into Catalog Manager, as explained in Chapter 13.*

What if you change your mind? You have two options. You can simply navigate to the section page in which the product was found originally and click the link—thus replacing it back where it started. Or you can go into the Contents page (click the **Contents** button on the Editor toolbar), and click the **Siberia** button you'll see near the top.

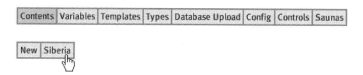

In the Exiles page that appears, you'll see the product page you just cut; it's "exiled" of course, because it no longer has a parent (if you'll excuse the mixed metaphor); it's no longer linked to from any other page.

Exiles

body-back-buddy item. page.

Click the link to the page and click the **Unexile** button on the Editor toolbar.

Now let's look at how to modify the store layout—how items are placed on the page, both in the Home page and in the catalog pages.

Chapter 16

Modifying Page Layout

In the previous chapters, you learned how to create pages by various methods and discovered some very basic techniques for defining what appears on those pages. In this chapter you're going to learn much more about page layout—how, for instance, you can use Store Editor's Contents-format and Contents-elements to define how product information appears on a section page. This can be a little confusing, as there are a number of settings that affect contents layout, but this chapter should help you figure it out if you take it slowly and spend the time experimenting a little.

Modifying the Section Page's Head and Contents Layout

A section/category page contains both a "head"—the section's Name and Image—and "contents." Merchant Solutions uses the term *contents* in various ways, but in the case of the section page, it means information about the products contained within the section. For each product, the section page can display various different content elements in different formats—the product Name, the product Icon image, the Abstract, the Order button, and so on. You can have just a little information, with most of the information displayed on the product page where the buyer would order, or instead have a lot of information, with the buyer able to place an order on both the section page and the product page. You can even discard your product pages entirely and simply let people order off the section pages.

The page content is configured using these settings, which are found in the Variables page:

Head-elements	Defines which section head elements will be displayed at the top of the section page. Select **Image** to include the section Image, and select **Display-text-title** to include the section Name (the Image is placed above the Name if both are selected). This has no effect on the Inset image, by the way, which displays regardless of this setting.
Head-style	Defines the placement of the section Name, Image, and Inset image at the top of the section page. You can set these to Left, Center, or Right.
Contents-format	Defines how the product elements are laid onto the section page.
Contents-elements	Defines which product elements—the Name, Abstract, Caption, etc.—are displayed for each product that is included in the section page.
Columns	The number of columns used to display product information.

These settings, by default, are stored in the Variables page; click the **Variables** button on the Editor toolbar button and search the Variables page to find them. You can see the effect of these settings in Figure 16-1.

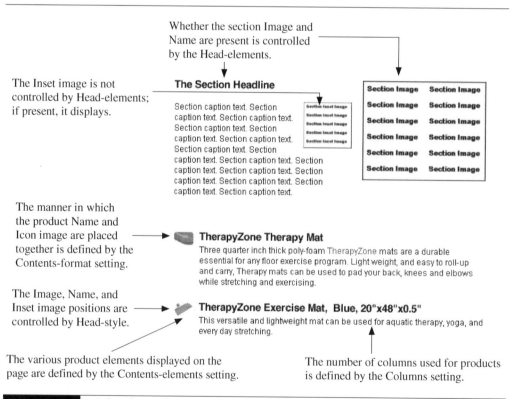

FIGURE 16-1   A few formatting choices for section pages

Choosing Product Layout with Contents-format

The Contents-format setting defines how the product information is displayed on a section page. As you can see in Figure 16-2, there are four different Contents-format layouts: Vertical (the contents are stacked, one element above another); Ell (an L shape, with an image and the text next to it); Wrap (the product Name and text wrapped around the image); and Pack (the product Images are packed together with no other information displayed).

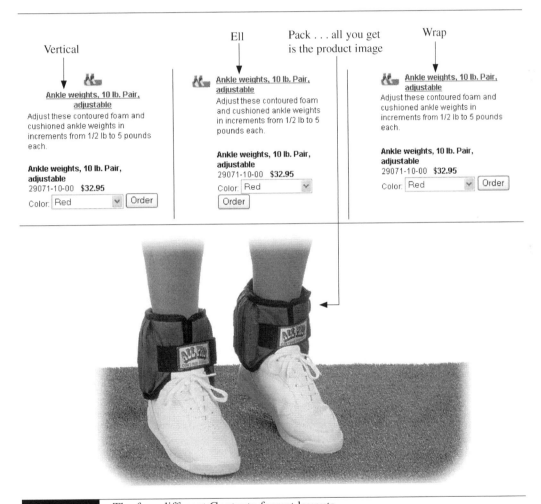

FIGURE 16-2   The four different Contents-format layouts

Picking Product Elements with Contents-elements

The Contents-elements setting in the Variables page defines which product elements are displayed on the section/category page.

tip   *Be careful with a Rebuild import (see Chapter 13). If you rebuild the database, all your section-page formatting will be lost.*

Image	The product's Icon image, if available; otherwise, a reduced-size product Image.
Bullet	If no image is available and Bullet has been selected, a bullet is used. By default, this is a small square (using the Home-button-color setting in the Variables page). You can upload your own bullet image if you wish (see the Bullet-image line on the Variables page).
Screen-text-file	The product's Name, shown as a text link. This is overridden by Display-text-file; that is, if Display-text-file is selected also, then Screen-text-file will *not* appear.
Display-text-file	The product's Name, converted to an image link.
Abstract	The product's Abstract text.
Caption	The product's Caption. If the product has an Abstract and if you select Abstract in the Contents-elements list, Caption won't appear even if selected.
Price	The product's Price. If the product also has a Sales-price, both are shown, with labels (*Regular price: $32.95 Sale Price: $19.00*)
Order	Select this, and all basic product information is displayed: the Name (as plain text, not a link), the product Code, the Price and Sales-price, the Options, and an Order button.
Contents	Select this, and any products associated with a product on the section page will be listed below the product itself. (That is, if a product ID has been entered into the product page's Contents field.) However, this does *not* include product accessories; an accessory will *not* be listed. (To learn about associating one product with another, see "Associating One Product with Another" and for information on accessories, see "Creating a Product Accessory" later in this chapter.)

You can select multiple elements in this list by holding the CTRL button and clicking; if you use a Macintosh, press the Apple button.

Overriding Head and Contents Settings

You've just seen how to modify section pages' Head and Contents settings—they are set in the Variables page. You can, however, override these settings in two ways:

- Use Leaf, an additional group of format settings.
- Override the settings for a particular page.

Using Leaf

The Leaf system provides another group of page-formatting settings for section and product pages. As you've just seen, the Variables page provides the following settings: Head-elements, Head-style, Columns, Contents-elements, and Contents-format. However, there's another group of these settings, found on the Config page: Leaf-head-elements, Leaf-head-style, Leaf-columns, Leaf-contents-elements, and Leaf-contents-format.

These settings are the same as the ones in the Variables page (with the exception—probably a programming oversight—that Leaf-head-style provides only two choices, Left and Center, unlike Head-style, which also has a Right setting).

 note *Leaf has no effect on the Home page. However, both Leaf and Variables settings work in product pages as well as section pages. By default, in fact, the product pages use the Leaf settings, not the Variables settings.*

Thus, you have two different design settings; some section pages may use one set, while others can use the other set:

- ■ If Leaf is set to **Yes** in a page, that page uses the settings in the **Config** page.

- ■ By default, Leaf is set to **Yes** in **product** pages, so by default, product pages use the Config settings.

- ■ If Leaf is set to **No** in a page, that page uses the settings from the **Variables** page.

- ■ By default, Leaf is set to **No** in **section** pages, so by default, section pages use the Variables settings.

Overriding Contents Layout

The third way to define these settings for a section page is to override those settings for a *particular* page. In other words, you can use the Variables settings, you can use the Leaf settings, or you can create settings specifically for a particular page. Here's how to override:

1. While viewing a section, click the **Layout** button on the Editor toolbar to see the Layout toolbar.

Put Contents		Alignment	Columns			Hide
On Own Pages	On This Pages	Left	Center	1	2	3

2. Click one of the buttons; it doesn't matter too much which, perhaps one of the Columns buttons.

3. At this point, Merchant Solutions automatically creates new fields in the section's Edit page. Click the **Edit** button on the Editor toolbar, scroll to the bottom of the page, and you'll see the settings under the **Custom properties** bar.

4. You can now set properties using these controls directly, or click **Cancel** at the bottom of the page to return to the section page and use the Layout toolbar to make changes:

■ Click On Own Pages to select the following Contents-elements: Image, Bullet, Screen-text-file, Abstract, and Price.

■ Click On This Pages to select the following Contents-elements: Image, Screen-text-file, Caption, and Order, and to set the page Template to nil.

■ Click an alignment button to change the Contents-format setting; click Left to select the Ell setting or click Center to select the Vertical setting.

■ Click a column number to change the number of columns used for the products listed in the section page.

You can also manually override whatever settings you want, not only the Head and Contents settings. Here's how:

1. Navigate to the section where you want to override a setting.

note *Remember that by default, the section settings are controlled by the Variables page. When you override a setting in a particular section page, you are, in effect, saying to Merchant Solutions, "Don't use the setting in the Variables page for x; use this instead."*

2. Click **Edit** on the Editor toolbar.

3. In the Edit page, click the **Override Variable** button.

4. In the drop-down list box you see, select the variable that you wish to override. For instance, let's say you want to have a custom background color on this particular page; select Background-color.

5. Click the **Update** button to return to the Edit page.

6. Scroll to the bottom of the page and you'll find a new item added to the Edit page, below the **Custom properties** bar. Use this new line to choose the custom settings for the page.

7. Click the **Update** button to save your changes and return to the section page.

Placing Products on the Section Page Only

You can set up your store so that product information is placed onto the section page—the products do *not* have their own product pages. Buyers will have to order the product directly from the section page. In fact, you can set individual products to work this way, or you can place all the products on a section page.

 note *This procedure ensures that a product doesn't have a product page, but it doesn't ensure that the necessary information, such as an order button, is displayed on the section page. Use the Contents-elements setting to do that. You cannot, however, differentiate between products on a section page; all the products on the page use the same Contents-elements setting.*

First, here's how to make sure that a product doesn't have a product page:

1. Navigate to the product's page.

2. Click the **Edit** button on the Editor toolbar.

3. In the **Template** field, replace "page." with "nil"—type it exactly like that, with *no* period after the letters.

4. Click the **Update** button. You'll return to the section page.

5. Click the **Up** button on the Editor toolbar to return to the section page.

 tip *To reverse the situation and ensure that the product* does *have its own page, replace "nil" with "page." in the Template field.*

Now, when you click the product name in the section page, you won't see the product page; you'll go directly to the Edit page.

There's a quick way to carry out this procedure for *all* products on a section page. Here's how:

1. Navigate to the section page.

2. Click the **Layout** button on the Editor toolbar. The Layout bar opens.

3. Click **On This Pages** on the Layout bar.

That's it, that's all it takes. Merchant Solutions automatically carries out the following actions for you:

- It changes all the individual product templates to *nil*.

- It creates the following Custom properties at the bottom of the section's Edit page: Head-style, Contents-format, Contents-elements, and Columns,

- It selects the following Contents-elements: Image, Screen-text-file, Caption, and Order.

note *In some cases, Merchant Solutions won't allow you to select On This Pages, if doing so will "orphan" a "grandchild." If the section page contains a product that itself has an accessory, that accessory will now be "orphaned"; there will be no way for a shopper to get to the accessory if product data is only displayed on the section page.*

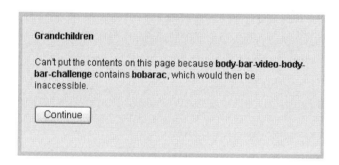

Creating and Editing Product Pages

You've already seen how to create product pages using Catalog Manager, and that's how we recommend you work with your products, unless you have just a small number.

note *If you modify a product in Store Manager, the changes will appear once you look at the product in Catalog Manager. Both systems load the data into the same database.*

You can also create products—and edit products that you created through Catalog Manager—from within Store Manager:

1. In the Home page, click the **Item** button on the Editor toolbar to create a product that is linked directly from the Home page; a button will be created for the product on the navbar.

2. Navigate to a section where you want to create a product, then click the **Item** button on the Editor toolbar.

3. Navigate to a product page and click the **Accessory** button on the Editor toolbar. This creates a special kind of product, covered under "Creating a Product Accessory" later in this chapter.

4. Navigate to the Contents page, click the **New** button at the top of the page, type a product ID, and click **Continue**.

Of course, you can also edit existing pages, even if you created them in Catalog Manager. Simply navigate to the page and click the **Edit** button on the Editor toolbar. When you create or edit product pages in Site Editor, you'll see some fields that were not present in Catalog Manager:

Type/Templates	Types and Templates are advanced features used in the early days of the Yahoo! product (Yahoo! Store) to provide advanced design capabilities. These days people who need more design flexibility use one of the HTML editors (StoreBuilder, Dreamweaver, or some other tool).
Family	You can forget about this; it's a "relic" from the early days of Yahoo!'s e-commerce product, related to associating products with each other. It's not commonly used these days.
Leaf	By default, this is set to Yes, meaning the product page uses some layout settings from the Config page.

Creating a "Link" Information Blurb

There are link to links, products, sections, accessories; if it has an ID, you can link to it.

 note *Using this method from the Home page will add a button with the link to the navbar; using this method from a section page adds a blurb with the link to the page itself.*

This following technique allows you to create a blurb on your section/category and product pages. This blurb will contain text, an image, and a link—on the heading and on the image—pointing wherever you want it to go, inside or outside your site:

1. Navigate to the page where you want to place this link and information blurb.

2. Click the **Links** button in the Editor toolbar.

3. Enter the following information:

■ **Name**   The text that will appear as a heading above the link Abstract.

■ **URL**   The URL of the web page that the link points to, either within your web site or to a page outside the site. If outside the site, make sure you precede it with **http://**; if not, the link is created to a non-existent page within your site.

■ **Image**   You can upload an image to go with the link blurb.

■ **Abstract**   This is the actual blurb, the text that appears below the Name and Image. It can be as extensive as you wish and can include HTML tags.

■ **Label**   You can probably ignore the **Label**; nobody seems to know what this is or when it appears!

4. Click **Update**. This is what your link looks like when placed onto a section or product page:

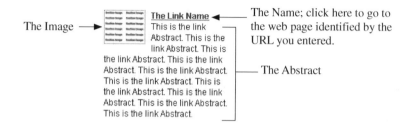

Creating a Product Accessory

A product accessory is a special kind of product. It's a product that is associated with another one and that appears on that product's page. A buyer can place an order for an accessory directly from the parent product's page—there's an Order button next to it. Accessories do not have their own pages; if you click on a link in Store Editor to an accessory, you'll end up in the accessory's Edit page.

Be careful with Rebuild (an import function described in Chapter 13). If you add an accessory to a product page and then Rebuild your database, the accessory is deleted from the database. Rebuild throws away the existing data and replaces it with the data from the new file.

*You will only see the **Accessory** button on the Editor toolbar if the Leaf setting on the product's Edit page is set to Yes. See the "Using Leaf" section for more information about Leaf.*

To create an accessory, simply navigate to the product page where you want to place it and click the **Accessory** button on the Editor toolbar. You'll see a normal product page, although not all fields are needed as it doesn't have its own product page. You can forget about the Label, Inset Image, and Icon Image, for instance, but make sure you have a Caption:

And while you could put a product name into the Contents field, this is pointless because the accessory doesn't have its own page to display any associated products, and the product you enter into Contents will not appear on the accessory's parent product page.

note   *The Accessory elements that are displayed on the product page are, by default, determined by the Leaf-contents-elements and Leaf-contents-format settings in the Config page, as discussed in Chapter 17.*

tip   *Another, safer way to associate products with each other is to enter information about the accessory in the parent product's Caption. You can then store this information in your database or spreadsheet so it is never removed. You can create links to other products within the Caption using normal HTML tags. URLs are created like this: http://www.yourdomain .com/productID.html.*

By the way, an accessory is not affected by the Contents choice in the Contents-elements list. When you choose Contents as one of the Contents-elements (the product elements) to be displayed in a section page, Merchant Solutions will include all the items listed in the product page's Contents text box on the section page, *except* accessories. That is, if the Contents text box lists other products that are *associated* with the product in question, the associated products will be listed on the section page under that product, but accessories will not.

Associating One Product with Another

You'll often find that two otherwise independent products are associated with each other. Your camping store may sell both groundsheets and tents separately, but sometimes people buy both at the same time. Your cooking store may sell bowls and spoons separately, but you may want to encourage people to buy both at once. Merchant Solutions allows you to associate products with each other, by inserting information from one product onto another product's page.

There are two ways you can do this:

■ Type a product code into the Contents box in another product's Edit page.

■ Use the **Copy** button on the Edit toolbar.

tip   *Don't remember the code of the product you want to associate? Either click Contents on the Edit toolbar and then copy the product code from the list, or refer to your original import spreadsheet or database.*

Using the Contents box is quick and easy. Simply open the product's Edit page, scroll down to the Contents box, and type the code of the product you want to associate with the current product. The products will be display in the order in which they appear in this Contents box.

The copy-and-paste method works like this:

1. Navigate to the product that you want to associate with another product.

2. Click the **Copy** button on the Editor toolbar. You'll see the Clipboard bar under the Editor toolbar.

3. Navigate to the product page with which you want to associate the product.

4. Click the link in the Clipboard bar. Merchant Solutions automatically inserts the copied product into the current page. (It has entered the code for the product into the current product's Edit page Contents field.)

5. The Layout bar automatically opens. In effect, Merchant Solutions has converted the current page to a section layout.

Modifying Product Page Layout

You've learned how to modify section/page layout in various ways. That's pretty much all you need to know about product-page layout, too, with a few minor differences:

■ Product pages can use Variables-page settings or Leaf settings, just as section pages can. But because Leaf is set to Yes by default, the product pages must use the Leaf settings.

■ The Contents-elements setting defines how associated and accessory products are treated. That is, if you have associated one product with another or created an accessory, Contents-elements defines which information for that ancillary product will be included on the product page.

In this chapter, you've seen how to modify page layout. In the following chapter, we'll look at how to modify design elements, such as text colors and buttons, but also how to add extra pages to the site to hold noncatalog information.

Chapter 17

Customizing the Site Design

Now that you've learned how to create pages and place elements onto those pages, let's look at how to define how the pages appear. What background colors do they use? What typeface for the various text elements? What color text? What color for text links?

In this chapter, you'll see how to define these things, and plenty more. Merchant Solutions provides a very quick way to change design elements—in literally seconds you can give your store a completely different appearance. But it also provides a hundred or more ways to tweak things very slightly, changing button designs, the text used on the buttons, the color of headings, and so on.

You'll also learn how to create additional, ancillary pages. Not category or product pages, these pages provide contact information, your privacy policy, and any other information you want to make available to visitors.

Modifying the Store's Graphic Design

Merchant Solutions provides tremendous flexibility in the design of your store: colors, fonts, image dimensions, and so on. There's so much flexibility, though, that it can take a long time to figure out exactly what everything does. We're not going to explain every design possibility, but we will look at the really quick ways you can change your site's design. Then we'll dabble a little in the more advanced features.

There are two ways to modify store design:

- The **Look** button—quickly select a design.
- The **Variables** button—modify scores of different design settings.

Quickly Selecting a Design

Merchant Solutions provides a way to select a different look for your site within seconds. The first appearance may not be exactly what you want, but you can then modify more design components using the Variables page, as we'll see next.

1. In Store Editor, click the **Look** button on the Editor toolbar. The Look bar opens:

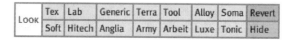

 tip   *You can ignore the Revert button—its usefulness is limited.*

2. Click the buttons to see the different designs. Each time you click, the store changes. When you have the design you want, click the **Hide** button to close the bar.

Clicking on a Look bar option changes several things:

■ The navbar button text size, color, and typeface

■ The navbar button color and design

■ The navbar background color

■ The content area background color

■ Heading text sizes, color, and typeface

■ Text color

These settings do not change layout; everything on the page remains in the same position. They only change design.

Modifying the Navbar Buttons

The buttons you see on the left side of your Store Editor when you first enter are the *navbar buttons*. The navbar is already configured for you—Merchant Solutions chose the buttons that will appear and the positions in which they will be placed. However, you can modify these in a number of ways, as we'll see right now.

Switching to a Horizontal Button Bar

You *may* wish to switch your navbar, removing the left-side navbar with a slim button bar at the top of the page . . . *may*, because this simply isn't appropriate for most stores. If you have a lot of buttons, they're not going to fit properly on a horizontal bar at the top—they will run off-page, to the right of the store, and make the store pages too wide. Try it and see if it looks good for your site:

1. In Store Editor, click the **Variables** button.

2. Find the **Page-format** line.

*In very long pages, in particular in this Variables page, use your browser's Search function to find the line you are looking for. It's much quicker than just scrolling down the page trying to pick it out! In Internet Explorer, select **Edit | Find**.*

3. Select **Top-buttons** from the drop-down list box.

4. Click the **Update** button at the top or bottom of the page. You'll be returned to the page where you were before, where you can see the new navbar position.

Adding, Removing, and Moving Buttons

Here are the buttons available for placement on the navbar:

- **Contents**   The Contents buttons are the buttons that point to pages that are children of your Home page. By default they are in Position #1, at the top of the list.

- **Download**   Don't use this button; it is left over from the old Yahoo! Store and not used in Merchant Solutions.

- **Email**   When a shopper clicks the Email button, his e-mail program opens with the Compose window, with your store's e-mail address in the To: field. (This is the Email field in the Variables page.)

- **Empty**   This is not a button, rather an empty space, such as the empty space that appears by default between the upper and lower buttons in the navbar.

- **Help**   This displays a generic Help page at http://stores.yahoo.com/help.html; it's not very useful, so you'll probably want to omit this button.

- **Home**   This takes the shopper back to your Home page.

- **Index**   This displays the store's Index page.

- **Info**   This is the store's Information page.

- **Mall**   This is the Y! Shopping button. Clicking this takes the shopper away from your store, to the Yahoo! Shopping Home page (http://shopping.yahoo.com/).

- **Next**   Clicking this takes the shopper to the next product in sequence.

- **Privacypolicy**   Clicking this opens your store's Privacy Policy page.

- **Register**   This allows someone to log into an existing customer account or register as a new customer.

- **Request**   Clicking this displays a generic page where a customer can request a catalog; this information is then e-mailed to the customer, using the Automatic Catalog Request Processing Email address in the Store Manager's Fax/Email page.

- **Search**   Clicking this opens your store's Search page.

- **Show-order**   When the shopper clicks this button, the items placed in the shopping cart are shown.

- **Up**   Clicking this takes the shopper to the parent page—if in a product page, up to the section page; if in a section page, up to the parent section or Home page.

Here's how you can control which buttons are placed onto the Home page's navbar, and in which position they appear:

1. In Store Editor, navigate to the Home page and then click the **Edit** button.

2. Scroll down to the **Buttons** line and click the **Change** button. You'll see the table shown in Figure 17-1.

3. To remove a button, delete the number next to the button (don't use 0, as this sometimes confuses Merchant Solutions).

4. To select the buttons you want and place them into the desired order, type numbers into the boxes; 1 for the first button, 2 for the second, and so on.

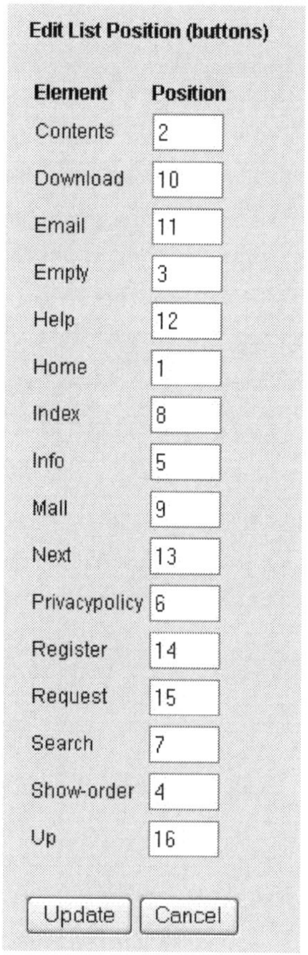

Edit List Position (buttons)

Element	Position
Contents	2
Download	10
Email	11
Empty	3
Help	12
Home	1
Index	8
Info	5
Mall	9
Next	13
Privacypolicy	6
Register	14
Request	15
Search	7
Show-order	4
Up	16

Update   Cancel

FIGURE 17-1   The table used for modifying the Home page's button positions

5. To insert a button, type a number into the button's text box; when you click the **Update** button, all the numbers will be reordered, leaving the inserted button in the correct position.

6. Click the **Update** button.

7. In the Edit page that appears, click the **Update** button.

How about the navbar used on pages other than the Home page? These are controlled by the Variables page. Click the **Variables** button on the Editor toolbar and then click the **Change** button on the **Nav-buttons** line.

Changing the Order of the Contents Buttons

Yahoo! uses the term *contents buttons* to refer to the buttons at the top of your navbar that point to section/category pages. How do you shuffle the order of these around? They are controlled by the Contents field in the Home page's Edit page; changing order here modifies the Contents button order not only in the Home page, but in every page in the store.

 note *Can't find the Contents field in the Edit page? You've probably got the Advanced Editor turned off. Exit the Edit page; if only one Editor toolbar is visible, Advanced mode is turned off. Click the little red triangle at the right end of the bar to turn it on. Better still, make sure it's turned on by default. Click the **Controls** button on the Advanced bar, select **Advanced** in the Default Editor Mode drop-down, and click **Update**.*

Navigate to the Home page and click the **Edit** button on the Editor toolbar. Find the **Contents** field and move the section/category names into the sequence in which you want them to appear in the navbar.

Changing Button Designs

If you don't wish to provide button images, there are still a number of other ways in which you can modify the look of the navbar buttons. Click the **Variables** button in Store Editor and look for these lines:

- Button-color
- Button-text-color
- Button-font
- Button-font-size
- Button-padding
- Button-edge-width
- Button-edge-color
- Home-button-color
- Home-button-text-color

■ Home-button-font

■ Home-button-font-size

note   *The Home-button variables only affect the navbar buttons if you use the horizontal navbar, set by choosing Top-buttons in the Page-format drop-down list box. If you don't use the Top-buttons, these settings modify the site Title (the Title is set at the top of the Variables page).*

As suggested by the button names, you can change the color of the button face, the text on the button, and the edge of the button. You can change the text size and typeface. You can modify the space between the text and the edge of a button (padding), and the space between buttons themselves (edge-width). You can also control the Home-button design separately from all the other buttons.

One element is very significant. Button-edge-color is a very misleading term; you can use this setting to define the color of the navbar on which the buttons sit.

Changing Button Labels and Using Images

You can change button names in a variety of ways, by changing text labels in some cases (some buttons can't be changed) or by providing button images.

■ **Contents buttons**   The contents buttons—the ones that point to the section/category pages—are already named for you, using the section/category names you create. You can change these by importing products into Category Manager with new section/category names in the *path* field of your data files, or by going into a section page and changing the Name field.

note   *If you set the Variables **Button-style** to **Icon**, any button for which you do not provide an icon will be a plain text button with no outline around the text.*

■ **Info, Privacy Policy, Request Catalog, Show Order buttons**   You can change the text used in these buttons. Click the **Variables** button on the Editor toolbar and search for the **info-text, privacy-policy-text, request-text,** and **show-order-text** lines. Enter the text you want to use and click **Update**.

■ **All buttons**   You can provide an image to be used for all your buttons. Click the **Variables** button on the Editor toolbar and search for the **Button Properties** section. Select a **Button-style** of **Icon** and upload the buttons using the **Upload** buttons. If you have provided Icon images for your section/category pages, they will be used as navbar buttons, too.

Changing the Function of the Y! Shopping Button

By default, your navbar contains a Y! Shopping button. This leads to the Yahoo! Shopping home page (http://shopping.yahoo.com/), so you'll probably want to remove it. The last thing you want is for visitors to your site to be distracted by this prominent button and then leave your site.

You can remove the button as explained earlier, of course, but you can also modify this button to link to any page you want inside or outside the site. Click **Variables** on the Editor toolbar and search for the **Mall-Image** line. Click the **Upload** button to upload a replacement image. On the line below, **Mall-url**, enter the URL of the page you want the button to link to.

Adding More Buttons

You can add more navbar buttons if you wish, pointing to pages within your site or outside.

1. Navigate to the Home page.

2. Click the **Links** button in the Editor toolbar.

 note *Using this method on the Home page adds a button with the link to the navbar; using this method in a section page adds a blurb with the link to the page itself.*

3. Type a link name; the text that will appear on the button.

4. Type the URL the link points to, either within your web site or to a page outside the site. If outside the site, make sure you precede it with **http://**; if not, the link is created to a non-existent page within your site.

5. If you prefer, you can upload an image file to be used as the button. (You'll also have to change **Button-style** in the Variables page to **Icon**.)

6. You can ignore the **Abstract** and **Label** fields if you only plan to use this link as a navbar button; the Abstract field is not used when creating a button, although it is used when creating a link in a section or product page. As for the Label field, it's probably never used under any circumstances!

7. Click **Update**.

In general, when you create a link on the Home page, it only appears on the navbar. However, there's one condition in which it also appears on the Home page itself: when you have the Contents option selected as one of the page elements that will be displayed (this setting is on the Home page's Edit page).

A link is an element that can be used in two places, on the navbar or on a section or product page. See Chapter 16 for more information about placing a "link blurb" onto a section or product page.

Using the Design Variables Page

Once you've picked a basic design, you can now modify the slightest detail. The Variables page offers almost 100 settings providing tremendous flexibility, from text and link colors to button sizes and fonts, from the currency symbol to the Sales Price label. Take a look for yourself; these settings are explained next. (In some cases, we've combined settings for the sake of brevity; for instance, we haven't described every setting related to buttons.)

- ■ **Title**   The store's name, which, by default, appears at the top of each page. When you create your Merchant Solutions account, your account name is placed here but you can change it. This text is not used if you are using a Name-image image (explained a bit later). The size of the Title is controlled by Banner-font-size, the color by Home-button-color, and the typeface by Home-button-font.

- ■ **Email**   The store's default e-mail address, used on the store Info page, and, if you use the Email button on the navbar, it is the address used when visitors to your site e-mail you.

- ■ **Background**   You can modify your pages' background color and define a background image if you wish.

- ■ **Text-color**   The color of the "body" text used in your pages.

- ■ **Link**   You can change the color of the links on the page, as well as the color of the links when they are clicked.

- ■ **Buttons**   Various settings let you change what the buttons in the navbar look like; the button text's font, font size, and color; the space around the text within the buttons; and the space between buttons.

- ■ **Buttons-edge-color**   This is actually the navbar background color, the color of the background under the buttons.

- ■ **Home-button-color**   The color of the Home button, *if* you set Page-format (explained further down in this list) to Top-buttons.

- ■ **Home-button-text-color**   The color of the Home button, *if* you set Page-format to Top-buttons; also modifies the color of the Title text.

- ■ **Home-button-font**   The typeface used on the Home button, *if* you set Page-format to Top-buttons; also modifies the typeface used for the Title text.

- ■ **Home-button-font-size**   The font size of the Home button, *if* you set Page-format to Top-buttons.

- ■ **Display-font**   The font size and typeface used in Title text.

- ■ **Text-font**   The font size and typeface used in body text.

- ■ **Labels**   The color, typeface, and font size of the text used for the product Label text when displayed as a "special" placed on the Home page.

- ■ **Banner-font-size**   The size of the text used for the store's name at the top of the site's pages (from the Title field).

- ■ **Emphasis-color**   The color used for emphasis text, in particular the Sale Price text.

- ■ **Thumb-height / -width**   These define the size of the section or product Icon image displayed on the section or product page.

- **Inset-height / -width** These define the size of the section or product Inset image displayed on the section or product page.

- **Item-height / -width** These define the size of the section or product Image displayed on the section or product page.

- **Page-format** The navbar format defines whether the buttons are on the side or top of the page.

- **Page-width** If using Side-buttons, this determines the width of the store pages; that is, how far the contents of a page will spread to the right. (If using Top-buttons, Page-width is ignored.)

- **Name-image** An image used in place of the Title text on interior pages (in the Home page you must ensure that Name is selected as one of the displayed Page-elements).

- **Head-elements** This defines which section-head elements will be displayed at the top of the section page. Select **Image** to include the section Image, and select **Display-text-title** to include the section Name (the Image is placed above the Name if both are selected). This has no effect on the Inset image, by the way, which displays regardless of this setting. See Chapter 16.

- **Head-style** Defines the placement of the section Name, Image, and Inset image at the top of the section page. You can set these to Left, Center, or Right.

- **Columns** The number of columns used to display product information.

- **Column-width** This modifies how columns of product data are formatted on section pages. It actually doesn't set column width. That's defined by the width of the product Label—above a certain minimum width, the wider the label, the wider the column. This Column-width setting, though, defines whether the text below the label conforms to the minimum column width (Fixed) or extends to the width set by the Label (Variable).

- **Row-pad** The vertical space between products listed in a section page.

- **Contents-elements** Defines which product elements—the Name, Abstract, Caption, etc.—are displayed for each product that is included in a section page. See Chapter 16.

- **Contents-format** Defines how the product elements are laid onto the section page.

- **Bullet-image** You can display a bullet instead of an image for each product on the section page (using Content-elements). It's a little square bullet or you can upload an image here.

- **Button-style** Defines what the buttons on the navbar look like: Text (just the text, no button image behind it); Solid and Incised ("3D" buttons, which look pretty much the same); and Icon. If you select Icon, button images that you have uploaded will be used in place of the text navbar buttons. If you've uploaded Icon images in section/category pages, those are used on the navbar as well.

- **Nav-buttons** These specify the buttons that are included on the pages, as well as their positions. This setting affects all pages except the Home page, which is controlled in the Home page's own Edit page.

■ **Button Image Uploads**　Set the Button-style to Icon, then upload button images for the Up, Next, Show Order, Home, Info, Privacy Policy, Help, Search, Index, Download, Register, Request, Email, and Mall buttons.

■ **Info-text**　The text used on the Info button (which leads to the Information page) if Button-style is not set to Icon. You may want to change it to *Information* or *About Us.*

■ **Privacy-policy text**　The text used on the Privacy Policy button if Button-style is not set to Icon.

■ **Request-text**　The text used on the Request button if Button-style is not set to Icon. (This button leads to a generic request-a-catalog page.)

■ **Mall-image/Mall-url**　You can create a new button, totally replacing the default Y! Shopping button; upload an image and specify a URL.

■ **Keywords**　Keywords that will be placed into a keywords meta tag at the top of every page in the site (<meta name="keywords" content="*keywords*">), read by some search engines to help them index pages. (Actually, this tag is not particularly important anymore, and using the same tag for all pages isn't ideal, anyway.)

■ **Head-tags**　HTML tags that will be placed at the top of the page. For advanced users, this field might be used to create the <meta name="description"> tag, for instance. You could also use it to place a banner across the top of the store.

■ **Final-text**　Another block of text into which you can add HTML. By default, it appears in all section and product pages, and can be added to the Home page if selected in the Page-elements (in the Home page's Edit page) field.

tip　*What if you want to use Final-text on the Home page but not on the section and product pages? You can remove it from section and product pages by overriding the variable (Chapter 16) for each page. That can be very laborious. A simpler way is to not use Final-text! Simply put the text you want on the Home page into another field, such as Intro-text.*

■ **Address-phone**　A block of text that can be placed onto the Home page using the Page-elements setting in the Home page's Edit page. You can use HTML tags.

■ **Price-style**　How Sale-price will be displayed. **Quiet** (prices in normal text, on product pages only); **Normal** (prices are displayed in bold); **Big** (prices are rendered into images). Sale-price is always displayed using Emphasis-color, one of the earlier settings.

■ **Regular-/Sales-price-text**　You can define the text that appears before the prices on your pages. For instance, rather than *Sales price:* you might use *Our price!:*

■ **Order-style**　Defines how product order information is laid out:

Wrist weights, 4 lb. Pair, adjustable 29073-04-00　Regular price: $22.95　Sale price: **$21.00**　Color:

[Red ▼] Size: [Small ▼] [Order]

Normal

Wrist weights, 4 lb. Pair, adjustable

29073-04-00   Regular price: $22.95   Sale price: $21.00   Color: [Red ▾]   Size: [Small ▾]

[Order]

Two-line

Wrist weights, 4 lb. Pair, adjustable

29073-04-00   Regular price: $22.95   Sale price: $21.00

Color: [Red ▾]

Size: [Small ▾]   [Order]

Multi-line

■ **Secure-basket**   This determines whether a secure server (an https server) is used while displaying items in the buyer's shopping cart. This isn't entirely necessary and even slows down page loading, but some buyers prefer to see this. The payment-transaction pages are always served from an https server.

■ **Compound-name**   If Yes is selected, accessory items placed into a shopping cart will show the parent product name, too.

■ **Order-text**   The text on the Order button.

■ **Show-order-text**   The text on the Show Order button.

■ **Families**   This is another "relic," related to the Family field you've seen elsewhere; you can ignore it.

■ **Cross-sell-text**   If you use the Cross-Sell Tool (see Chapter 21), this is the text used to introduce the complementary products.

■ **Currency**   The currency symbol you want to use in your store; by default, $.

■ **Thousands mark**   The character—by default a comma—used to divide groups of three digits in your prices; for instance, 5,000.

■ **Decimals mark**   The character—by default a period—used to denote the decimal place in a number, such as 15.56.

■ **Quantity-text**   The character used to separate a quantity and price when using quantity pricing, by default a / symbol (as in 4/$20). See Chapter 13 for information on setting up quantity pricing.

■ **Minimum-order**   This is the minimum order, in dollars. Set this to 50, for instance, and the store won't let the buyer check out if the total charge, before shipping, is less than $50.

tip   *Remember, you can override settings on particular pages. For instance, if you sell mainly tangible products but have one downloadable product, you could set that one product to use a No setting in Need-ship. Or if all products but one are immediately available, you can set the Availability text for a particular product. See Chapter 19 for more information.*

- **Minimum-quantity**   Set to 1 by default, but this allows you to automatically enter a quantity into the shopping cart. Set it to 10, for instance, and when the buyer clicks the Order button, the Quantity field in the shopping cart will show 10.
- **Availability**   Text that appears above the order information on a product page, letting buyers know that the product can't ship immediately.
- **Need-ship**   If set to No, the product can be purchased without a shipping address. If selling downloadable products or subscriptions, for instance, you could set this to No.
- **Need-bill**   If set to No, the product does not require a billing address.
- **Need-payment**   If set to No, the product does not require payment; it's a free product.
- **Personalization-charge**   This is the charge for product personalization, using the Monogram and Inscription features (see Chapter 13).
- **Ypath/Shopping-url**   These are "relics" of earlier days; you can ignore them.
- **Publish-timestamp**   This is a UNIX code indicating when the store was last published. It's unintelligible to ordinary people, and you can ignore it.

 *It's possible to override variables for one particular section page. Open the page, enter the Edit page, and click **Override Variable**. Remember that if you delete a product or section, you lose the settings, including overridden variables! And that means that if you import products and do a Rebuild (see Chapter 13), you are going to lose all your overridden variables because Rebuild deletes items and then re-creates them. So, if you do override variables, make sure you always do an Add import.*

Adding Ancillary Pages

Merchant Solutions has a number of ancillary pages, of which two are required—Yahoo! will not allow you to open for business without creating an Info page and a Privacy Policy page.

The Info page is intended to provide basic store information to customers. You can put anything you want here, but Yahoo! does demand certain information: your street address and phone number, an e-mail address at which you can be contacted with questions about your store and products, your shipping rates and methods, and refund and return policies.

You must have this information, but you may want to add other things, too. Consider adding information that builds credibility—memberships in trade associations, Better Business Bureau, and so on—and other contact methods, such as Instant Messaging, fax, and so on.

 Remember, you can change the text on the navbar's Info button—perhaps to Store Info or Information—in the Variables page; look for the Info-text field.

To edit the Info page, open the page—click the Info button on the navbar—then click **Edit** on the Editor toolbar. You can upload an image (which appears at the top right) and enter text into three text fields. You can, of course, enter HTML into these fields.

There's one more field that is automatically dropped onto the page. The text in the Variable page's Email text box is placed onto the page immediately after the Info page's Address-phone field and before the Info field. If you don't want this e-mail address appearing here—perhaps you have built a table of contact information that you are placing into one of the other fields—override it using the **Override Variable** button at the top of the Edit page (see Chapter 16).

Yahoo! demands that all stores must contain a Privacy Policy page, which should "inform customers what personal information is collected and how it is used." In fact, the Privacy page contains a note about Yahoo!'s privacy policy, which you are not allowed to modify and cannot remove. It's popular these days for sites to post long, complicated privacy policies. Yahoo!'s is almost 1,400 words long. There's no reason a privacy policy can't be short and sweet, though, and in any case, you're already covered by Yahoo!'s policy. These things are good to include:

- We collect information we need to process a purchase, to ship your products, and to make contact with you if there is a problem with the order.

- We don't rent, sell, or share your private information, except where necessary to process and ship your order.

- We limit access to your information only to trusted employees who need the information in order to process and ship your order.

To edit the Privacy page, enter the page and click the Edit button. The only field you can enter here is the Info text. However, you can use HTML tags in this text to format the text any way you wish, and even to add images.

Creating a Feedback or Catalog-request Form

There's a very simple way to create a feedback form. Yahoo! calls this form a *catalog-request form*, but you really can use it for various purposes: feedback, information request, subscribing to a newsletter, and so on.

 tip *You can also create links from any of your pages to the Request page. Here's how to find the URL you have to use. In Store Editor, look in the browser's Address bar for the yhst number on any page. Then add that number to the end of* http://order.store.yahoo.com/cgi-bin/ wg-request-catalog?. *For instance, if the yhst number is yhst-35484225783552, then the URL is* http://order.store.yahoo.com/cgi-bin/wg-request-catalog?yhst-35484225783552.

Yahoo! Merchant Solutions creates this form automatically; whether you customize it and use it or not, it's always there. You can get to it by turning on the Request navbar button. (In the Home page's Edit page and in the Variables page, open the Buttons table and add the Request item.) You can also create a link to it from any page by entering it into a text field in an Edit page, or by creating a Link element (see Chapter 16).

You can also customize the form. Most of this isn't done in Store Editor, though; all but the first item are handled through Store Manager.

1. Change the text on the button pointing to the form; in the Variables page, use **Request-image** or **Request-text**.

2. To set the e-mail address to which the message is sent, click the <u>Fax/Email</u> link and enter the information into the **Automatic Catalog Request Processing Email to** field.

3. Set the text that appears in the browser's title bar while the form is displayed in the **Catalog Request Form Title** field of the Customize Your Order Form page; click the <u>Order Form</u> link.

4. Add extra fields to the form; click the <u>Edit Extra Fields</u> link in the same page.

5. Add a text message at the top of the page; use the **Message** field.

6. Add check boxes to the form to let people subscribe to your newsletter, to request a paper catalog, to request a call from a sales person, and so on; use the **Request Items** field.

Creating More Pages

You can create more pages, if you wish, for a variety of purposes. For instance, A2BScooters .com—which we looked at in several earlier chapters—created, in addition to the section pages and normal ancillary pages, several more pages: Our Price Guarantee, Free Shipping, Link to Us, Scooter Laws, Safety and Scooters, and About A2B (see Figure 12-1).

How did they do this? Simple; they created new sections. A section page doesn't *have* to contain products, it can contain whatever content you want. Name the section with the text you want to appear in the navbar, and then put whatever text or HTML content you want onto the page, in the section's Caption text box.

You can also create however many layers of subsections; a button on the navbar may lead to a *More Information* page, for instance, which can then link to as many subsection pages as you wish.

Publishing Your Work

Remember that before your work appears in your store, you must publish it. All the product information you've entered, the section pages you've created, the design settings you've made . . . none of this is "live" until you publish it. Simply return to the Home page and click the **Publish** button on the Editor toolbar.

Of course, your store is not ready to go yet. You still have to define how the "backend" works—how the transaction processing functions. In the following chapter, you'll learn how to set up a credit-card merchant account, order forms, and notification e-mail messages.

Chapter 18

Defining Payment Methods and Your Checkout Process

You've finished your store, at least the piece that's visible to the buyer. Now there's plenty more work to do. The first thing you may want to do is get started on setting up a credit-card merchant account, so you can process credit-card orders. In fact, Yahoo! won't allow you to open your store until you have a merchant account working. In this chapter, you'll learn what a merchant account actually does and how to get one. You'll also learn how to set up payment processing in Merchant Solutions and configure the credit-card antifraud tools. Fraud is a huge problem for many businesses, so it's important to understand what you can do to minimize it.

In addition, you'll see how to set up various order-form options, and how to ensure you receive order notifications so that you know when you have an order waiting to be processed.

Setting Up a Credit-card Merchant Account

Before you can open a Merchant Solutions store, you *must* have a credit-card merchant account; Yahoo! won't allow you to open until you do. You cannot set up the merchant account until, in theory, you are ready for business. You must be "ready for business with clear product and pricing information available for viewing." We recommend you set up the account as soon as possible, as it can take a little while to get sorted out. So, as soon as your store appears to the outside world to be ready, you should begin the process.

Credit-card Transactions Explained

Here's how a credit-card transaction works, as you can see in Figure 18-1. When someone purchases something with a credit card online, that information is sent to a *payment gateway*. The gateway sends the information on to one of the *credit-card networks*. There is just a handful of different networks—when your card is swiped at a store, the credit-card swipe terminal sends the information on to one of these networks. In effect, the payment gateway in an online transaction takes the place of the swipe terminal in a brick-and-mortar store transaction.

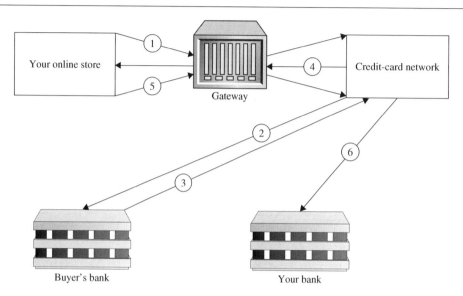

1. Your store sends a message to the credit-card gateway, which passes it on to the credit-card network.
2. The network checks with the customer's bank to see if it will cover the transaction.
3. The bank sends a message back, approving the transaction.
4. The network sends a message back to your store, letting it know it can complete the transaction.
5. The store lets the network know the transaction has been completed.
6. The network begins the process of transferring money to your account.

FIGURE 18-1   How credit-card transactions are processed

Your merchant account identifies you as the merchant. The buyer's credit-card number, of course, identifies the buyer. The credit-card network sends the information to the appropriate credit-card company, which checks the credit card to see if it's valid and has sufficient funds for the purchase. If everything's okay, it authorizes the transaction, holding the funds temporarily. Later, usually at the end of the day, the transaction has to be settled; at that point, the credit-card company takes the money from the credit card and transfers it to your bank account (or, at least, begins the process; it actually takes a day or two—perhaps as many as five days—before the money appears in your account).

So, you can see that a merchant account is required to identify you and tell the credit-card companies where to put the money.

Already Got a Merchant Account?

If you're setting up an existing business online, you may already have a credit-card merchant account. You *may* be able to use it with your store, depending on a couple of things: the network compatibility and the account policies.

If you're setting up an existing account to work with Yahoo! Merchant Services, the bank or company that provides the merchant account must now provide MID (merchant ID) and TID (terminal ID) numbers. You'll have to provide the company with information about Merchant Solutions: the product name and ID, and the vendor name and ID. (To find this information, click **Pay Methods** *in Store Manager and then click the* Set up processing through FDMS *link; you'll find the information in the Setup page.)*

Merchant accounts are set up to work with a particular credit-card network, of which there are several. Yahoo! Merchant Solutions sends transactions out over a First Data Corp. network, known as *FDMS Nashville.* If your current merchant account sends information over a different network, you *will not* be able to use it with Merchant Solutions—you'll have to apply for another one.

However, even if your merchant account *does* work with FDMS Nashville, you may not be able to use it. Some accounts are restricted to specific types of transactions. If your merchant account only allows "swipe" or credit-card-present transactions, you are not supposed to carry out transactions in which you do not see the credit card. Check with the bank or company that set up your merchant account.

Merchant Account Fees

There are all sorts of fees associated with merchant accounts. Compare carefully and make sure you are absolutely clear about exactly which fees are going to be charged.

- **Setup Fee**   The fee charged for the privilege of setting up an account.

- **Discount Rate**   The percentage fee that you will be charged for a transaction; if the rate is 2.29% and the transaction (including shipping and handling) totals $100, you are charged $2.29. The discount rate varies depending on the card type used. (The rate typically quoted is for Visa and MasterCard, but American Express, Discover, and others have different rates.)

- **Termination Fee**   Watch for this one! Most merchant accounts charge a fee— sometimes hundreds of dollars—to close the account.

- **Transaction Fee**   A fixed sum charged, in addition to the discount rate, for each transaction. Usually around 15 to 25 cents, but again, it varies depending on the card used.

- **Monthly Fee**   Sometimes called a statement fee or service fee. You'll pay this every month, regardless of the number of transactions.

- **Monthly Minimum**   The minimum discount-rate fee you'll pay; if your transaction discount rates don't total this or more, you'll still pay the minimum.

- **Chargeback Fee**   The fee you'll pay if a transaction is charged back to you; if someone claims they never received the product, for instance, or that the card was used fraudulently, your account is charged for the transaction *and* the chargeback fee.

- **Online Access Fee**   There may be a fee to use a merchant account's online tools.

■ **Equipment Lease or Purchase**   Some unscrupulous companies charge for "equipment," claiming that they are providing the equipment that transmits the transaction to the credit-card network (the payment gateway). These charges can sometimes amount to thousands of dollars (although this practice is probably dying out).

■ **Other Stuff!**   Ask for a full schedule of fees, so you know what else you may be charged for—there are different rates for different types of transactions, for instance— sales, credits, authorizations, and so on. Some companies will provide a list of five different fees and claim that's the full list; it isn't. A full schedule includes many more fees, but some companies (such as 1st American, mentioned in the next table) won't show you the list until *after* you apply.

warning   *Merchant account rates vary tremendously. If you are a long-term brick-and-mortar merchant and have never sold online, you may be used to paying way too much for your merchant accounts. E-commerce has led to great price competition, so it's now possible to get relatively cheap merchant accounts. Whichever company you are already using or plan to use, compare pricing!*

The following table shows examples of the two companies recommended by Yahoo!. Other companies may be comparable, or may have significantly higher fees.

Fee	Paymentech	1st American Option 1	1st American Option 2
Setup Fee	$0	$0	$95
Termination Fee	$0	$0	$0
Discount Rate (MasterCard)	2.69%	2.29%	2.29%
Transaction Fee (MasterCard)	20 cents	25 cents	25 cents
Monthly Statement Fee	$22.95	$19.95	$9
Monthly Minimum	$15	$20	$20
Chargeback Fee	$15	$25	$25

Setting Up Credit-card Transactions

Yahoo! works primarily with a merchant account company called Paymentech. In fact, Paymentech manages the payment gateway (discussed earlier) and sets up merchant accounts. However, if you are rejected by Paymentech, you may be able to set up an account through another company. Yahoo! suggests you try 1st American Card Service (http://www.1stamericancardservice.com/), or that you go to the First Data web site and try the list of companies provided (http://www.fdms .com/section.asp?m=25&s=117). You may also want to check another service, even if Paymentech *doesn't* turn you down, to see if you can get a better deal. Click the Pay Methods link in the Order Settings column in Store Manager to apply for an account.

 note *When you set up an account, it will be automatically able to handle MasterCard and Visa transactions. Other cards are optional; if you want to accept American Express and Discover, for instance, make sure you ask for these. Yahoo! Merchant Solutions can also accept Carte Blanche, Diners, Optima, and JCB.*

Once you've set up a merchant account, you have to enter the information into Store Manager, so it knows what information to send to the credit-card network with every transaction.

1. In Store Manager, click the Pay Methods link.

2. In the Merchant Account Signup and Setup area of the Payment Methods page, click the Set up processing through FDMS link.

3. Very carefully enter the information you have been provided into the Setup Merchant Account Through First Data page (see Figure 18-1), and click the check boxes next to the credit-card types. Do not check any credit card that you cannot accept; if you do, when Merchant Solutions tests the connection it will fail.

4. Click the **Setup** button, and Merchant Solutions will access the credit-card network to test the information you've entered.

Configuring Credit-card Verification (Risk) Tools

Credit-card fraud is an unfortunate—and at times significant—cost of doing business. Fraud in online transactions is around 12 times higher than for in-store purchases, and over three times higher than mail-order and phone sales; in total, a little over 1% of all dollars charged are done so fraudulently.

 tip *Using these fraud-reduction tools does not guarantee that you won't be a victim of fraud! It also doesn't indemnify you in any way. If you ship a fraudulently purchased product, you still end up losing (the product and the chargeback fee from the credit-card company), however careful you are.*

For some businesses, in fact, fraud is *very* significant; for others, it's a minor cost. If a credit card is used fraudulently and you ship the product, you lose three ways. The owner of the credit card will eventually complain to the credit-card company, which investigates. And if you can't prove the product was delivered to the card owner, they'll refund the money. You'll pay back the purchase price, you'll pay back the shipping cost, *and* you'll pay a *chargeback fee*, probably $20–$30. (The credit-card companies love to advertise that if someone uses your card fraudulently, they'll cover your losses. Actually, it's the merchants who cover your losses!) What's worse, if a merchant's chargeback rates are consistently high, they can be fined or even lose their credit-card merchant account altogether.

One risk tool, IP Blocking, allows you to stop people using certain IP (Internet Protocol) numbers from placing orders at your store. (Every computer connected to the Internet at any moment has a unique IP number identifying the computer.) At this stage, you are unlikely to know what numbers to block, so we're going to ignore it for the moment. For more information, see Chapter 20.

So it's in your interest to reduce fraudulent transactions as much as possible. Merchant Solutions provides two credit-card tools to help you do that:

- **AVS: Address Verification System**   AVS compares the billing address with the address on file at the credit-card company.

- **CVV: Card Verification Value**   The CVV is a three-digit number on the back of a Visa or MasterCard credit card, or a four-digit number on the front of an American Express card. As it's not part of the actual credit-card number and so never appears on transaction paperwork or in transaction databases, it's harder to steal. The theory is that if someone can provide the CVV number, there's a good chance that he has the actual card in his possession.

Understanding Address Verification

AVS looks at the billing address a buyer enters into your order forms and compares it to the information on file. You can then decide what to do according to the response that is returned:

- Street address OK, ZIP code bad

- Street address bad, ZIP code OK

- Both street address and ZIP code bad

- System is unavailable (sometimes AVS isn't functioning)

- Verification information not available (the network is unable to access address information for some cards, in particular foreign cards and debit cards)

Unfortunately, AVS doesn't work for foreign transactions.

You can choose how to handle each of these responses:

- **Flag the transaction.** The order will appear as *Pending Review* so you will be able to confirm the transaction, perhaps by calling the buyer. In addition, the particular AVS response code will be displayed, so you know what the problem is.

- **Accept the transaction.** For instance, if the ZIP code is correct but the street address bad, you may want to accept the transaction without flagging it.

note *How much are your products worth? With very high-cost products, you'll probably be more careful about fraudulent transactions. Also, some products have very low fraud rates—books and classical music, for instance—while others have much higher rates (such as golf clubs).*

It's sometimes hard to decide how to handle these transactions; some merchants are so paranoid that they tighten down the fraud tools as far as they will go. But it's worth understanding that sometimes AVS will return bad responses in cases in which no fraud is involved. Perhaps someone has moved recently or mistyped something or mixed up cards with different billing addresses. Bad AVS does *not* always indicate fraud. For some businesses, simply rejecting all bad AVS responses will reduce sales more than it reduces fraud.

Understanding Card Verification Value

If you turn on CVV—and you probably should—the buyer will be prompted to enter a three- or four-digit code when using a Visa card, MasterCard, or American Express card. The CVV system then checks the number provided by the buyer against the number on file. There are three bad CVV responses:

- Code doesn't match
- CVV system not currently available
- CVV number not provided or not available for that card type

As with AVS, you get to choose how to handle each. You can flag or accept the transaction.

Selecting Risk Settings

Here, then, is how you go about selecting your risk settings:

1. In Store Manager, select the Risk Tools link.

2. In the Risk Settings page, click the Settings link.

3. In the Settings page, check the **Yes, enable Risk Tools** check box.

4. If you wish, you can set an **Order Minimum**. Leave it set to 0.00 to use AVS and CVV for all orders, or set it to a number and orders above that dollar value will use AVS and CVV.

5. Select the **AVS Rules**; for each AVS response, select whether you wish to Flag or Accept the transaction.

6. Select the **CVV Rules**; for each CVV response, select whether you wish to Flag or Accept the transaction.

7. We recommend that you leave the **Yes, make CVV required on checkout** check box checked; if you clear it, transactions will be processed even if the buyer doesn't enter the information.

8. Click the **Update** button.

Selecting Payment Methods: Credit Cards, PayPal, and More

Once you've set up your credit-card merchant account, you also need to make sure the payment method actually appears on the web site. This is done in the Payment Methods page.

There are other ways to accept payments, too: PayPal, purchase orders, COD, fax, e-mail, phone, and so on. We'll look at these in Chapter 20. However, note that all these methods—including PayPal—require human intervention. None are as convenient as credit cards, which is why most merchants prefer credit-card transactions.

 note   *PayPal is a very popular option these days for merchants. However, note that PayPal is not built into the Merchant Solutions store. You can set up a PayPal payment method but will then have to check your PayPal account manually to ensure that the payment has been received; that is, Merchant Solutions does not get an automated confirmation from PayPal.*

Most merchants will want to avoid some or all of these non-credit-card transactions. One method that has an extra advantage, however, is phone orders. If you prominently display a phone number on your web site, you may find that you actually don't get many phone calls but that the number of online credit-card orders increases. Making it clear that you're available, that a buyer can call and talk to someone, increases the "comfort level" and credibility of your store.

In order to specify which payment methods you want to use, click the <u>Pay Methods</u> link in Store Manager and scroll down the page. Simply click Yes next to each payment type you want to use—make sure you only select the credit cards that you have already set up in your credit-card merchant account. If you wish, you can type **PayPal** into the **Add Other** text box, then click **Add** and, in the screen that appears, click **Done** (don't make any changes in this screen). This adds PayPal to the list but as mentioned before, you should remember that this is a manual process. You will have to get the buyer to PayPal your payment before shipment.

When you have finished in this page, click **Update**.

Setting Up Your Order Forms

Now let's set up how your order forms function. Click the <u>Order Form</u> link on the Store Manager page (under the Order Settings column), and you'll see the Customize Your Order Form page. These are the options available to you:

- **Enable new checkout flow**   Leave **Enabled for all orders** selected. The new checkout flow was introduced years ago, but the old flow is still available for long-term merchants who wish to continue using it.

- **All forms use**   Select this whether buyers should enter their names into a single name field or into separate first and last name fields. The latter is generally the best choice.

 tip   *As you make changes, you can see the effect by clicking the **Preview Order Forms** button at the top or bottom of the page.*

- ■ **Currency**   Select the currency you are using.

- ■ **Cart Look**   This defines whether the shopping-cart pages look like the store you created using Store Editor, or whether they use very simple "generic" pages, which you may want to select if you are not using Store Editor to build your catalog pages. Click the Preview Order Forms button to see the difference.

- ■ **Checkout branding**   You can choose to put your domain name or a store logo at the top of the checkout pages.

- ■ **Privacy Policy URL**   The URL of a page containing your privacy policy, which will be displayed in the checkout pages. Leave this blank if you want to use the page created in Store Editor.

- ■ **Information Page URL**   The URL of a page containing your privacy policy. Leave this blank if you want to use the page created in Store Editor.

- ■ **Continue URL**   The URL of a page displayed when visitors click Continue Shopping. If you don't enter anything, the Continue Shopping link returns the shopper to the previous product.

- ■ **Final URL**   The page displayed when shoppers click Keep Shopping on the order-confirmation page. If you don't enter anything, your store's Home page is used.

- ■ **Customer Rating Enabled**   If this is turned on, Yahoo!'s customer-rating system is turned on so customers can rate their experience shopping with you.

- ■ **Email Comments To**   If you don't want the rating information sent to the e-mail address in the Yahoo! account associated with this store, enter the address you want to use here.

- ■ **Gift Wrap**   If you offer gift-wrapping services, select Yes.

- ■ **Price**   Enter the price for gift wrapping, and whether you charge per order or per item.

- ■ **Gift Message**   Select Yes if buyers will be able to enter a short gift message.

- ■ **Shipping Info Message**   A short message that goes at the top of the Shipping Address box on the checkout's Shipping Form. You can use HTML in this field if you wish.

- ■ **Edit Standard Fields**   Click this link to determine which fields should be included when you export XML data. (You must also select the **Export Form Fields Set to Display (Yes)** check box on the Field Length Limits page.) You can export data in various formats from Order Manager (see Chapter 20).

- ■ **Edit Extra Fields**   Click this link to add more fields to the shipping-information box. If selling very large products, for instance, you might add a comment box into which the buyer could add the best time for delivery.

- ■ **Billing Info Message/Edit Standard Fields/Edit Extra Fields**   These options work in the same way as for the Shipping options but appear on the Billing form.

- ■ **Disable Comments**   The Billing page contains a Comments box at the bottom, allowing buyers to enter special instructions. It's a good idea to leave this turned on, but you can turn it off if you wish.

■ **Order Confirmation Message**   This is the message that appears at the top of the order-confirmation page. You can enter HTML if you wish.

■ **Order Status Message**   The message at the top of the order-status page. This is a page that buyers can view after completing a transaction so that they can track their orders. This field can include HTML.

■ **Catalog Request Form Title**   This is *not* anything to do with the order form. It's the text that appears in the browser's title bar when a visitor is viewing the Catalog Request form, displayed by clicking the Request button on the navbar. (The Catalog Request is e-mailed to the address on the Fax/Email form.)

■ **Message**   The message that appears above the Catalog Request form; you can enter HTML here.

■ **Request Items**   For each line you enter into this box, you will get a check box that the buyer can select. For instance, you might have a check box to let people subscribe to your newsletter, one to request a paper catalog, another to request a call from a salesperson, and so on.

■ **Edit Extra Fields**   Click this link to add more fields to the form.

■ **Multiple Ship To Enable**   Turn this on if you want to allow buyers to ship products in a single order to different addresses.

■ **Field Length Limits**   Click this link if you want to change the text-entry limits on fields in the Shipping and Billing pages, if you want to use the Young America fulfillment company's (www.young-america.com) address format, or if you want to turn on the feature that allows you to specify which fields are included in an XML export file.

■ **Order Button**   This defines what happens when the buyer clicks on the Order button for a product that is already in the shopping cart.

■ **Enable Got Customer Email Collection Check Box**   This is used when you sign up for a *Campaigner* e-mail marketing account (provided by a company called *Got*). In Store Manager, click the Email Marketing link in the Promote column. Select **Yes** to add a check box to your checkout process, allowing people to choose to receive e-mails from you.

■ **Enable Webloyalty Thank-You Reward Banner On Confirmation Page**   Select this to turn on the Webloyalty system, which displays a banner on your order-confirmation page allowing buyers to opt to receive a "reward." (You can see a demo here: http://clientdemo.webloyalty.com/yahoo/.) The reward is some kind of free membership in a discount club for a limited time. There's no real benefit to the merchant to set this to Yes; you won't earn commissions on sales.

■ **Item Options Validation Current Setting**   If you have created all your product options properly, you shouldn't have to change this setting. We recommend you do not change this setting, as it opens your store up to security vulnerability, which could potentially be used to commit fraud against you (although admittedly it's very unlikely). This was added to Yahoo!'s store some time ago to plug a potential security hole in which someone could use options to submit an order at a much lower price than the real one.

Setting Up Notification and Feedback Messages

It's now time to define the Fax/Email addresses and settings. Click the <u>Fax/Email</u> link under the Order Settings column in Store Manager. You'll see the screen in Figure 18-2.

note *You don't need the credit-card number in the confirmation message. You'll learn how to process orders online in Chapter 20.*

This page lets you define how order notifications and catalog requests are sent to you. An order notification is information about a recent order, sent to you so that you know you have an order ready to process and ship. By default, it doesn't provide all the information—it doesn't include credit-card information *unless* you set up encryption, which most merchants do not do (as it can be a little complicated). A *catalog request* is information entered by a buyer into the Catalog Request page, although it makes more sense to think of this as a feedback form (see Chapter 17).

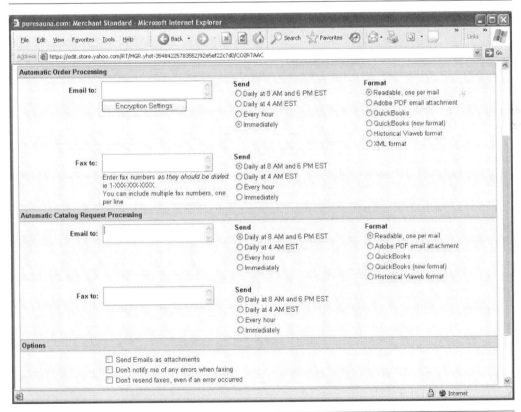

FIGURE 18-2 The Fax/Email page

In each case, the settings are very similar, with the exception of the Encryption Settings.

- **Email To** The e-mail address you want the order notification or feedback message sent to. You can send messages to multiple addresses, separating them with a comma and a space.

- **Encryption Settings** Click this if you want to set up encryption so that you can receive credit-card numbers in the e-mails. This is *not* necessary because you will process the orders online.

- **Send** Select the time at which you want the messages sent; many merchants want them sent immediately, but it's possible to have them sent at a particular time of day.

- **Format** Select the format in which you want to receive e-mailed information. You can choose just plain text, with each message in an individual e-mail. Or you can select another format—Adobe Acrobat PDF, two different QuickBooks formats, the old Viaweb format (Viaweb was the company that originally created the Merchant Solutions software), or XML. If you select one of these formats, you could choose to have the information sent periodically, in which case information will be grouped together.

- **Send Emails as attachments** Select this, and the plain text messages will be sent attached to your e-mail message, not displayed inside it. You'll have to open the message in another program to read it.

- **Don't notify me of any errors when faxing** Select this, and you won't see notifications when faxes can't get through. Notifications are displayed at the bottom of this page.

- **Don't resend faxes, even if an order occurred** Select this, and Merchant Solutions will not try again if faxes can't get through on the first attempt.

There's a little more configuration to do. In the next chapter, you'll learn how to configure shipping and taxes, and how to work with automated inventory tracking.

Chapter 19

Configuring Shipping, Taxes, and Inventory

So you've created a store. You have products, categories, and various information pages. You've set up your payment methods and your order forms. Finished? Not quite. You still have to set up various details: where you are willing to ship, what shipping methods and rates you will use, how you will handle sales tax, what will be in your confirmation e-mails, and how you will manage inventory.

Specifying Where You Ship—Foreign Orders

You need to define what countries you are willing to sell to, so that your customers see the correct address options when they check out. Where you are willing to ship to is dependent to a great degree on what kind of product you are selling. Is it very expensive to ship overseas? Will the product require large import duties when arriving in the country? Is it a product with a high fraud rate? When a buyer claims a credit-card transaction was fraudulent, you lose the price of the product and the cost of shipping, and also you must pay a chargeback fee. So, overseas shipments are even more expensive as a loss than domestic shipments. In addition, foreign orders have a much higher fraud rate, perhaps 2.5 times the domestic rates (although rates vary greatly in different areas around the world). Indeed, one study found that 10 percent of Internet merchants that used to ship overseas have *stopped* doing so because fraud losses outweighed the profits.

Still, many businesses do significant trade overseas; 10 or 25 percent of orders going outside the United States is by no means an unusual amount. Here's how to set your country choices:

1. In the Store Manager, click the <u>Foreign Orders</u> link.

2. In the Foreign Orders page, click the right option button to see these choices:

   ◾ **Default List of Countries**   The list of around 70 countries that appears by default. These are countries that Yahoo! says are low-fraud countries, and in general that's true. However, there may be some countries on the list that are relatively high-fraud countries—Egypt, for example, is on the list yet it has quite high rates according to at least one study.

   ◾ **US Only**   If you will only ship within the United States, select this.

   ◾ **All Countries Except Selected**   Select this check box to choose countries you *don't* want to ship to; this is useful if you want to ship to most locations with only a few exceptions.

   ◾ **Only Selected Countries**   Select this check box to choose countries you *do* want to ship to; this is convenient if you want to ship to a small selection of countries.

   ◾ **Complete List of Countries**   If you are willing to ship *anywhere*, select this.

3. Click the **Update** button.

Setting Up Shipping Methods and Rates

One of the most complicated things to deal with is shipping products to buyers. You need to define what methods will be used: what companies and what particular services from those companies, and how much you will charge. You will configure these settings through Shipping Manager. Click <u>Shipping Manager</u> in the Order Settings column of Store Manager.

Using UPS OnLine™ Tools

Yahoo! has integrated UPS OnLine Tools into Merchant Solutions, providing a very simple way to manage shipments if you choose to ship via that service. The tools help you print UPS labels, provide address validation, help buyers select a shipping method, and insert tracking numbers into confirmation messages.

note   *You can use the UPS OnLine Tools with any Merchant Solutions package. However, high-volume merchants who want to integrate with UPS WorldShip (which we don't cover here) must have the Merchant Solutions Professional package.*

Before you can use UPS OnLine Tools, you must have a UPS account; visit https://www.ups .com/myups/info/openacct to do so. Register with UPS by clicking the <u>Shipping Manager</u> link in the Order Settings column of Store Manager, and then on the Shipping Manager page, click the UPS Registration link.

When you complete the UPS registration, UPS options will automatically be integrated into Shipping Manager, as you'll see when you set up your shipping methods.

Creating Shipping Methods

Begin by creating the shipping methods you want to provide—downloadable, air, ground, Federal Express, UPS next day air, and so on. Click the Shipping Methods link in Shipping Manager, and then click the **Edit** button in the Ship Methods page; you'll see the page in Figure 19-1.

On this page you are simply telling Merchant Solutions what shipping methods you want to use. Don't worry about how much will be charged for each method; you'll deal with that next. Right now you are defining which methods will be presented to the buyer as a shipping choice.

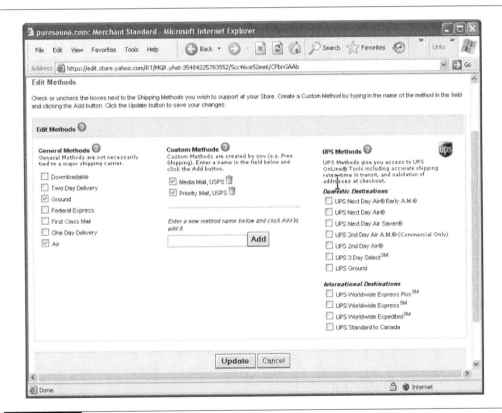

FIGURE 19-1   The Edit Methods page

The following are your choices:

- **General Methods**   These are nonspecific, predefined terms that will appear in the Choose Shipping Method drop-down list box during checkout. *Downloadable*, of course, refers to a product that will be downloaded and not shipped. If you feel the descriptions are not specific enough—you'd rather say *Fedex Ground* than *Ground*, for instance—or if they simply don't match what you want to use—*US Postal Service Media Mail*, for instance, or *Priority Mail*—you can create your own names under Custom Methods.

- **Custom Methods**   Type a term and click **Add** to add it to the list. It will appear on the page above the text box. (You can delete it by clicking the little trash can icon.)

- **UPS Methods**   If you signed up to use the UPS OnLine Tools, you'll see the list of UPS Methods. Simply check the ones you want to offer.

*The order in which the items are listed in the Ship Methods page is the order in which they appear in the Choose Shipping Method drop-down list box in the checkout pages. If you want to change the order, click the **Change Display Order** button.*

When you click **Update**, the methods you selected are added to the Ship Methods page.

Defining Shipping Rates and Creating Rules

Now that you've defined the shipping methods you want to use, you can specify how much the buyer will pay you for each method. This can be a little time-consuming because you have to add a number of rules. For instance, if you ship anywhere in the world, you'll want to include a variety of shipping methods to accommodate people in different regions around the world. But then you'll also want to have different shipping charges. You'll charge a Canadian who's selecting Global Priority Mail less, for instance, than someone in the United Kingdom, because your charge is less for Canada than for the UK. So, before you begin creating your shipping-rate rules in Merchant Solutions, you should spend some time figuring out which method can be used for each delivery area, and how much will be charged in each delivery area.

Merchants often make money on shipping charges—actually charging more than it really costs to package and ship the item—but there's a limit to how far you can take that. You don't want your shipping charges to be so much that they discourage the purchase!

When you're ready, here's how to set up the shipping-rate rules.

1. Return to Shipping Manager and click the <u>Shipping Rates</u> link.

2. In the ship rates page, click the **Add Rule** button.

3. Select **Anywhere** if the rule can be used in any location to which you ship, or select **Specific Location** if you want to specify where the rule applies, and then choose one of these options:

- Select **Inside** and choose one or more countries if you are specifying which countries the rule applies to. Then select, from the list, the country or countries to which the rule applies.

- Select **Outside** and then, from the list, choose **US United States** to specify that the rule applies to all shipments overseas (of course, we're assuming here that you're in the U.S., but you can specify any other configuration if you need to).

4. If you selected Inside the United States or Inside Canada, you can now specify *where* in the country the rule applies, either by selecting the states or provinces or by entering specific ZIP or Post codes. If you want the rule to apply to the entire country, select **Any State** or **Any Province**.

5. Click the **Next** button.

6. In the next screen, select the shipping method this rule will use. For instance, if setting up a rule for shipping via Priority Mail to Europe, you might select Global Priority Mail (assuming you have created this method in the Ship Methods process). See Figure 19-2.

7. Click the **Next** button.

8. In the next page, you'll select the type of calculation you want to use for this rule:

- **Flat Rate Charge** Merchant Solutions uses a flat rate—$5, $12, or whatever you specify—as the shipping charge. The charge can be per order, per pound, or per item.

- **Percentage Charge** A shipping charge based on a percentage of the order charge. If you say shipping is 10%, then on a $200 order the charge will be $20.

Step 2 of 5 : Add Rule - Select Method(s)

Selecting methods gives you the ability to apply a shipping charge to a particular shipping method or to all of your shipping methods. You can configure your Ship Rule to apply to all of your shipping methods or a specific method. When finished, click the Next button.

Select Method

When customer information matches:

Location - **Inside United States, Canada (Any State, Any Province)**

And Ship Method matches:

UPS Next Day Air® Early A.M.®

If you don't want this rule to apply to all methods, select the desired method for this rule. Otherwise you can leave it set to "Any Method."

Cancel   Previous   Next

FIGURE 19-2 Selecting the shipping method to be used for this rule

- **Rate Table**   This is a more complicated method in which you can define the charge based on the order value, the number of items in the order, and the shipping weight (*if* you provided shipping weights when entering your products into Catalog Manager; see Chapter 13).
- **UPS Real-Time Rates**   If you registered for the UPS OnLine Tools and specified a UPS method, you can have UPS calculate the rates for you.

9. Click the **Next** button.

Let's look at each of the shipping methods in turn.

Using a Flat Rate Shipping Method

After you've clicked **Next**, the Flat Rate Details page opens. Enter how much you want to charge. For instance, you might charge a flat $3 **Per Order**; then another $1 **Per Item**. Or perhaps you could simply charge $7 **Per Pound**. Charge any combination that works for you.

Using a Percentage Shipping Method

This is a very easy method to use. Simply type a percentage into the text box. Typing **10**, for instance, causes the shipping charge to be $15 on a $150 order.

Creating a Rate Table

The rate table allows you to create more complicated shipping rules that vary depending on various criteria and at various levels. For instance, you could base shipping on the value of the order, with a maximum shipping charge; $5 for the first $50 of value, $7.50 up to $100, and $10 for a shipment that is valued at $200 or above.

Perhaps you want to charge based on the weight of the shipment or the number of items. Perhaps you might charge a flat rate for the first five items, another rate for an order of 10 items, and still another rate for orders of 15 or more.

Simply select what the rule should be by clicking the **Based On** drop-down box: Taxable Amount, Nontaxable Amount, Amount, Weight, or Items. Now enter your rates into the boxes below. The table in Figure 19-3, for instance, shows a rule that charges the following:

- $5 for an order of five or fewer products
- $10 for an order of 10 or fewer products
- $15 for an order of 11 or more products

 tip   *If you don't have enough rows, click the <u>Add Additional Rows</u> link to extend the table.*

Using UPS Real-Time Rates

If you selected a UPS Shipping method, all you need to do is to click the **UPS Real-Time Rates** option button in the second step of creating rules and click **Next**. There are no configuration

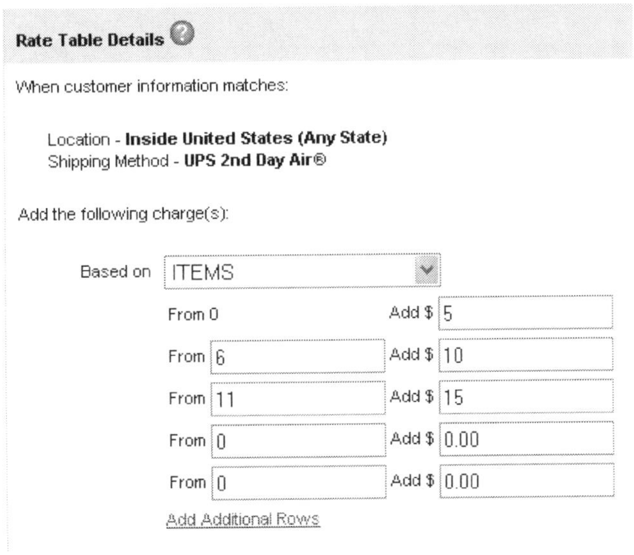

Rate Table Details

When customer information matches:

Location - **Inside United States (Any State)**
Shipping Method - **UPS 2nd Day Air®**

Add the following charge(s):

Based on ITEMS

From 0   Add $ 5
From 6   Add $ 10
From 11   Add $ 15
From 0   Add $ 0.00
From 0   Add $ 0.00

Add Additional Rows

FIGURE 19-3   A rate table configured for a shipping charge based on the number of products in the order

settings; if you select it, then the UPS rate tables will be used. The page that appears shows you your UPS account information and reminds you that you must provide shipping weights for your products.

What if you want to charge more for the shipment than UPS charges? After all, it will cost you more to ship the product than UPS will charge you—you have the cost of packaging and the time it takes to pack the product. In order to manage this, you will create *another* rule for the shipping method.

For instance, let's say you selected UPS Second Day Air. You would create one rule using the UPS Real-Time Rates rule type. Then you would create *another* rule using one of the other methods. For instance, you might add a $5 Flat Rate Charge. When Merchant Solutions calculates shipping for an order for which the buyer selected UPS Second Day Air, it adds the charge provided by the UPS OnLine Tools, and then adds $5.

Combining Methods and Finishing the Process

After you've selected and configured the rate type—and clicked the **Next** button, of course— you'll see an option that allows you to decide whether or not the rule should be combined with another.

By default, with the **Apply ONLY this rule, even if other rules match** check box not selected, the rule *will* be combined with others. In the earlier UPS example, you combined the

UPS Real-Time Rates rule with a Flat Rate rule; leave this check box unchecked and these rules will be combined. Check it, though, and if two rules match, only this one will be used; the other will be ignored.

Why would you want to ignore some rules? Let's say you set up a rule for the entire United States and another rule for just within your state. A shipment into your state would match both rules, so you would want to ignore the United States rule.

tip *Once you have set up your shipping methods and rates, you should test them. Test these, as well as sales tax calculations, by clicking the Shipping & Tax Test link in Shipping Manager, or the Order Settings column of Store Manager. See "Using the Shipping & Tax Test Tool" later in this chapter.*

Configuring Shipping Settings

Once you've set up the methods, rates, and messages, you can define how all this comes together to function in your store. Most of these settings are related to UPS, but the first setting is important for *all* stores. Click the Settings link in Shipping Manager. You'll see the options shown here:

- **Shipping Calculations** This drop-down defines whether shipping calculations are made or not. You can select **No shipping charges** (the system assumes that no shipping charges are necessary); **Tell customer that shipping may be added later** (the system won't add charges but will display a message telling the customer that shipping charges may be added to the total shown); **Calculate in real time; OK if no matching rule** (shipping charges are added, and the order will always be accepted, even if the selected shipping method doesn't match the buyer's shipping location); and **Calculate in real time, error if no matching rule** (charges are added, but if the buyer selects an inappropriate method, he'll see an error message).

- **UPS Branding** Check this box to place the UPS logo during checkout.

- **Address Validation** Select the check box to turn on Address Validation, a UPS tool that checks to see if the buyer's address is valid (only if using a UPS shipping method with a delivery in the U.S.).

- **Time in Transit** Select to display an estimated delivery time (if using UPS).

- **Rates and Services** Select to display the shipping rates (if using UPS).

- **Shipping Location** This is merely a reference field to ensure that the correct UPS shipping location is entered.

- **Ship-To Address Type** If your customers are primarily business, select **Commercial**; otherwise, select **Residential**.

Shipping Options	
Service	Business Days
UPS Ground	5
UPS Next Day Air®	1

Shipping Options	
Service	Cost
UPS Ground	$8.00*
UPS Next Day Air®	$15.99*

* Includes Shipping & Handling Fees

- **Account Type**   This is the account type you selected when you set up your UPS account; it determines the UPS rate chart used.

- **Allow Additional Insurance**   Select **Yes** if you want the rates to automatically include shipping insurance, based on the purchase total.

- **Reference Number**   You can determine what reference number will be sent to UPS so that you can reconcile orders and shipments on UPS documentation later. You can create a combination of your domain name and order number if you wish, or just select the order number and leave the other field blank.

- **Label Format**   Select what type of printer you'll be using. If using an Eltron label printer or compatible, select **UPS Thermal Printer (Eltron)**; for any other kind of printer, select **HP Compatible LaserJet or Ink Jet**.

Defining Shipping Confirmation Messages

This is the final step in setting up shipping, configuring the confirmation messages sent to buyers. Click the Shipping & Order Status link in Shipping Manager to see the Shipment Status page.

- **Shipment Tracking**   Make sure this check box is selected or shipment tracking will not function—shipment-status e-mails will not be sent to buyers.

- **Order Confirmation Email**   In order to have order-confirmation e-mails sent to your customers immediately after they place their orders, you must enter an e-mail address here. This will be the Reply To address in the message they receive. It might be orders@*yourdomain*.com, for instance; make sure this is a valid e-mail address for which you have created an account.

- **Bounced Message Email**   If someone enters a bad e-mail address, the confirmation e-mail *may* bounce back to you. This is the address to which these bounces will be sent; bounce@*yourdomain*.com, for instance.

- **Confirmation Email**   This is the message at the beginning of the confirmation e-mail; it's rather basic, so you may want to customize it, e.g., *Thank you for your purchase at . . ..* Click **Preview Email** to see what the message looks like.

- **Status Update Email**   This is the message at the top of a status-update e-mail sent to the customer, when the shipping status changes.

- **XML Updates**   An advanced feature that allows a sophisticated merchant to send an e-mail to Yahoo! to update order status.

Managing Sales Tax Rates

Here's something many small businesses forget about in their early days—sales tax! In fact, the whole issue of sales tax is rather confusing, so here's a quick summary of your obligations.

In the U.S., local government has the right to collect sales tax on products sold within their borders, and most do; the state, city, and county can all collect tax. In some cases there are even special-district taxes; several cities may get together and start a new tax to fund, for instance, a rapid-transit system throughout the region.

The situation is further complicated by the fact that different products—and, in some states, services—have different tax rates. And some products are exempt from all sales tax, or exempt from state sales tax but not from local tax, and so on. In fact, the U.S. probably has the world's most complicated sales-tax system. Unlike European nations, that generally have a single sales-tax rate, every order your deliver potentially has a different tax rate.

 note *This situation could change; but, quite frankly, it's not likely to change any time soon. There is no current legislative process working to change it.*

However, at the current time there is one thing that makes things simpler for you. In most cases, *you don't have to collect sales tax for every location to which you deliver!* It all depends on what's known as nexus. If you have a nexus in a state, you must collect sales tax in that state. What, then, is a nexus? In general, *nexus* is a physical presence. What's that mean? Well, that depends on which state you're talking about! Different states define a nexus differently. However, in general, a nexus exists for you in a state if

- You have a store in that state.
- You have employees working in that state.
- You have some kind of office location or other property in that state.
- At some point during the year, you employ someone, in some capacity, working within that state to solicit sales—such as setting up a booth at a convention.
- You, an employee, or an agent, at some point during the year, visit a customer in that state.

If your business fits some of these conditions, you *may* have a nexus. If you have a store in a state, there's no need to wonder; yes, you have a nexus. But if your business occasionally visits a convention in a state . . . well, maybe, maybe not. In Florida, no; in California, possibly, depending on the number of days in total you have a "presence" in the state.

So how do you handle sales taxes? Here are some points to consider:

- If you think it's possible that you may have a nexus in a state, contact the state and find out if you actually do. (Contact the state's Department of Revenue or similar.)
- If you discover you do have a nexus in the state, you're going to have to find out what the sales tax rates are.
- Find out how you have to collect and remit the taxes.
- Register with the state and get a sales tax license.
- Get all the numbers, then read on and find out how to set it all up in Yahoo!.

 tip *Here's a good place to start on your hunt for state tax authorities, the Federation of Tax Administrators: http://www.taxadmin.org/fta/link/.*

Okay, so now you've discovered that you have to charge sales tax for your products in, say, Colorado. The tax rate varies throughout the state. Strictly speaking, you have to pay a different tax rate depending on the delivery location—the place in which the buyer lives. Here's what the situation looks like in Colorado:

- Sales tax is due on most "tangible personal property" sold for 17 cents or more.

- The base state sales tax is 2.9%; all sales must be assessed that rate.

- On top of the 2.9% is a city, county, and, in some cases, a special-district sales tax.

- Under Colorado law, you must collect sales tax dependent on the location of your nexus and the delivery—you collect tax for the locations you *share.* If you have an office in Denver, and deliver by mail or UPS to Colorado Springs, you just collect the state sales tax, 2.9%. But if the buyer is also in Denver, you must collect all the sales taxes in that area: a total of 7.6%.

- Thus, if you have a location in Denver, some of your sales in Colorado would be charged at 2.9%, some at 7.6%.

Setting Up Sales Tax in Merchant Solutions

Here's how to set up sales tax rates in Merchant Solutions. As an example, we'll assume that you are in Denver, Colorado, and want to set up two rates: one for deliveries within Denver, and another for deliveries to other locations within Colorado.

Begin by finding out what ZIP codes are contained within Denver. A number of web sites can provide this information. Search Yahoo!, for instance, for *zip codes denver*. You might also try http://www.melissadata.com/ and http://zipcodes.addresses.com. We found 75 ZIP codes, a range from 80201 through 80299. (Yes, that's more than 75 numbers, but some are unused.) Now, let's begin to set up the tax rates:

1. In Site Manager, click the Tax Rates link.

2. Click the Use the Auto Setup Wizard link.

3. Currently, Merchant Solutions only calculates taxes in the U.S., so when asked where you are based, there's only one check box; click **Next**.

4. You'll see a list of states. Click the state in which you have to collect sales tax; if you have to collect in multiple states, hold the CTRL key and click each one (on the Mac, use the Apple key).

5. Click **Done**.

6. Merchant Solutions has now set up a very basic sales-tax profile for each state, but you need to go in and modify it. Click the edit link on the state line.

7. In the Edit Rule page, shown in Figure 19-4, you can ignore the Country box; United States is already selected. (In theory, you create a tax rule that sets up a tax rate for a particular country.)

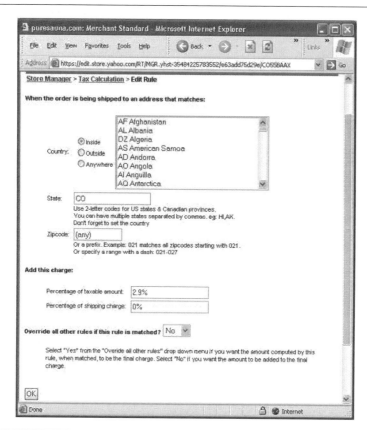

The Edit Rule page, where you define the sales tax for a state

8. Ignore the **State** box as well; the state abbreviation should already be here.

9. We'll ignore the **Zipcode** box, too. We're setting a tax rate for the entire state, so leave *(any)* displayed.

10. In the **Add this charge: Percentage of taxable amount** text box, type the tax rate for the state; in our example, 2.9%.

11. If sales tax is charged on shipping, enter the amount into **Percentage of shipping charge** (it's not in Colorado).

If you want to combine two rules, make sure both Override drop-down list boxes are set to No. If you want them to stand alone, make sure both are set to Yes.

12. The **Override all other rules if this rule is matched?** drop-down list box allows you to define how multiple rules are managed. You can tell Merchant Solutions to combine two rules or make them stand alone. For instance, one rule might define the tax rate for the entire state while another defines the *additional* tax rate for a particular area within the state, in which case the rules must be combined. That's what we're going to do here. We'll leave this drop-down set to No, meaning that another rule—which we'll create in a moment—can also enter into the calculation. This will mean that everyone in Colorado pays 2.9% *and* people in a particular area will pay an additional sum.

13. Click the **OK** button.

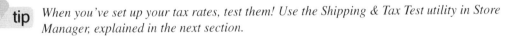

> tip   *When you've set up your tax rates, test them! Use the Shipping & Tax Test utility in Store Manager, explained in the next section.*

You've created one rule to set up tax, in this example, in Denver. Now we have to set up sales tax for the rest of the state. In this example we are going to specify that people who have their orders delivered in Denver will pay an additional sales-tax rate.

1. In the Tax Calculation page, click the **Add New Row** link.

2. In the New Tax Rule page, leave **Percentage** selected (most sales taxes are percentages, not flat rates), and click **Next**.

3. In the next screen (bizarrely named Customer Matching), make sure **US United States** is selected in the **Country** list box and that the **Inside** option button is selected:

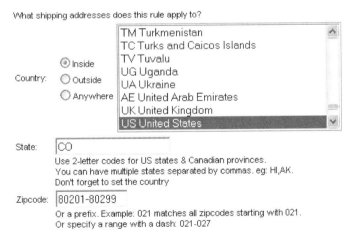

4. Enter the state two-letter code into the **State** text box.

5. Enter **80201-80299** into the **Zipcode** text box; we're going to set a tax rate for these ZIP codes, the codes that cover Denver.

6. Click the **Next** button.

7. In the page that appears, enter **4.7** into the **Percentage of taxable amount** text box.

8. Click the **Done** button.

That's it; you've set up the tax rates for Colorado. In Denver—the ZIP code range entered into the **Zipcode** text box—purchases are assessed the 2.9% state rate *and* the 4.7% Denver rate. Outside those area codes, just the 2.9% rate is assessed. And outside Colorado entirely, no tax is added to the calculation.

There's one more thing to do, though. Having defined the tax rates, you now have to ensure they are used in the checkout system. You must select the correct option from the **Tax Calculation for Customers** drop-down list box on the Tax Calculation page.

■ **Calculate in real time**   The tax rules you have used will be used during the checkout.

■ **Nothing is taxed**   Your tax rules will *not* be used—no tax will be added to the transaction.

■ **Tell customer that tax may be added later**   Your tax rules will *not* be used—no tax will be added to the transaction. However, a message is displayed informing the customer that you may have to add sales tax to the order before shipping.

Make sure you click the **Update** button after making this selection.

Using the Shipping & Tax Test Tool

Merchant Solutions provides a great little testing system for your shipping and tax calculations. It's a good idea to use this—spend enough time to make sure you've checked a wide range of possible shipping locations and items, weights, and order values. A mistake in your tax and shipping settings could prove expensive.

Click Shipping & Tax Test in Store Manager to see the test tool. Play with this for a while. Enter different amounts in the **Taxable**, **Non-Taxable Amounts**, and **Item Counts** fields, different **Ship Methods**, and so on. When you click the **Calculate** button, the results are shown below. Make sure they make sense in every case, and if you find a problem, go back to taxes and shipping to find the error.

Configuring Inventory Options

Your final step before opening for business is to tell Merchant Solutions what sort of inventory-management system you'll use. What do we mean by inventory management? Your inventory is your stock of products, and *inventory management* in this context means, essentially, figuring out how your store knows which products are available or which are not . . . better still, how many of each product you have in stock. In addition, you can have the inventory system send you e-mail alerts when stock levels fall below a certain amount.

Click the <u>Configure Inventory</u> link in Store Manager to see the three Inventory Options:

Inventory Options

Change Inventory Feature   ⦿ None
○ Real-time inventory
○ Database inventory

- **None**   This is the default, and most small merchants use this method. There is no inventory management. You'll have to physically modify a product's settings to show it as not available if a product is out of stock, put a message onto your product saying it's not yet available, or perhaps take the order and let the buyer know it's not yet available. You won't receive notifications if stock levels fall below a specified limit.

- **Real-time Inventory**   You'll need someone who can write a program that will check with an inventory application running on another web server. This option is beyond the scope of this book; it's an advanced method that is only used in special circumstances and requires programming skills.

- **Database Inventory**   This option adds an <u>Inventory</u> link to Store Manager, leading to a page where you can modify product quantities by hand, or import a file containing stock levels for each product.

 note   *Many merchants, especially existing offline merchants just beginning to sell online, really don't need to worry about inventory levels. Their online sales are a small proportion of their offline sales, and so have little effect on inventory levels.*

Configuring Database Inventory

Small merchants will generally use either no inventory management or the Database Inventory system. To use the latter, follow these instructions:

1. Click the **Database Inventory** option button.

2. Click the **Modify Settings** button. You'll see the settings in Figure 19-5.

3. If you want to see e-mails warning you of stock levels falling too low, select **Yes** in the **Send email alert** box.

4. Set the warning level in the **Alert Threshold** box; if you want to know when stock drops to 5 or below, type **5**.

5. Enter the e-mail address to which the warning messages should be sent in the **Email to:** box.

6. Select a time at which the message should be sent in the **Send** column.

FIGURE 19-5   Setting up Database Inventory

---

7. An In Stock column, shown next, can be displayed to the buyer when he places something into the shopping cart. If you don't want this column, select **No** in the **Display Inventory Column** drop-down list box. Or select one of the **Yes** options; **with Quantity** means the column actually shows the actual number in stock, while **with Availability** means the columns shows only *Yes* or *No*.

Your Shopping Cart					
Item	**Options**	**Unit Price**	**Qty.**	**In Stock**	**Subtotal**
Joe's Original BACKTEE [Remove]	Color: Red Size: Small	14.99	1	Yes	14.99

8. Select **Yes** in the **Quantify can Exceed Availability** drop-down list box if you want to allow buyers to place an order for an item that is out of stock. If you select **No**, the item appears in the shopping cart when the buyer clicks the product's **Order** button, but it will be removed from the shopping cart as soon as he returns to shopping or tries to check out.

9. The **Default inventory quantity** drop-down defines how the system handles products for which there is no inventory information stored in the database; if you select **Zero**, the system assumes that the product is out of stock. If you select **Infinity**, it assumes it is always in stock.

10. Click the **Update** button.

Entering Inventory Data

You've set up how the Database Inventory system works, but right now your system has no inventory information. Here's now to enter it:

1. In Store Manager, click the Inventory link in the Process column. (This link doesn't appear if you don't have Database Inventory configured.) The Inventory page appears.

2. Click the **Edit** button if you want to modify inventory levels by hand. You'll be able to type a number into each product's **Quantity** field separately.

3. If you want to import your inventory levels, click the **Upload** button. You'll be able to upload a .csv file, similar to the one discussed in Chapter 13, but this particular file must contain only two columns, Code and Quantity.

Opening for Business

You're ready for business! Or at least should be if you've done everything we've covered so far. You need to complete these steps:

1. Enter products into the product database.

2. Create and customize your store pages.

3. Create and customize the two ancillary required pages, Info and Privacy Policy.

4. Set up a credit-card merchant account.

5. Set up all your store settings, from what the order form looks like to inventory settings.

Now, here's what you have to do to actually open for business:

1. Go into Store Editor and click the **Publish** button on the Editor toolbar.

2. Return to Store Manager and click the Publish Order Settings in the Order Settings column.

3. Look near the top of Store Manager for the Open for Business link. If you've completed all the required steps, you should see this link in the yellow box above the columns of links.

4. Click the <u>Open for Business</u> link and follow the instructions; you'll have to provide your credit-card merchant account information to prove that you have set up a merchant account.

5. You'll be informed when your information has been reviewed and the site is up and running!

Once your store is up and running, you should try a test order or two to learn how to process orders. Move on to the following chapter to learn about this.

Chapter 20

Processing Orders

You've finally reached the point to which you've been heading all through the process of building a store: processing orders! In this chapter, we'll look at how to handle an order once a buyer has come to your store and bought from you. We're going to discuss how to review the orders, how to check "flagged" orders (Yahoo! automatically flags some orders according to your preferences about handling AVS and CVV codes), and how to process credit-card payments—including how to modify charges and cancel orders. You'll also learn about processing other forms of payment—fax, phone, and mail orders—and payment methods such as PayPal and COD. Finally, you'll see how to manage your shipments, including using the integrated UPS tools.

Reviewing Your Orders

Click the Orders link, under the **Process** column, in Store Manager, and you'll see something like the screen in Figure 20-1.

You have a few options here:

- **View a specific order.** The most recent order number will be shown, but you can enter any number and then click the button.

- **View a range of orders.** If you have several unprocessed orders, the numbers will be shown here. Click **View** to see them all on one page.

- **Summarize a range of orders.** You'll see one line per order, showing the customer name, the city and state, number of items, order value, date, its status (Pending Review, On Hold, etc.), and the amount of the order that has been shipped.

- **Print a range of orders.** You can choose to print full-order information, an invoice, or packing slip.

- **Export a range of orders.** You can export information in a variety of formats: MS Excel, MS Access, CSV (a text file with comma-separated values), M.O.M. (Mail Order Manager software), QuickBooks, PC Charge (a credit-card processing program), XML, or Plain Text.

- **Order Lookup.** Enter any piece of information—a fragment of the street address, a buyer's last name, an order date, and so on—to find matching orders, up to one year old. (You can search on credit-card numbers for orders up to 30 days old.)

Let's take a look at an order page. Simply click the top **View** button. You'll see a page like that in Figure 20-2.

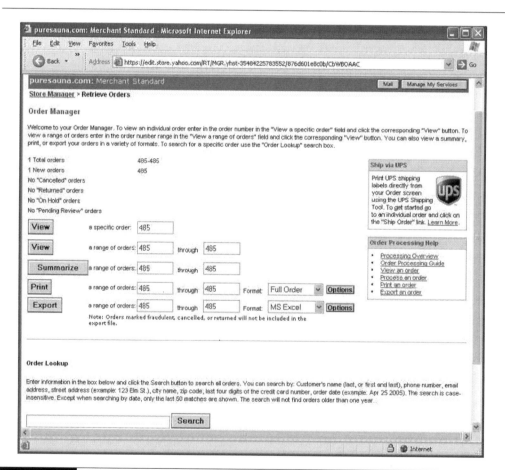

FIGURE 20-1   The Yahoo! Merchant Solutions Order Manager

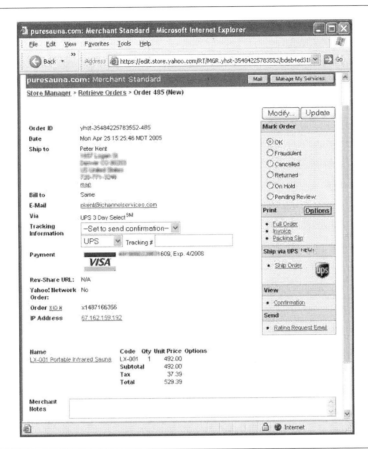

FIGURE 20-2 A sample order in Yahoo! Merchant Solutions Order Manager

Here's the information you'll find in this page:

Order ID	The order identification number, which comprises the store ID (yhst-35484225783552 in this case) and the specific Order ID (485 in the example).
Mark	This line only appears if you use the **Mark Order** option buttons on the right side of the page, or if Yahoo! automatically marks the order as **Pending Review**, based on the AVS and CVV information (see "Checking Flagged Orders" later in this chapter).
Date	The time and date the order was processed.
Ship To	The shipping address.

Bill To	If the customer used a different billing address you'll see it here.
E-mail	The customer's e-mail address.
Via	The chosen shipping method.
Tracking Information	Selecting an option from this drop-down will send a confirmation message to the customer when you click the **Update** button. You can tell the customer that the order has shipped, will ship within a particular period, or that the item is no longer available.
	In addition, you can enter the shipping method and a tracking number here. (It will be saved when you click **Update**.) If you use the Ship Order link in the **Ship via UPS** box on the right to prepare a shipping label, the UPS tracking number will be placed here automatically.
Payment	This shows the payment method including, if applicable, the credit-card number.
Rev-Share URL	If you created a tracking link that was used to access your account for this order (see Chapter 21), the tracking-URL information is shown here.
Yahoo! Network Order	If the order came from Yahoo!—for instance, if the buyer arrived through a Yahoo! search—you'll see information here.
Order XID#	This is an ID used by Commission Junction to identify affiliate-generated orders (see Chapter 21).
IP Address	This is the IP (Internet Protocol) number of the computer used to place the order. If you decide that this order is fraudulent, you can block orders from this IP number; click the number to open the blocker (see later in this chapter).
Product Information	The order information—the items that have been ordered, the subtotal, tax, and total.
Merchant Notes	You can enter a note here if you wish; this note is saved when you click the **Update** button.
Mark Order	You can classify an order in various ways—by default, it's set to OK, but you can change it to Fraudulent, Cancelled, Returned, On Hold, or Pending Review. The choice is set when you click the **Update** button.

 tip   *If you cancel any transactions, remember to use the Cancelled setting; if you don't do so, you'll get charged the transaction fee for that order. (Yahoo! charges a 1.5% fee for every transaction in a Starter store, 1% for the Standard store, and .75% for a Professional store.) Marking orders as Fraudulent and Returned also avoids paying these fees, although if you kill a lot of orders using these statuses, Yahoo! may investigate to ensure that you are not doing so merely to avoid the fees.*

Print	Clicking a link here creates an Adobe Acrobat PDF document containing Full Order information, an Invoice, or a Packing Slip.
Options button	Click this button to change the print format to PostScript, an earlier version of PDF (2.0), or HTML.

Ship via UPS	Click the <u>Ship Order</u> link to print UPS shipping labels.
View	Click the <u>Confirmation</u> link to open the Confirmation page that the customer saw when completing the transaction.
Send	Click the <u>Rating Request Email</u> link to send an e-mail to the customer asking for a rating; the customer will be able to rate your store, from Poor to Excellent, on five different criteria.

Notice also the two buttons on this page:

Modify	Click this button to see a page in which you can change almost anything about the order; the buyer's address, the shipping method, the items ordered and pricing, and so on.
Update	Click this to save the changes you made to the Order page; for instance, select a Tracking Information option and click **Update** to send an e-mail to the buyer with shipping information.

Checking Flagged Orders

In Chapter 18 you learned about using "Risk Tools"—the AVS (Address Verification System) and CVV (Card Verification Value). If the customer enters invalid information, the order will be handled in one of two ways, depending on what you chose in the Risk Tools page:

- ■ **The AVS or CVV information is ignored.** The order will be given a status of OK.

- ■ **The order is flagged.** It will be marked as **Pending Review** in the Orders page. You'll see it listed on the Pending Review line in Order Manager.

No "On Hold" orders

1 "Pending Review" order   485

tip   *Read Yahoo!'s detailed information before deciding how to handle orders with bad AVS and CVV codes.*

If you have chosen to run the risk tools—to flag some orders—Yahoo! will mark orders that have problems as **Pending Review**. Here's how to deal with them:

1. In the Order Manager page, click the link pointing to the Pending Review order. The Order page will open; you'll notice that the **Pending Review** option button in the **Mark Order** box is selected, and the **Marked** line, below the Order ID, says "Pending Review."

2. Look at the AVS and CVV codes under the credit-card number on the **Payment** line.

3. Based on these codes, decide what course of action you want to take; contact the buyer or process the order as normal. (If you choose to contact the buyer, you may wish to place the order **On Hold**—click that option button, then click the **Update** button.)

These are the **Card Verification Values** you may see in the **Payment** area:

- **M** Match; there's no problem.

- **N** Incorrect code. This could be a mistake on the part of the buyer, but could be an indication of fraud.

- **P** or **X** System unavailable. *Not* an indication of fraud, but then neither does it provide information suggesting that the transaction *isn't* fraudulent.

- **S** or **U** The system is not providing CVV information for some reason. As above, not an indication of fraud.

The **Address Verification Codes** are more complicated, unfortunately. The AVS checks the street address and ZIP code; these are the codes returned for **U.S. credit cards:**

- **YYY** Valid street address and five-digit ZIP code

- **YYX** Valid street address and nine-digit ZIP code

- **NYZ** Valid five-digit ZIP code, invalid street address

- **YNA** Valid street address, invalid ZIP code

- **NNN** Invalid street address and ZIP code

- **NYW** Valid nine-digit ZIP code, invalid street address

- **XX** Card number not on file

The previous codes—with the exception of the first two, of course—may indicate a possible problem. The following do not; for some reason, no AVS information is available, but that isn't an indicator of fraud:

- **XXU** Address information not verified

- **XXR** System unavailable

- **XXS** Service not supported

- **XXE** Address verification not allowed for this card type

- **XX** No response from AVS

These are codes you may see for **foreign credit cards**. The first few are good codes, of course:

- **YYD** Valid street address and postal code

- **YYM** Valid street address and postal code

- **YYF** Valid street address and postal code (United Kingdom)

These may indicate a problem:

- **YNB** Valid street address, invalid postal code

- **NYP** Valid postal code, invalid street address

- **NNC** Invalid street address and postal code

The previous codes may indicate a possible problem; the following do not—for some reason no AVS information is available, but that isn't an indicator of fraud:

- **NNI**   Address information not verified
- **XXG**   Non-AVS participant

tip   *Remember, bad codes do* not *always indicate fraud. There are many reasons that people may enter bad address and CVV information.*

There are many decisions to be made here, depending on the type of products you are selling—in particular the value—and where you are sending them, your willingness to take a risk, and so on. We recommend that you thoroughly read all the fraud information and devise some sensible processes and standards for managing these codes.

Processing Credit-card Payments

Most of your orders will probably be placed using a credit card. Here's how to process these orders:

1. Enter the **Order** page.

2. Review the order information to ensure that it looks okay.

3. Find the Transaction Control Panel at the bottom of the order.

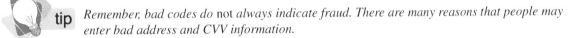

4. Click the **Sale** button. If the transaction is processed correctly, the Order page will now show "Charged" on the **Payment** line.

5. When you have processed the payment, return to the order form to prepare the shipment. If shipping via UPS, use the Ship Order link in the **Ship via UPS** box to create your mailing labels (see "Shipping Your Order" later in this chapter).

Note that at the point you click the Sale button, and the payment is processed correctly, the money the buyer owes to you is reserved—your money is secure, and you can go ahead and ship the product. Technically speaking, though, the process isn't quite finished. Credit-card orders have to be "settled." Typically merchants submit a batch of orders to be settled at one time, generally once a day, and the Merchant Solutions software automates this process for you; each evening Yahoo! automatically submits all your orders—the *batch*—for *settlement*. You could, if you wish, submit a batch of orders sooner, by clicking the Submit batch link, but there's no need to do so.

Modifying Charges and Canceling Orders

What if you need to change the payment sum? Perhaps someone called in, and asked you to change the shipping method, or add an item. Perhaps you haven't processed the payment . . . or perhaps you have. And how about canceling an order? The following methods can be used to change or cancel a payment:

- **To change the payment, if you haven't yet processed.** Simply modify the sum in the Transaction Control Panel, and then click **Sale**.

- **To change the value, if you've already processed the order but the batch has not been settled.** Click the **Void Sale** button to void the original transaction, then enter the correct value and click the **Sale** button.

- **To change the value, if the batch *has* been settled.** Return to Store Manager, and click the Manual Transactions link under the Process column. (This link only appears once you have your credit-card merchant account set up.) This takes you into a form where you can manually process credit-card transactions. Enter the information and click **Sale** to charge more, or **Credit** to refund money.

- **To cancel a payment, if the batch has not been settled.** Click the **Void Sale** button (this button appears only if you have already processed the order). This removes the transaction from the batch, so it won't be submitted for settlement.

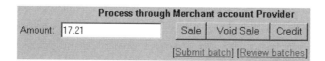

- **To cancel a payment, if the batch *has* been settled.** Go into the Manual Transactions page (from Store Manager), and issue a credit. This form does contain a Void Transactions box, but this won't work if the transaction has already been settled.

Processing Fax, Phone, and Mail Orders

You may choose to accept fax, phone, and mail orders if you wish. The best way to process these orders is to enter them directly through your store. Actually enter your store as if you were a customer, choose the items, and enter the shipping and payment information into the checkout pages.

 tip   *If you process an order like this, you should probably type a quick note into the transaction's* **Merchant Notes** *field—Phone order entered by Joe, for instance.*

It is possible to charge somebody's card using the manual-transaction form (the Manual Transactions link under the Process column in Store Manager). But the problem with doing this is that you won't have a record of the actual sale, only the credit-card transactions. If you enter it into the store directly, you'll have a full record, and can manage the confirmation e-mails, shipping labels, tracking number, and so on fully.

Processing PayPal and Other Forms of Payment

Credit cards are the easiest way to take payments—indeed you must have a credit-card merchant account before you can open your store. However, as you saw in Chapter 18, you can set up other methods: Bill Me, COD, Purchase Order, PayPal, and so on.

note *We're assuming that you have set up PayPal as a payment type, using the **Add Other** text box in the Payment Methods page (see Chapter 18).*

Here's how you would process PayPal payments; other methods are going to be very similar—you'll process the payment "offline," then come to the Orders page to mark the order as complete:

1. When you review the order, you'll notice PayPal set as the **Payment** type. (Ignore the expiration date; this is simply the default expiration date used if someone enters a credit card.)

   Payment   PayPal ppal@ichannelservices.com, Exp. 4/2008

tip *Alternatively, consider sending a PayPal invoice. Log into your account, click the **Request Money** tab, and then click the **Create an Invoice** subcategory below the tab. The buyer will be able to click a link in the invoice e-mail to view a payment page in a web browser.*

2. PayPal is not fully integrated into Yahoo! Merchant Solutions, so you need to take a few additional steps. You must request payment via PayPal immediately (the longer you let things slip, the less likely you are to get paid!). Click the buyer's e-mail address, and send an e-mail asking for payment, and explaining how. You need to provide the e-mail/ ID of your PayPal account, and you should also probably provide a link to PayPal to speed up the process.

   E-Mail   pkent@ichannelservices.com

3. When you receive the payment, return to the order form to prepare the shipment. If shipping via UPS, use the Ship Order link in the **Ship via UPS** box to create your mailing labels.

4. Return to the Order page.

5. From the **Tracking Information** drop-down list box, select Shipped.

6. Click the **Update** button at the top of the page.

Shipping Your Order

You learned how to set up shipping methods in Chapter 19. Once you have processed the transaction and you are sure that you have been paid, you can go ahead and ship the package. Once it's shipped, follow these steps:

1. Go to the Order page.

2. Select the shipping method you used from the smaller **Tracking Information** drop-down list box.

3. Enter the tracking number, if available.

4. Select Shipped from the larger drop-down list box.

5. Click the **Update** button. The customer will be mailed a shipping-notification message, which includes the shipping method and tracking number.

Shipping via UPS

Merchant Solutions has integrated UPS shipping, making it very easy to print shipping labels for that service. Click the <u>Ship Order</u> link next to the UPS logo to see the Create a Shipment page.

This is very straightforward. Simply make the appropriate shipping choices—the address type, the packaging type, dimensions, and weight, and whether you want a Saturday Delivery (the shipping type is already set from the order).

On the following page, you'll be able to review the shipping information; when you click the **Ship Now** button, the shipping information is sent to UPS, and on the third page you can click the **Print UPS Label** button to open a window containing a label that you can print. If you now return to the Order page, you'll see more UPS information.

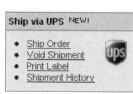

You now have four options:

Ship Order	Click here to go through the shipping process again.
Void Shipment	Click this link to void the shipment; information is sent to UPS to cancel it.
Print Label	Click here to see the label again so you can print it.
Shipment History	Click here to see the time and date that the shipment was processed (and voided if that's the case); you'll also find the tracking number, the shipping service, and the shipping price.

Blocking Fraudulent Orders

If you are the victim of fraud, or perhaps receive an order that you decide might be fraudulent and have decided not to fulfill it, you may want to block the IP number from any future transactions.

warning *Be careful about blocking IP numbers. Many, perhaps most, IP numbers are shared. For instance, if someone dials into their ISP—AOL, for instance—the ISP assigns an IP number to the computer. When the user disconnects, the IP number is assigned to another computer. Thus blocking the IP number doesn't really help in this situation; the next time the user connects, he will have a different IP number, and the one you would be blocking would be assigned to another, totally innocent person.*

An IP number is an identifier; every computer connected to the Internet, at any given moment, has a unique IP number identifying it. When someone purchases from your store, the IP number of the computer used to make the purchase is saved with the transaction; you'll see it on the **IP Address** line on the Orders page.

Here's how to block an IP number if you've decided the order is fraudulent:

1. Click the IP number in the Orders page, and the IP Blocking page opens.

2. At the bottom of the page you'll see information about the computer used to place the order. For instance, you may see an Org. Name line something like *Comcast Cable Communications, IP Services*—in other words, this would be a computer connected through a broadband ISP. In this case, the computer probably keeps the same IP number for an extended time; had this been an AOL subscriber who dials in, the IP number would change each time the person connects.

3. If you are sure this order is fraudulent, contact the ISP to report it.

4. If you wish to block the IP number, to ensure the computer cannot be used again to buy from you, click the **Add** button.

5. Click the **Done** button to finish.

tip *The maximum number of entries in the IP Block List is 100; these can either be ranges or individual IP numbers. Only ten can be added at a time.*

There's another way to block numbers or ranges of numbers. Click the Risk Tools link in the Store Manager page, and then click the IP Blocking link to get to the IP Blocking page. Enter a range of IP addresses into the **IP Addresses** box (for instance, 216.109.112.0–135), click the **Add** button, and then click the **Done** button.

IP blocking is really quite tricky. In fact, unless your business is particularly hard hit by fraud, you'll probably end up ignoring it. Unfortunately, it's not practical to block entire swathes of the globe, but it may be possible to block particular countries.

Of course being able to handle incoming orders is all very well . . . but you need orders first! In the following chapters you're going to find out how to generate sales in your store.

This page intentionally left blank

Chapter 21

Promotion Strategies and Tools

Opening your store for business is all very well, but how are you going to get people to visit your store? And how are you going to encourage them to buy from you?

We'll be looking at ways to get traffic from the search engines, and various other sources, starting in Chapter 22. Before we get there, though, let's look at a variety of promotional and marketing tools provided by Yahoo! Perhaps one of the most important tools Yahoo! provides is quick access to the Yahoo! Shopping directory; you can quickly feed data into Yahoo! Shopping, which can then direct people to your store (you'll pay between 10 cents and 80 cents each time someone clicks a link to your site).

There are other useful tools, though. Coupons and discounts can be very effective—you can even combine a discount with a tracking link to promote a special discount offer through a club, a discussion group, or a friend's web site. You'll also learn about affiliate programs, e-mail marketing, and Merchant Solutions' statistics.

Submitting Data to Yahoo! Shopping

Yahoo! maintains a huge directory of products that is used when people search through the Yahoo! Product search or directly at the Yahoo! Shopping site.

Yahoo! doesn't provide buyer's guides for all categories, just for a few basics, such as books, CDs, electronics, and video games.

In addition, if you provide the correct product information, your products may also appear in the Yahoo! Shopping Buyer's Guides. These are comparison charts that allow buyers to compare specific products across various merchant sites. You'll have to provide particular product information that will allow Yahoo! to exactly match products; ISBN numbers for books, manufacturer's part numbers, UPC codes for many other products, and so on.

The products in this directory have been placed there by their merchants, through the Product Submit program. Each time someone clicks a link to a merchant's store, the merchant pays Yahoo! a sum dependent on the category in which the product has been placed—as a Merchant Solutions client, you'll pay 20 percent less than the normal rates, which vary between 12 cents and 80 cents.

There are other, optional costs. You can choose to upload a store logo, for instance, or display your store name in bold text, both of which give you priority placement when your product turns up in a search-results page.

To sign up for a Yahoo! Shopping account, click the Yahoo! Shopping link in Store Manager, and follow the instructions. You must enter Yahoo! Shopping this way in order to ensure you get your 20 percent discount.

Preparing Product Data

Yahoo! Shopping can pull your product data directly from Merchant Solutions' Catalog Manager. In fact it will check your product data several times a day, to make sure it has the latest information.

Before you can submit data to Yahoo! Shopping, you need to prepare your data. There are a number of fields that you *must* provide, and others that you *should* provide. Remember that the more information you provide about your products, the more likely they are to be found. Why? Because if someone searches using a particular word or code, and that word or code isn't in your product information, your product won't be found. For instance, people sometimes search using manufacturer's codes. If you don't include them, your competitors' sites may be found, but yours won't!

Notice that Yahoo! Shopping doesn't pull the Sale-price field! If you're using both the Price and Sale-price fields in your Merchant Solutions store, you'll have to stop doing so, and put the price at which you sell the product in the Price field. If you don't, Yahoo! Shopping will list the more expensive price, rather than the one at which you actually sell the product.

This is the information that is required (the first three are already in your product database):

- **code**
- **name**
- **price**

- **product-url** This tells Yahoo! the page on which the product information is found on your web site.

- **medium** Only required for music or video, this field can be *CD, Cassette, MiniDisc, LP, EP, 45, VHS, Beta, 8mm, Laser Disc, DVD,* or *VCD.*

- **merchant-category** The category in which the product is placed in your store.

There are other product fields that are useful; fields that are required for inclusion in the Buyer's Guides, in appropriate categories, but that should be included if at all possible because the more information the more likely your products are to be found.

- **upc** Universal Product Code (the number on a barcode)

- **isbn** For books, the ISBN number

- **brand** The brand name (Levi's, Guess, and so on)

- **manufacturer** The product's manufacturer

- **manufacturer-part-number** The manufacturer's part number

- **model-number** The manufacturer's model number

- **ean** The European Article Numbering code

- **classification** One of these product classifications*: new, used, refurbished, open box, returned, damaged, overstock,* or *liquidation*

- **gender** For gender-specific products: *men, women, unisex*

- **age-group** The age for which the product is intended: *infant, toddler, child, pre-teen, teen,* or *adult*

- **age-range** The age range for which the product is intended, such as *0–6 months, 9 months – 2 years, 2–4 years, 8 years and up*

- **size** The product size; a numeral or word (*small, medium, large,* and so forth) or code (*S, M, L, XL,* and so on)

- **style-number** The manufacturer's style code

- **condition** The product condition: *new, like new, very good, good,* or *acceptable*

- **yahoo-shopping-category** The Yahoo! Shopping category in which you want to place the product

You may have some products that use some of these optional fields, and others that use different fields. That's okay. In your data file you'll create columns for all the fields you need, and leave particular fields blank if they're not appropriate for a particular product.

But how do you get these fields into your product information? You learned about Catalog Manager in Chapter 13 . . . but you didn't learn about most of these fields. They're not in the default product table in Catalog Manager, in fact.

You'll need to check your product table in Category Manager to see which fields are present, add the ones that are not, and then add or import the appropriate product information.

Adding Data Fields

Here's how to find out if the product fields you need are present in your data table.

1. In Store Manager, click the <u>Catalog Manager</u> link.

2. In Catalog Manager, click the <u>Manage Your Tables</u> link.

3. Click the table containing your product data (probably *default-table*; we won't be discussing how to create new tables in this book).

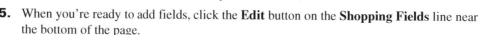

4. The Edit Table page shows you all the fields in the table. Compare this table with the list of fields you'll need for Product Submit; you'll probably have to add *merchant-category* and, if selling music and videos, *medium*. You may also want to add other fields, such as *upc*, *isbn*, *brand*, and so on.

5. When you're ready to add fields, click the **Edit** button on the **Shopping Fields** line near the bottom of the page.

6. In the Shopping Fields page, select a field you want to add from the drop-down list box, and then click the **Add Field** button.

 You must publish your Catalog Manager changes, otherwise they won't appear in Yahoo! Shopping.

7. When you've added all the fields you need, click the **Update** button.

8. In the Edit Table page, click the **Save** button.

Categorizing Products

Product placement, or categorization, is important. Where your products are placed will determine how much you will be charged for each click, and how people find the product if they browse through the store.

There are two ways to categorize products within Yahoo! Shopping. Yahoo!'s staff will review your choice, and may change it, by the way; they want to make sure you're placed into the correct category.

First, you *must* provide the **merchant-category** information. This does not define where you think the product should be placed; rather, it tells Yahoo! where you have placed the product in your own store. For instance, you might have used the *path* field (see Chapter 13) to specify that a product is in the Clothing:Mens:Shoes category. You would enter **Clothing > Mens > Shoes** into the **merchant-category** field (while the *path* field uses the colon to divide categories and subcategories, in the *merchant-category* field you must use a space, the > character, and another space).

If you wish, you can stop there and let Yahoo! decide where to place the product. Since Yahoo! Shopping has a very limited set of product categories, this product might end up in either the **Apparel** category or the **Apparel > Shoes > Athletic** category, depending on what type of shoes they are.

 tip   *You can find a list of Yahoo! Shopping categories at the following web site: https:// productsubmit.adcentral.yahoo.com/sspi/us/category_definitions.html.*

You may, if you wish, tell Yahoo! which category you think the product should be placed into in the Yahoo! Shopping store. To do this, use the **yahoo-shopping-category** field. If you want to ensure the product is placed into the **Apparel > Shoes > Athletic** category, enter that into the **yahoo-shopping-category** field. Of course, whatever you enter here has to be the name of a valid Yahoo! Shopping category.

Creating the Product-url Field

After a few minutes of using Yahoo! Shopping, you'll notice that when you follow a product's link you eventually end up at the merchant's store, and on the appropriate product page. In some places, clicking a product name takes you to the store; in others, clicking <u>Check Store</u> takes you there. But either way, you reach the product page, not just the Home page.

When you feed data to Yahoo! Store, you have to feed a URL for every product—that is, the URL of the page that holds the related product information. That's done using the **product-url** field. Don't worry, you don't have to look at every page in your site and figure out which URL is used for each product. Here's a (relatively) simple way to get this information into your import spreadsheet, for example.

1. Copy the ID column and paste it into a word processor.

2. Using the word processor's Search and Replace functions, copy your base store URL— **http://store.*yourdomain*.com/**—at the beginning of every line. For instance, if the ID is **09870987**, you end up with **http://store.*yourdomain*.com/09870987**.

3. Use Search and Replace to paste **.html** at the end of every line. Now you should have **http://store.*yourdomain*.com/09870987.html**. That's the URL of the product.

4. Copy the entire column of data.

5. Paste the data into a new column in your spreadsheet, and then name the column **product-url**.

Importing and Publishing Your Data

In Chapter 13, you saw how to import data from a database or spreadsheet. You can do the same thing to publish your data. Add all the new fields you need—*merchant-category, product-url, isbn, upc,* and so on. Then import the data exactly as you did before.

Once you've imported the data, make sure you also publish it. Until you publish the Catalog Manager data, it won't be available to Yahoo! Shopping.

Using Coupons and Discounts

Coupons can be a great way to promote your store. These are, in effect, "digital" coupons. You define a particular coupon number—N09827340978, for instance, or whatever you want to use—which can then be printed on paper, entered into an e-mail, read to a customer over the phone, embedded into an attractive coupon "image" and temporarily posted on your web site, entered into messages posted in online discussion groups, and so on.

How can you use coupons? Send a coupon to buyers in a follow-up message, thanking them and offering a discount on their next order or on a friend's order. Put a paper coupon in the box along with the product you are shipping. Announce a special-promotion coupon in a discussion group. E-mail old customers with a coupon code for a special offer.

Here's how to create your coupons. Begin by clicking the <u>Coupon Manager</u> link in Store Manager, under the Promote column. You'll see the Coupon Management page (Figure 21-1) and these fields:

Field	Description
Enter Coupon Code	The code that the buyer types in during the checkout process. Type a code, any code (as long as it begins with a letter, and contains only letters, numbers, hyphens, and underscores). It can't exceed 128 characters, but you'll probably never want to create a code that long anyway. The code could be A09870987, Zoui897_1, T-9078-098, or whatever you wish.
Good for	Select the discount value. A fixed dollar **Amount**; a **Percent** of the order value; or **Free Shipping**. Make sure you enter the appropriate value *and* select the appropriate option button.
Minimum Purchase	If you wish, you can specify that the buyer must purchase a minimum amount ("10% discount on all orders over $100," for instance).
Expiry	In most cases, you'll want coupons to expire eventually; maybe have them only last a week, or a month. Either way, you should select an expiration date.
Target Items	Leave this text box blank if you want the discount to apply to all products. Otherwise, enter the product item codes into the text box, separated by commas (no space). You can also select a product from the drop-down list box (each time you choose one, the code is entered for you . . . if you add one accidentally, simply delete the text). Or click the <u>Browse for an item</u> link to open a tool in which you can browse categories to find the products.
Attach To Links	Leave this blank if you want someone to be able to type the coupon code during checkout. Only use this in the text box if you want to associate a discount with a particular source. For instance, if you have a partner site and have offered a discount to that site's visitors, attaching the link to the discount activates the discount automatically when someone arrives from that site. See the following section for more information about Links.

Once you've created the coupon, it's immediately live. There's no need to "publish" the information.

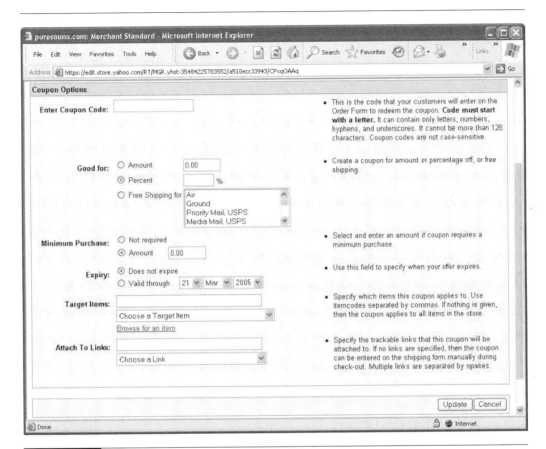

FIGURE 21-1   The Coupon Management page

Creating Affiliate, Discount, and Tracking Links

Merchant Solutions allows you to create special links that can be tracked for three purposes:

- **Affiliate Links**   You can pay other sites for sending buyers to you; these *affiliate* sites earn a commission on sales.

- **Discount Links**   You can create links that automatically provide a discount to all visitors arriving through the links, using a coupon created earlier (see "Using Coupons and Discounts" earlier in this chapter).

- **Promotion Tracking Links**   You can create links for use in tracking responses to advertising, PR, and various promotions.

An *affiliate* is a person or company who sends visitors to your site in return for a commission on any purchases made by those visitors. For instance, someone clicks a link at an affiliate site, comes to your site, and buys $100 worth of products. If you've agreed to pay a 7.5 percent commission, you now owe the owner of the other site—the affiliate—$7.50.

A *discount link* is one that provides a discount to anyone who arrives at your site when they use it. What would you do with such a link? Here are a few ideas:

- E-mail special-offer discounts to old customers—put the link in the e-mail.

- Provide a discount to members of professional associations and clubs; those groups can put the link on their web sites.

- Place ads on other web sites for discounts at your store. Put the link in the ad.

A *promotion tracking link* is one that you use to track the effectiveness of an advert or promotion of some kind. You don't provide a discount or commission; you just use the link to track how much traffic arrives at your site through the link.

Merchant Solutions provides a very simple link-tracking tool; you can create a link and assign a commission level to that link. Any sales from buyers coming through that link will be commissionable. Or you can assign a coupon discount to the link. Here's how to create these links:

1. Click the <u>Create Links</u> link under the Promote column in Store Manager.

2. Type the name of the affiliate web site and click the **Create new trackable link for:** button.

Create new trackable link for:	

(name of site which will link to you)

3. You'll see the information in Figure 21-2.

First Link	This is the link you must give to the affiliate. When visitors click this link, come to your site, and buy a product, you owe the affiliate the commission. This link takes visitors to the Home page, but you can tell affiliates they can direct buyers to particular pages if they replace *index.html* with the filename of a different page.
Second Link	This link takes affiliates to a page in which they can see statistics about traffic from their sites and any sales and commissions.
Link Name	This is the name you entered on the previous page; you can change it if you wish.
Auto Merchandise Credit	This is the commission that will be paid to the affiliate for any sales. Enter the percentage commission you want to pay into the **of sales** box. If you wish, you can also pay a fee for visitors sent to your site, even if those visitors don't make a purchase. For instance, if you type $10 into the **per thousand visits** box, you'll owe the affiliate $10 for every 1,000 potential buyers that arrive at your store through the link.

Buyer Discount	If you wish, you can provide a buyer discount to people arriving through the link. This allows you to "automate" coupons. Enter the number of the coupon you've already created into the box.
Linker sees	This determines what information is shown to the affiliates on their statistics pages—you can display just the number of visits ("hits" as the drop-down says, though this is not the correct term) and the order totals; or you can also display a list of all the orders, showing each order total and various buyer information. You should probably not select this option, as this page is not password protected.

4. Click the **Email Instructions** button. This opens a window in which an e-mail message is displayed. You can quickly e-mail the instructions on how to use the link to the affiliate.

5. When you click **Send**, you return to the previous page.

6. Click **Update** to complete creating the link.

When you need to monitor your links, click the Track Links link in Store Manager. The page that appears will provide a list of each link, showing how many "visits" have come through the link, the amount of sales through the link, and the "credit" owed to the merchant.

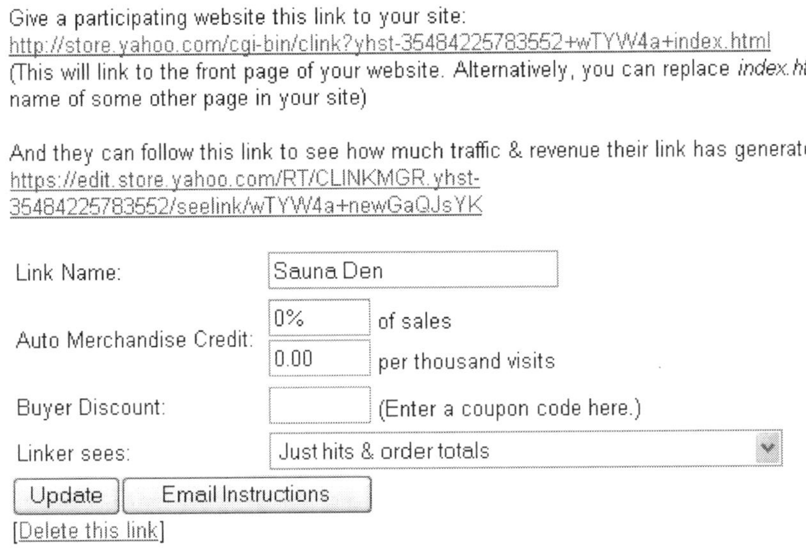

Give a participating website this link to your site:
http://store.yahoo.com/cgi-bin/clink?yhst-35484225783552+wTYW4a+index.html
(This will link to the front page of your website. Alternatively, you can replace *index.html* with the name of some other page in your site)

And they can follow this link to see how much traffic & revenue their link has generated:
https://edit.store.yahoo.com/RT/CLINKMGR.yhst-35484225783552/seelink/wTYW4a+newGaQJsYK

Link Name:	Sauna Den	
Auto Merchandise Credit:	0%	of sales
	0.00	per thousand visits
Buyer Discount:		(Enter a coupon code here.)
Linker sees:	Just hits & order totals	

[Update] [Email Instructions]
[Delete this link]

FIGURE 21-2   Creating a new trackable link

note *The trackable links we've just looked at provide a great way to create "discount" links and to track promotions, but they're not a great affiliate tool, for a number of reasons. The statistics are crude, they don't provide automatic affiliate-account setup, they don't provide the many sophisticated tools provided by real affiliate software. In fact, you may find it hard to recruit affiliates, because the system is so crude. For information on setting up a more sophisticated affiliate system, see Chapter 27.*

Using E-mail Marketing

E-mail marketing can be a very effective way to generate sales for many businesses. Yahoo! provides an integrated tool, *Campaigner*, that you can use to manage an e-mail account. This system lets you:

- Place a sign-up form on your web pages encouraging visitors to join your mailing list.

- Add a "sign up for our newsletter" option in the shopping-cart checkout. (See the Enable Got Customer Email Collection check box on the Customize Your Order Form page.)

- Add a list of e-mail addresses directly. If you've been using another e-mail system to send customers e-mails, you can import them.

- Create attractive, colorful e-mail messages from provided templates.

- Enter trackable links to pages on your site; you'll be able to see reports showing who clicks which links.

tip *Merchant Solutions collects e-mail addresses from customers and people who use the "request" tool (the Request A Catalog Or Feedback Form tool). This is an old, crude system that allows you to export a list which you could then use in some other e-mail system (such as Campaigner). Simply click the <u>Mailing Lists</u> link under the Promote column in Store Manager, and then click the <u>Export to Excel</u> link.*

For $10 a month, you can send 500 messages; for $25 a month you can send 2,500; $40 buys 5,000 messages; and $75 gets you 10,000 e-mail messages. You might consider using this system to sign up prospects and customers, and send them special offers each month. If you'd like to give it a try, you can do so for free. In fact as a Yahoo! merchant member you can use the system free for three months. Click the <u>Email Marketing</u> link under the Promote column in Store Manager.

Setting Up Cross-sell Products

The term *cross-sell* is a merchandising term meaning to sell an additional product to someone who is already buying something else from you. If someone has just placed a tent into their shopping basket, perhaps they may be interested in a protective groundsheet. If someone has just ordered a book on baking cakes, perhaps that buyer may be interested in the cookie trays you stock.

note *Some of the features you'll learn about in this chapter will not work in the Starter Merchant Solutions package. Cross-sell, Coupons, Gift Certificates, and Trackable Links only work in the Standard and Professional package. In addition, some of the reports and statistics you'll learn about are not available in the Starter package.*

Yahoo!'s cross-sell tool allows you to present ideas for additional purchases when someone places an item into the shopping cart (see Figure 21-3). You can

- Provide special discounts on the cross-sell purchase
- Set time limits—for seasonal promotions, for instance
- Create a cross-sell table in a spreadsheet and upload it into the cross-sell tool

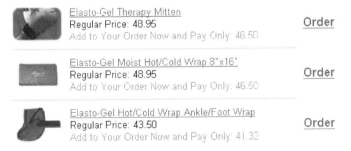

FIGURE 21-3 Three cross-sell items in a shopping cart

Here's how to use this tool:

1. Click the Cross-Sell link in Store Manager under the Promote column.

2. Click the Get Started Now link in the first page you see.

3. Click the **Create Entry** button to see the Cross-Sell table (Figure 21-4).

4. Select the item for which you want to set up cross-sell from the **Purchase Item** drop-down list box. When a buyer orders this product, the cross-sell items you define beneath it will be used.

5. If this is a temporary cross-sell promotion, enter the **Start Date** and **End Date** (in the format mm/dd/yyyy, such as 10/17/2006).

6. Select up to three cross-sell products from the **Cross-Sell Items** drop-down list boxes, or use the Browse for an item link to access a tool that lets you see products listed by category.

7. If you wish, you can enter a **Discount**. If the buyer purchases the cross-sell item at the same time as the original purchase item, the price of the cross-sell item is reduced by the amount you enter here. This can be a percentage or dollar amount, so you must enter a dollar sign or percent sign: $5 or 7%, for instance.

8. You can add more cross-sell items if you wish. Click the Add a Cross-Sell Item link and another row will be added. Note, however, that only three cross-sell items are displayed at any time, so if you create more, only three will be selected, randomly.

9. Click the **Create Entry** button to finish. The system checks that the rules are valid, and then displays a confirmation table.

Please review the information below and select "Add".

- **Add** will add new rules and update existing rules in your cross-sell table.

You attempted to load 3 rules.

- All the rules were successfully validated.

Purchase-Item Code	Cross-Sell-Item Code	Start Date	End Date	Discount
66400-00-00	66001-00-00	(No Start Date)	(No End Date)	5%
66400-00-00	66805	(No Start Date)	(No End Date)	5%
66400-00-00	66807	(No Start Date)	(No End Date)	5%

10. Click **Add** to finish.

Purchase Item			Start Date *(optional)*	End Date *(optional)*
Elasto-Gel Hot/Cold Wrap, 6" x 16"		Browse for an item	(mm/dd/yyyy)	(mm/dd/yyyy)

Cross-Sell Items			Discount *(optional)*	
Elasto-Gel Moist Hot/Cold Wrap 12"x12"		Browse for an item	5%	(% or $ off)
Elasto-Gel Moist Hot/Cold Wrap 8"x16"		Browse for an item	5%	(% or $ off)
Elasto-Gel Hot/Cold Wrap Ankle/Foot Wrap		Browse for an item	5%	(% or $ off)

(enter $xx for dollar discount, or xx% for percentage discount)

Add a Cross-Sell Item

[Create Entry] [Cancel]

FIGURE 21-4   Entering cross-sell products

tip   *Cross-sell settings do not need to be "published." As soon as you enter the rule, it's available to the store.*

You can also create cross-sell rules in a spreadsheet and afterward upload them—it's often quicker to do this. First, download a copy of an existing rule to see how the data file is formatted. Click the **Download Table** button in Cross-Sell Manager. Create a file with all the information, and then upload it using the **Upload Table** button.

	A	B	C	D	E
1	purchase-item-code	cross-sell-item-code	start-date	end-date	discount
2	66400-00-00	66001-00-00	10/17/2006	1/2/2007	5%
3	66400-00-00	66805	10/17/2006	1/2/2007	5%
4	66400-00-00	66807	10/17/2006	1/2/2007	5%

note   *Yahoo! promotes a number of marketing tools, some of which offer discounts to Merchant Solutions members. Go to the **Manage My Services** page and look at the **Promote Your Business** column.*

This page intentionally left blank

Part III

Using Google Pay Per Click and More to Grow Traffic

This page intentionally left blank

Chapter 22

Google AdWords and Other Pay Per Click Programs

Pay Per Click (PPC) is big business. In fact, it's the primary manner in which Google makes money—almost *all* its income, 98 percent, comes from PPC—and is very important to Yahoo! as well. Pay Per Click has brought mass-media advertising to small businesses. Businesses that would never have spent money on radio, TV, or newspapers, are now spending it on PPC . . . and sometimes even making a profit!

Sometimes? Well, the fact is that PPC doesn't work for everyone, as you'll learn in this chapter. You need the right combination of gross profit per sale, Pay Per Click price, and web-site conversion ratio. If you *don't* have the right combination—and many businesses simply don't—PPC will lose you money. Get everything lined up just right, though, and PPC can provide a regular, predictable flow of profitable business to your web site.

What Is PPC?

Pay Per Click refers to an advertising mechanism in which advertisers pay each time someone clicks their ad. More specifically, though, these days it refers to ads displayed on search-engine results pages.

You can see an example in Figure 22-1. At the top of the search results are two small ads—shown on a light blue background in this instance. In the top-right corner, notice the words *Sponsored Links*. More ads appear down the side of the page—again with the words *Sponsored Links*, but this time above the ads.

Each time someone clicks one of these links, the company that placed the ad is charged. How much? Somewhere from 5 cents (on Google) or 10 cents (on Yahoo!) to many dollars! Some PPC ads cost as much as $50 per click, occasionally even more!

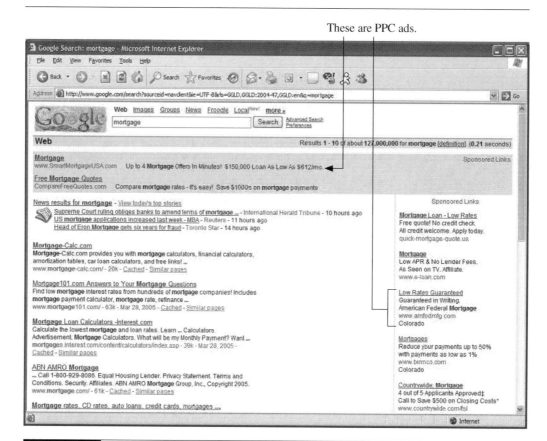

FIGURE 22-1   A Google search-results page, showing AdWords PPC ads

Because large PPC systems generally "feed" a variety of sites, when you buy ads through a system such as Google or Yahoo! Search Marketing Solutions, your ads may end up on many different search sites. But you may also have your ads distributed elsewhere, like on the pages of thousands of different web sites, thanks to the Google AdSense distribution program.

PPC advertising has a number of advantages:

■ **It's very quick.** You can start getting results from the search engines in a day or two (in theory, a few hours, but in most cases it takes a little longer to get everything sorted out).

■ **It's reliable.** Using PPC to get traffic to your site is very reliable. You can generate a lot of traffic, and always appear for appropriate searches in the major search engines . . . if you're willing to pay enough.

■ **It's easy to measure.** You can see just how much traffic you're getting, and even figure out how much of the traffic turns into business (see Chapter 24).

The PPC Systems

There are *many* PPC systems, but only three big ones, and a few "second-tier" systems:

- ■ **Google AdWords**   Perhaps the best-known PPC system is Google AdWords (http:// adwords.google.com/). Since Google is the single most important search engine, this system displays many millions of PPC ads every day.

- ■ **Yahoo! Search Marketing Solutions (formerly Overture)**   This system is also huge, and displays many millions of ads each day (www.overture.com/). Overture was the original PPC search-engine company.

- ■ **MSN adCenter**   MSN, Microsoft's online service, actually gets its PPC ads from Yahoo! at present. However, it's in the process of building its own PPC system and by the summer of 2006 will probably have stopped using Yahoo! ads entirely.

The "second-tier" systems include services such as FindWhat (www.findwhat.com/), LookSmart (www.looksmark.com/), Enhance (www.enhance.com/), ePilot (www.epilot.com/), Espotting (www.espotting.com/), and Kanoodle (www.kanoodle.com/).

Others also exist. In fact, there are literally hundreds of PPC systems . . . most of which are not worth dealing with. For example, when you figure the time it takes to configure the systems, it's not worth the small amount of admittedly cheap clicks you'll get—and some that border on the fraudulent (you'll get little or no traffic from them, but will pay a setup fee that you'll never see again). In general, you'll want to avoid very small PPC systems, and stick to the first- and second-tier systems.

Understanding the PPC Process

The basic process of using Pay Per Click is pretty simple.

1. Decide to which pages you want to direct traffic from your ads. You can bring traffic to any page you wish, not just the home page.

2. Register with a PPC system—you'll provide a credit card to be used to pay for the ads—and "load" the account with some money to begin with.

3. Write one or more PPC ads (carefully follow the system's ad guidelines, or the ad won't be placed).

4. Associate keywords with your ad—that is, decide which keywords will "trigger" your ads to appear.

5. Place a bid on each keyword for each ad—in other words, tell the PPC system how much you are willing to pay every time someone clicks your ad.

6. Turn on the ad campaign and wait for the traffic to appear.

Understanding Conversion Ratio, Click Value, and ROI

There's one huge disadvantage to PPC ads, though . . . they cost money. Sometimes a lot of money. Often, in fact, so much money that you will lose money if you buy PPC ads! In order to use PPC, you really must understand *Conversion Ratio*, *Breakeven Click Value*, and *Return on Investment* (*ROI*):

- **Conversion Ratio**   The proportion of visitors to your site who buy from you. This is the foundation of any click-value or ROI calculation.

- **Breakeven Click Value**   The "breakeven" value of a click is the maximum sum you can pay for a click and not lose money. Of course, you want to pay as little as possible, but there's a point at which a click doesn't make you money and doesn't lose you money. If you go over the price, however, you start losing.

- **Return on Investment**   The amount of money you make after investing in advertising, typically expressed in terms of the sum returned for every dollar invested. If you pay $1,000 for ads, and make a profit of $10,000, your ROI is $10 per $1 invested.

You need to consider these things three times:

- **When you have no background information**   When you first begin considering PPC ads, you may not know what your *conversion ratio* is. That is, you don't know how many people coming to your site will buy from you. You can, however, do a simple "guesstimate" to figure out whether PPC will work for you. At this point, you can decide if PPC is worth doing.

- **When you know your conversion ratio**   Once you understand what your conversion ratio really is, you can calculate more accurately whether PPC will work for you. At this point, you'll have a much better idea of the likelihood of success.

- **When you're running a PPC campaign**   Once you're buying PPC ads, and people are coming to your site, you can calculate ROI exactly. It's then that you'll know exactly whether (under current conditions) PPC works for you.

In order to calculate click value and ROI, you must first know—or estimate—your *conversion ratio*. The conversion ratio is the relationship between the number of people carrying out some process and the number of those people who move on to the "next step." For instance:

- If 100 people see an ad, and three click the ad, the "conversion" is 3:100, or three percent.

- If 100 people come to your web site, and ten sign up for a newsletter, the "conversion" is 10:100, or 10 percent.

- If 100 people come to your web site, and one buys a product, the "conversion" is 1:100, or 1 percent.

Of course, it's the last of these that we're most interested in. Of all the people who come to your site, how many will buy? This conversion ratio is the core of any ROI calculation.

Calculating Click Value and ROI with No Background

Unfortunately, you're probably in a situation in which you simply don't have the information to accurately calculate click value and ROI. You have to guess. Here's what most people do: they think, "For every 100 people I can get to the site, I'll sell to, say, 20 of them." Based on that, they look at the cost of clicks, and get excited . . . there's a lot of money to be made! So let's look at more realistic numbers.

Assume that for every 200 people who visit your site, *one* will buy. If you're lucky, it will be more. If you're unlucky, it will be less. But a conversion ratio of 1:200 is not an unreasonable number.

Many people are shocked when they see this number. 1 in 200 . . . half a percent! How can that be right? You must understand that conversion ratios are very low. If you own a retail store and sell to 20 percent of all the people who walk into your store, you shouldn't use that as an online-store conversion-ratio estimate! Online conversion ratios are *much* lower than offline ratios.

 We're not saying that online stores never have better conversion ratios than 1 in 200 or 1 in 100—many have much *higher conversion ratios. The world's top retail stores average perhaps 4 percent and sometimes, very rarely, reach over 20 percent. But such stores are in the minority. In general, online retail conversion ratios are small fractions.*

Calculating Gross Profit

In order to calculate these important numbers, you need to know your gross profit per sale. We're talking *gross profit*, not *revenues*. If you sell a product for $50, your gross profit is *not* $50—after all, you first have to buy or create the product. Here's how to calculate gross profit:

+	The order total
+	The shipping and handling fee
=	Revenues
–	The credit-card transaction costs or other transaction costs (such as PayPal transaction cost)
–	The e-commerce system transaction costs (some e-commerce systems, such as Yahoo! Merchant Solutions, charge a fee for every sale)
–	The sum you paid for the products you sold
–	The price you paid to ship the products to you, including shipping insurance
–	The cost of the packaging used to ship the products
–	The cost of the labor to pack and ship the products
–	The shipping fee
–	Any other per-product costs you had to pay
=	Gross Profit

In other words, gross profit is what is left over from the sum you received for the products you sold after subtracting all the costs directly related to selling the products.

The calculation above doesn't include click costs, though; we're assuming that you're trying to calculate the gross profit of a sale, before you have begun your PPC-advertising campaign. Of course, if you are paying for clicks to generate the sale, you must also subtract the cost of those clicks.

Calculating Breakeven Click Value

So, here's how to calculate breakeven click value. Let's use some sample data:

- Click conversion rate: out of every 200 people clicking a PPC ad and arriving at your site, one will buy.
- Average profit per sale, before advertising costs: every sale brings $150 in gross profit.

The calculation is very simple. Divide the average profit by 200 (in order to make one sale, you must get 200 clicks): $150/200 = 75 cents.

What does this mean? If you spend 75 cents for every click—that is, 75 cents each time you use a PPC ad to bring a visitor to your site—and you sell to one person in 200, you'll break even. You won't make money on the sales, but you won't lose money on the products sold, either.

What's the ROI?

What's the ROI on an advertising campaign in which you pay the maximum click value? Nothing. You have no return. The profit you make on the sales goes to paying the investment in the advertising. Here's how to calculate ROI:

Gross profit derived from the advertising divided by the sum spent on advertising

In the previous example, the advertising cost was $150 (200 clicks at 75 cents), and the profit, after subtracting the cost of the advertising, was $150.

$150/$150 = $0

Consider another scenario. This time you spend 40 cents per click; you still need 200 people to come to the site for each sale (so you spend $80 on clicks), and the gross profit, before click costs, is $150.

$150 − $80 = $70

$70/$80 = $0.875

In other words, for every dollar you spend, your ROI is $0.875.

Calculating Click Value and ROI Later

If you're already in business and selling through your online store, you should have a closer estimate of your conversion ratio. From there, you should be able to figure out the real conversion ratio. It won't necessarily be the same as the conversion ratio you'll get from your

PPC campaign; for many reasons the PPC conversion ratio could be higher or lower. But at least you'll have a real number to work with, rather than a pure guess.

How do you figure out your conversion ratio? Look at your web site statistics and find out how many people visited your store over a particular period. For instance, choose your last month of operations, and look for a statistic such as:

■ Unique Visits

■ Unique Visitors

■ Customers (an ambiguous term, but unfortunately the one used by Yahoo! Merchant Solutions)

tip *If you're using Yahoo! Merchant Solutions, click the* Reports *link in the Statistics column and look for the Customers statistic.*

Once you know how many people have visited your store during that period, you need to find out two more things:

■ The number of orders taken through the store

■ The average *gross profit* on each order

Now you can calculate your conversion ratio. To do so, divide the Number of Visitors by the Number of Orders. For instance, if you had 1,538 visitors one month, and you processed 12 orders, your conversion ratio is 1:128. That is, you need 128 visitors in order to make one sale.

The average gross profit number, of course, allows you to figure out your *breakeven click value*. For instance, let's say:

■ The average gross profit on the orders is $35.

■ For every order you needed 128 visitors.

■ Thus, your breakeven click value is 27.34 cents. If you pay more than this for every click, you'll lose money.

This is still just an estimate, of course, because until you run a PPC campaign, you don't know if the conversion will be worse, the same, or better.

Once you actually run the PPC campaign, you can get exact numbers. You won't care so much about breakeven click value anymore because you'll be able to see your ROI and determine whether you're making money. You'll know just how much you're spending for each click, and you'll also know your conversion ratio, under two conditions:

■ If you're sure you're getting all your site visits from PPC campaigns, then you know all your sales are derived from PPC advertising and you can accurately calculate your ROI. If you get traffic from various sources, though, you can't do this, unless . . .

■ You install software that tracks sales from your PPC campaigns. We'll look at this in Chapter 24.

So, Can You Make Money?

Many readers, after thinking about the last few pages, are probably now in shock, especially if they've run a few numbers through their heads. They remember that

- A click costs at least 5 or 10 cents through the major PPC systems, and often much more.
- Conversion rates are often 1:100 or 1:200.

How on earth can I possibly make money with PPC? The simple answer is, in many cases, you can't. Here's an example. Let's say your product will give you a gross profit of $10, before paying for the PPC costs. Not an unusual sum—many products are in this ballpark, such as books, music, small gifts, and so on. Let's give you a fighting chance, and assume you'll have a conversion ratio of 1:50. And we'll assume that you can buy clicks for 10 cents:

- 50 clicks are needed for one sale.
- 50 clicks cost $5 (50 × 10 cents).
- Thus one sale costs $5, so your ROI is $1 for every $1 spent on advertising ($10 pre-advertising profit = $5 profit after advertising; $5/$5 = $1).

You're making money, but unless you sell a lot of whatever this is, you're not getting rich. So let's see what happens when you change just one thing in the calculation. Let's try separately altering the conversion ratio, the click cost, and the gross profit per sale and see how each affects the equation.

- Your conversion ratio is 1:100—you just broke even.
- Your conversion ratio is 1:200—you just lost $10.
- Your click cost is actually 30 cents a click—you just lost $5.
- Your click cost is actually 50 cents a click—you just lost $15.
- Your gross profit is actually $6—you just made $1.

The fact is, PPC *doesn't work for everyone!* In particular, you'll have trouble making PPC work if:

- Your products have low gross profits.
- Your web site has a low conversion ratio.
- Click costs are very high for the keywords you want to use.

Remember:

- High Gross Profits + High Conversion Ratios + Low Click Costs = Good!
- Low Gross Profits + Low Conversions Ratios + High Click Costs = Bad!

Any one of these elements can cause a problem. If all three are bad, you're in real trouble!

Understanding Keywords

A *keyword* or *keyword phrase* is a word or series of words typed into a search engine by someone seeking something. Keywords are used to trigger the display of your PPC ads. You'll "bid" on keywords—for instance, you might bid, say, 55 cents for the term *camping equipment*. When someone types *camping equipment* into their browser, the PPC system looks at all the bids for that keyword phrase, and places the ads on the results page accordingly—most systems place the highest bid at the top of the list, as in Figure 22-2, although Google uses other characteristics. More importantly, ads that people click more frequently get a rank "boost" in the system.

If someone clicks this ad, the
advertiser pays 36 cents.   This one is 35 cents a click.

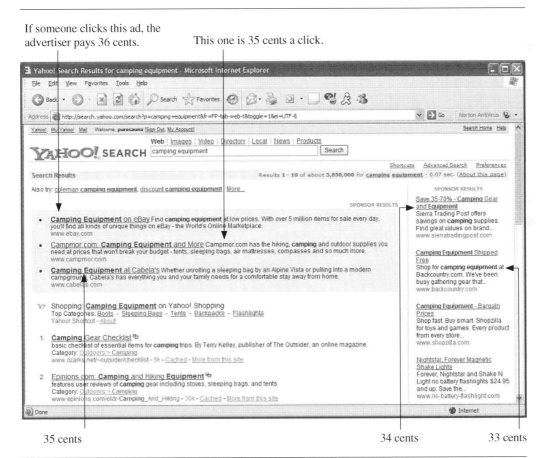

35 cents   34 cents   33 cents

FIGURE 22-2   Yahoo! places ads according to the amount of the bid.

As you can see, keywords are essential. In fact, you have to pick the right keywords, because

- The right keywords bring the right people to your site; you don't want to pay for people who won't buy!
- Some keywords are more expensive than others. Some keywords might be several dollars, while similar ones might be ten cents.

Here's an example, taken from Yahoo! Search Marketing Solutions (www.overture.com), for top bids at the time of writing:

vioxx	$11
vioxx attorney	$38.06
vioxx attorney denver	10 cents

Keywords are critical! Before you can begin a PPC campaign, you must understand the keywords.

Broad vs. Narrow Terms

You can bid on broad terms, or you can bid on narrow terms (or both, of course). Each has advantages and disadvantages:

- Broad terms (for example, *vioxx*) tend to be expensive.
- Broad terms often attract people who are not looking for what you're selling. Use the term *golf*, and you'll get people who want golf vacations, golf lessons, golf equipment, and so on. So you'll end up buying clicks for people who aren't even interested in your stuff.
- Narrow terms are often cheaper than broad terms. *Golf* is currently $1.51, while *golf equipment* is 42 cents, and *golf equipment denver* is 10 cents on Yahoo! (this isn't always the case, as shown by the *vioxx attorneys* example earlier).
- Narrow terms are more likely to attract the right people, saving you from paying for worthless clicks.

Doing a Keyword Analysis

If keywords are important, how do you know which keywords to use?

1. Guess.
2. Take your guesses and run them through a keyword-analysis tool.

Do *not* stop at Step 1! If you guess, you'll guess wrong!

tip

Wordtracker is almost certainly the best keyword-analysis tool around (www.Wordtracker .com). It's the system used by most search-engine professionals because you can do more with it, more quickly. We don't have room to describe this tool, but it's worth spending a few hours and doing a really good analysis with this tool.

We'll look at a free way for carrying out a keyword analysis, though ideally you should use Wordtracker, which you can "rent" for around $8 a day (one day's usually plenty). The following's a simple procedure that uses your brain power and Yahoo!'s Keyword Selector Tool.

1. Quickly write down all the obvious keywords, the ones you've already thought about. If you're selling golf equipment, an obvious choice might be *golf equipment* . . . and *golf clubs, golf balls, golf cart*, and so on.

2. Now think from your customers' point of view. Put yourself in their shoes . . . can you think of terms they might use?

3. Ask employees, partners, family . . . what other terms can you come up with?

4. Go back over your list, and add plural versions of singular terms and singular versions of plural terms.

5. Look for words that are likely to be frequently misspelled, and add them, too. (Some words are misspelled as much as one third of the time they're used, so these represent a significant opportunity for reaching people.)

6. Go to the Yahoo! Search Marketing Solutions web site (http://searchmarketing.yahoo .com/) and find the Keyword Selector Tool. (Unfortunately, Yahoo! keeps moving things around; sometimes it's easy to find, other times it's hidden away. Dig around and you should eventually find it; look for the Advertiser Center or something similar.)

7. Type a keyword into the text box and press ENTER.

tip

Google also provides a free keyword-analysis tool, though it's also hidden away a little. Go to adwords.google.com and begin setting up a Google AdWords campaign—quickly enter a little fake data so you can move through the steps and you'll find a <u>Keyword Tool</u> link in the **Choose Keywords** *step.*

8. The tool returns a list of similar keywords and the number of times the keyword has been used in a prior month on the Yahoo! PPC network (see Figure 22-3).

9. Look down the list for terms to add to your own list. Enter another term, including terms you find in this list, into the text box at the top and try again.

This tool will give you ideas for keywords, and some notion of how often searchers use a particular term. It won't tell you how much the term will cost, though.

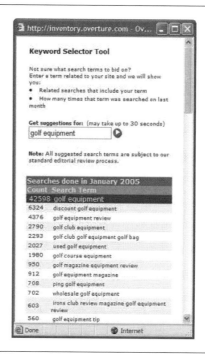

FIGURE 22-3   The Yahoo! Keyword Selector Tool

Checking Bid Prices

Here's how to quickly view bid costs for a few keywords.

1. At Yahoo!, in the Advertiser Center, click the <u>View Bids Tool</u> link to open the View Bids window (see Figure 22-4; note that this tool is also hidden away now and then).

2. Type the term you want to check into the first text box, copy the security code into the second text box, and press ENTER.

3. Yahoo! returns the first 40 PPC ads, along with the bid price. (See Figure 22-5.)

What exactly is a bid price? It's the maximum amount that an advertiser is willing to pay for a click; it's *not* always what the advertiser actually pays. The actual cost is only one penny above the next bid. For instance, in Figure 22-5 advertiser #2 may pay 91 cents, while #1 may pay 92 cents . . . but both are willing to pay much more, if necessary, to hold their high positions.

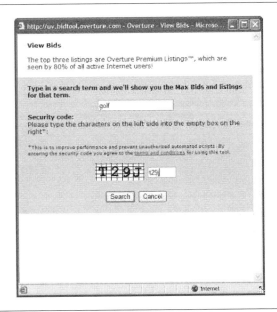

FIGURE 22-4   The View Bids window

This is the bid—the maximum that the advertiser is willing to pay for a click.

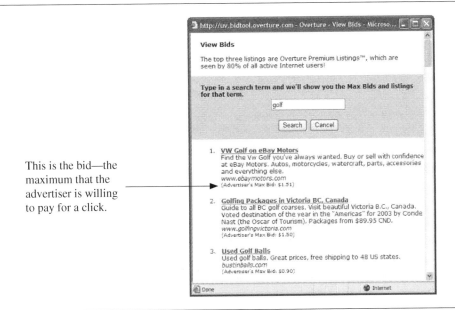

FIGURE 22-5   The View Bids tool showing a list of bids, along with the bid prices

This page intentionally left blank

Chapter 23

Setting Up a Google
PPC Campaign

In this chapter, we'll examine how to set up your first Pay Per Click (PPC) campaign, using Google's popular AdWords program. Google is selling billions of dollars worth of "clicks" each year through this system . . . in fact, it's the only advertising system Google has at present. Google has never been enthusiastic about banner ads, though for a while it did sell fixed-position text ads at the top of search results pages. But in 1994, it dumped those and went to a pure PPC model. Currently the only way to advertise on Google is through its PPC program (unlike some other search engines, it doesn't sell "paid inclusion" or "trusted feed" services, which the founders of Google believe to be unethical).

Getting Started

We're going to jump right in and begin setting up our ad campaign on Google.

1. Start by opening https://adwords.google.com/ in your browser, and click the **Click to begin** button.

2. In the first step, you'll select location information (see Figure 23-1). In the list box, click the language you want to target (Google has services targeting dozens of countries and language groups). If you want to select multiple languages, press the CTRL key (the Apple key on the Mac) while you click.

3. In the large box, select the location *type* you want to use.

    ▓ **Global or nationwide**   Your ad will appear on results pages worldwide or in a specific country (you'll select the country in the next step).

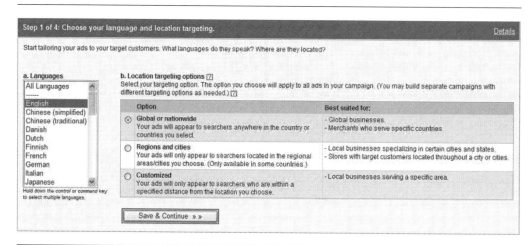

FIGURE 23-1   Begin by selecting location information.

- **Regions and cities**   You'll be able to select a particular region or city, which is great for brick-and-mortar businesses, though not so important for the average e-commerce site.

- **Customized**   A refinement of the "region" choice that lets you specify a distance from your location; again, useful for brick-and-mortar stores.

Selecting a Location for Your Ads

Let's look at how to set up the three different location options. If at all possible, it's worthwhile defining your location choices, because the fewer ads shown outside your location, the more efficient your ad campaign will be.

- If you only ship within, say, the United States and Canada, you don't want to display your ads to people in other countries.

- If you're advertising to get people to the type of business that can draw from a wide region, such as theaters, museums, amusement parks, and so on, you won't want people outside your region to see the ad; you'll probably want to use the **Regions and cities** choice, which allows you to select states and major metropolitan areas.

- If you're trying to get people to your retail store, with a more restricted range, you only want a limited number of people viewing the ad; thus, you may want to use the **Customized** choice, which lets you specify a distance from an address, ZIP code, or even a longitude or latitude.

Selecting the World or Specific Countries

Select **Global or nationwide** to see the **Choose Your Countries** page. If you don't care where the ad appears, you'll leave All Countries selected, of course. But that shouldn't be the case. If you don't ship your products to a particular country, you don't want to waste money on ads targeting that country.

Select the countries in which you want your ads displayed—hold CTRL (or the Apple key on the Mac) to select multiple countries—and click the **Add** button. Then click the **Save & Continue** button.

Selecting a Region or City

You can specify a particular state or major metropolitan area. Select **Regions and cities** to see a box in which you can select a country.

tip *You can only select a region or city in a single country; you couldn't, for instance, select Vancouver, Canada and Seattle, United States. If you want to do this, you'll have to set up this campaign for one country, and then go back later and create a separate ad campaign.*

Select the country and click **Save & Continue**. In the page that's displayed, you can select the states and regions in which you want your ads to appear. What if the choices aren't precise enough? Perhaps you want to exhibit your ad to people in Lakewood, CO, but the only choice you have is Denver, CO, the larger metro area. In such a case, click the browser's Back button twice and select **Customized**.

Selecting a Very Precise Region

You can be very precise about the area in which your ad is displayed. But remember that Google doesn't know for sure exactly where everybody is, so this is not terribly accurate.

Select the **Customized** option, and you'll see the box in Figure 23-2.

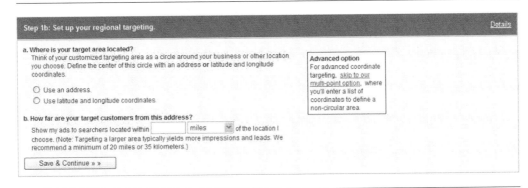

FIGURE 23-2   You can very precisely define a location.

There are three ways to define a precise location:

- Enter an **address** or **ZIP code** and a distance from that position.
- Enter **latitude and longitude coordinates** and a distance from that position.
- Click the skip to our multi-point option link and enter coordinate boundaries of an area.

Creating Your Ads

When you select your region and click **Save & Continue**, you'll find yourself in **Step 2: Create Ad Groups** (see Figure 23-3).

tip

We'll talk more about writing ads, including the "editorial guidelines," later in this chapter in the section "Writing Effective Ads."

You're actually creating an ad here. You can see a sample ad (the Got Widgets? ad below the first text box). This sample ad has a Headline, a Description line 1, a Description line 2, and

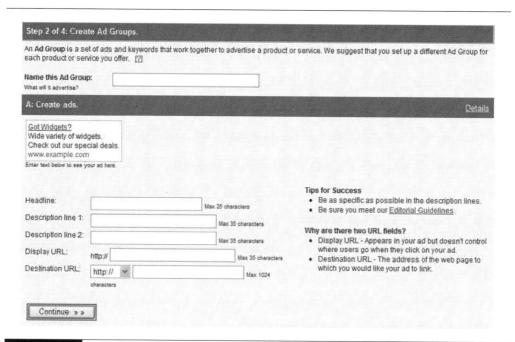

FIGURE 23-3   This is where you create your first AdWords ad.

a Display URL, corresponding to the following text boxes, which describe the information you need to fill in.

Name this Ad Group	This is just a reference name for your own use; it doesn't appear in the ad itself.
Headline	This is the first line of the ad—in blue, underlined text, on which the link is placed (up to 25 characters).
Description line 1	The first line of the ad (up to 35 characters).
Description line 2	The second line of the ad (up to 35 characters).
Display URL	The URL that appears, in green, at the bottom of the ad (up to 35 characters). This is *not* the URL that the searcher actually lands on when clicking the ad; it's generally the site home page.
Destination URL	This is the actual page that the ad points to, and it can be virtually as long as you wish (1,024 characters). You can (you *should*) in most cases point to a particular page within your site. You can also add a tracking code (something we'll discuss later in Chapter 24), so you can see when traffic arrives at your site from this ad.

Figuring out how to say what you need to say in 95 text characters takes time! Don't rush this; make sure you get it right. See "Writing Effective Ads" later in this chapter for more information.

Entering Keywords

When you click the **Continue** button, a page displays where you should enter the keywords.

 tip *Keywords are not "case sensitive." Type* shoe *and Google matches the ad with* shoe, Shoe, *and* SHOE.

We discussed keywords in Chapter 22, so you probably already have your keyword list; simply paste your keywords into this text box. You can also use the Keyword Tool link to do some of your keyword analysis right now. When you're ready, click the **Save Keywords** button to continue.

 tip *You should enter similar keywords. Later, you can create more ad groups, generating various groups of similar keywords (an* ad group *is a group of keywords matched to one or more ads).*

Bidding on Keywords

On the following page (Figure 23-4), you'll be able to bid on the keywords you entered.

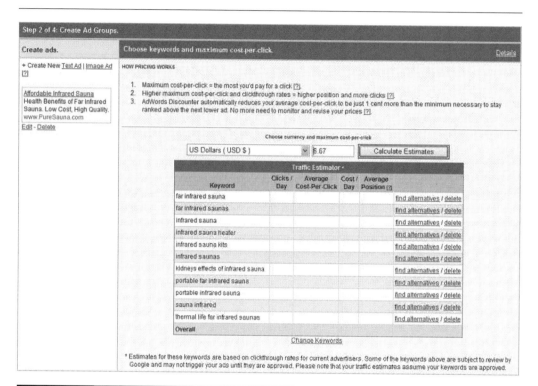

FIGURE 23-4 Here's where you assign the bid for a keyword.

Before starting, click the **Calculate Estimates** button. Google has already suggested a click bid based on current conditions for the keywords you've entered, so clicking the button shows you what you'll get based on Google's recommendation (see Figure 23-5).

The Google table shows the following information:

Keyword	The keywords you entered.
Clicks/Day	For each keyword, the number of clicks you're likely to get each day.
Average Cost-Per-Click	The average price you'll pay for each click.
Cost/Day	The sum you'll pay each day; look at the bottom of the column to see your total daily cost.
Average Position	The average position where your ad will sit in the list of PPC ads on the search results page.
Find Alternatives	Click this link to open the Keyword Tool and find related keywords.
Delete	Click this to remove a keyword from the list.

				Traffic Estimator •		
US Dollars (USD $)		⌄	2.00		Recalculate Estimates	
Keyword	**Clicks / Day**	**Average Cost-Per-Click**	**Cost / Day**	**Average Position**		
far infrared sauna	2.1	$1.71	$3.59	5.6	find alternatives / delete	
far infrared saunas	1.1	$1.61	$1.77	4.8	find alternatives / delete	
infrared sauna	8.1	$1.59	$12.81	5.5	find alternatives / delete	
infrared sauna heater	< 0.1	$0.05	$0.00	1.0	find alternatives / delete	
infrared sauna kits	< 0.1	$0.05	$0.00	1.0	find alternatives / delete	
infrared saunas	4.6	$1.75	$8.04	5.4	find alternatives / delete	
kidneys effects of infrared sauna	< 0.1	$0.05	$0.00	1.0	find alternatives / delete	
portable far infrared sauna	< 0.1	$0.05	$0.00	1.0	find alternatives / delete	
portable infrared sauna	0.5	$1.31	$0.66	3.9	find alternatives / delete	
sauna infrared	< 0.1	$0.00	$0.00	-	find alternatives / delete	
saunas	80.0	$1.23	$98.40	2.0	find alternatives / delete	
thermal life far infrared saunas	< 0.1	$0.05	$0.00	1.0	find alternatives / delete	
Overall	**96.4**		$1.30	$125.24	2.6	

FIGURE 23-5   Clicking the Calculate Estimates button shows you the likely effect of the maximum bid.

Too expensive? Enter another value into the text box and click the button again.

Remember, the maximum bid is not what you'll usually pay; it's what you're telling Google you're *willing* to pay. But you never pay more than one penny above the ad below you. For instance, the following table shows an example of five people bidding on a keyword:

	Price Paid Per Click	Maximum Bid
Advertiser 1	$0.89	$20.00
Advertiser 2	$0.88	$3.00
Advertiser 3	$0.87	$1.35
Advertiser 4	$0.86	$1.00
Advertiser 5	$0.85	$0.85

note   *Google actually doesn't base ad position purely on bid. It also factors in the "pull" of the ad. Ads that get clicked upon frequently get an extra boost in the rankings and may actually end up above ads with a higher maximum bid.*

Try reducing your bid. As it goes down, your cost per click and cost per day goes down, too. On the other hand, so does your average position, and the amount of traffic you'll get to your site.

When you've finished here, click the **Save & Continue** button, and Google asks if you want to create another Ad Group. If you wish you can finish setting up your account, and add another Ad Group later; click the **Continue to Step 3** button.

Specifying Your Daily Budget

Next, you'll see the page in which you can enter your daily budget, the most you're willing to spend each day. This is a good way to avoid surprises! Actually you may still be charged more each day, due to general fluctuations in searches, but overall you'll be limited to around this sum each day over a month.

Entering Your Account Info

That's it. You've now created an ad group for your first ad campaign. Next, you need to input basic account information. Enter your e-mail address (twice, to confirm you entered it correctly), then create a password and enter that twice, too. When you click the **Create My AdWords Account** button, Google now sends you a verification e-mail.

> **tip** *Google uses two related terms,* Ad Campaign *and* Ad Group. *A campaign is an advertising "project" that targets a specific region and contains one or more ad groups. An ad group is a group of keywords to which one or more ads have been assigned. If you use multiple ads for a single group of keywords, Google rotates the ad; the reports will show you which ad is most effective. (The term* ad group *is really rather misleading; you may find it easier to think of an ad group as a* keyword group—*a group of keywords with one or more ads—and there are good reasons to combine the keywords with no more than a single ad. See "Creating New Ads" later in this chapter for more information about the pros and cons of having multiple ads in a single group.)*

When you receive your e-mail, click the link in the e-mail to verify the account. Then you can go back to the main AdWords page (https://adwords.google.com/) and log into your account.

Modifying Keyword Characteristics

Your account has been set up, but the ads are not yet running. They won't, in fact, until you "activate" the account. That's okay in many cases; perhaps you want to spend more time creating ads and looking around the system. In fact, we recommend you look at one or two more things (described next) before entering your billing information (as soon as you do that, your ad "goes live").

■ **Individual bid prices**   You can change bid prices for individual keywords.

■ **Keyword matching**   You can define how Google treats the keywords you selected.

tip   *If you want to stop a campaign or ad group from running, select the check box next to the campaign or group name, and then click the **Pause** button.*

Log into your account, and you'll see the table shown in Figure 23-6, which lists the Ad Campaigns you've created.

tip   *Want to create a new ad campaign? Look for the Create new AdWords campaign link just above the Campaigns table, under the **Campaign Management** tab.*

The table in Figure 23-6 is a summary of the ad campaign, showing various statistics (we'll look more closely at these in Chapter 24). For now, we need to look at how to modify keyword characteristics.

Changing Bid Prices for Specific Keywords

We saw how to set a bid price for an entire ad campaign, but you can also specify bid prices for individual keywords. The following steps outline how:

1. Click the campaign name in the Campaign table (Figure 23-6).

2. In the Campaign Summary table (Figure 23-7), click the name of the ad group containing the keywords you want to modify.

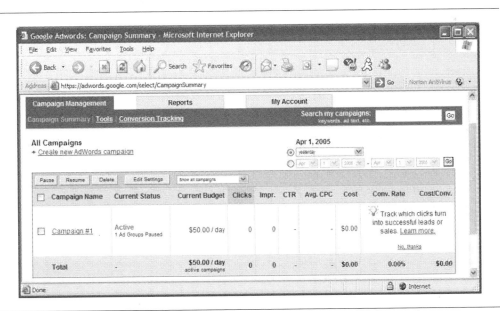

FIGURE 23-6   The Campaign Management table, which lists your PPC campaigns

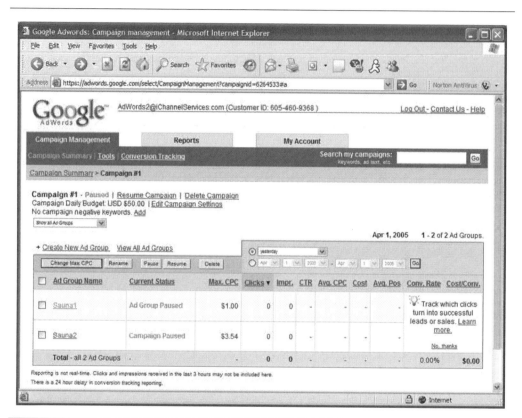

FIGURE 23-7   The Campaign Summary table lists the ad groups inside the campaign.

tip   *There's another way to change individual keyword bids. Select the Ad Group name, click the check box next to the keyword you want to modify, and then click the **Edit CPCs/URLs** button.*

3. Click the Edit Keywords link on the Ad page.

4. In the keyword table that appears (Figure 23-8), you can specify different rates for each keyword phrase, like this:

keyword**bid**

For instance, *far infrared sauna***2.50** means "set this keyword to a maximum bid of $2.50."

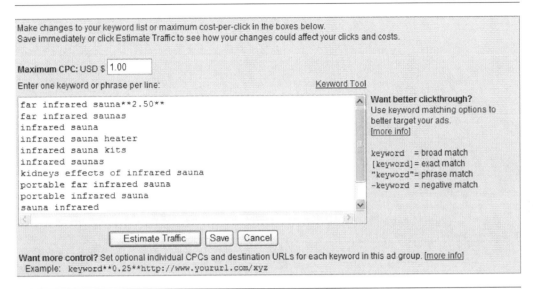

Make changes to your keyword list or maximum cost-per-click in the boxes below.
Save immediately or click Estimate Traffic to see how your changes could affect your clicks and costs.

Maximum CPC: USD $ 1.00

Enter one keyword or phrase per line: Keyword Tool

```
far infrared sauna**2.50**
far infrared saunas
infrared sauna
infrared sauna heater
infrared sauna kits
infrared saunas
kidneys effects of infrared sauna
portable far infrared sauna
portable infrared sauna
sauna infrared
```

Want better clickthrough?
Use keyword matching options to
better target your ads.
[more info]

```
keyword   = broad match
[keyword] = exact match
"keyword" = phrase match
-keyword  = negative match
```

Estimate Traffic   Save   Cancel

Want more control? Set optional individual CPCs and destination URLs for each keyword in this ad group. [more info]
   Example: keyword**0.25**http://www.yoururl.com/xyz

FIGURE 23-8   Change your keyword settings here.

Changing Target URLs

You can change the URL that a keyword points to, also. You may want people who come to your site after entering one keyword to go to Page A, and those who enter another keyword to go to Page B, for instance.

In the same keyword box, enter the information like this:

keyword**bid**targeturl

For instance: far infrared sauna**2.50**http://www.pursauna.com/abc

If you don't want to specify a different bid, just leave that space empty, like this:

far infrared sauna** **http://www.pursauna.com/abc

Keyword Matching Techniques

There's one more keyword adjustment we can make: changing the way in which Google matches the keywords you enter with the keywords typed into the search engine by people searching through Google.

By default, the keywords you entered are used in a "broad match" method of matching up your ad with the searches, but there are three other methods:

- **Broad match**   This, the default, can lead to high CPCs (Costs Per Click), and should only really be used with multiphrase terms. If your keywords are, say, *infrared sauna*, your ad will be included in the results whenever someone includes the words *infrared* and *sauna* in their search, even if in reverse order or combined with other words.

- **Phrase match**   A phrase match ensures that your ad only appears when someone uses the terms in the order in which you entered them, although they may be combined with other words. If your keyword phrase is *infrared sauna*, the ad appears if someone types *infrared sauna* or *cheap infrared sauna*, but not for *cheap sauna infrared*.

- **Exact match**   An exact match is one in which your ad is included in results only if the searcher entered the exact phrase you bid on, with no other words included, and in exactly the same order.

- **Negative match**   A negative match tells Google *not* to include your ad in the results if the word is included in a search. For instance, let's say you want to display an ad when someone searches for the term *mesothelioma*, but *not* when the search is for a mesothelioma attorney; simply add *-attorney* to the list and your ad is never matched for searches that include the word *attorney*.

The following table shows how to code the search terms:

Broad Match	*infrared sauna*	Match with any search including the words
Phrase Match	*"infrared sauna"*	Match with any search that includes the words in this order
Exact Match	*[infrared sauna]*	Match only with this exact search phrase—in this order, and with no other words included
Negative Match	*-attorney*	Do not match with any search that includes this term, even if other keywords match

*tip   You can quickly add negative keywords to an entire Ad Campaign, rather than just an Ad Group. Choose the **Campaign Management** tab at the top, click the <u>Tools</u> link, and then click the <u>Edit Campaign Negative Keywords</u> link.*

Understanding Expanded Matches

By default, any keywords that are set to *broad match*—and by default that's all of them, unless you change them to *precise* or *exact*—use *expanded matching*.

Expanded matching takes your keywords and looks for *similar* terms:

- If you entered a plural term, Google matches your ad with the singular term.

- If you entered a singular term, it matches with the plural.

- It matches the ad with synonyms.
- It matches the ad with related terms.

If you'd like to see expanded-match terms, use the Google Keyword Tool; the terms it shows you when you enter a keyword are the expanded terms.

Creating New Ads

You'll want to experiment with different ad text. Does the word *Cheap* work better than the word *Affordable* or the term *Low Cost?* Do the ads work better when you include a time-sensitive offer (*Reduced Prices for 30 Days*), and so on.

You can actually create several ads for a single ad group, and then be able to see the results for each individual ad. However, there is one problem with doing this. As you'll see in the next chapter, you'll want to keep a careful eye on the results provided by each ad/keyword combination. Some ads perform very well with some keywords, but not with others. If you have multiple ads for a group of keywords—multiple ads in a single ad group—you can see how each ad performs for the entire group of keywords, and you can see how all the ads combined perform for a particular keyword. However, at present, you cannot see how an individual ad performs for an individual keyword. One ad may do very well for keyword-phrase A, and badly for B, yet one of the other ads in the group might do very well for B, and badly for A. If you group ads together in an ad group, you'll never know.

You can create new ads in this way:

- **To add an advert to an ad group**, open the group and click the <u>Create New Text Ad</u> link. (To edit an ad, click the <u>Edit</u> link; if you have multiple ads in a group, you'll find it at the bottom of the page under the picture of the ad.)

- **To create an ad alone, using the keywords from an existing ad group**, you'll have to simply create a new group—there's no shortcut to duplicate the group and change the ad. Click the <u>Create New Ad Group</u> link in the Campaign Summary page, and copy and paste the keywords from the first ad group to the new one.

Turning Off "Content" Placement

As you learned in Chapter 22, Google AdWords ads can appear in two places: in search-result pages, and in *content* pages (pages on non-search sites).

By default, Google will distribute your ads throughout its entire network, both search pages and content pages. We recommend you turn off the content network when you begin. You can turn it on later, perhaps, but when you're trying to find out if PPC works for you, you'll increase your chance of success by *not* using content distribution, because content sites are likely to be less effective than search-engine ads. The following outlines how to turn off the content distribution:

1. Click the **Campaign Management** tab.

2. Click the name of the campaign you want to modify.

3. Click the Edit Campaign Settings link.

4. Clear the **content network** check box.

5. Click the **Save All Changes** button.

Writing Effective Ads

Creating an AdWords ad is an art, not a science. You have just 95 text characters to play with. Invariably, you'll find that you can't quite say what you want to say, and have to keep experimenting to get your message across. Unfortunately, your ads have to do two things:

■ Encourage potential customers to click the ad

■ Discourage people who are not customers from clicking the ad

 note *You can also create image ads—look for the Create New Image Ad link at the top of the Ad Campaign table. These do not appear in Google. They are used for content-match placement, on content pages, not search-result pages.*

Unlike most forms of advertising, when you create PPC ads you don't want everyone to be attracted to the ad, you only want good prospects. With a TV or print ad, it makes no difference how many people pay attention to the ad, even if most will never buy from you; the more the better. With a PPC ad, though, you pay—sometimes a lot of money—each time someone takes real interest in your ad. So you need an ad that works well to encourage the *right* people, and discourage the *wrong* people.

This is where a good keyword analysis comes in (as we discussed in Chapter 22). If you have a really good idea of what words people are using when searching for your products, you cannot only bid on those keywords, but also use those words in your ad. This way, the people you're interested in will see the words they already have in mind.

The following are a few things to remember.

■ **Don't mislead people.** If you imply, say, that you are giving something away just to get people to your site, you're paying for wasted clicks.

■ **Be as clear as possible.** Clarity reduces costs, while ambiguity increases costs by bringing the wrong people to your site.

■ **Sell the sizzle.** Remember, you're advertising. Give people a *reason* to come to your site and buy, such as: save money, make money, lose weight, get healthy, end your back pain . . .

- **Use attention-grabbing words.** New, Cheap, Free, Sale, Low-Cost, and so on. You must do this, of course, without breaking Google's guidelines (see the next section).

- **Think about what makes your site/offer stand out.** What makes you special compared to other businesses selling similar products. Are your products cheaper? Stronger? Tastier? More popular?

- **Make it clear that your product costs money.** This is important for many businesses that are competing against companies which give away products. If you sell software, for instance, you don't want people coming to your site if they only want free software.

- **Abbreviate.** Look for ways to remove unnecessary words, such as conjunctions. You have 95 characters, including spaces! Make every character count.

- **Use calls to action.** Employ lines like "See the Details Now," "Read More Here," "Learn More Today," and so on.

- **Use the keywords.** Placing the primary keywords from your keyword list in the ad has proven to help ad performance. Searchers will see their keywords bolded in the search results, drawing their eye to your ad.

You're not just creating one ad, though. You should experiment with multiple ads. You can even assign several ads to each group of keywords, and Google will show you which ad performs best for each keyword.

Google's Editorial Guidelines

Further complicating the process is the fact that you have to comply with Google's Editorial Guidelines. Google, of course, has a number of concerns:

- They want to sell as many "clicks" as possible.

- They want the search results seen by searchers to be as "relevant" as possible, to keep searchers coming back to use Google.

- They don't want advertisers to mislead people.

- They don't want results pages to look trashy, like if you have e-mail spam Subject lines displayed in your e-mail program.

Their guidelines were created with these ideas in mind. Spend a little time reading them before you create your ads. The guidelines demand such things as **clear, "standard" punctuation** (only one exclamation point is permitted per ad, and not in the title; no repeated punctuation—????, for instance); **standard capitalization** (www.PureSuana.com is okay, while WWW.PURESAUNA.COM is not; don't capitalize unnecessarily or excessively, such as FAST AND FREE RESULTS!); and **Limit Repetition** (don't repeat words unnecessarily or in a "gimmicky" way such as Free, Free, Free . . .).

Going "Live"

When you're ready to make your ad campaign live, and finally see the ads published in Google's search results, follow these steps:

1. Select the **My Account** tab near the top of the page.

2. Click the <u>Billing Preferences</u> link under the tabs.

3. Follow the instructions to provide your billing information.

4. Return to the Campaign Management table. All ad campaigns shown as **Active** (in the **Current Status** column) will now go live, possibly within seconds or a few minutes.

5. If an ad campaign has been paused, click the check box next to the ad and click the **Resume** button.

You can't just set a PPC campaign up and let it run. You have to monitor it carefully. We'll look at that subject in the following chapter.

Chapter 24

Managing Your PPC Campaigns and Measuring Results

Once you set your PPC campaign running, you'll probably be tempted to look at it every few minutes. In fact, large PPC campaigns have to be monitored almost continually. If you are paying half a million or a million dollars a month on PPC ads, you'll probably want to ensure that things are running smoothly. The average small-business owner doesn't have time to do this, of course. But you can't just walk away either, and then come back a month later. PPC campaigns take work; you need to see where your ads are sitting—if they drop too low you won't get any clicks. Keep an eye of the click cost, and, most importantly, figure out your Return on Investment.

Viewing PPC Results

The first thing you'll want to do is view the results of your PPC campaign. Begin by logging into your AdWords account. The very first screen you see will show you a quick summary of each of your campaigns (see Figure 24-1).

 note *By default, this table shows you yesterday's results. Use the date controls above the table to pick another date range if you wish.*

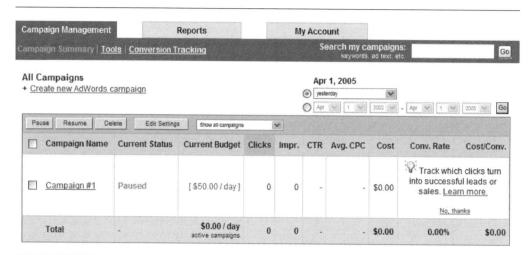

The All Campaigns table shows what's going on in each of your campaigns.

For each campaign, you can see various statistics from yesterday:

Clicks	The total number of clicks on all the ads included in the campaign, for all the keyword matches.
Impr.	The total number of *impressions*—that is, the total number of times that the campaign's ads were displayed on a web page.
CTR	The *click-through rate*—the percent of ads that were clicked on. If the CTR is 0.5 percent, your ads were clicked on once for every 200 times they were displayed. (Not an uncommon rate.)
Avg. CPC	The average price you paid for a click.
Cost	The total amount of money you spent for this campaign.
Conv. Rate & Cost/Conv.	These columns are not enabled initially; rather, you'll see a promotional blurb for the tracking service. We'll look at this under the section "Entering Conversion Values" later in this chapter. These are *Conversion Rate* and *Cost Per Conversion*, showing you how many clicks turned into sales.

A campaign summary is useful, but you can't use it to carefully manage a PPC campaign. You also need to see how each keyword and each ad performs. Click the name of the campaign, and you'll now see a similar table, this time showing summaries for each ad group in the campaign (see Figure 24-2).

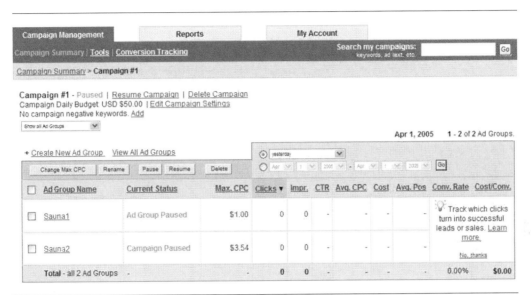

FIGURE 24-2   Similar statistics are shown for each ad group.

You have much the same statistics here, in addition to the following:

Max. CPC	The maximum bid you set
Avg. Pos	The average position your ad held during the time period

We're still not quite there yet. Click the name of an ad group to see the stats for that particular group (see Figure 24-3).

Let's take a look at the information that can be found there:

Keyword	The statistics for a particular keyword—that is, the cost of the click through when the ad was displayed after being matched with that keyword, and so on
Status	There are four possibilities:
	Normal: Your ads are being matched with this keyword.
	In trial: Your ads are still being matched with this keyword, but may not be soon (see the section titled "Managing Bad CTRs" later in this chapter).
	On hold: Your ads are not being matched with this keyword any longer, though they may be if Google runs out of ads that perform better.
	Disabled: Your ads will no longer be matched with this keyword.
Max. CPC	Your maximum bid for this keyword
Clicks	The total number of clicks your ads receive after being matched with this keyword

Impr.	The total number of *impressions*—that is, the total number of times that the ads were displayed—after being matched with this keyword
Ctr	The *click-through rate*—the percent of ads that were clicked after being matched with this keyword. Very low click-through rates will lead to this keyword being disabled.
Avg. CPC	The average price you paid for a click after the ad is matched with this keyword
Cost	The total amount of money you spent for ads matched with this keyword
Avg. Pos	The average position your ad occupied once matched with this keyword
Conv. Rate & Cost/Conv.	See the section "Entering Conversion Values" later in this chapter for information on *Conversion Rate* and *Cost Per Conversion*.

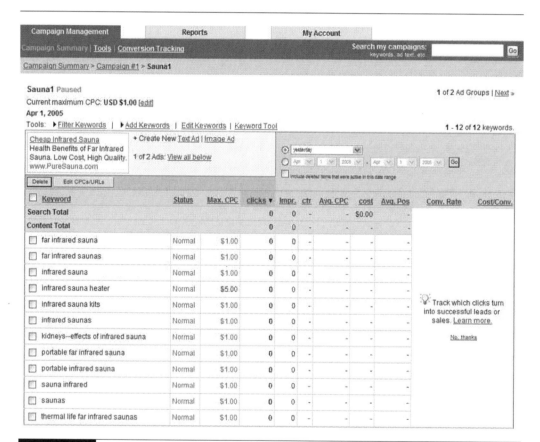

FIGURE 24-3   The Ad Group table, where you can monitor particular ads and keywords

Managing Bad CTRs

One of the first things you're likely to notice is that some of your keyword matches have been *Disabled*, or perhaps are *In trial* or *On hold*. What is this all about?

 tip   *Remember, despite people talking, in shorthand, about ads becoming* disabled, *it's not the* ad *that's disabled, it's the keyword match that's disabled. The ad may still appear for other keyword matches.*

Google wants your ads to perform above a certain level. They want the CTR—*click-through rate*—to be above half a percent. In other words, if your ad is clicked once or more every 200 times it's seen when matched for a particular keyword, you're okay. Drop below that rate, and the ad gets onto the *In trial* list. *In trial* is a warning that your CTR for that keyword matching is too low, and may also slow the delivery of the ad a little; Google will favor ads with CTRs exceeding 0.5 percent for that keyword over one they think is probably lower.

Once Google is sure that the ad's average CTR is 0.5 percent for that keyword match, it will give the ad an *On hold* status. Basically, Google won't match the ad with the keyword unless "space becomes available"—in other words, if it can't find anything better.

Finally, the ad is placed into the *Disabled* status for that keyword, where the ad will never appear for that keyword match. In fact, a keyword match can become disabled if the ad has not been matched with the keyword over the last 90 days.

Why Does Google Do This?

Why does Google penalize ad matches with low CTRs?

- **Profitability**   They would rather display an ad that is likely to be clicked upon than one that isn't; remember, they're paid when someone clicks, not when an ad is displayed. Dropping ad/keyword matches that don't perform well leaves room for better performing (in other words, more profitable) ads.

- **Relevance**   Google assumes that if people don't often click the ads, the ads are not "relevant" to the keyword match. Google wants to please people who search at the site by providing search results that are as relevant as possible.

- **Profitability II**   If ads drop too low because the price is below everyone else's, eventually they'll be dropped. The simple fact is that the lower you are on a page, the less likely your ad will be clicked. Penalizing ads with low CTRs forces advertisers to bid more in order to stay in the game, encouraging more competitive bidding.

How to "Fix" Low CTRs

Remember, the CTR (click-through rate) is for a particular ad/keyword match. What, then, can you do about that match's CTR? There are several components to a CTR, including the following:

- **The ad text**   The words seen by the searcher
- **The keyword**   The keyword phrase the searcher typed

- **The audience**   The locations in which the ad is being shown
- **The bid**   How much you're willing to pay for a click, which affects how high on the page it appears

The first two items are fixed. You can't modify an ad/keyword match by creating another ad or picking another keyword, of course, since you've just created a new match.

What, then, can you do about a low CTR? Well, the following list offers some suggestions.

- **Let it go!** Perhaps it really is a bad match that isn't worth pursuing. Instead, create new matches—put together a different ad for the keyword, or modify the keyword and use it with the same ad.

- **Raise your bid.** Increasing the bid will increase the ad position, although the low CTR will create a penalty (remember, ad position is a function of both the maximum bid and the CTR—so sometimes ads appear *above* ads with a higher bid).

- **Consider targeting a different audience.** Use the ad in a different region. Perhaps people in some of the locations in which the ad is displayed are less likely to click for some reason. Ads for discounts on ski tickets are likely to work better for people in Colorado than in Florida, for instance.

Tracking Conversions

The statistics we've seen so far are useful, important even . . . but they're nothing compared with the ad/keyword match's Conversion Rate and Cost Per Conversion:

- **Conversion Rate**   This is the percentage of people clicking the ad who carry out some useful action on your site: buying from you, contacting your sales people, signing up for a newsletter, and so on.

- **Cost Per Conversion**   This is the click cost for each sale.

Focusing on CTR while ignoring Conversion Rate is a *big* mistake! In fact, increasing CTR can in many cases actually *decrease* Conversion Rate and *increase* Cost Per Conversion. It's quite possible to tweak your ad in a way that makes your offer more attractive to people who see it . . . and thus brings more people to your site who are not going to buy from you or do anything else of use to you. You multiply the number of useless clicks—which you still have to pay for, of course—thus increasing the cost of each sale.

You really should turn on conversion tracking. The following explains how.

1. Click the <u>Learn more</u> link in the **Conv. Rate / Cost/Conv.** column.

2. You'll see a page of background information. Click the **Start Tracking Conversions** button.

3. You'll see the first step in setting up your tracking (shown in Figure 24-4).

Track which clicks turn into successful leads or sales. <u>Learn more.</u>

No, thanks

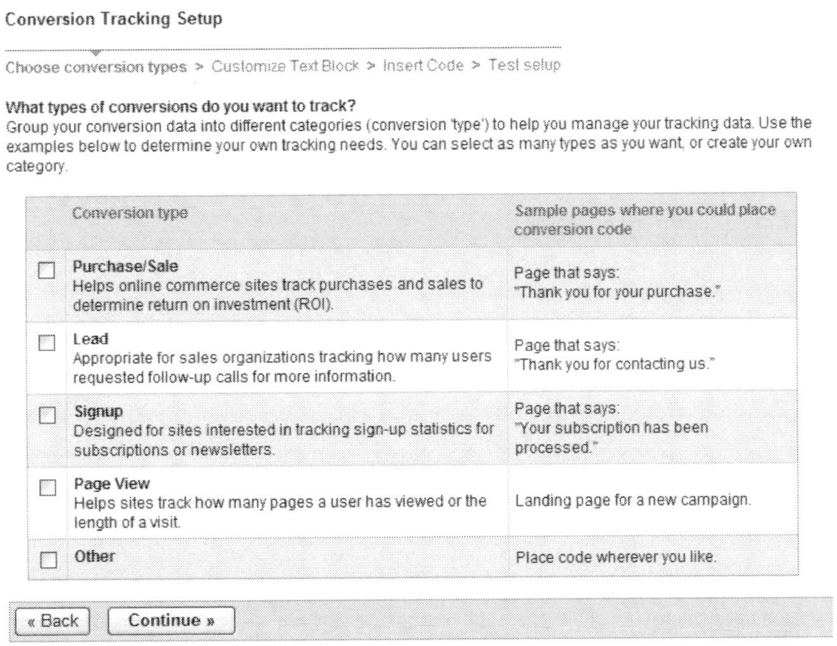

Conversion Tracking Setup

Choose conversion types > Customize Text Block > Insert Code > Test setup

What types of conversions do you want to track?
Group your conversion data into different categories (conversion 'type') to help you manage your tracking data. Use the examples below to determine your own tracking needs. You can select as many types as you want, or create your own category.

	Conversion type	Sample pages where you could place conversion code
☐	**Purchase/Sale** Helps online commerce sites track purchases and sales to determine return on investment (ROI).	Page that says: "Thank you for your purchase."
☐	**Lead** Appropriate for sales organizations tracking how many users requested follow-up calls for more information.	Page that says: "Thank you for contacting us."
☐	**Signup** Designed for sites interested in tracking sign-up statistics for subscriptions or newsletters.	Page that says: "Your subscription has been processed."
☐	**Page View** Helps sites track how many pages a user has viewed or the length of a visit.	Landing page for a new campaign.
☐	**Other**	Place code wherever you like.

[« Back]   [Continue »]

FIGURE 24-4   Select the types of conversions you want to track.

4. You can track various types of conversions, not merely sales, such as the following:

Purchase/Sale	Tracks how many of the ad clicks lead to sales
Lead	Tracks how many ad clicks lead to requesting information
Signup	Tracks how many ad clicks lead to someone signing up for a newsletter subscription, subscribing to a web site membership, or some other form of signup
Page View	Tracks what people who click an ad do, how long they stay on the site, and how many pages they view
Other	Tracks some other form of action—placing the code on a page tells you how many people who click the ad arrive at the page, so placing the code on a page at the end of some kind of sequence allows you to track who has completed the sequence

5. Select the type of conversions you want to track, and click the **Continue** button. You should see the screen in Figure 24-5.

Conversion Tracking Setup

Choose conversion types > **Customize Text Block** > Insert Code > Test setup

Customize your 'Google Site Stats' text.
On the webpage to which you add the conversion tracking code, a small 'Google Site Stats' text block will appear to customers who have clicked on your ad. Customers can click the 'send feedback' link to learn more about the tracking process and tell us about their experience.

[!] This text must appear as is. Please do not alter your conversion tracking code or this tracking text after the setup process. [?]

1. Choose text format (one line or two).

○ Google Site Stats
   send feedback

◉ Google Site Stats - send feedback

2. Customize the background color. Preview your selection.
Click desired color, or enter your own: `#33CC66`

Preview:
Google Site Stats - send feedback   You'll specify the language of this text in the next step.

[« Back] [Continue »]

FIGURE 24-5   Specify the format of the Google Site Stats block.

6. Google requires that you place a small *Google Site Stats* block on your tracking pages—the code you're provided with in a subsequent step does this automatically. The text block appears, for instance, on your sales-confirmation page. This page allows you to customize that block. You can select the format—a one-line or two-line block—and you can select a background color. (You'll see the effect of your choices in the Preview block at the bottom, above the **Continue** button.)

7. Click the **Continue** button and you'll be shown the page with the code snippets (see Figure 24-6).

8. In Step 1, **Select your conversion page language** defines the language used for the *Google Site Stats* text block. Select a language if necessary, and the page reloads.

If you're using Yahoo! Merchant Services, the confirmation page is an https:// page, so you must select the https:// security level. If you're tracking on multiple pages, you need to know how each page is delivered. If some use https:// and others use http:// you'll have to do this step twice. You cannot take code from this page after selecting an https:// security level and place it on an http:// page, or vice versa.

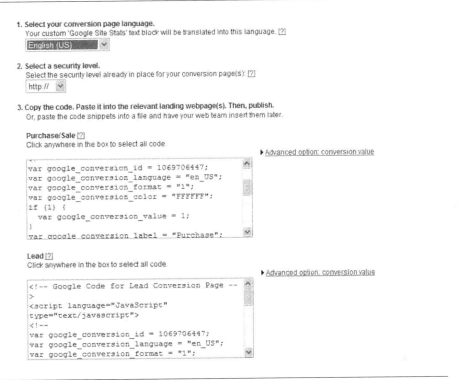

1. Select your conversion page language.
Your custom 'Google Site Stats' text block will be translated into this language. [?]

English (US)

2. Select a security level.
Select the security level already in place for your conversion page(s): [?]

http:// ▾

3. Copy the code. Paste it into the relevant landing webpage(s). Then, publish.
Or, paste the code snippets into a file and have your web team insert them later.

Purchase/Sale [?]
Click anywhere in the box to select all code.

▸ Advanced option: conversion value

```
var google_conversion_id = 1069706447;
var google_conversion_language = "en_US";
var google_conversion_format = "1";
var google_conversion_color = "FFFFFF";
if (1) {
   var google_conversion_value = 1;
}
var google_conversion_label = "Purchase";
```

Lead [?]
Click anywhere in the box to select all code.

▸ Advanced option: conversion value

```
<!-- Google Code for Lead Conversion Page --
>
<script language="JavaScript"
type="text/javascript">
<!--
var google_conversion_id = 1069706447;
var google_conversion_language = "en_US";
var google_conversion_format = "1";
```

FIGURE 24-6   Grab your code snippets from this page.

---

9. In Step 2, **Select a security level** defines whether the page on which you are placing the code will be a secure page (https) or not (http). To make sure, load the page in your browser, directly off the web site, and see how the sales-confirmation page has been delivered. Look in the Address bar; you'll see either *https://* or *http://*. Then return to this process and select the matching entry in the **Select a security level** drop-down list box.

10. If you wish, you may enter a **conversion value** (we'll discuss this in a moment in the section "Entering Conversion Values").

11. Click inside the **Purchase/Sale** text box and then copy the text. (In Windows, you can just press CTRL-C.)

12. Paste this text into a text file and save the file on your computer hard drive.

13. Copy the other text blocks in a similar manner.

14. Click the **Continue** button at the bottom of the page.

15. The following page is a confirmation page. If you wish, you can end here. If you are running PPC campaigns through other systems you can also use Google to track these. Click the **Continue to Cross-Channel Setup** button.

Entering Conversion Values

During the process in which you grabbed the code, you saw an option in which you could enter a *conversion value*. Google Adwords doesn't know how much your conversions are worth to you . . . unless you tell it. This option allows you to add value information to the code you will be adding to your pages.

Click the Advanced option: conversion value link, and the text box shown at right opens (it may already be present).

Into this box, you can type a number. It might be a monetary value—10, for instance, means that the conversion is worth ten dollars. Perhaps you

▼ Advanced option: conversion value
How much is each conversion worth to you? Provide a value, or enter a variable to capture each conversion's value. Then click 'Refresh.' [?]

Value: $ | 1.0 | Refresh
See examples

regard each signup to a newsletter to be worth $10, or each sale is worth $10—say, if you only sell one product, such as a newsletter subscription. (Don't enter anything but a digit.)

tip | *Need to get the code again, perhaps to code a different page? The original Learn more link, where you began this process, has disappeared, and the Conv. Rate and Cost/Conv. columns now show the actual data. Under the* **Campaign Management** *tab, click the Conversion Tracking link. Then click the Get conversion tracking code link.*

But what if you don't know how much a sale is worth? Each sale is generally different, after all. In such a case, you may be able to enter a variable value—*Sales_Value*, for instance. If you're not the programmer who built the site, you need to speak to the one who did!

If tracking pageviews or signups, for example, you can also leave the digit 1 displayed; the conversion "value" is then 1, a way to track how many signups you've had.

When you've entered the value, click the **Refresh** button and *then* grab your code snippets. Google will have added the conversion value to the script.

The Conversion Value statistics are not displayed in the normal Campaign and Ad Group tables. Rather, they appear in the Reports area, under the **Reports** tab at the top of the AdWords page.

Placing the Conversion-tracking Code into Your Site

Now you have to place the code you were given into your site. The way this is done varies, depending on the system you're using, so you should probably review the *Conversion Tracking Guide*, which you can find by clicking the **Campaign Management** tab, clicking the Conversion Tracking link, and then clicking the Setup guide link.

tip *The general rule is that the code is placed into your HTML page immediately above the </body> tag. But see the* Conversion Tracking Guide *before getting started.*

If you're using Yahoo! Merchant Solutions, though, here's how to add the code to your store.

1. In Store Manager, click the Order Form link at the top of the Order Settings column.
2. Find the **Message** text box in the **Order Confirmation** area.
3. Grab the **Purchase/Sale** code you grabbed earlier (see Figure 24-6).
4. Paste this code into the bottom of the **Message** text box.
5. Click **Done**.
6. On the Store Manager page, click **Publish Order Settings** at the bottom of the Order Settings column to add the code to your live store.

That's it. You've added the code, and AdWords will now fill in the Conv. Rate and Cost/ Conv. columns in your reports. Unfortunately, with Merchant Solutions you won't be able to add a variable value for the conversion value (this is explained for other systems in the *Conversion Tracking Guide*), so either the value will be 1, or it may be an average value you entered. You *won't* get the actual value from each order passed through to the conversion-tracking system.

Using Trackable Links

If you're using Yahoo! Merchant Solutions, you should create a trackable link for each ad you create. (See Chapter 21 for information on creating and tracking links.) This link is placed into the **Destination URL** field for the ad—it's the link that the ad actually points at. When someone uses that link, Yahoo! keeps track of the information. Not only will you be able to see how many people click the ad, you'll also be able to see how many sales were made using it, and the total value of all those sales, something Google's system *won't* be able to tell you.

If you're not using Yahoo! Merchant Solutions, you may still be able to use some kind of tracking system that can provide you with total sales per ad. Talk with your site developer or e-commerce service provider, or check the documentation.

Using Other Tracking Tools

You can track results from Pay Per Click campaigns in many other ways. Virtually all commercial web "metrics" tools—such as WebTrends, ClickTracks, Omniture, and Urchin— include sophisticated tools for tracking traffic. These are far better tools than Google's basic conversion-tracking tools, of course. For instance, ClickTracks can even show you what links people have clicked, depending on the PPC ads through which they arrived.

note *Though Google requires a blurb on every page, with a* send feedback *link, other tools don't. Google's tracking tool is free, however, while you have to pay for most others.*

In addition, you can purchase specialized software—or rent it by the month—designed for tracking PPC campaigns. Using one of the major search engines, search for terms such as *ppc tracking* or *ppc statistics.*

Using the Conversion Information

The conversion information is critical, because it gives you the most important feedback: how much money does each ad (combined with each keyword) make for you.

> **tip** *If you combine a single ad with a single keyword—that is, each ad group contains a single ad and a single keyword—you can use trackable links in Merchant Solutions that will tell you exactly how much money each keyword-match combination makes. Unfortunately, this is not practical in most cases. Tracking of this kind is possible with more sophisticated e-commerce systems, however.*

AdWords show you the percentage of people who click the ad to reach your sales-confirmation page—that is, the conversion rate. It also shows you the cost of each conversion. (See Figure 24-7.) If, for instance, 100 people click your ad, at an average click cost of 87 cents, you've just spent $87. If your conversion rate is, say, 1.33 percent, your cost per conversion is $65.41.

■ If an ad/keyword combination works very well, producing high conversion, yet has a low position on the search-results page, consider paying more to push it up in the list of sponsored ads on the search-results page so you get more people clicking it. These people are likely to convert well, as your statistics already show.

■ If conversions from an ad/keyword combination cost more than your gross profit on the transaction, stop using it. You're wasting money.

■ Consider shifting funds from low-performing ad/keyword combinations to high-performing combinations in order to move them up the ranks.

■ Keep a record of good combinations so you can use them on other PPC systems. (However, different PPC systems may provide different results.)

Keyword	Status	Max. CPC	clicks ▼	Impr.	ctr	Avg. CPC	cost	Avg. Pos	Conv. Rate	Cost/Conv.
Search Total			0	0	-	-	$0.00	-	0.00%	$0.00
Content Total			0	0	-	-	-	-	0.00%	$0.00
far infrared sauna	Normal	$1.00	0	0	-	-	-	-	0.00%	$0.00
far infrared saunas	Normal	$1.00	0	0	-	-	-	-	0.00%	$0.00

FIGURE 24-7 You can see exactly the cost of each conversion.

Remember your ROI (Return on Investment) calculations from Chapter 22. You already know how much a conversion should be worth, so these conversion numbers will tell you if your PPC campaign is profitable or not . . . and if it is, how profitable. If you're making a few cents profit per transaction, it still may not be worthwhile.

There's another thing to consider about poor conversion rates, something that's rarely discussed. The single most important factor in low-conversion rates is bad site design! Hundreds of millions of dollars have been spent on PPC to bring people to web sites that do a terrible job of converting visitors to sales. It's easy to blame the Pay Per Click advertising in general, or the keywords you used, or the words in the ad . . . but what about your web site? If the site does a lousy job, your PPC conversion numbers will be lousy, too.

Watching for Click Fraud

Be on the lookout for *click fraud*, fraudulent clicks on your PPC links. Click fraud is a huge problem for the PPC networks, and happens for two reasons:

- **Competitors** Business owners sometimes click ads that sit higher than them in the ranks in order to grab a higher position by forcing the competing ads out—either by running through the competing ad's budget or by simply frightening the business owner into dropping the bid.

- **Sites scamming the search engines** Owners of sites that run AdWords ads on their sites (through the AdSense program), or a similar PPC distribution program, sometimes click links appearing on their sites in order to push up their income. (Sites using AdSense earn a commission each time an ad is clicked.) This is particularly a problem for keywords that are very expensive.

Sometimes the clicks are manual; someone literally sits in front of a computer and clicks the links. In other cases, programs are used to click particular ads.

note *Click fraud is so serious it "threatens [Google's] business model," according to Google's Chief Financial Officer George Reyes.*

How big is click fraud? According to some estimates, perhaps 20 percent of all clicks in certain very competitive advertising categories are fraudulent. Other analysts claim that 20 percent of *all* clicks are fraudulent.

So how can you deal with it? First, remember that just because some clicks may be fraudulent, it doesn't mean PPC can't be profitable. You might consider fraudulent clicks as simply a cost of doing business, just as real clicks from people who *are* interested in your ad but *don't* buy from you are also worthless to you. What counts is the ROI (Return on Investment)—does your ROI "work" for you? (See Chapter 22.)

Of course, in some cases click fraud becomes so serious it can't be ignored. Indeed, it makes a PPC campaign totally unprofitable. So how to avoid the dangers of click fraud?

- **Rely on the search engines.** The search engines all claim to have antifraud departments, and Google recently began filing lawsuits against people it claims are using click fraud. On the other hand, the problem is way too big for serious PPC advertisers to rely on search engines.

- **Check for unusual activity in your hit logs.** If you see a sudden huge jump in traffic to your site coming from your ads, you may be the victim of crude click fraud.

- **Consider using a fraud detector.** If you have a significant PPC budget, you should seriously consider using a fraud-detection tool. There are a number of these, such as ClickDetective, Click Defense, Click Risk, Clicklab, and WhosClickingWho. These systems look for people clicking your ads repeatedly; some fraud detectors even claim to be able to identify when people click just once or twice a week.

- **Don't bid on really expensive keywords.** If your keywords are $50 a click, you'd better believe you're a prime target for fraud! If you *must* use these keywords, you *must* use a fraud detector.

If you're sure you're the target of click fraud, contact the PPC network. They *will* issue refunds if you push hard enough and convince them you really have been scammed, though they've also been criticized for not being very responsive, too.

Chapter 25

Selling Through Shopping Directories: Froogle, Yahoo! Shopping, and More

Google, Overture, and MSN are not the only PPC games in town—you shouldn't forget the shopping directories. Systems such as Yahoo! Shopping, Shopping.com, PriceGrabber, and mySimon are Pay Per Click product-search directories. Some are integrated into major search engines—search for a product at Yahoo! for instance, and you may find links into the Yahoo! Shopping area, and results from PriceGrabber appear in Ask Jeeves, DogPile, and Metacrawler. Others are integrated into major content sites—results from mySimon and Shopper.com appear in CNET.com, for instance.

If you're interested in the PPC game, you really should check out the shopping directories. They often provide lower-cost clicks—in fact, a couple of directories, Froogle and Google Catalogs, don't charge *anything*. They are easier to use, and in most cases do not use a bidding system—you pay a flat rate per click. And they are easy to work with; once you've prepared to feed data to one of the sites, it doesn't take long to feed that data into the other sites (some, however, charge setup fees). In fact, you may even hear a rep from one of these companies say something like, "If you're already feeding data to Yahoo! Shopping, we can use that data feed."

How to Work with the Shopping Directories

The shopping directories are search engines, but specifically for merchandise. They are giant catalogs of products (see Figure 25-1).

 tip *Many online buyers are very price sensitive. If your prices are significantly above everyone else's, marketing through the shopping directories probably isn't going to work for you. We discussed price sensitivity in Chapter 1.*

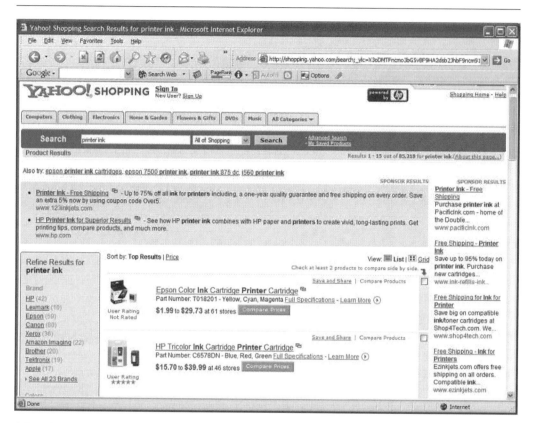

FIGURE 25-1 You can get to Yahoo! Shopping directly, at shopping.yahoo.com, or simply click the little Products link before you search at Yahoo!.

From the merchant's point of view, there are really three types of shopping directories:

■ **Free directories** You provide your data, and the directory sends traffic to you at no cost. Not surprisingly, there aren't many of these. Most notably they include Froogle (Google's directory), Google Catalogs, and PriceSCAN.

■ **Fixed-click price** Most directories are fixed-price directories. You'll pay for every click, as with the Pay Per Click systems we've already seen. But there's no bidding; it's a fixed rate per product category.

■ **PPC bidding** These systems (such as BizRate and Shopping.com) have a minimum click rate, but the actual rate you pay depends on the bidding; merchants bid for position.

Is it worth working with the shopping directories? Maybe. As with all other forms of marketing, you don't know what works until you try it. The advantage of the shopping directories is that even if they don't work, you probably haven't invested much time and effort into trying them. It should be possible, in most cases, to get set up with several directories very quickly.

Many merchants have seen the shopping directories as some kind of guaranteed business source. Just feed data into the directories, and watch the business roll in. The reality may be very different. Here are some real numbers from a luxury-goods merchant using Yahoo! Shopping:

Clicks from Yahoo! Shopping	2,278
Number of sales	7
Conversion rate	0.3%
Cost of clicks (@ 40 cents/click)	$728.96
Total value of sales	$2,532.00
Average sale	$361.71
Average cost per sale	$130.17
Average cost per sale, as a % of sale	36%
Return on investment	$3.47 for every dollar spent on clicks

Not a resounding success. Did the merchant make money? After paying their cost of goods, they probably did, but not much. Their results through Froogle were even lower, a conversion rate of under 1/10 of a percent; on the other hand, the Froogle traffic is free.

Does that mean the shopping directories don't work? No, absolutely not. Other businesses can and do get much better results. Why?

- Perhaps their web sites are better designed and do a better job of converting visitors to buyers.

- Perhaps their pricing is more competitive (the merchant that provided these numbers definitely has a pricing problem).

- Perhaps they are up against less competition.

- Perhaps they are in a category with products that sell online more often.

What will you need in order to work with the shopping directories? Basically, a "data feed," information about your products that is fed to the directories.

If you are using Yahoo! Merchant Solutions, you've already learned about feeding data to Yahoo! Shopping (see Chapter 21). That shopping directory can pull data automatically out of Merchant Solutions. Of course, if you aren't using Merchant Solutions, you can still feed data to Yahoo! Shopping. All these directories can work with simple delimited text files.

What's a delimited text file? It's a text file that contains information about each of your products, with each field of data separated by some kind of common character—a tab or a comma:

 tip *Using text files to feed data to directories works well for small businesses. Many larger businesses, with more sophisticated technical departments, may already be using a database system for managing product data.*

The easiest way to create such product-data files—the data feed files—is in a spreadsheet program such as Microsoft Excel. (We discussed this issue in Chapter 13.) There's a catch, though. Each system has its own data-file criteria—different required fields and different headings for the fields. Here's the simplest way to manage this:

1. In the first worksheet in the spreadsheet program, save all your product data, with all the product information that's available.

2. Create worksheets for each of the shopping directories you're going to work with.

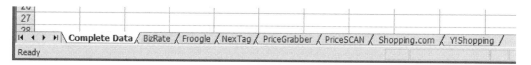

3. In each of the secondary worksheets, enter the correct heading names for the data columns, according to the shopping directory's required format.

4. Reference data from the main worksheet to the secondary sheets, so that when you change any numbers in the primary sheet the changes appear in the secondary sheets. (See your spreadsheet program for information on how to do this; this is not merely copying the information, but referencing the information.)

5. When you need to export data to a directory, save the entire document to ensure all recent changes are saved, then save the specific shopping-directory sheet in a .csv format (Comma Delimited). In Microsoft Excel, for instance, do a File | Save As, and pick the .csv format. When you do this, Excel only saves the data in the currently displayed sheet.

tip *If your company publishes a paper catalog, send it to Google! They'll add it to Google Catalogs. See catalogs.google.com for more information.*

Using Froogle

Froogle is Google's shopping directory (www.froogle.com). The banner at the top says that the system is in "beta," which means it's prerelease test or experimental software. But it's been that way for a couple of years now, and millions of people already use Froogle (see Figure 25-2). Furthermore, Google often places links from its main search-results pages, at Google.com, into Froogle.

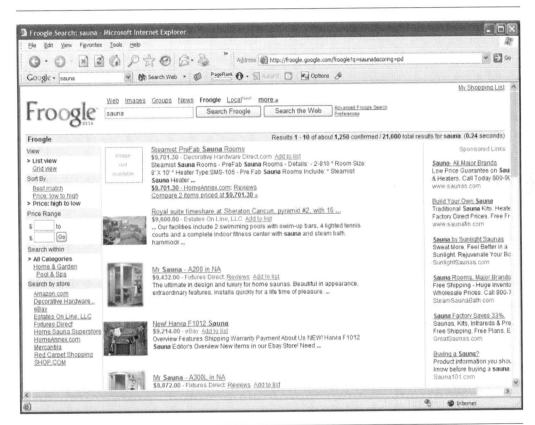

FIGURE 25-2   Froogle is a very convenient shopping directory . . . and it's free to you.

To sign up, visit Froogle and look for the <u>Information for Merchants</u> link at the bottom of the Home page. You have to provide a *very* simple data-feed file—Froogle only wants a little information. For each product you'll provide the data in the following table:

product_url	The URL of the product's page
name	The product name
description	The product description
image_url	The URL of the product image
category	A category name
price	The product's price

This data is transferred to Froogle using an FTP program, a tool frequently used by web designers to transfer files to web sites.

Using Yahoo! Shopping

We looked at Yahoo! Shopping in Chapter 21. Yahoo! Merchant Services provides a convenient way to transmit data to Yahoo! Shopping—the directory can pull the information directly out of Merchant Services' Catalog Manager. If you're not using Merchant Services, you can still use Yahoo! Shopping, of course, but you'll have to submit a data-feed file to the system.

Yahoo! Shopping is a major system, of course, because Yahoo! itself is the world's most popular web site. So this directory could, potentially, send a lot of traffic to your site. Yahoo! charges a simple click fee based on the product category; there's no bidding for position on this directory. Remember, if you use Yahoo! Merchant Solutions, you'll get a 20% discount on these fees.

Other Shopping Directories to Work With

There are a number of other systems you might want to check out:

PriceGrabber, http://www.pricegrabber.com/	Shopping.com
Shopzilla, Shopzilla.com	PriceWatch.com
NexTag.com	PriceSCAN.com
PriceSaving.com	

tip   You can find many more directories in Yahoo! Directory (http://dir.yahoo.com/Business_and_Economy/Directories/Companies/) and Google Directory (http://directory.google.com/Top/Shopping/Directories).

There are *many* other shopping directories. Some may be worth listing in, if they are specialty directories related to your business. However, many are not worth dealing with; they won't send you much traffic, so you'll waste a lot of time signing up for all these directories.

Chapter 26

Improving Natural
Search Engine Ranking

You've learned how to get traffic from the search engines—by paying for it. But there's another way to do it. Remember, many results displayed on a search-results page are *not* PPC ads! On Google, for instance, you might find two paid ads at the top and eight down the side . . . but ten *free* search results in the body of the page. If you can place *your* pages in this free area, you can get free traffic to your site.

Why You Must Understand the Search Engines

Most small businesses that employ web-designer firms to build their sites, or that have designers on-staff, rely on the designers for search-engine optimization. The fact is, though, that very few web-design firms or web designers understand search-engine optimization, even if they say they do. (For competitive reasons, most design firms claim to understand this subject; they don't.) It's essential that *someone* on your team *does*.

> **note** *The term* search-engine optimization *means the process of helping a web site rank well in the search-engine search results. The term* optimize *originally meant to create a web page in such a manner that a search engine is likely to think it is very relevant for a particular keyword or keyword phrase.*

This chapter is not a comprehensive description of search-engine optimization—there are entire books written on the subject. But it will give you a good start, outlining the basic rules. Sometimes getting free traffic—by placing your pages into what are known as the *organic* or *natural* search results—is very easy. (For example, we know for a fact that you can easily rank well for the search term *pet cosmetics*, perhaps even within a few days.)

Usually, however, if you are in a very competitive situation, ranking well takes time and energy . . . and perhaps a lot of both. For instance, if you are selling a book about buying a mortgage, the chance of ranking well on the keyword *mortgage* is highly unlikely. Perhaps there's a related term you could target, such as *buying mortgage advice*. But even to rank well on a term like that would be very difficult (3.6 million pages indexed by Google contain those words).

Unfortunately, much of search-engine optimization is guesswork. The search-engine companies don't want you to know how to make a page rank well in the search engines; they regard that as manipulation. Thus there is a lot of conjecture in this business, and a lot of downright misinformation. It's complicated, but if you want to try to get free traffic from the search engines, you have to at least understand the basics.

Understanding Search Engines

Let's begin by learning exactly what search engines are and what they do. First, it's important to understand the difference between a *search engine* and a *directory*.

- **Search Engine**   A system that "indexes" web pages—it looks at millions of pages (Google currently indexes over eight *billion* pages!) and stores information about those pages, in some cases even keeping a copy of many of the pages. The three big search engines are Yahoo! (www.yahoo.com—see Figure 26-1), Google (www.google.com), and MSN (www.msn.com).

- **Search Directory**   A system that categorizes web *sites*, not pages. The directory has no idea about the content of particular pages within the site; it just knows what the site is about. Yahoo! had the first massive directory on the Internet (dir.yahoo.com—see Figure 26-2). Google also has a directory (dir.google.com), but MSN does not currently have one.

Remember, search engines *index the content of individual web pages; search* directories *categorize web sites.*

We're primarily interested in the search engines—the web-page indexes—for a couple of reasons:

- Indexes are now used far more than directories; most search traffic goes through the indexes, *not* the directories.

- There's not much you can do to optimize your site for the directories—the large directories are human-edited; someone actually looks at your web site and decides where to place your site in the directory, and what text will appear in the listing. You can suggest text, but the editors may not accept it.

This is an introduction to search-engine optimization. This is a big, complicated subject . . . to do really well, you may *need to understand more. Sometimes ranking well is very easy. Follow these basic rules and you may find your site on the first page of the search results at major search engines. In many cases, however, you're up against a lot of competition, and ranking well is very difficult. One of the authors of this book, Peter Kent, is also the author of* Search Engine Optimization for Dummies *(Wiley Publishing, Inc., 2004), which provides a more detailed path to search-engine success.*

Enter a search term here.

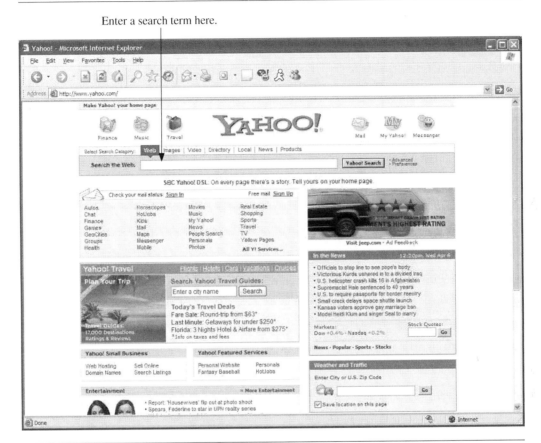

FIGURE 26-1   Yahoo!'s search engine. Type a keyword here and Yahoo! searches through the content of billions of pages.

So the search engines come to a web site and start reading pages. They index the text on the page, and, using very complicated (and secret) computer-programming algorithms, they attempt to match pages with searchers' queries. When someone searches for the phrase *shoes denver*, for instance, the search engine attempts to find the most relevant pages for that search. That's a complicated thing to do—Google, for instance, has around three quarters of a million pages with the words *shoes* and *denver* in its index.

How do search engines find your pages? They use "searchbots" that follow links all day long (that's the great thing about "bots"—they never need to rest). They travel from page to page to page, reading and indexing every page as they go. (You'll learn how to get them to arrive at your site under "Registering with the Search Engines" later in this chapter.)

Browse through the directory here.   Search through the directory here.

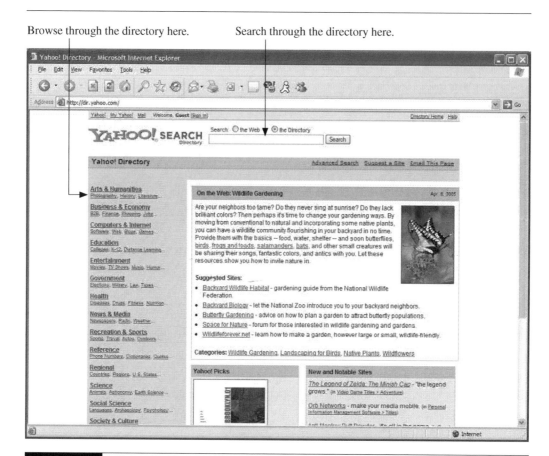

FIGURE 26-2   Yahoo!'s directory. You can browse through the categories or search for a web site, but the directory does not contain information about individual pages, only web sites.

Your goal is to appear at the top of a search-engine results page when someone searches on your top term (see Figure 26-3). Even if you're not top, but in the first few positions, you can still get a lot of traffic. If you drop "below the fold," though (below the area of the page visible without scrolling), traffic drops off dramatically. And if you're on page 2, even at the top, you'll see only a small fraction of the traffic garnered by the #1 position.

By following a few basic rules, you can create sites that will be indexed by the search engines. And by creating pages that are "search-engine friendly," you have a good chance of ranking well and getting traffic when people search for the keywords to which your site is related.

You want *your listed* page here!

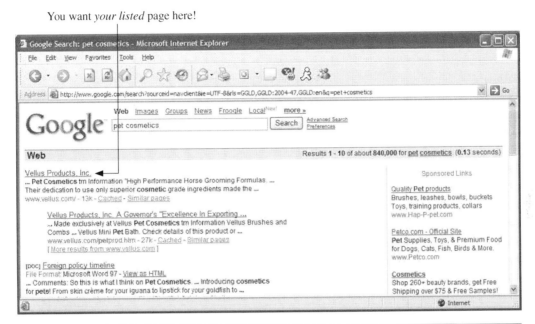

FIGURE 26-3   Here's where you want to be when someone searches for, say, *pet cosmetics*.

Understanding the Keywords

The foundation of a search-engine optimization program, as with a PPC campaign, is keyword choice. You *must* understand what keywords people are using to search for products such as yours.

note   Optimizing *a page means placing keywords into the page in such a manner that search engines will read the page and think that it is highly relevant for a particular phrase—that is, a page that searchers will find useful when they are searching using that keyword phrase. You can optimize a page only for a single keyword phrase at a time; thus, if you have many keyword phrases you're interested in, the ideal is to create pages for each phrase and optimize each one.*

We looked at how to research keywords in Chapter 22. We want to reiterate in this chapter that you should do a good analysis. If you don't have a really good idea of which keywords are important to you, you won't know how to optimize your pages for the right keywords. And nobody actually knows the important keywords just by guessing, however well they know the business they are in.

As we mentioned before, we believe you shouldn't rely merely on the Overture or Google keyword-analysis tools. You should use the real thing, a full-blown analysis tool such as Wordtracker.com, which can be "rented" for under $8 a day. (All you need is one day.)

Making Sure Search Engines Can Index Your Pages

The first thing to consider is that if search engines can't read your pages, they can't index them. They won't be included in the search engine index, and so have no chance of appearing if someone searches for a term related to your products and services.

 Just because a page is in the index, doesn't mean it will appear in the search results. The first step is to make sure it will be indexed . . . but you also have to create it in such a manner that it has a good chance of appearing high in the search results.

When are search engines unable to index your site? When you have very complicated URLs. For instance, a page may not be indexed if its URL looks like this:

```
http://www.domainname.com/Catalog/Catalog.asp?PageLevelID=548&bRange=2750
&tRange=8975
```

 Here's a rule of thumb. If you have one or two database parameters in a URL—one or two = signs or? characters—the page is probably okay; the search engines will quite likely index it. If there are three or more, though, you may have a problem. However, there are a number of technical reasons why search engines won't index pages with very complicated URLs, which we don't have space to cover here.

This URL references a page that is "databased"; the web server sends a "query" to the database, asking for the page. Each = sign in the URL indicates a different "parameter" in the query.

Another issue that causes problems is that of the *session ID*, a piece of code that is used to track a particular *user session* as the site visitor moves through the web site. It might look like this:

```
http://www.domainname.com/index.jsp;jsessionid=S8HFB9876R9BSD9876WR9B
```

 If you see the word sessionid *in a URL, it's a session ID string! (But some URLs that* don't *include that term may also be session IDs.)*

If your pages use session IDs, two problems can occur:

- Search engines may not index the pages.
- If they *do* index the pages, the URL in the search results page probably won't work correctly.

note   *Pages created using the Yahoo! Merchant Solutions e-commerce system do* not *have these problems. They* can *be read and* are *indexed in the major search engines.*

Both these issues are problems with e-commerce products; the first is very common with all types, including "off-the-shelf" systems, while the second is more common with more sophisticated custom systems.

How do you know if your site, or a product you are considering using, has this problem? Find out if pages created by the system—either on your site or on other companies' sites using a system you are evaluating—are indexed by the major search engines.

tip   *Here's a quick trick to see if a site is indexed by the search engines. Search for this:* site: domainname.com. *The search engine returns all the pages on the site it knows about. This trick* won't *work on all search engines, but it will work on Google, Yahoo!, and MSN.*

Avoiding the Basic Mistakes Before You Start

There are a number of other basic mistakes made by businesses when they build their web sites, in fact more common mistakes than the above indexing problem. Luckily, they're all easy to avoid.

Frames

The term *frames* refers to creating "subwindows" within a browser window and placing documents inside (see Figure 26-4).

Framed sites have three main problems:

- They are typically built in such a manner that search engines are not provided with all the information they need to index each page separately.

- When a page *is* found in the search engines and someone clicks to visit the site, the page is displayed *outside* the frame setup (without the normal navigation, for instance).

- If you use a PPC system (see Chapters 22 and 23), you can't link to the product page because in a frame situation you can't see the content-page's URL; again, linking to the page breaks it out of the navigation.

Frames are a big mistake, and rarely needed. There isn't much you can't do without frames that you can do with them, anyway. Avoid them if you can. If it's too late—you already have a framed site—we recommend you read a book on search-engine optimization that addresses this issue, or find expert help.

Invisible Navigation Systems

Some navigation systems cannot be read by the search engines. Search engines do not read JavaScript and DHTML, for instance, two coding systems often used to build drop-down menus (see Figure 26-5). Thus, if your site's entire navigation structure is built using this sort

There's a vertical navbar frame here.

There's a horizontal frame across the page here.

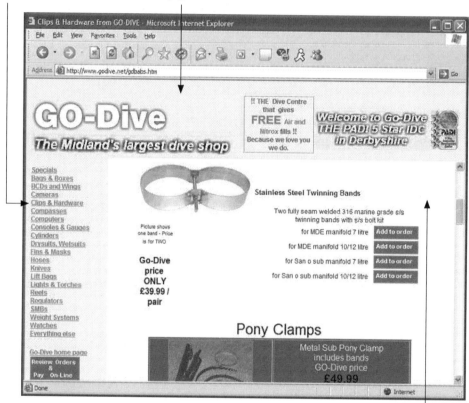

This white area is a separate frame, too—you can see the scroll bar acts only within this frame.

FIGURE 26-4   This is a framed web site, with three frames within the browser window.

of programming, the only pages the search engines will ever reach are the ones linked to from *outside* your site; the search engines will generally *not* be able to enter the site and move through it, indexing all the pages.

note   *The button navbar used by stores created with Yahoo! Merchant Solutions do not have this problem; search engines* can *read this bar.*

The fix is easy. Simply ensure that you have plain old text links in the body of the page, or perhaps a little plain-text navigation area at the bottom of the page.

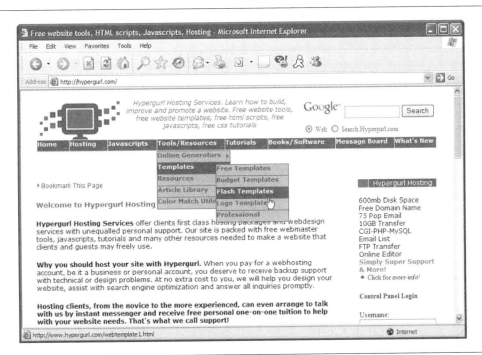

FIGURE 26-5   This drop-down navigation system was built using JavaScript, so search engines will never see it.

tip   *Consider creating a sitemap page and ensuring it can be reached easily from your home page, then link to every page in your site from that sitemap. This is a great way to provide easy access for the search engines.*

Images and an Absence of Text

Search engines need text to read. If you don't give them text, there's nothing much for them to index. And text means actual typed words on a web page, not words appearing in images.

Many designers create much of the site in an image-editing program, then drop the images into pages. Some sites even contain *all* or most of the text in the images. Apart from the fact that in most cases this is a very inefficient way to build a web site and that doing so creates very large, slow-loading pages, it also creates pages with nothing for the search engines to index . . . pages that won't rank well in the search results.

Let's say you have a stock-photo business; you don't need many words, you just need to present the pictures on your web site and let visitors pick the ones they want. However, the fact is that without text, search engines don't have anything to index, so if you provide hundreds of pages with nothing but pictures, you're not giving the search engines enough to work with.

All these rules are dependent on how much competition you are up against. If very few other web sites are competing for the search keywords you are after, you can get away with breaking some rules . . . you may be able to rank well with very little effort. Don't bet on it, though!

Macromedia Flash

Macromedia Flash is often used by designers to create attractive, interactive components inside web sites. On occasion it is used to create an entire web site—all the pages are inside the Flash file, and all the navigation between the pages, too . . . everything's inside the Flash file.

While there are very good reasons for using Flash, there's also a reason that designers don't like to discuss:

Flash is often used because designers like to use Flash.

In other words, it's often used for no good reason. It's often used when HTML could easily be used in its place, and the average site visitor wouldn't even notice the difference.

Both Yahoo! and Google, in their Advanced Search pages, allow you to select from one of seven different file formats—you can, for instance, search for an Adobe Acrobat PDF file or a Microsoft Excel spreadsheet file. Flash is not *one of the file formats listed.*

This wouldn't matter too much, except there are real consequences to using Flash in place of regular HTML on a web site—search engines won't index the site well. While search engines sometimes do index the content of Flash files, their main concern is the content of HTML pages. You can virtually guarantee that if the only thing you provide to the search engines are Flash files, your site will not rank well! That's not to say you should never use Flash; just that if you do, you should think about providing text to the search engines in some other way. (Actually, there are other consequences, among which is the fact that Flash sites are often more expensive to modify and maintain.)

File and Directory Names

When you are creating your site, consider using keywords in your file and directory names. The search engines index the names, so you can sometimes get a little boost from that. You can also include keywords in a domain name, of course.

Let's say you are creating a page related to one of your pet-cosmetic products, the rodent eyeliner. You could create a directory and filename like this:

http://www.PetCosmetics.com/pet-cosmetics/rodent-eyeliner.html

Note also that we've separated the words in the folder and filenames with hyphens, not underscores. This is the preferred way to do this, because the search engines will recognize the two words in each item (pet and cosmetic, and rodent and eyeliner) as separate words. If you use an underscore the search engines see them as one word, with the underscore as just another character in the word.

Optimizing Pages for Particular Keywords

As we mentioned before, this is a text game; you need plenty of content (that is, *words*) typed into your pages. Why exactly is that? Well, search engines try to match keywords typed into the search engine with words from the web pages, in order to index. If they can't find the keywords, they have nothing to match.

Furthermore, there are other criteria. The engine can't simply give someone every page with the keywords in them; it has to rank those pages somehow. And it uses criteria such as these:

- How often does the keyword appear in the page? (More is better, within reason.)
- How many pages in the site contain the keyword?
- How many links point to the page with the keyword in the link text?
- Is the keyword in the page's <TITLE> tag? How close to the beginning of the title?
- Is the keyword in any headings in the page?
- Is the keyword in any body text in the page? Is it near the top of the page?
- And more . . .

tip *You may have a list of 50 keyword phrases you've decided to focus on . . . but you can't optimize all your pages for all 50. One strategy is to create a page for every keyword you are interested in, optimize the page for just that keyword, but then ensure some of the other keywords are also included in the page.*

As you can see, you need text. You can use the text in your pages to give the search engine clues as to what the page is all about, by where and how often you place the keywords in the page.

note *This description refers to some HTML-coding terms. You cannot optimize web pages without understanding HTML, and we don't have room to teach it, so we're going to assume a basic understanding of HTML tags.*

Here's a simple summary of the process. Let's say we're optimizing for the term *Pet Cosmetics* (which, admittedly, isn't used as a search term very often for some reason!):

1. Pick the keyword phrase for which you want to optimize a page.

tip *Place the <TITLE> tag immediately below the <HEAD> tag at the top of the page.*

2. Ensure that the keyword appears at least once in the page's title (created using the **<TITLE></TITLE> tags**). The title is the text that appears in the browser's title bar when the page is loaded. The keywords can appear twice if you wish, at the beginning and end of the tag, with various other keywords in between—no more than around 50–70 characters, like this:

```
<TITLE>Pet Cosmetics. World's best makeup for pooch or kitty. Best
Pet Cosmetics available</TITLE>
```

3. The page description is indexed by the search engines, and sometimes even displayed on the search-results page. Create a **DESCRIPTION** metatag using the term, starting with the term. Again, use it a couple of times, mixed in with other keywords, to a maximum of around 250 characters, like this:

```
<META NAME="description" CONTENT="Pet Cosmetics. The world's best
Pet makeup - lipstick for cats, eyeliner for dogs, blush for
gerbils. We're the Pet Cosmetics leader in the Chicago area, with
Pet Cosmetics for all types of pet, including cat makeup, dog
makeup, rodent makeup, alligator cosmetics, and more.">
```

4. Create a **KEYWORDS** metatag containing the keyword and other related terms. Limit the tag to around 10 or 15 words, and don't use too much repetition. Something like this could work:

```
<META NAME="keywords" CONTENT="Pet Cosmetics cat makeup dog makeup
rodent eyeliner gerbil blush dog cosmetics pet makeup">
```

You can forget about other metatags, such as the REVISIT-AFTER tag, although many web designers will tell you they are important. As far as the search engines go, they have little or no effect.

5. Use the keywords in the **ALT attribute of IMAGE tags**. The ALT attribute creates the "pop-up" text that appears when you point to an image in a web page. For instance, on a product picture you might have this:

```
<IMG SRC="dog-lipstick.jpg" ALT="Pet Cosmetics - Dog Lipstick">
```

6. Put the keywords into the headings on the page, using **<H> tags**. If a search engine finds keywords in a heading, it will consider it to be one of the more significant terms on the page. For instance:

```
<H1>Pet Cosmetics for every Pet - Dog, Cat, and Rodent</H1>
```

7. Put the keyword into the **body text**, and use it multiple times. Don't overdo it; if the text sounds clumsy, like you've been using the keyword over and over again—because you have!—you've almost certainly gone too far.

8. Place the keyword into **bulleted lists**, **italic text**, and **bold text**, and in some places use the keyword in title text (*Pet Cosmetics* rather than just *pet cosmetics*)—stressing the term in some way may give the search engine a clue that it's important.

If you have a brick-and-mortar store, include location information on your pages, too, such as the full address and ZIP code. "Geo" searching is getting very good these days, and people are beginning to search with keywords in combination with city names and ZIP codes. Include this information and you have a very good chance of ranking well.

9. Use the term in a **Comment tag** a couple of times, like this,

```
<!-- Pet Cosmetics Page Begins Here -->
```

and,

```
<!-- Pet Cosmetics Page Ends Here -->
```

Understanding the Role of Links

Links are very important, both incoming links—links pointing to your site from other web sites—and internal links—links pointing between pages within your site. Links are valuable for several reasons:

- ■ **Links act as "votes" for a web page.** Links from other sites pointing to your site act as votes telling the search engines that your site is important. The more links—in particular from other sites with lots of links pointing to *them*—the more important.

- ■ **Links tell search engines what the page is about.** Search engines don't just follow links, they read the text in the links to get an idea what the referenced page is all about.

- ■ **Links help search engines find your site.** So they'll come to your site and index it (see "Registering with the Search Engines," next).

Thus, links are critically important; they can be the difference between a #1 position in the search results and a #100 position. In fact, in some cases it doesn't matter *what* you do to your pages; you will *not* rank well unless you have a lot of good links:

- ■ **Use links within your site.** Make sure you have lots of interlinking between pages in your site, and make sure you include good keywords in the links. Don't just say, for instance, *To see our latest pet cosmetics prices, <u>click here</u>*. Make sure the keywords are included in the link, like this: *To see our latest <u>Pet Cosmetics prices, click here</u>*.

- ■ **Get links from other sites to yours.** Make sure, whenever possible, that you get keywords in these links.

Perhaps the best-known example of the power of links is the *miserable failure* search. Search for this term at Google, Yahoo, and MSN, and the very same page comes first in the search results (see Figure 26-6).

Note that the biography of George Bush does *not* contain the phrase *miserable failure*. In fact, it contains neither the word *miserable* nor the word *failure* anywhere in the page . . . there is nothing on the page to indicate to the search engines that it is relevant in any way for the term *miserable failure*.

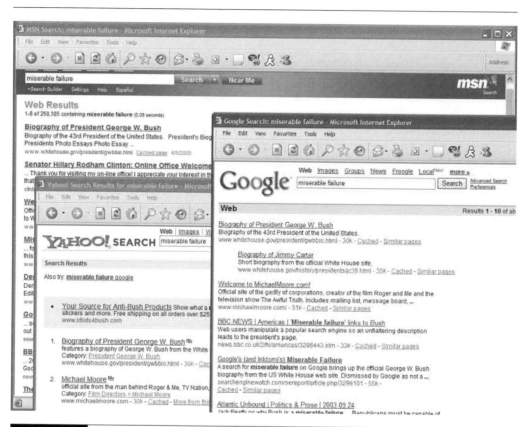

FIGURE 26-6   The *miserable failure* search term has much the same effect in all three of the major search engines.

Yet it ranks #1 . . . entirely because of links. A concerted link-building campaign by people angry at George Bush for various reasons led to the page's prominence. Look at the search results though, and you'll see a number of other pages, which also don't contain the words *miserable failure*. These pages are related to Michael Moore, Jimmy Carter, and Hillary Clinton. A counter-campaign by Bush supporters pushed these pages high up in the results for this term but was still unable to garner enough links to push George Bush's page down for anything but a few days.

This example shows you two things:

■ Links are *very* important!

■ Links are *very* important to all three major search engines in the same way!

Getting Links to Your Site

So where do you get links from? How can you get other web sites to link to yours? There are many ways. Here are a few ideas:

- **Anyone you know who has a web site** Friends, family, employees, the mailman, etc.

- **Associations and clubs** Use these if you are a member.

- **Suppliers** If you are selling another company's products, see if they'll link to you.

- **Yahoo! and the Open Directory Project** If you can afford it, get a link from Yahoo! Directory (dir.yahoo.com; it's $300 a year), and submit your site to the Open Directory Project (www.dmoz.org; it's free, but often takes a long time to get in). The Open Directory Project feeds data to hundreds of web sites, including the Google Directory.

- **Other directories** There are *hundreds* of small general and specialized directories; many will give you a link for the asking. Find the Search Directory or similar category at Yahoo! Directory and Google Directory (dir.google.com).

- **Send out press releases.** Make sure you put a link in them, and they'll often end up on web sites linking back to you.

- **Create your own "blog" and point to your site from your blog messages.** Try using, for instance, Blogger.com, which is owned by Google. The search engines often index blogs and will find the links.

- **When you respond to blogs or leave messages in forums**, include a link to your site.

 tip *Remember, keywords are important. When you ask anyone for a link, suggest to them what the link should look like . . . exactly what words should appear in the link text.*

Registering with the Search Engines

One of the great myths of the search-engine business is that in order to get into the search engines, you need to "register" with them. You *can* do so if you wish—you can go to the search engine's web site, find the "add url" page, and register your URL. It won't do any harm, but it may not do any good, either. The search engine *may* come to your site or it may *not*. And it may take a long time to make up its mind.

 note *If you want to register directly with the major search engines, just in case, try these links: www.google.com/addurl.html, search.msn.com/docs/submit.aspx, and submit .search.yahoo.com.*

There's a quicker way to get indexed. It's possible using this method to get indexed literally within a few hours in some cases. It's a two-step process:

1. Create a link to your site from another web site that you know is already indexed.

2. Create some more links from other web sites.

Actually, if you stop at Step 1, you've still probably done enough—the search engine will find your site eventually. But creating multiple links from multiple sites helps in a few ways:

- The more links to your site, the sooner the search engines are likely to find it and arrive at your site.

- The more links to your site, the more often they will "trip over" links to the site, and thus the more often they are likely to come to your site.

- The more links to your site the more important the search engines will think your site is; you may get a boost in the ranks because of it.

Chapter 27

Using Affiliate Programs and Other Marketing Techniques

As we've discussed in the first chapter, successful businesses try different strategies to reach customers. So far you've learned, in Chapter 21, about using the Yahoo! Shopping directory, and you've also learned about search-engine Pay Per Click campaigns. And in Chapter 26, you learned about using "natural" search-engine results.

But is that enough? You may not be able to make money using PPC, and search-engine optimization can be incredibly difficult in some cases, so you can't stop there. In any case, if you don't understand your other options you may be missing a huge opportunity. There are many ways to reach customers online—as with offline businesses, "one size does not fit all." It's important to keep learning and exploring, and to experiment with different ways to market your store. You don't know *what* will work until you try it, so you have to try many things. Who knows, you may hit a gold mine and take a small "hobby" business and turn it into something really big.

Using Affiliate Programs

Affiliate programs are a proven method for making money online (although that doesn't necessarily mean it's easy money). Most of the Internet's large online businesses use affiliate programs as one of their promotional tools.

An affiliate program is a system through which you pay other web sites for channeling buyers to your site. Affiliates may be paid for

- Each sale made at your web site (this is the most common form of commission).
- Each time they send a visitor to your site.
- Each time they send a lead to your site.

Yahoo! has integrated the Commission Junction affiliate system into the Merchant Solutions e-commerce product. Click the <u>Affiliate Link</u> in the Promote column of the Store Manager page.

Traffic from one site to another is generally tracked through one of two methods:

■ The affiliate is given a special link with a code in it identifying the affiliate; when someone clicks on that link, special tracking software places a "cookie" on the visitor's computer and can follow the visitor through the site; if they buy, credit is assigned to the affiliate.

■ The affiliate places a small piece of code onto their web pages; when someone opens the page, a "cookie" is placed onto the person's computer; if that person then visits your site, they can be identified as "belonging" to the affiliate.

All affiliate systems use "cookies"—there's really no way around it.

How do you create an affiliate program? Somehow, you need software to track visitors to your site and to manage the process of recording sales and assigning payments to the appropriate affiliate. You can either use an affiliate service, which runs all necessary software for you, or you can install software on your own server.

■ The quickest way is to sign up with one of the **major affiliate services**, primarily LinkShare (www.LinkShare.com) and Commission Junction (www.CommissionJunction.com). These companies have come to dominate the business.

■ You can use one of the **smaller affiliate systems**, such as FusionQuest (www.fusionquest .com) or Affiliate Tracking Network (http://www.affiliatetracking.net/).

■ You can **install affiliate-tracking software** on your own server. There are *many* different packages available.

As usual, there are advantages and disadvantage to all these methods:

	Major Affiliate System	Smaller Affiliate System	Your Own Tracking Software
Search-engine ranking	You'll get no search-engine rank boost, because the links point at the affiliate system, *not* your site.	You *may* get a boost; some of the smaller systems provide a way to direct links directly to your site, not to their server.	Links will point to your site, and so may help with ranking; however, there may be technical problems if search engines pick up the links—when people go to your site through the search-engine links, you pay commission!
Installation/ Monthly fee	Very expensive.	Much more affordable.	Large up-front cost, saves money in the long run.

	Major Affiliate System	Smaller Affiliate System	Your Own Tracking Software
Software management costs	Low management expense; they manage the system for you.	Low management expense; they manage the system for you.	High management costs; you have to manage the system.
Accounting management	They will figure out which affiliates are owed, and process the checks each month.	They may manage payments for you, or you may choose to do it yourself.	You'll have to manage the accounts and payments yourself.
Access to an affiliate network	Have hundreds of thousands of affiliates already signed up.	Some have tens of thousands of affiliates.	You'll have to find your own affiliates.
Management tools	Have very sophisticated management tools.	The smaller systems and purchased software vary, but generally aren't so sophisticated.	

tip *When you are shopping for an e-commerce system, you might want to consider affiliate-program integration. The e-commerce system has to be able to pass the purchase information back to the affiliate system, so that the system can figure out how much is owed to which affiliate. Many e-commerce systems make it very hard to integrate an affiliate program, providing no way to pass that information through. Many others will only work with one or two affiliate systems. Yahoo! Merchant Solutions has been configured to work with Commission Junction, for instance.*

Using one of the major services is a good way to get started, but can be very expensive. For instance, if you want to work through Commission Junction, you can expect the following expenses:

- $2,500 setup fee
- $250 per year
- $3,000 deposit toward commissions
- 30% commission (for every $1 paid to an affiliate, a 30-cent fee is paid to Commission Junction)
- $500 monthly minimum—even if you don't pay a single affiliate, you'll pay Commission Junction a $500 monthly fee
- No maximum monthly commission

Consider that $500 minimum. If you pay affiliates a 10% commission, you have to make almost $17,000 in sales before you reach the Commission Junction's commission minimum.

The smaller systems let you get started at a much lower cost (but they don't have the large networks of affiliates that Commission Junction and LinkShare can provide). For instance, here's what you'll pay for the basic FusionQuest (www.fusionquest.com) service:

- $195 setup fee
- $19.95 per month

In addition, if you want access to their network of affiliates (around 40,000), and if you want them to process payments to affiliates for you, you'll pay this:

■ 10% commission (that is, for every $1 paid to an affiliate, a 10-cent fee is paid to FusionQuest)

■ $0 monthly minimum

■ Maximum monthly commission of $650

 You need lots *of affiliates to create an effective program, preferably thousands. Most affiliates will send you very little business; you'll probably find that 90% of your business comes from 5% of your affiliates.*

Don't think that an affiliate program is a quick fix, though. It can take considerable work to make it worthwhile. The main problem is recruiting affiliates to your program. Here are a few ideas:

■ Commission Junction and LinkShare, and some of the smaller affiliate systems, have networks of affiliates to which you can promote your program (Commission Junction has hundreds of thousands—they reported 350,000 in 2002, so it's probably considerably bigger now; FusionQuest, a much smaller system, has around 40,000). Investigate the different ways you can promote to them, and make sure you are listed in the system's merchant directory.

■ List your program with the various affiliate directories (there are around 50 of them). There are services, such as AffiliateFirst (www.affiliatefirst.com), that will register your program in these directories for you very affordably.

■ Seek out sites that attract the sort of people you want to attract, and invite them to join your affiliate program.

■ Consider using a service such as LinkProfits.com to help you track down and sign up good affiliates.

■ Make sure you have a page on your site, with relevant keywords in combination with the words *affiliate* and *associate*, so that people searching for affiliate programs and selling products like yours can find you.

 Around 50% of the Internet's top 300 merchants work with Commission Junction.

Should you use an affiliate network? Perhaps, *if* you are willing to invest not just money but time in making it work.

Using Coupon and Discount Sites

There are thousands of coupon and discount web sites. Just search one of the major search engines for *coupons discounts*, for instance, and you'll see. Some merchants have used these systems very successfully. The jeweler Mondera.com, for instance, has made a concerted effort to target these systems, and consequently has links to its site on thousands of pages across the Internet.

Many of the coupon and discount sites are affiliates; they sign up with the merchants as affiliates, provide discounts to people who enter their site, and still get a commission when a sale is made. Some businesses will provide special discounts on a few specific products in order to work through these sites, rather than site-wide discounts, so they don't see too much of a reduction in revenues. Remember, do the sums right; make sure you can afford both the reduced income due to any discount offered, and the affiliate fee that a coupon/discount site might require.

Promoting Through Newsletters

Whatever you are selling, there's an e-mail newsletter read by your customers. Some newsletters have tens, even hundreds of thousands of subscribers. Promoting through e-mail newsletters can be incredibly effective; it's a very cheap way to reach large numbers of people very quickly.

First, you need to find e-mail newsletters read by your prospects. Here are a few places to find them:

- **New List** (http://new-list.com)
- **E-Zine List** (http://www.e-zine-list.com)
- **Newsletter Access** (http://www.newsletteraccess.com/)
- **NewJour** (http://gort.ucsd.edu/newjour/)
- Remember the search engines!

We recommend that you create a directory of useful newsletters; you'll want to reach these people a number of times. You should then contact these people, with a number of suggestions:

- **Let them know you exist**, using a simple, informal PR piece. Remember that anyone who is publishing a newsletter needs content! They need information. If you hit them at the right time with the right story, you may get picked up.
- Later, announce a **special offer or discount**.
- Suggest a **giveaway, a contest of some kind**. You might promote a single drawing for a product to a single newsletter if it's very large, or perhaps promote the drawing to several newsletters at once.
- **Announce new products.**
- Approach the newsletter and **suggest a revenue-sharing proposition** of some kind, in which the newsletter earns commissions on sales. If you have an affiliate program, the newsletter editor can sign up through that; if you are using Yahoo! Merchant Solutions, you can create a trackable link (see Chapter 21).

note *We're assuming here that you have something to say! If you don't have a "good story," there's nothing you have that you can promote. We suggest you read a good book on guerrilla PR to understand how to position a story that is likely to be picked up. Think about what you are doing: Are your products cheaper? Better? Do you have a wider selection? Are they very hard to find? Why should people visit your site? Do you provide useful information in addition to the products?*

A word of warning about promoting to newsletters. You'd better do it right. If you don't have a story that is of interest to the newsletter's readers, you are not a useful information source to the editor; you are merely a nuisance.

Creating Your Own Newsletter

Some merchants use a newsletter as a way to promote their products. This can be a very effective marketing tool, but there are a few things to remember:

- ■ It's a **lot of work** putting together a regular newsletter.

- ■ You'd better **be sure you can put together a newsletter that is truly worth reading**; the Internet has plenty of web sites and newsletters that are *not* worth reading—it doesn't need more.

- ■ It's **a lot of work promoting the newsletter** to new subscribers.

tip *If you're working with Yahoo! Merchant Solutions, you can get a 3-month free trial of the e-mail tool, Got Campaigner (see Chapter 21).*

The bar has been raised very high in recent years. There is so much online content now, and people are so swamped with e-mail, that it's much harder now to make a newsletter work than it used to be. A newsletter that can act as a successful marketing tool must have these:

- ■ **A large subscriber base** In general, newsletters with only a few hundred subscribers probably don't do their owners much good.

- ■ **A loyal readership** You need people to actually open and read the newsletter. "Open rates" have declined precipitously recently, so only a small number of e-mail newsletters are opened.

- ■ **Quality** It needs to be good, so good that readers will sometimes forward copies to friends and colleagues.

If you *do* decide to create a newsletter, you may want to consider it as part of a three-pronged campaign, combing the newsletter with search-engine optimization and content syndication. Every time you write an article, it appears

- ■ In your newsletter,

- ■ On your web site, providing well-keyworded content for the search engines to read (see Chapter 26), and

- ■ In your syndication library, so other web sites can use it (see next).

Content Syndication

Another strategy used successfully by many online marketers is that of *content syndication*, which provides "content" of some kind—generally articles, but in some cases other things such as interactive "Flash-based" games and utilities—that other web sites and newsletters can use. In return, you get

- **A link to your web site**, to bring people to your site
- **Links that the search engines read**, helping to push you up in the search-results ranks (*if* you create the syndicated content in the right way)
- **Your company logo**, splattered across the Internet

tip   *Please, if you can't write, don't bother! We can show you some absolutely awful examples of newsletter articles and syndicated content that never should have seen the light of day, written by business people who are simply wasting their time. Ask someone totally objective— ideally* not *friends or family—to tell you if your writing works.*

There are several ways to provide syndicated content to other sites:

- **You host the content.** Other sites can link to a page on your site, or frame the content on their site. Not a very effective way to do it; most sites don't like it, so you won't get many using your articles.

- **Use "browser-side includes."** You can give a little bit of JavaScript to the sites that want to use your content—the script "pulls" the article off your web site and places it into the other site automatically when the page is loaded. This method does nothing for your search-engine rank, though, because search engines don't read JavaScript and therefore will never see your article on the other site.

- **Use "server-side includes."** This is another way to automatically pull data from your site and place it into another page. It works well and will be read by the search engines . . . but it's complicated to use and explain to other web-site owners.

- **Utilize RSS feeds.** We don't have space to go into this, but it's worth watching. It's really exploding on the scene. Although it's probably not appropriate for most businesses at present, it will be a viable option very soon.

- **Cut and paste.** This is the preferred method. Provide HTML code that people can paste into their site. It *will* be read by the search engines, and while you have less control—the user may change it—in most cases, people will abide by your rules and include the links and images you require.

tip   *For an example of a simple cut-and-paste syndication system, view this site: http://shaneco .com/synd/.*

As mentioned before, you can get triple use out of whatever you write; use it on your web site and in your newsletter, as well as syndicating it. And think, while you are writing, about the purpose and style:

- **Include good keywords** to attract the search engines (see Chapter 26).
- **Include multiple links to your site,** with good keywords in them, so wherever the search engines find your writing, it benefits you.
- **Of course, write well!** The better the writing, the more it will be read and recommended to others.

How do you reach people to let them know about your syndicated content? You can announce it in various directories of content, such as Amazines.com, Bullmarketer.com, ConnectionTeam .com, EzineArticles.com, and Freesticky.com. You'll also find a lot of discussion groups in Yahoo! Groups (groups.yahoo.com) related to free content. But think about all the ways you already "touch" people . . .

- If you have an affiliate program, let your affiliates know.
- If you publish a newsletter, discuss the syndicated content.
- Let the people who buy from you know . . . many may have web sites.
- Let newsletter editors know about it.
- Mention it in discussion groups (see next).
- Mention it on the home page of your web site, and lead people to a content "library" area.

Internet marketing is a cumulative, overlapping process. You'll discover many different ways to reach people online and promote different things through different channels. It all hooks together.

Marketing Through Discussion Groups

The Internet is far more than just web sites—the online discussion groups are hugely important. It's possible to promote products through discussion groups, if it's done subtly.

There are a number of different types of discussion groups:

- **Newsgroups**   In order to read newsgroup messages, you originally needed a special newsgroup reader, and such readers are still available. (For instance, visit http://www .forteinc.com/ to learn about Agent and the free version, Free Agent.) However, you can also read newsgroup messages through the Web, at sites such as Google Groups (http:// groups.google.com/).
- **E-mail discussion groups**   These work via the e-mail system. You send a message to the group, and that message is sent on, via e-mail, to all members, who can then respond by e-mail.
- **Web forums**   There are many web-based discussion groups, too; messages are posted and read through forms on a web site.

We recommend you do *not* simply post ads to discussion groups. That's a great way to get yourself banned immediately! However, many people have promoted their businesses more subtly, by becoming loyal members of particular groups related to their businesses:

■ There's nothing wrong with **including a "signature" block at the bottom of each message**, which contains information about your business and a link to your site. (Just make sure you don't post worthless messages just for the sake of including your business info.)

■ **Become a group "expert"**; give advice and answer questions. It's possible to become one of the "go-to" people in the group. Such people often get a lot of exposure for their businesses.

■ When **someone asks a very specific question** ("Where can I buy . . .", "What's a good price for . . ."), respond with a fair, balanced answer, and don't be scared to mention that you, too, sell these products.

So where do you find discussion groups? Try these places:

■ **Lycos Discussion Search** (http://discussion.lycos.com/); a great system that has indexed messages from many different web-based discussion groups

■ **Yahoo! Groups** (http://groups.yahoo.com/)

■ **Network54** (http://www.network54.com/)

■ **Google Groups** (http://groups.google.com/). Not only can you read newsgroup messages, but you can also join web-based and e-mail discussion groups.

■ **MSN Groups** (http://groups.msn.com/)

■ **AOL Groups** (http://groups.aol.com/)

■ **Coolist** (http://www.coollist.com/)

■ **ListTool** (http://www.listtool.com/)

■ **Tile.net** (http://www.tile.net/). A directory of newsgroups and e-mail newsletters

You can also find discussion groups by searching the major search engines and directories. Should you get involved? Probably only if you're willing to spend a few minutes every day in these online discussions, and would enjoy doing so. And be careful! Discussion groups can be addictive and soak up a *lot* of time!

Creating Your Own Discussion Group

It's very easy these days to set up your own discussion group. Visit the group systems at Google, Yahoo, and MSN for instance. But should you do so? Perhaps, if you think that there's a need for a discussion group among the clients you want to attract, nobody else is doing it well, and you are willing to invest the time and effort to do it.

Actually, once set up and promoted to enough people, a discussion group doesn't have to take much work. Most of the work is done by the participants, and in many cases you can even recruit participants to help moderate the group (to stop fighting that breaks out, to delete obscene or obnoxious messages, and so on). Many companies have used discussion groups to promote their businesses. One classic example that got significant press coverage a few years ago is the StudioB discussion list for computer-book authors (http://www.studiob.com/). This is the most important discussion list for this profession, and it is owned by a literary agency that represents computer-book authors. We know, from our personal contacts with StudioB, that this discussion list had a very real impact on the growth of the business.

Chapter 28

Selling Through Amazon and Other Merchant Programs

In the previous chapter we looked at shopping directories, systems that funnel traffic to your site and charge you a fee for the sale. There's another class of site that you should consider working with, the merchant sites. These systems sell your products on their sites. They don't channel people to your site; rather, the transaction is processed right there on the merchant site. The merchant site—Amazon.com, Half.com, PriceGrabber, or one of several others—processes the transaction through its own e-commerce software and credit-card merchant account, then the information is e-mailed to you. You ship the product, and the merchant site sends the payment to you . . . minus their commission, of course.

Selling on Amazon.com

Amazon.com wants to sell *everything*. In fact, the average person has no idea of the breadth of products that Amazon sells. They may have begun with books, and moved into music fairly quickly, but you can also buy clothing, diamonds, food, industrial supplies, pet supplies, Segway transporters, musical instruments, and plenty more. (Amazon says they sell "millions" of different products.)

 tip *As with the shopping directories, price is very important when selling through the merchant sites. If you are selling products that are the same or similar to other merchants, and your pricing is not very competitive, you'll have trouble succeeding through these systems.*

Amazon doesn't stock all of these products; rather, they partner with other stores in various ways. Certainly, they have partnerships with major companies, such as Toys R Us, Harry and David, and JCPenney. But they also sell products that are shipped by many small companies, including small, one-person operations. These companies are placing their products on Amazon's pages, in various ways (Figure 28-1).

Click one of these <u>used and new</u> links to view other merchants' products.

Click an **Add to Cart** button to buy from one of these merchants.

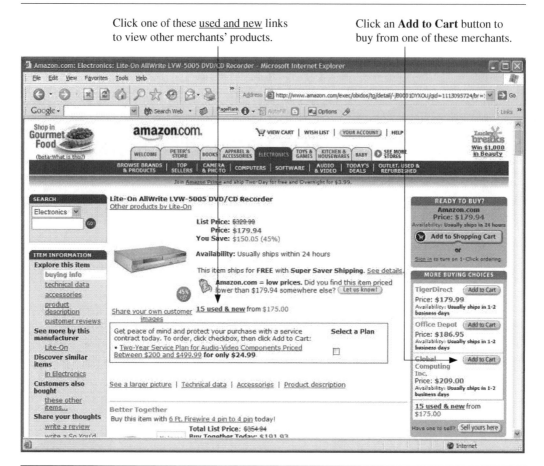

FIGURE 28-1   Amazon displays products from other merchants.

If you click on one of the <u>used and new</u> links, Amazon displays a page showing the product on offer from different merchants. They'll list the "Featured Merchants" near the top, but scroll down a little and you'll find the regular guys. These are listed by price, with the lowest price first.

Different Ways to Sell Through Amazon

Amazon.com actually has a number of different ways for merchants to sell through their store.

■ **Amazon Marketplace**   This is really intended for the sale of used and collectible items, although you can sell new products. In fact, it's designed to be possible for individuals to sell their own "stuff." On virtually every page you'll see a  **Sell yours here** button. Your listings will appear in the used & new page linked from the main product page.

■ **Marketplace Pro Merchant**   With this program you can upload data into Amazon Marketplace en masse, and Pro Merchants are more likely to be selling new items.

■ **zShops**   This system (www.zshops.com) is an online discount store comprised of products entered into the Amazon Marketplace; if you are a Pro Merchant you'll get your own mini store within zShops (see Figure 28-2). Some product pages within the main Amazon site do have a little zShops link, but probably few people notice this.

This link appears on some search-results pages, and takes you to a zShops page listing Marketplace merchants selling this product.

This link appears on the product page, and takes you to products listed by Marketplace merchants.

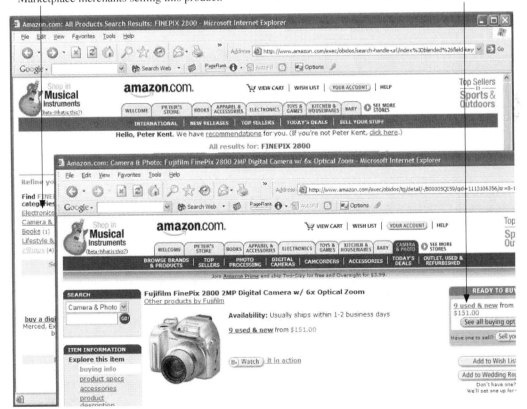

FIGURE 28-2   An Amazon zShops store

■ **Amazon Auctions**   Amazon has its own auction site (auctions.amazon.com), although it's not terribly well known.

■ **Amazon Advantage**   If you publish books, music, videos, and DVDs, Amazon has another program for you, Amazon.com Advantage. This program puts your products into Amazon's inventory, allowing them to sell and ship directly.

Amazon has *not* done a great job at clarifying all this. It's very easy to get confused when you dig through the jumble of diverse and contradictory information related to all the different ways to sell through the company. (Perhaps this is Amazon's way of ensuring the survival of the fittest; if you can figure it all out, they'll let you sell.)

Forget for now about zShops. It's essentially a compilation of Amazon Marketplace product listings. So the primary way to sell through Amazon is with a Marketplace account, and if you want to be a regular merchant selling a lot of product through this system, you'll probably need a Merchant Pro account.

Becoming an Amazon.com Marketplace Pro Merchant

To get started with Amazon Marketplace Pro Merchant, visit the Amazon.com home page and look for the little Make Money box on the left side; click the <u>Marketplace</u> link and look for the Pro Merchant information. Follow the instructions to set up a Pro Merchant account.

When Amazon sells one of your Marketplace listings, it processes the order and transfers the money to your bank account (every 14 days) minus certain charges.

■ A 99-cent flat fee per transaction

■ For computer equipment, a 6% fee

■ For photographic equipment, cell phones, and electronics, an 8% fee

■ For musical instruments, a 12% fee

■ For everything else, 15%

However, note that Amazon provides a shipping credit; they charge the buyer a shipping charge, and also pay you for shipping. For instance, if you are shipping a book within the U.S. using standard, media mail, they'll pay you $2.26. If shipping a computer they'll pay you $4.04 plus 45 cents per pound (you have to define the shipping weight when entering the product).

tip   *Is your pricing competitive? You don't always have to have the rock-bottom lowest price. But if you're not close to the bottom, you probably won't do well selling through Amazon Marketplace. Note that Amazon has some pricing rules, which can be summarized as follows:*

■ *You must sell your products at or below the Amazon price.*

■ *You cannot sell your products anywhere else on the Internet at a lower price.*

However, if you have a Pro Merchant account, you don't have to pay the 99-cent fixed fee—but you will pay a $39.95/mo. membership fee. Sell 40 products a month, and you've saved the fee. But there are other advantages to the Pro Merchant account:

■ You can use the **Inventory Loader** to upload data about thousands of products at a time. Without a Pro Merchant account you'd have to enter each product into a form, one by one. The Inventory Loader is essentially a system similar to the Upload function in Yahoo! Merchant Solutions' Category Manager (see Chapter 13), in which you upload a spreadsheet or other data file into Amazon Marketplace.

■ You can create and customize a **zShops storefront**. Some merchants don't maintain any other store on the Web; they simply work from zShops.

■ You can upload any number of products; there's **no limit to your Amazon listings**.

By the way, although Amazon.com makes it easy to join and get started, they are actually more selective than one might imagine, based on size of your listing. If you upload five or ten products, fine . . . but if you upload 50,000 products, you're going to get a call from them, and be vetted. In some cases, very large merchants are denied access—they have their Merchant Pro accounts shut down.

Using PriceGrabber

PriceGrabber.com, mentioned in the previous chapter, is both a shopping directory and a merchant site. Which method of working with PriceGrabber should you choose? Remember, as a shopping directory, they'll charge you per click. As a merchant site, they'll charge you per sale (7.5 percent). You may find it more profitable to go one way or another! If your web site's conversion rate is low, you may find that you spend a lot of money on clicks for every sale—in which case it would be better to use PriceGrabber as a merchant site. The decision depends on your product price, gross profit, and conversion rate.

Using Half.com

Half.com was such a popular merchant site that it couldn't remain independent—it was purchased by eBay in 2000 with the intention of integrating it into eBay and then closing it down. However, it's still so popular that eBay finally cancelled the October 2004 closing, and announced that it would keep it open indefinitely. eBay stated that Half.com was continuing to grow more than they expected, and that Half.com members provide eBay with almost half of its books, music, video, and games listings.

 note *There's a certain amount of Half.com/eBay integration. When you search at Half.com, you'll see an **On eBay** tab, which shows you matching listings on eBay. Half.com isn't promoted in the same way on eBay, though. (Perhaps this will change now that eBay has decided not to close Half.com.)*

Half.com allows merchants and individuals to sign up and list products very quickly, and unlike eBay, doesn't charge a listing fee; rather, they charge a fee based on the sales price, declining with sales volume.

Transaction	Commission
Up to $50	15%
$50.01–$100	12.5%
$100.01–$250	10%
$250.01–$500	7.5%
$500.01 and more	5%

However, here's one real problem with Half.com: there's no simple way to upload large numbers of products to the Half.com inventory. Once you're established as a reliable merchant, you can increase the quantity for each product, but what you can't do is list large numbers of different products quickly; each has to be typed in one by one!

Using Overstock.com

You've probably seen the Overstock.com TV ads; they've been spending tens of millions of dollars on television advertising recently, pushing the company with a mixture of sexual innuendo and low prices (see Figure 28-3). Unlike Amazon, Overstock isn't looking for products so much as merchants. If you have single items to sell, Amazon will take it. But Overstock is building relationships with merchants with large inventories.

Overstock says it's "an Internet leader for name-brands at clearance prices." They offer "top-quality name-brand merchandise at 40–80% off, every day of the week." The company name and the blurb imply that the products are all, well, overstock or clearance items, but in fact many merchants are simply using Overstock as another low-price sales channel. They sell through Overstock the same products they sell on their stores, except at a lower price. (We discussed the issue of different pricing models in Chapter 1.)

Overtock.com can move *a lot* of product. But they won't take just anyone. They want to know you can deliver. This is not an automated signup, like setting up an account with Amazon. You'll have to contact Overstock (look for the Have Products to Sell? link), and discuss with them the products you want to sell, how many you have available, the different prices at which the products are sold, and so on.

FIGURE 28-3   Overstock.com is looking for merchants, not products. They want to build long-term relationships with merchants.

Using uBid.com

uBid.com is an unusual system (see Figure 28-4). It's a business-to-consumer auction site, selling brand-name products—around a billion dollars' worth so far—to four-and-a-half million buyers. Every merchant is vetted, transactions are processed by uBid itself, and a 250-person customer-service department aims to ensure that every transaction goes smoothly.

note   *Products sold on uBid.com generally have no reserve and a $1—or very low—minimum bid price. Auctions are generally multiple-item auctions—sometimes hundreds of items. As with eBay, there's a "buy it now" function that allows people to bypass the auction process and buy a product immediately.*

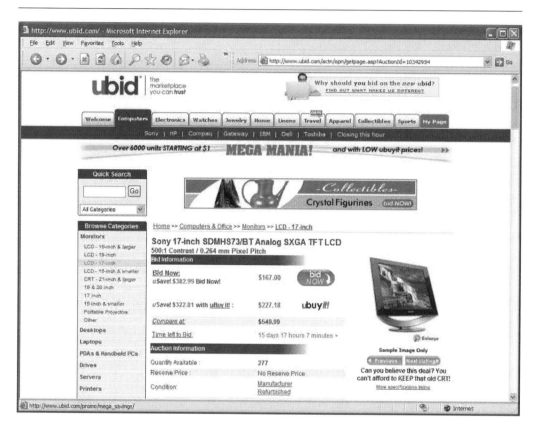

FIGURE 28-4   The uBid system, perhaps the only business-to-consumer auction site

uBid provides three ways to work with them: you can manage your own auctions, have them manage the auctions but send you the orders, or have them manage the entire process, from sale to shipping. There's no automatic signup, of course, because uBid wants to know who you are and ensure that you have a reliable supply of items to sell on their site.

Using SmartBargains.com

SmartBargains is another major system that you won't get into without personal contact; there's no automatic merchant signup, and when we requested information about selling through SmartBargains.com, we were given the e-mail address of the Executive Vice President & Chief Merchandising Officer. It's an important system, though, partly because it feeds data to AOL's Instore.com shopping site.

You're not getting into SmartBargains.com if you sell a couple of homemade candles a week. But if you can reliably supply large quantities of products, then you should probably consider talking with them.

Using Other Merchant Sites

You may be able to find other specialty merchant sites. One that comes to mind is Djangos.com. This company had 300 brick-and-mortar stores in the U.S., and a very active online store. It will buy your CDs and DVDs, one at a time if you wish. It also has a special program through which it buys collections of 400 or more at a time, and takes a commission from the sales price as each one is sold. But Djangos has also had drop-ship relationships with merchants, in which they e-mail orders to the merchants as they come in.

 In 2001 Yahoo! launched Yahoo! Warehouse, a merchant site intended to compete with Half.com. However, it was integrated into Yahoo! Shopping and no longer exists as an independent entity.

Are there other merchant sites out there suitable for your business? Perhaps. The Internet is a big place, so you may be able to find stores, specializing in your type of products, that will take orders for you.

This page intentionally left blank

Chapter 29

Cross-site Merchandising and Promotions

The Internet is often thought of as a *sales channel*, one way among many in which a company reaches customers and distributes its products. But in fact it should really be thought of as several sales channels. Many successful online businesses end up with multiple sales channels:

- Sales made through a brick-and-mortar store
- Sales made through eBay
- Sales made through a web site
- Sales made through a merchant site, such as Amazon.com Marketplace
- Customers found through shopping directories, such as Yahoo! Shopping and PriceGrabber

If you find yourself in this situation—or considering opening a new sales channel—you need to consider how all these sales channels work together; or if, in fact, they all have to operate separately.

Understanding Channel Conflict

If you have an offline business and are planning to take it online, or even if you have one online channel and want to open another, you have to understand what is known as *channel conflict*. This refers to the incompatibilities between two channels. The most likely cause of channel conflict when you open an online store is pricing. You may find that the prices in your offline store are simply too high for the Internet. You can't sell online with your offline prices . . . and you don't want your offline customers to know just how low your online prices are!

Or perhaps you have a web store and now want to sell through Amazon.com. Amazon has certain price demands on Marketplace merchants (see Chapter 28); you can sell for *more* elsewhere, but you can't sell for less. In this situation you wouldn't want people arriving at your web site to know that you sell the products cheaper on Amazon, if that's the case.

For various reasons, companies may want to sell through different channels at different prices. This is not unusual, and nothing illegal, immoral, or fattening. Many, many companies do this in the real world. How do companies deal with the channel-conflict issue?

- Some companies have chosen to run, in effect, **two or more separate businesses**, a low-priced online business under one name, and a higher-priced business offline under another name. Or perhaps an offline business, a business running a web store, and another business selling through low-cost channels such as the shopping directories and the merchant sites.

- Other companies have chosen to bypass the problem by **differentiating their online business** in order to avoid price competition. For instance, a jewelry company may choose to focus on the uniqueness of its designs, so it doesn't have to compete dollar-for-dollar with other online businesses.

Using Your Brick-and-mortar to Promote Your Online Site

Let's say, however, that you don't have to worry about channel conflict; there's no need to have different pricing in each "channel." Instead, let's consider how an online channel can benefit an offline company:

- **Your customers can see your products any time of day or night;** they don't have to wait until business hours.

- **They can view your products wherever they are;** they don't have to visit your location.

- **They can indulge their desire for instant gratification;** people want information *now*, when they think about it, not when they have time to visit your store or when the post office finally delivers a catalog.

- Customers who have never heard of you and may never drive by your store can **find your products**.

- **Customers can shop "together" even if they are in different cities.** Grandparents can buy for grandkids, fiancés can shop for their wedding together even when apart, and so on.

- **Customers can always get to the very latest catalog,** seconds after it's published.

- **You can attract customers who are searching online,** who might otherwise go elsewhere.

- **You can process an online order cheaper than an offline order.**

- **Customers often research online, then go to the store to buy.** If you don't provide this opportunity, you may lose a sale to a company that does.

How about the other way around? How can an offline channel help an online store? Plenty of ways—your offline business is already in front of customers and prospects in many different ways. In fact, if you already have an offline business you are way ahead . . . you can now promote your online business at almost no cost!

- **Put a sign up outside your business** (see Figure 29-1). In effect, you are handing out a business card to everyone who drives by . . . when they get home, they know just how to reach you.

- **Put a sign up inside your business;** make sure that anyone walking into your store cannot possibly leave without knowing that you have a web site and remembering your domain name.

This little .com sign *can't* be expensive . . . but is seen by millions of people every year.

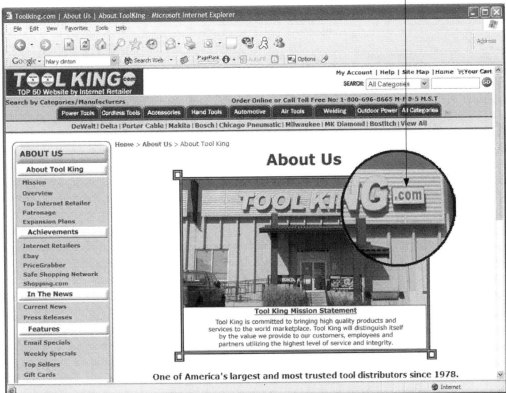

FIGURE 29-1   We zoomed in on this photo on the ToolKing.com About Us page so you can see the low-cost little .com signed added to the store name on the building.

- **Put your URL on *everything*:** product packaging, business cards, invoices and other paperwork, print ads, TV and radio ads, and more.
- **Give people a *reason* to come to your site;** when you use your URL in ads, for instance, explain *how* the site can help: "See our entire inventory online, at . . ."
- **Place fliers on your store's countertops promoting the online store,** and make sure every customer leaves with one.
- **Put magnet signs on your car or delivery trucks.**
- **Give buyers at your store a discount coupon for the online store.**
- **Drop a fridge magnet** with your URL into every customer's bag.

While writing this bulleted list, an ad came on TV for an organization called The Neptune Society. An 800 number was prominently displayed . . . but no URL. The organization does have a web site, though . . . so why no URL?

Of course larger, more sophisticated businesses can play other games:

- **Buy online; return to a brick-and-mortar.**
- **Buy gift cards online, use in the brick-and-mortar,** and vice versa.
- **Use instant-win codes.** Your brick-and-mortar store gives a scratch-card to every buyer; the buyer enters the code into a form on the web site to see if it's the winning number.

Giving People a Reason to Visit Your Site

Many merchants simply provide the site's URL and think that's enough to get people to the site. But you really should give people a *reason* to visit the site; an *address* is *not* a reason. The goal is to put into your customers' minds either a very specific reason, or perhaps a more general tagline.

For instance, here are some specific reasons:

- "Visit our store to see our online-only offers"
- "Enter the drawing to win a *xxxx* on our web site"
- "Sign up for our special-offers bulletin online"

A more general "tagline," good for signs, business cards, invoices, and so on, might be something like this:

- "See our latest, up-to-the-minute pricing and offers on our web site"
- "Window-shop at www.domainname.com!"
- "Instant catalog delivery, at www.domainname.com!"

Using Your Online Site to Promote Your Brick-and-mortar

You can also use your online store to push people to your offline store, of course. Many merchants do more business from the offline store after a buyer visited the online store than they do in the online store itself. In fact, the Internet generates more offline sales than online sales overall. Recent studies have shown the importance of the *W2S shopper* or the *off-channel shoppers*.

A study commissioned by ShopLocal.com, for instance, found that in the fourth quarter of 2004, 83 million Americans had researched products online, then made purchases both online and offline (they referred to these buyers as W2S, or Web-to-Store, shoppers). On average they

- Spent $250 online
- Spent $400 in a brick-and-mortar store on products they researched online
- Spent an *additional* $200 in the stores when buying the researched products

As you can see, the average buyer was spending $250 online and $600 offline as a result of their online research. The study had this to say:

"W2S shoppers rely on the Internet nearly twice as much for local purchasing information compared to traditional shopping media, such as newspaper advertisements and inserts; local TV and radio ads; and other media."

Another study, by Forrester Research, came to similar conclusions, about what they termed *off-channel shoppers*:

- Most Internet users are off-channel shoppers.
- They spend more money offline after researching online than they spend online.
- Almost half of these buyers purchase additional products when they visit the store.
- Forrester Research estimated that the Web was generating over $100 billion in offline sales.

If you own both an online and offline store, you can't ignore these numbers. As one merchant told us recently, "We don't know how much brick-and-mortar business our online store is generating, but we know it's big; we keep seeing people walking into our stores with printouts from our web store."

How, then, do you use an online store to generate business offline?

- **Do all the things we mentioned under "Using Your Brick-and-mortar to Promote Your Online Site."** It's a two-way street, and if your customers don't know your store exists, they can't use it to see what products you have.

- **Make sure you include a *good* store locator.** Make it easy for site visitors to find your store address *and* maps and directions. By the way, this also helps you make online sales. As we mentioned elsewhere, simply placing a phone number on a site can increase sales, as it improves credibility. Making it quite clear that you are a well-established offline store boosts credibility, too.

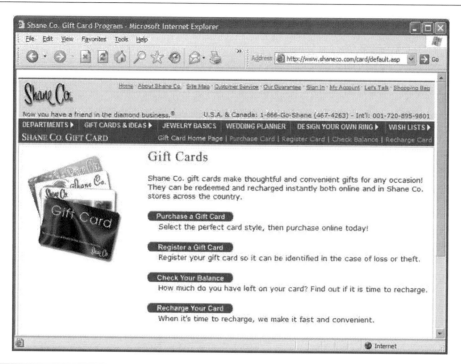

FIGURE 29-2   ShaneCo.com lets its customers buy their gift cards online and use them in both the online store and the offline stores.

- **Provide as much information about your products as possible.** Help your customers do their research.
- **If possible, use cross-channel tools.** Allow your customers to buy and recharge their gift cards online, and use them in both the online and offline stores (see Figure 29-2). Online gift registries and wish lists are also tools that "off-channel" shoppers can use.

Using eBay to Push Visitors to Your Web Site

If you are an eBay merchant, you can use the tremendous popularity of this site to generate business for your web store, or even your offline store. However, eBay doesn't want you to simply use their auctions as a way to push people to your store, which seems fair enough. (And they also have an important pricing rule, the same as Amazon's: you can't sell a product on your site for less than you list it in your eBay store.)

But that doesn't mean you can't use eBay to promote your web site; in fact, eBay is pretty liberal in what they do allow. There are several things you can do:

■ You can't overtly promote your web site from an item listing page, but you *can* **link to a page on your site that describes the product**. That page can even link to other pages on your site, as long as the primary purpose of the page is to describe the product, not push people to other areas of your site.

■ **You can promote your site from your About Me page,** as long as you don't directly promote a particular product on the About Me page.

■ **You can link to your site from your eBay Store,** as long as you don't promote a particular non-eBay product in your store or links to a non-eBay product on your site.

■ **When you send a confirmation message** to an eBay buyer or auction winner, you can promote your site.

■ When you ship a product to an eBay buyer, **you can promote the site in a packing insert**.

■ You can, if given permission, **keep in contact with existing clients** (see Chapter 21).

Many merchants have tried a variety of tricks to use eBay to generate traffic to their web sites. There's probably nothing you can think of that eBay hasn't seen. You cannot, for instance, sell very low cost "catalogs" through eBay that are intended to push people to your site; it's already been tried! eBay is, quite reasonably, doing its best to reduce site "pollution." If you place a listing on the site, eBay wants a genuine listing, not a weak attempt at Internet marketing.

Using Your Site to Help eBay Sales

Some merchants do all their selling through eBay. They may maintain a web site, but they use the eBay e-commerce tools to manage actual transactions. eBay provides a tool called the **eBay Merchant Kit** to help you place information about your current auctions inside your web site (see Figure 29-3). Of course, there are certain rules. For instance, if you want to use the Merchant Kit, you can't display other, non-eBay products on the same page.

It's very simple to use; eBay provides a web-based "wizard" to configure the products you'll show on your site. The wizard then provides a little piece of HTML that you drop into a web page on your site, something like this:

```
<script src="http://syndicate.ebay.com/ebayshop/ebayshop.dll?GetSellerList
&uid=poiupp&fontsize=2&numofitems=50&billpoint=1&highlight=1&fontface=
verdana&sortby=endtime&sortdir=asc&siteid=0&catid=0"></script>
```

You can literally create this code snippet and get it into a page on your site in a minute or two.

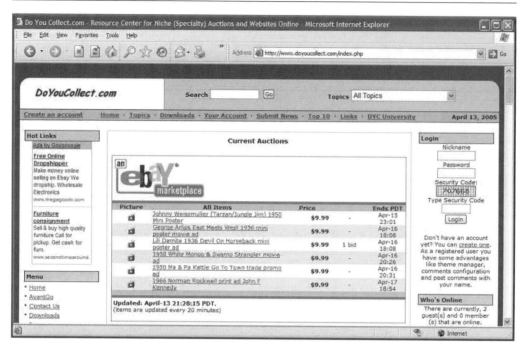

FIGURE 29-3   This site has used the eBay Merchant Kit to drop a list of their current auctions into the site; it probably took a couple of minutes' work.

Index

383

28947122R00242

Made in the USA
Charleston, SC
26 April 2014